Regulating Fraud

MICHAEL LEVI

REGULATING FRAUD

White-collar crime and the
criminal process

TAVISTOCK PUBLICATIONS
London and New York

First published in 1987 by
Tavistock Publications Ltd
11 New Fetter Lane, London EC4P 4EE

Published in the USA by
Tavistock Publications
in association with Methuen, Inc.
29 West 35th Street, New York, NY 10001

Printed at the University Press, Cambridge

British Library Cataloguing in Publication Data

Levi, Michael
    Regulating fraud: white collar crime and
    the criminal process.
    1. White collar crimes
    I. Title
    364.1'68   HV6635
    ISBN 0-422-61160-3

Library of Congress Cataloging in Publication Data

Levi, Michael.
    Regulating fraud.

    Bibliography: p.
    Includes indexes.
    1. White collar crimes—Great Britain. 2. Fraud—Great Britain. 3. Criminal
justice, Administration of—Great Britain. 4. White collar crimes—United
States. 5. Fraud—United States. 6. Criminal justice, Administration of—United
States. I. Title.
    K5215.L48   1987   345.41'0268   87-9994
    ISBN 0-422-61160-3   344.105268

Contents

Acknowledgements

Many people have given a helping hand in the lengthy preparation of this book. Among the multitude of academic colleagues who have been pressed into reading chapters in draft, often at short notice in what sadly turned out to be wildly over-optimistic deadlines, I am particularly grateful to David Sugarman for his critique of my original introduction. This spurred me on to produce the much fuller account of the legislative process that is now Chapter 4, though he is not responsible in any way for this final version. Many thanks are due also to Phil Fennell for his comments on an earlier draft of Chapter 4 and to Robert Reiner for his comments on the draft manuscript. The other distinguished commentators suggested little in the way of revision, so I will maintain their anonymity: this should protect them from any public embarrassment – though not private blame, for I am not one of those who hypocritically accept full responsibility for the deficiencies of others – if and when any critical reviews come out!

As for the research that went into the making of the book, I thank the Commonwealth Secretariat and Law Ministers for commissioning my research into fraud trials (and prosecution departments around the world for supplying the data); the Home Office Research and Planning Unit, accountants Arthur Young, and the Police Foundation for funding and sponsoring the survey of *The Incidence, Reporting, and Prevention of Commercial Fraud*; the Home Office Statistics Department and Fraud Squads in England and Wales, most particularly the Metropolitan and City of London Company Fraud Department, for supplying me with what must have seemed to be absurdly irrelevant data and for making constructive comments about it; and Lloyd's, The Stock Exchange, and the Securities and Investments Board, for some very helpful information about their enforcement procedures and sanctions.

On a personal as well as an institutional note, I am particularly grateful to Claire Austin of the Home Office and to James Morgan of Arthur Young for their time and efforts on the research study of *The Incidence, Reporting, and Prevention of Commercial Fraud* (1986); to Barry Rider of the Commonwealth Commercial Crime Unit and Jesus College, Cambridge, for his constant encouragement; to Commander

Malcolm Campbell, Chief Superintendent Mike John, and Chief Inspector Phil Whittick (and other colleagues in the Metropolitan Police Fraud Squad); to Superintendent John Todd of the City of London Fraud Squad; to Vince Carratu, of Carratu International; to David Chaikin of the Australian Attorney-General's Department; and to a number of other insiders in the public and private sector who prefer anonymity, for many stimulating conversations. Kevin Heal and Gloria Laycock of the Home Office Crime Prevention Unit, and Trevor Benn of the Home Office Statistics Department, also smoothed my path in this delicate area of research. However, none of the persons above bears any responsibility for the interpretation I have placed upon the data or upon the conversations that I have had with them: that is the author's burden alone.

The financial crisis in the higher education sector made it pointless to apply for my theoretical entitlement to sabbatical leave in order to complete this book. My thanks instead (and anyway), go to my wife and partner, Penny, and to our horse, Seven Up, for putting up patiently with my long absences at the word processor, on research trips away, and at those gastronomic rituals which professionals and businesspeople call 'working lunches' and which we academics would prefer to label 'fieldwork', because it sounds like even less fun. (I suppose that wild mushrooms in raspberry vinegar would be the closest I ever came to a field on any of these projects! Those who lament the paucity of research on upperworld crime might use culinary incentives as a redistributive mechanism to move criminologists away from their traditional concentration on juvenile delinquency.) My students deserve some gratitude for not pointing out too often that my office looks as if burglars had wrecked it: actually, my hope was to deter burglars by inducing them to believe that someone had got there before them. Indeed, I think that I have now found the definitive solution to the problem of office burglary though, like many solutions to crime, it may not have much general appeal to people other than those doing the recommending.

The editorial staff at Tavistock – Caroline Lane, Tamar Miller, and Juliet Aitchison – coped heroically and tolerantly with the gradual expansion of this book from the rather more modest scale I had originally anticipated. The constant drip of new data must have made their task seem like a Department of Trade and Industry insider dealing enquiry, even if they remain disappointed at my holding back on the ultimate foolproof fraud – I need something in reserve for my old age! Finally, though he played no part in these recent pieces of research, my thanks go to Richard F. Sparks both for first kindling my interest in fraud at Cambridge way back in 1972, when virtually no other criminologists (or, fraudsters themselves excepted, other *non-*

criminologists) were doing any thinking about it, and for the model he offered in the rigorous self-criticism and clarity of his own writing. If this work bears any comparison whatever with what he would have produced, then my efforts will have been worthwhile.

Michael Levi
University College, Cardiff.
January 1987

The author and publishers would like to thank the following for permission to reproduce copyright material: all Home Office material is reproduced with the permission of the Controller of Her Majesty's Stationery Office.

Table of statutes

Table of cases

Glossary of financial terms

AIBD   Association of International Bond Dealers: the organization of dealers in Eurobonds, first formed in 1969. They are members of the Securities Association self-regulatory organization.

AFBD   The Association of Futures Brokers and Dealers. This Self-Regulatory Organization comprises firms advising, dealing, and broking in futures and options (except for individual stock options).

Big Bang   The term used to describe the revolution in UK financial markets on 27 October, 1986, when The Stock Exchange abolished fixed minimum commissions on the sale and purchase of securities, and shifted from single capacity to dual capacity. More generally, the term also refers to the introduction of a new electronic price information system and to the entry of large American and Japanese firms into the UK securities business, when for the first time they have been allowed to become Members, i.e. outright owners rather than just minority shareholders of firms that are Members of The Stock Exchange. By contrast with the United States, where the Glass-Steagall Act forbids banks to underwrite corporate securities (including commercial paper) and Japan, where the Securities Law similarly forbids banks from underwriting securities, banks (both domestic and foreign) operating in Britain *are* permitted to underwrite and deal in securities, reflecting greater British confidence that banks can be trusted not to get themselves into financial trouble through these diversified tasks.

broker   A recognized agent – personal or corporate – in securities, currencies, and/or commodities who acts as a middle-person between buyer and seller. In the UK, prior to Big Bang, he acted only as a retailer for a client and did not quote prices himself or operate on his own account in money markets. From 1986, he has been able to act as a broker/dealer rather than simply as a broker.

Chinese Walls   In the brave new world of financial services, many of the major firms are conglomerates that have corporate finance and specialist advice sections (such as on mergers/take-overs) traditionally associated with merchant banking. If those who work in the section on take-over advice – perhaps working for the target or the bidding company – talk to their colleagues in the securities dealing section, this might lead the latter to buy or sell shares (whether on their own *personal* account, for the financial conglomerate itself, or for the company for whom they are acting) in which they would not otherwise have traded. Consequently, firms in this position are required to set up so-called Chinese Walls, policed by corporate compliance officers, to *try* to ensure that the different sectors of the same company do *not* conspire with each other or even talk carelessly about deals. These are backed up by 'house rules' involving the threat of dismissal for those who are caught – if any.

cold calling As defined in s.56 of the Financial Services Act (1986), this means 'a personal visit or oral communication made without express invitation' for the purpose of inducing people to invest.

debenture In international markets, these are bonds secured only against the unpledged assets and general standing/goodwill of the company. In UK markets, however, they are bonds secured against the assets of a trading company, and rank higher in priority than ordinary unsecured trade debts.

dual capacity The ability to act both as agent (on behalf of clients) and principal (on one's own account) when dealing in securities. This is the aspect of post-Big Bang conduct that generates alarm about investor protection risks, for all Stock Exchange firms will be able to act with dual capacity if they wish, rather than as independent brokers and jobbers.

equities Shares in a company.

Eurobond A bond traded internationally in a Eurocurrency denomination; this is a currency held by a non-resident of the country of that currency.

Eurodollar US dollars that are held by non-residents of the US, normally in the form of a deposit with a bank outside the US or with the foreign branch of a US bank.

FIMBRA Financial Intermediaries, Managers, and Brokers Regulatory Association. A Self-Regulatory Organization for firms whose main business is that of an independent intermediary advising on and arranging deals in life assurance and units in authorised unit trusts, and providing investment advice and management services to retail customers. Some members advise on and arrange securities transactions as an incidental activity.

IMRO Investment Management Regulatory Organization. The Self-Regulatory Organization for firms with investment management as their main activity. This includes the management and operation of regulated unit trusts, investment trusts, and pension funds.

insider dealing/insider trading This is defined differently from nation to nation, and in 1986, some countries such as New Zealand do not prohibit it at all under the criminal law. However, the essence of insider dealing legislation is to prohibit the use, when trading in securities is undertaken by certain categories of 'insiders' such as company directors, of price-sensitive information that is not known to the general public. Chinese Walls may minimize leakage to other sections of the company, but they will not prevent self-dealing by insiders, often via nominees (or 'tippees'). For example, directors who know that the market has undervalued or overvalued shares in their company or in a company for which they intend to bid may purchase (or sell) shares before the public is given information that will change the rating that is given to the shares. In Britain, this is prohibited by the Company Securities (Insider Dealing) Act (1985).

ISRO The International Securities Regulatory Organization, which in 1986 merged with The Stock Exchange to form The International Stock Exchange, whose SRO is The Securities Association.

jobber A 'wholesaling' firm that commits itself to buying from and selling to brokers particular securities at a price that it quotes. Acting as a principal rather than as an agent, it makes its profits on the spread between the buying and selling prices. This formerly specialized function has now been replaced by the 'market makers'. Since October 1986, all price quotes have been automated.

LAUTRO The Life Assurance and Unit Trust Regulatory Organization. The Self-Regulatory Organization for insurance companies and friendly societies in respect of their retail marketing of life assurance products and of the retail marketing by those who operate the schemes of units in regulated collective investment schemes. This is the only SRO whose members are permitted to sell investments by 'cold calling' persons who have not initiated contact with them.

Market Maker   A Stock Exchange firm that commits itself to *always* being ready to deal in a range of stocks in which it is registered with the exchange.

RPB   A Recognized Professional Body, such as the Institute of Chartered Accountants or The Law Society, whose disciplinary standards are recognized by SIB as adequate.

SEC   The US Securities and Exchange Commission, a federal policing body with extensive powers, charged with supervision of the US securities industry.

securities   A general term for financial instruments including bonds, shares, and stocks.

SIB   The Securities and Investments Board. The organization given delegated powers by the Secretary of State for the Department of Trade and Industry (DTI) under the Financial Services Act (1986) to authorize (or not authorize) persons and companies to sell investments. In this capacity, it can license self-regulatory organizations (SROs), recognized investment exchanges (RIEs), clearing houses, and recognized professional bodies (RPBs). It can investigate and prosecute cases of fraud. It has the power to vet the rule books of SROs and direct registrants to ensure that they provide for adequate investor protection, and it can de-register them if they fail to meet the standards it requires. It has immunity from being sued for performance (or non-performance) of its regulatory functions. Its stated aim is to ensure uniformity to minimum supervisory standards throughout the financial services markets, though individual SROs can provide extra benefits – for example, compensation for investors – if they wish. Its members have to be approved by the Government and the Bank of England, and are principally representatives of commerce and industry: this has led to some controversy, not least when John Kay, the former head of the Institute of Fiscal Studies, a respected non-Left critic of government taxation policy, was *not* approved for membership by the Conservative Government in 1986. The rule book of the SIB has to be vetted by the Director General of Fair Trading to see whether its rules are anti-competitive, and the Secretary of State for the Department of Trade and Industry must then take the decision whether any anti-competitive element is outweighed by the need for investor protection.

single capacity   The situation in which a securities dealer is able to act either as an agent or a principal, but not both.

SRO Self-regulatory organization. An organization that gathers together firms in a common area of activity – for example trading in financial futures – and has the task of approving which firms shall be authorized to deal in securities and of monitoring their integrity and solvency according to rules drawn up by itself and approved by SIB. Because of the breadth of their activities, major financial conglomerates are members of more than one SRO. Like the SIB, SROs have legal immunity from lawsuits in respect of their regulatory activities.

stag A dealer or investor who buys a new issue with the intention of selling it immediately at a profit on the issue price. Under some circumstances, where the securities are obtained by fraudulent means, this can be a criminal offence.

The Securities Association The SRO for firms dealing and arranging deals in securities of all kinds, including international bonds and equities, related matters such as warrants and options on individual stocks, and giving incidental advice and management in those areas. This was formed following the merger between The Stock Exchange and the International Securities Regulatory Organization.

Preface
The academic context of this study

'One of the things that most struck me about [the lecturer] at the time had been his casual use of the word 'criminal'. In my opinion, and, I think, in that of most modern lexicographers, a criminal is one who commits a serious act generally considered injurious to the public welfare and usually punishable by law. [Professor] Krom seemed to believe that anyone possessing the imagination and business planning skills needed to evolve a new way of investing time and money in order to make a profit, was automatically a criminal. The wretch need not have committed any illegal act to earn him the distinction. If he had been original and his orginality had succeeded, that was enough. For Krom he stood condemned.'

Eric Ambler, *Send No More Roses*

This is a book about crimes committed by and against business: how common they are, what their effects are, how seriously they are regarded, what political, economic, and organizational factors influence legislation and the implementation of legislation against them, and how people think they could be and should be controlled. The controversial and ambiguous criminological term 'white-collar crime' in the sub-title of the book is used here in the sense employed by Wheeler, Weisburd, and Bode, who state that 'white-collar crimes, for our purposes, are economic offenses committed through the use of some combination of fraud, deception, or collusion' (Wheeler, Weisburd, and Bode, 1982:642). Such crimes come in many forms: they include acts as diverse as the setting up of businesses to obtain large quantities of goods on credit without intending to pay for them; the use of mail-order businesses to obtain money for goods that one does not intend to supply; the pocketing by brokers or other trustees of funds that they have promised to invest; the diversion of funds to one's own account by means of computers; the illegal use of private inside knowledge to make a profit on share-dealing; and the non-declaration of taxable commercial sales to the tax authorities. The control of employee pilferage and of 'corporate crimes' such as bribery and health and safety at work offences will be examined at various points in the text, but the principal focus will be upon fraud in business.

There is a growing tendency among 'white-collar crime' academics to differentiate between crimes *by* business and crimes *against* business: the former are labelled 'corporate crime'; the latter 'white-collar crime' (D. Smith, 1982). But useful though this distinction is, it may overstate implicitly the homogeneity of 'crimes *against* business'. Even if one excludes from consideration many forms of business 'malpractice' that are either not criminal at all or whose criminality is ambiguous, to write about 'commercial fraud' is to write about a number of very different sorts of activities: there are frauds by businesspeople against each other; by businesspeople against investors – who by volume of securities traded are predominantly institutions or professionals – as well as against small investors, consumers, and tax authorities (who may be regarded as 'corporate crime' rather than 'white-collar crime' victims); and by directors and employees against their companies. Nor is the social-class composition of 'white-collar criminals' simple: they include members of 'the upperworld' and 'the underworld', and comparatively junior employees. Even upmarket-sounding crimes like insider dealing – where shares are bought or sold unlawfully on the basis of confidential inside information – may be committed by the company chairman or the company typist.

To seek to capture the motives, methods, and control mechanisms of all conduct falling within this category would take far more space (and cost readers far more money) than is feasible. Rather, the aim of this book is to examine some key empirical and theoretical issues in the impact and control of business crime, within the context of North American and European research carried out (1) into the incidence and impact of different types of fraud, and (2) into the functioning of commercial organizations and the multifarious parts of the criminal justice process. Much of the British research has been conducted by me during the 1980s, and is published here for the first time. Among the topics covered in relation to fraud will be the influences upon legislation against it, and the extent, the impact and perceived seriousness, the auditing, the policing, the prosecution, the trial, and both the formal and informal sanctions that are applied in respect of different types of fraud. I have tried to systematize and review salient sections of the scattered literature on these topics, much of which is comparatively inaccessible both to academics and to practitioners. It is my hope that this will help readers both to understand more clearly the issues involved in regulating crime in the upperworld, and to form their own views concerning how to deal with an aspect of criminality that not only involves the most intricate *methods* of crime commission but also is more closely embedded than are most crimes into the fabric of 'normal' commercial life.

An occupational hazard of specialized academics is to assume too much knowledge on the part of their audience. This is particularly the case when one is working in an interdisciplinary field which incorporates accountancy, criminology, economics, law, politics, and sociology. However, in writing this book, I have tried to bear in mind the great variations in the backgrounds of what I hope will be its readership. I doubt that many businesspeople or practising lawyers and accountants will be familiar with theoretical accounts of the relationship between economic interests and law – discussed, and criticized, in Chapter 4 – but the analysis of pressure-group politics in commerce should be of interest (and even of practical use) to those outside the rarified circles of sociologists of law. Likewise, few students or colleagues in criminology, sociology, or law – other than those looking apprehensively or longingly at early retirement schemes, or searching for ways of funding their further studies – will be familiar with what the Eurobond market does, or indeed with much of the commercial context of business crime control. Consequently, I have tried to avoid the use of unnecessary jargon, and have provided a brief glossary of those economic terms that may be useful to professional people, to colleagues, or to students. If I have got the balance between clarity of writing and subtlety of analysis wrong, I apologize. But I have made the effort.

In Britain, business crime has been neglected by most academics and activists on the left as well as those on the right: it comes as no surprise to find no discussion of it in contemporary analyses of the crisis in policing, and it does not figure as 'crime' in the outpourings of the 'left realist' solution to 'losing the fight against crime' (Lea and Young, 1984; Kinsey, Lea, and Young, 1986). For the left, this probably reflects the political focus of *praxis* which makes 'poor man's law' a more relevant and worthy subject than 'rich man's law' (Cain, 1975:61; Sugarman, 1983:214). Similarly, authors on the right of the political spectrum have tended to be more concerned about public-order issues such as street crime, industrial picketing, and political demonstrations: Wilson (1975), for example, dismisses white-collar crime as irrelevant to what he sees (and thinks that the public sees) as the 'real' crime problem. This neglect has had several regrettable results for the development of criminology, sociology of law, and crime policy in Britain (though this is less true of the United States). Insofar as students, administrators, and the concerned public learn anything at all about 'crimes of the powerful', they tend to get their information and ideas either from the well-written, provocative, but grossly oversimplified account in the only current student criminology text in Britain to incorporate such material (Box, 1983) or from American work which – the Thalidomide and Third World pharmaceutical scandals excepted – tends to be very insular in its neglect of political and corporate malpractice outside North America: see, for example, J. Coleman (1985a); Ermann and Lundman (1982). Furthermore, much of the case study material focuses on conflicts between big business, on the one hand, and workers, consumers, or the environment on the other, neglecting the conflicts *between* capitalists and between government and various groups of capitalists which are an important feature of the commercial world. In doing so, it contributes towards an over-coherent view of the interests of 'the powerful' and oversimplifies the nature of power relations in society.

It has become conventional wisdom in some criminological circles to lament the dearth of research on crime in the business world (Braithwaite, 1982a; Kramer, 1984). This is often bound up with criticism of the conservatism of what Lea and Young (1984) have referred to patronizingly as 'administrative criminology'. However, particularly in the United States, whether one is discussing offences committed by or solely against businesspeople, the research and public interest explosion has been impressive. Some of the empirical work on business crime has been of uneven quality, using variegated (and sometimes less than explicit) operational definitions of 'crime', but there is no doubt of its existence or of the important contributions it makes towards our understanding of the social and organizational processes involved in sifting 'white-collar crime'. (See, in particular, Clinard *et al.* 1979; Geis, 1984; Mann, 1985; Reiss and Biderman, 1980; and Shapiro, 1983). In the Third World, the principal focus of both functionalist and radical analysts has understandably been on political corruption, but there have been some intriguing forays into fields as varied as corporate crime in the pharmaceutical industry (Braithwaite, 1984) and breaches of professional ethics by lawyers touting for clients (Gandhi, 1982).

In Britain, there have been several valuable case studies of commercial and professional scandals by journalists, but academic analysis has been rather patchy. Nevertheless, contemporary work includes scandals and fraud perpetrated in the City (Clarke, 1981, 1986; Leigh, 1982), bankruptcy fraud (Levi, 1981), corruption (Doig, 1984), health and safety at work (Carson, 1981), pollution (Gunningham, 1974; Hawkins, 1984; Richardson, Ogus and Burrows, 1983), fraud on consumers (Cranston, 1979), exploitative landlords (Nelken, 1983), and workplace crime and the 'underground economy' (Ditton, 1977a; Henry, 1978, 1981; Mars, 1982; Mattera, 1985). As regards *fraud*, there is an intriguing bifurcation in the sort of offences that are studied. On the one hand, there is an understandable tendency to focus upon prosecuted and and unprosecuted crime in high places: that, after all, is the 'sexy' side of power, greed, and capitalism. On the other, there is a tendency to present subversively non-judgemental portraits of workers' 'fiddles' which are entertaining to read and easy for readers to identify with. Some regard these as proto-political acts: Mattera (1985:62) asserts that fiddles 'are perhaps best viewed as a covert form of struggle by workers'. (See also Scraton and South, 1984.) This accords with a 'history from below' perspective in which employee theft and fraud are seen not as a burden upon business which, due to the 'excessive power of the unions', has to be tolerated, but rather as something akin to an heroic struggle by the workforce against the hegemony of bourgeois ideology and against capitalist expropriation of surplus labour value. In this book, I do not explore fraudsters' own perspectives on what they are doing (as was done in Levi, 1981), and to that extent the work is a 'history from above'. What it does seek to do is to describe and analyse the ways in which a wide spectrum of fraud offences – from high-level City scandals to worker and social-security fraud – are regulated (or ignored). It thus examines the way frauds are treated by different segments of powerful groups in the corporate, political, and criminal justice spheres.

It is paradoxical that for all the criticisms of the alleged narrow quantitative empiricism of American social science, in the 1980s, US sociology and criminology journals have included many articles on white-collar crime issues. By contrast, the readers of articles in the mainstream British sociology and criminology journals might be forgiven for being unaware of the explosion of research and writing on corporate and governmental crime: since 1970, in the field of fraud and white-collar crime, setting aside the 'underground economy' which *has* been a popular field for writing, the *British Journal of Criminology* has published only five articles – on the enforcement of factory legislation (Carson, 1970), the sentencing of tax offenders (Deane, 1981), 'regulatory agency policing' (Hutter, 1986), credit-card fraud in Canada (Tremblay, 1986), and the Roskill Report on fraud trials (Levi, 1986b); the *Howard Journal of Criminal Justice* has published three – on sentencing fraud (Levi, 1979), on class bias in prosecutions (Sanders, 1985), and on fraud prevention (Smith and Burrows, 1986); the *British Journal of Sociology* has published one on corruption (Chibnall and Saunders, 1977); and *Sociology* has published one, on research methods in white-collar crime (Braithwaite, 1985a). However, this is largely a reflection of the methodological difficulties of working in this field, the topics that have been of interest to British criminologists, and what areas the suppliers of research moneys have wanted to see examined. With the exception of an interesting small-scale analysis of fraud prevention in large organizations by two Home Office researchers (Smith and Burrows, 1986), the research reported here represents the *only* work on commercial fraud that has been funded by the British Government, and until the Economic and Social Research Council funded three business crime projects on its 1984–85 Crime and Criminal Justice Initiative, there had been no *non*-governmental sponsored research into 'up-market' fraud either.

Criminological research and theorizing, then, tends to reflect definitions by 'the public' and by state agencies of what the principal social problems are. The moral and empirical definition of what the police, courts, and prisons are doing is an important arena for ideological struggle and interpretation, however, and those who oppose official criminal justice practices equally concentrate their attention on public order and street crime issues, albeit for 'demystificatory' purposes. It is interesting that the outlets for journal publications also tend to mirror the divisions in the legal process as defined by the state. Thus, the focus of the British and (apart from the Austrian *Kriminalso-ziologische Bibliografie*) most European 'criminology journals' has been on the aetiology of criminal (and particularly juvenile delinquent) behaviour outside and inside the penal system, on penal reform and, more recently, on 'the police' (including, occasionally, some non-police agencies such as the Post Office). Since, as we shall see later in this book, the decarceration of business criminals has not been a major problem for the penal process, the 'domain assumptions' of these journals tend to exclude the topics of fraud and business regulation.

Very few British sociologists or psychologists have displayed much empirical interest in commercial crime. Instead, those – in Europe and Australasia, but less so in North America – who write about law-making and law-violation within the upperworld tend to have a legal background and will seek publication in socio-legal journals of varying degrees of radicalism, such as the *Journal of Law and Society*, the *International Journal of the Sociology of Law*, and *Contemporary Crises*; in the mainstream business-oriented law journals such as the *Company Lawyer* or the *Journal of Business Law*; and, since 1984, when more criminal lawyers began developing an interest in commercial crime, the *Criminal Law Review*. In the United States, particularly, there is a burgeoning interest in the area of 'regulation' among administrative lawyers and socio-legal scholars, but this too seems often to by-pass criminology and find its place in the specialized 'regulation' journals such as the *Law and Policy* and the *Negotiation Journal*, plus the less conservative University Law Reviews. So there is some kind of 'interaction effect' between past editorial policies, the images of journals, and the sorts of articles that are sent to them, which produces a self-fulfilling prophecy not unlike the processes involved in the creation and maintenance of 'problem housing areas': we both gravitate and are propelled towards those with whom we feel most comfortable. (For a critical general review of the development of British criminology, see Sparks, 1983.) American criminology seems to have overcome its label of being oriented towards petty juvenile crime: whether the Europeans will do so remains an open question.

There is no automatic relationship between social harm and what the criminal law prohibits: anyone writing about 'crime in the suites' walks a narrow (if not frayed to the point of extinction) tightrope between the Scylla of being attacked for accepting existing legal and enforcement agency definitions of crime and the Charybdis of being attacked for using 'crime' as a term of propaganda to condemn alike both lawful and unlawful corporate behaviour to which the criminologist has taken exception. This dilemma is exemplified, on the one hand, by Nader's (1986:1362) criticism of Shapiro's study of the Securities and Exchange Commission (SEC) – which deals with securities fraud in the United States – as being a 'narrow book about a broad and important topic' and, on the other, by the complaints of Jones and Cassidy (1986) that Fisse and Braithwaite (1983) had treated legal definitions in far too cavalier a manner and had mislabelled their product *The Impact of Publicity on Corporate Offenders* when very few of the corporations discussed had been convicted. Orland takes to task the $247,000 government-funded study by Clinard *et al.* (1979) entitled *Illegal Corporate Behavior* in the following terms:

> 'The result is a study of neither corporate crime nor corporate wrongdoing. Rather it is a study of federal administrative regulation of large corporations. The Clinard tabulation of violations is nothing more than a collection of discretionary decisions to initiate formal or informal non-criminal agency procedures against a particular corporation for a particular event; it appears that less than 1% of these 'violations' involve accusations of crime as Congress, lawyers, and the courts have defined crime. . . . The Clinard study asserts that corporate crime is prevalent by pointing to a large number of incidents that have nothing to do with criminal law and even less to do with crime.'
>
> (Orland, 1980:500)

As Pepinsky (1974) has observed, there has been a tendency to redefine the field of 'white-collar crime' so that it refers to 'exploitation' rather than 'crime' (in the technical legal sense), though this was a danger – and/or, to many, a benefit – inherent in Sutherland's original use of the expression (1983). I have side-stepped *some* of these definitional debates by focusing primarily on the regulation of financial fraud rather than on the sorts of corporate acts that are dealt with by administrative agencies, almost entirely outside the criminal justice system. Nevertheless, analogies will be made between the treatment of fraud and that of corporate 'regulatory offences', and I have no doubt that my use of the term 'crime' in this book will meet with a critical fate not dissimilar to the works mentioned above: perhaps this is a testimony to the ideological and moral significance that is attached to the social label of 'crime'.

The preparation of this book has taken place against a background of major changes both in the organization of the financial sector of the economy and in the criminal justice response to fraud. Despite these changes, and despite the inaccessibility and complexity of much of the research material – both documents and people – it would have been comparatively easy to write a book which focused exclusively on the regulation of commercial fraud. However, although this is not an *apologia* for the kind of sloppy thinking that is all too prevalent in the white-collar crime debate, there is a paradoxical sense in which the neat pigeonholing of crimes into different compartments can perpetuate their divisions and make it more difficult for practitioners and students to think laterally about issues of fairness and consistency. As a reaction to this, what I have aimed for is something more ambitious: to place the control of fraud within the context of the control of other forms of crime and the political economy. The chapters that follow will discuss (but alas, will not be able fully to explain) the ways in which 'social harms' in the business sector come to be criminalized, both in the 'law in books' and in the 'law in action', by legislators, judges, and law enforcement agencies.

The sorts of behaviours that constitute 'commercial fraud' (1) in criminal law, and (2) in the practices of reporting, policing, prosecuting, and sentencing, vary over time and place to a greater extent than do more 'traditional' sorts of property crime such as burglary and robbery. One of the aims of this work is to describe and to begin to account for *changes* in enforcement practices in Britain and in the United States, for it is important that we should not be trapped into a static and dated conception of commercial crime control as it was in the 1930s or even in the immediate post-Watergate era of the early 1970s: because white-collar crime was once neglected by law enforcement agencies does not *necessarily* mean that it still is neglected; nor, for that matter, can we assume that because it came to be more heavily policed in the 1970s (in the United States), this will always be the case in the future (see Sutherland, 1983; Katz, 1980).

The boundaries of criminology are in many respects artificial ones. The criminal law and its enforcement processes are only part of the means by which social regulation is accomplished: as both conservative and revolutionary writers from Durkheim and Marx onwards have observed, patterns of social and economic interaction, of routine social surveillance, play a key role in the creation of what Foucault (1977) has termed the 'disciplinary society'. All sectors of society are not subjected to equal measures or methods of surveillance, however, and some attention will be paid to disciplinary rules enforced (or not) by self-regulatory bodies; to settlements under civil law; and to the conditions under which civil and criminal law are activated. Public law (such as criminal law) is commonly thought to be the sole arena in which the state asserts its independent interest. But private law is also the product of state intervention: the state determines the substantive and procedural rules under which civil disputes are resolved, and the very fact that the parties are permitted to resolve their conflicts without the state being represented explicitly does itself reflect a particular (if often unselfconscious) view of the proper boundaries of public policing.

Those studying 'rich man's law' should focus not only on criminal law but upon private law, particularly contract law, and upon informal settlements. Sugarman (1983) has shown how fruitful such a perspective can be, and in an ideal world – or at least one where university cutbacks did not rule out the possibility of sabbatical leave – I would have liked to have researched and written more about the interaction between civil and criminal law in the regulation of commercial life. Nevertheless, although I have written something about this interaction, limitations of space and time have led me to focus primarily on describing and accounting for the operation of the *criminal* justice system in relation to fraud and, moreover, to focus upon this relationship in the 'modern' period from the Second World War to the present, largely ignoring its detailed historical development. These important omissions must await further projects.

Nineteen eighty-five and 1986 have witnessed a large number of changes in legislation, in the organization of the financial sector, and in the organization of the business regulatory system in Britain. The wave of scandals currently sweeping the financial services sector in Britain and the United States has made it particularly difficult to decide at what point to finish the book, but in the belief that the main outlines of legislation and control systems in relation to fraud have now crystallized for the 1980s, I have drawn the line at April 1987, with the passage of the Financial Services Act (1986) and the House of Lords stage of the Criminal Justice Bill (1986). Quite apart from the civil law and historical aspects which I have deliberately omitted from the analysis, there undoubtedly will be points of detail that will alter. The most major possible change is that in the aftermath of revelations about how major figures in the City assisted Guinness – and perhaps other companies – in illicit share support operations during take-over bids, a collapse in the political viability of self-regulation by the City of London or a Labour victory in the general election may lead to the deprivatization of investor protection: the potential impact of this upon fraud is discussed in Chapter 8. But I hope that readers will agree that what I *have* dealt with does form a significant and interesting object of study in its own right. For, in both a theoretical and a practical sense, it is important that we should do justice to the subject of white-collar crime.

1 Introduction

Most crime, whether measured by official statistics or by studies of the 'dark figure' of unrecorded crime, is property crime. Most of the property crimes that come before the courts and which are reported by the media involve the involuntary transfer of goods or money, normally by stealth, more rarely by intimidation or violence. Fraud, then, is an unusual type of crime because the fraudster gets the victim to part with his property voluntarily, albeit (by definition) under false assumptions about the transaction. The fraudster may be likened to Milton's sorcerer, Comus, who exults in his ability to 'wind me into the easy-hearted man and trap him into snares'.

Fraud is often depicted as a 'new crime: as a 'twentieth century crisis' (Bequai, 1978). We shall examine the extent to which it may properly be regarded as a modern 'crisis', but it is a mistake to view it as a *new* phenomenon. Activities such as forgery and counterfeiting – particularly the debasement of coinage – were problems for the Roman and the Byzantine states, and in England, were prohibited as early as 1292 by the *Statutum de Moneta*: the Statute of Purveyors of 1350 made them treasonable offences. The obtaining of goods and money by false pretences has been prohibited under Anglo-Saxon common law and statute law since at least the middle ages. Insolvency frauds that would be considered as being substantial if they occurred today were carried out in the nineteenth century. (See Levi, 1981; Styles, 1983; and Sugarman, 1983 for some relevant historical discussion. Styles' analysis of the period 1550–1780 demonstrates the considerable amount of embezzlement and pilfering by 'out-workers' in the woollens trade that existed even before the era of the factory and the creation of an industrial proletariat.)

Yet to state that there is nothing new about fraud is not to show that it is not the *modern* crime *par excellence*. With some honourable exceptions (Hall, 1952; McIntosh, 1975), an aspect of crime too often neglected by criminologists is that as the forms of social and economic organization change, the forms of criminality change. It appears to be mere tautology to state that there could be no autocrime without the invention of the car, no computer fraud without computers, and no credit-card fraud without credit cards, but the dynamics of crime are not simple truisms. Just as – however distressingly – not all those people who experience a 'need' to be rich will actually become rich, so too there may be a gap between the number of people who – if they are not prepared to go 'straight' – may need to change the pattern of their criminality and the number who will actually be able to achieve this goal. In reality, then, not all would-be fraudsters will be able to achieve their ambitions. However uncomfortable it may be for those who wish to blame *either* 'the offender' or 'the victim', if we wish to account for patterns of victimization, we must try to integrate both potential offender and potential victim conduct.

General changes in the distribution of goods and money can have major – and often unanticipated – effects upon crime: for example, improved protection for cash kept in safes has undoubtedly increased the relative attractiveness of armed robbery, as almost the only vulnerable points for criminals are cash in transit or in the tills. (The kidnapping of managers' families may not be sufficient, because as a security measure, the manager may not have the ability to open the safe on his own.) As the carrying of cash becomes less common – only the prevalence of the 'black economy' sustains its popularity! – intending criminals are forced towards the exploitation of 'plastic money', even though they may come by it as a result of traditional crimes such as muggings, thefts from offices, and burglaries. 'Long-firm fraud', in which sham businesses are set up as fronts to obtain large quantities of goods on credit from manufacturers, has long been a growth point for the more sophisticated 'villains' (Levi, 1981). During the 1980s, it has become a common pastime for 'retired' armed robbers in search of less physically and emotionally demanding activities (and lighter sentences). It seems, therefore, that for adults in all socio-economic groups, particularly if greater success is achieved in the prevention of autocrime and burglary, fraud will become the modal crime of the future.

Barriers to entry – whether technological or social – are an important feature of crime for gain. If one cannot make use of stolen 'plastic money' (or cannot find anyone to buy it), there is little point in mugging people whose disposable assets can be accessed only through their credit and cheque cards. If one cannot operate and obtain access to a computer, computer fraud is impossible. Unlike 'mugging', commercial fraud is not an 'equal opportunity crime' and to the extent that there is disadvantage or discrimination by class, gender, ethnicity, or religion in occupying particular roles, the opportunities for particular types of fraud are correspondingly restricted. Neither physical opportunity nor technical knowledge are *sufficient* to explain involvement in crime, but it is not solely because of their innately superior morality that there are so few female and/or black management fraudsters in Britain or even in the United States! (See Carlen, 1985, and Zietz, 1981, for some relevant data on female fraud.) In short, opportunities for crime may exist in a theoretical sense, but people have to find ways of using cars, computers, and credit cards for crime, just as over the last century, they had to find new ways of cracking open safes as safe technology improved.

Sometimes, technological changes can make old kinds of crime more freely available. An example is the development in the mid–1980s of Quick Response Multicolour Printers, whose laser scanners are so sophisticated that they can even reproduce the tiny blue and red silks that are embedded in green US dollar bills and recreate the slightly raised ink of the engraving process. When these mass photocopiers become readily available – probably in 1987 – they will transform counterfeiting from a highly specialized craft to a form of crime that will be open to all. Organizational changes in markets also can make fraud easier: an example is the so-called 1986 'Big Bang' when The Stock Exchange in Britain shifted from 'single capacity' – brokers do not hold shares on their own account but act only for their clients, and buy or sell shares only through separate firms called 'jobbers' – to 'dual capacity', whereby the same firm can both make markets and deal on behalf of clients. Technological developments intended for ordinary commercial transactions can facilitate their tasks: examples include not only computers but also international direct-dialling telephones, telexes, computer-aided despatch systems, and facsimile senders, which all enable fraudsters to distance themselves geographically from their targets. The spread of offshore banking and investment schemes has benefited multinational corporations and fraudsters alike: provided that they have confidence that they themselves will not be defrauded, both are inclined to move to where costs and levels of regulation are lowest.

Economic changes are important, too, in altering the desirability of particular *forms* of fraud. In the mid–1980s, documentary fraud in the shipping of goods has taken over from faked insurance claims for allegedly lost vessels and from overstated claims for vessels sunk deliberately into trenches deep in the ocean. The reason is that due to the excess of supply over demand in the market, ships themselves have become so cheap that they are worth less than their cargoes. So as long as this oversupply continues, scuttling – at least without first offloading the cargo – will remain relatively unprofitable. The faking of documentation may require skills that the simpler 'scuttlers' do not possess, and this may constitute a technical barrier to entry for some (though not many!) potential maritime fraudsters.

The growth of recorded fraud and convicted fraudsters

The twentieth century has witnessed a vast expansion in recorded fraud and in the number of offenders who are officially dealt with for fraud. This is a trend that fraud shares with other forms of crime. There is a great deal of disagreement among historians over the extent to which rises in recorded crime reflect (1) 'true' increases in the amount of law-breaking, (2) the growing enthusiasm of state bureaucracies to claim competency at finding 'professional solutions' to crime, and (3) the increased willingness of victims of all social classes to use the police to deal with their conflicts, albeit that different crimes have different reporting and recording rates (Foucault, 1977; Gatrell, 1980; Reiner, 1985, Chs 1 and 2; Sparks, 1982).

There has been an increase not only in the absolute but also in the *relative* importance of fraud, which was a mere 0.5 per cent of indictable crime in 1898 but had risen to become 4.6 per cent of indictable crime by 1968 before falling to 3.8 per cent of 'notifiable offences' in 1985. (The offences included within the category of fraud remained fairly stable throughout the period up to the substantial changes in the law of fraud brought about by the Theft Act, 1968.) The number of recorded offences of fraud quadrupled between 1938 and 1968. Since then, the fraud figures have stabilized, although some of this stability may be more apparent than real, due to the 'crime-deflating' effects of changes in recording procedures in 1980, when the Home Office, in an attempt to improve consistency, directed that 'continuing offences' should be recorded as one offence rather than as a multiplicity of offences.

The current official recording procedure is that if someone steals a cheque book and cashes thirty cheques, it should count as one recorded crime rather than as thirty. Before this, informed sources suggest that if the cheque offences were cleared up, they would have been put down as thirty; if they were *not* cleared up, they would count as one! Even now, the situation is complex, and is expressed with modest understatement as follows:

> 'The recording of offences of fraud and forgery often requires difficult judgments to be made as to what constitutes one offence. Cases may involve a large number of instances of deception or forgery and sometimes, several offenders acting together, perhaps in different groups on different occasions. Because of these problems the recorded numbers are particularly sensitive to variations in recording practice.'
>
> (Home Office, 1985a:29)

The effects of these changes are impossible to quantify, but there is no reason to suppose that the drop in 'false accounting' from 5,227 in 1979 to 2,382 in 1980, and in 'other fraud' from 97,438 in 1979 to 93,187 in

1980, were due to a falling off in the amount of fraud. Bearing in mind the statistical *caveat* above, it is noteworthy that recorded fraud has increased by an average of 5 per cent annually since 1980. The figures are set out below in *Table 1*.

Given the unpredictability of the time-lagged effect on involvement in fraud and, particularly, on the filtering of cases through the policing and prosecution process, it would be hard to build up an econometric model of the relationship between fraud and the volume and/or profitability of business. Furthermore, problems of reporting behaviour and of policing resources and attitudes – discussed in later chapters – would bedevil the validity of any such model. However, not surprisingly, the increases this century in the number of recorded frauds have been accompanied by rises in the number of convicted offenders. At the end of the First World War, there were 1925 people convicted for fraud and false pretences, of whom 354 were convicted in the higher courts of Assize and Quarter Sessions. This figure rose to 2749 in 1938, to 2954 in 1948, to 4188 in 1958, and to 9267 in 1968 (of whom 1200 were convicted at the Assizes and Quarter Sessions). So the numbers convicted of fraud almost quintupled, while the numbers convicted of fraud at higher courts more than trebled, over the 50–year period to 1968. Again, changes in the Theft Acts (1968 and 1978) make comparison difficult, and the extensive range of offences in the Home Office classification of 'other fraud' is particularly unhelpful, but there has been a substantial rise in convictions over the past ten years, mostly for relatively minor frauds rather than for major scandals that attract media attention and which, as we shall see in later chapters, are seldom prosecuted. *Table 2* sets out the increase in numbers convicted of or cautioned for fraud during the past decade.

As I noted when considering the recent changes in recorded fraud, the effect of administrative changes has been to deflate rather than to inflate the *offender* statistics in this area. For example, approximately 140 offenders were 'lost' as a result of changes in indictable offences brought

Table 1   *Recorded fraud in the 1980s*

	1980	1981	1982	1983	1984	1985
frauds by company directors, etc.	30	30	24	45	71	37
false accounting	2 382	2 415	2 667	2 292	1 883	1 823
other fraud	93 187	96 065	111 290	109 615	112 214	120 758

Source: Home Office (1986d)

Table 2   *Offenders found guilty of or cautioned for fraud, 1975–85*

	fraud by company director	false accounting	other fraud	bankruptcy offence
1975	21	552	15 837	43
1976	27	599	17 138	58
1977	31	570	16 998	30
1978	39	622	16 002	42
1979	26	703	17 457	68
1980	44	765	20 636	95
1981	39	818	21 200	89
1982	53	715	22 826	70
1983	59	734	23 200	115
1984	69	687	23 149	122
1985	84	734	22 468	165

Source: Home Office (1986d)

about by the Criminal Law Act (1977). Although it is possible that these statistical rises in both fraud and fraudsters dealt with officially may be due to increases in the levels of formal social control of fraud, this does not appear to be a plausible explanation, particularly for the past decade. There have been no significant legislative changes bringing previously uncriminalized activities within the ambit of the criminal law. There has been a modest rise in Fraud Squad manpower nationally over this period – from 232 in 1971 to 588 in 1986 – but such squads tend to deal with lengthy investigations into relatively small numbers of people. Nor is there evidence of major changes in victim reporting policies, the *proactive* redirection of CID manpower into fraud investigation, or more active prosecution policies on the part of the police, the Department of Trade and Industry, or the Director of Public Prosecutions, that could enable one to explain away all the rise in fraud and fraud convictions as a mere artefact of reducing the 'dark figure' of fraud and unprosecuted fraudsters. There *have* been some slight changes in policing, as we shall see in Chapter 5. However, it appears that the rise in fraud is a real one. Indeed, this is consistent with the arguments set out earlier which seek to account for why fraud can be expected to become an increasingly popular form of crime.

The growth of fraud internationally

Internationally, a similar process of growth of recorded fraud and convicted fraudsters has occurred. Here, the absence of research makes it harder to assess the extent to which changes in crime rates may be largely artefacts of changes in law or policing resources. However, the figures are interesting nonetheless. In Hong Kong, the Independent Commission Against Corruption has prosecuted 1478 persons for corruption in the private sector since its inception in 1974, with a conviction rate of 76 per cent. Prosecutions have risen from 17 in 1974 to 96 in 1976, to 113 in 1980, to 284 in 1983, and to 311 in 1984. In Eire, there has been a substantial rise in recorded fraud, which has doubled during the 1980s. North America and Continental Europe have also experienced a recorded fraud boom.

Fraud data from the United States are poor, partly because the Uniform Crime Reports – focusing as they do upon personal and household victimization of a more conventional kind – do not include it. However, in the period 1973–82, fraud experienced the largest percentage rise of any category of arrests (88.8 per cent); forgery and counterfeiting arrests came a close second (72.6 per cent); and embezzlement also rose 10.1 per cent over this period (US Department of Justice, 1985:464). It is largely an artefact of the differential nature of US federal, state, and local jurisdictions, but embezzlement and fraud was the largest single category of criminal case filed in US District (Federal) Courts in 1983: 22.1 per cent of all cases filed, compared with 6.7 per cent for forgery and counterfeiting; 9.8 per cent for larceny and theft; and 6.4 per cent for homicide, robbery, assault, and burglary combined.

In Canada, frauds accounted for 8.7 per cent of property crimes and 5.7 per cent of Criminal Code violations reported by the police in 1984. Credit-card fraud has increased by 25 per cent per annum since 1978. In 1984, it accounted for 13.25 per cent of fraud, and cheque-card fraud traditionally accounts for about 60 per cent of fraud in Canada. So three-quarters of recorded fraud is banking-related, generally of a relatively minor kind.

In Sweden, recorded fraud other than embezzlement increased from 14,653 cases in 1950 to 91,080 in 1984. Embezzlement has increased over the same period from 5469 to 8959 cases. The number of recorded frauds has actually dropped during the 1980s, possibly due to changes in recording procedures.

Elsewhere, the information is patchy. I have been unable to obtain from Interpol any data more recent than 1982, and it is far from certain that the numbers are compiled accurately. National classifications of the denotation or boundaries of fraud differ also. Indeed, it seems almost certain that the differences between the fraud rates per 100,000 population of the different countries set out below are the result of variations in classification systems (and in police resources and recording policies), and that they do not provide a properly comparable data base. For example, to take advanced industrialized nations alone, it is implausible that citizens of Sweden should be on average 3 times as likely as those of Australia to be the victims of fraud; or that the Swedes should be 4 times as likely as the English and Welsh, and 44 times as likely as the Italians to be fraud victims! Consequently, it may be as well to focus upon the intranational change rather than international comparisons.

But bearing in mind these reservations, over the period 1977 to 1982 (except where stated, because 1982 data are not available), the rate of recorded fraud offences per 100,000 population rose most dramatically in Austria, from 212 to 264; in Belgium, from 4.5 to 14.6; in Korea, from 119 to 218 (in 1981); in Denmark, from 140 to 235; in Spain, from 21 in 1978 to 42 in 1982; in Finland, from 323 to 586; in Japan, from 61 to 89; in Lebanon, from 6 to 17 (in 1981); in Monaco, from 375 to 528; in New Zealand, from 415 to 646 (in 1981); in the Netherlands, from 25 to 39; in Scotland, from 208 to 309 (in 1981); in Northern Ireland, from 97 to 179; in Senegal, from 13 to 23; in Singapore, from 37 to 80; in Sweden, from 693 to 1168 (in 1981); and in West Germany, from 434 to 602.

On the other hand, the rate of recorded fraud per 100,000 population actually *fell* in the Bahamas, from 205 to 139; Chile, from 130 to 105; Taiwan, from 12 to 7 (in 1981); Israel, from 296 to 205; Italy, from 41 to 26; Malaysia, from 16 to 12; Qatar, from 12 to 6 (in absolute numbers of offenders, from 36 to 18!); and Zambia, from 79 to 9. So the global picture is not wholly consistent, but it does generally suggest a rise in the rate of fraud.

Perceptions of the growth of fraud

The rise in recorded fraud has been accompanied by business perceptions of an increase in the risk of fraud. In a 1985 questionnaire and interview survey, 8.9 per cent of respondents thought that fraud was very much more common now than ten years ago; 58.9 per cent thought it was much more common; and only 30.4 per cent the same. Only one person thought that fraud had actually decreased in the last decade. The survey sample (Levi, 1986a) comprised executives from security and financial director upwards to company chairman in 74 companies, sampled from the *Financial Times* index to provide a cross-section of all private-sector companies quoted on The Stock Exchange, and was carried out in collaboration with the accountancy firm, Arthur Young. Because of the small numbers, statistical analysis is of doubtful utility here, but there was no clear relationship between level of reported victimization and perceptions of the growth of fraud.

In the telephone survey of 401 companies of mixed size by Consensus Research (1985) in November 1985, 54 per cent of respondents stated that they thought that company fraud had increased over the past five years; 28 per cent that it had stayed at the same level; only 1 per cent that it had decreased; with 17 per cent don't knows. However, it is important to qualify this by the observation that when asked how serious their *own* company's fraud problem was, only 4 per cent stated that they regarded it as very serious; 5 per cent fairly serious; 30 per cent not very serious; 61 per cent not at all serious; and 1 per cent don't know. Indeed, of the 65 companies who answered 'yes' to the question 'Do you think that fraud may *currently* be taking place in your company?', only 12 (18 per cent) described their company's fraud problem as either serious or very serious. Fraud problems, then, are something that do happen, but they happen to other people!

It is interesting that over two-thirds of the senior executives who responded to my survey (Levi, 1986a) thought not only that fraud in general had increased but also that some particular type of fraud had become a special problem in the last decade. Of those who thought this, the perceived growth areas mentioned were in computer fraud (45.5 per cent), credit/cheque-card fraud (25 per cent), expenses/embezzlement (9.1 per cent), and a smattering of others referred to by only one or two executives, including frauds in the spheres of commodities, property valuation, investment, tax, and consumer fraud. It is arguable that the executives do not have an accurate picture of the growth of fraud. Nevertheless, whether perceptions of increased risk are derived from direct experience or from the media and political attention that fraud has received during 1985 and 1986, the results of these surveys (and from research on attitudes to fraud discussed in Chapter 3) indicate that businesspeople do see fraud as a significant general problem in commerce today.

When interviewed, what did executives see as being the growing problems areas in relation to fraud? Only one person – an investment banker – mentioned computer fraud, stating 'computers are the things that really frighten me. This is because they are technical and therefore it might be difficult for somebody to understand what frauds are being perpetrated and also because of the scale on which a fraud might be perpetrated.' A more common area of concern was about corruption in purchasing. One industrialist stated that his competitors were doing far more than giving the odd side of smoked salmon or bottle of champagne, and this left him in both a moral and legal dilemma. A common distinction was made between dealing in Britain and overseas. It was stated that in Britain, unless your competitors were screwing you into the ground by bribery, you should avoid it (and certainly purchasing officers should not solicit or accept bribes), but overseas, you had to pay large 'commissions' in order to do any business at all. We will examine the social and political implications of this later, but it is encouraging to see such cultural relativism in commerce! American-based corporations, who were also more ready to report frauds committed against them, expressed more disapproval of corruption overseas than did British-based companies: it is possible that this may be the result of conditioning by the Foreign and Corrupt Practices Act (1977). (See also the excellent American study of bribery by Reisman, 1979.)

The media and commercial crime

Although there is much dispute about the importance of the media in influencing legislation, policing, and public perceptions of and attitudes towards crime, there can be little doubt that press, television, and radio interest does play *some* role in defining (and thereby moulding) 'the crime problem'. Media interest in business crime has increased considerably since the 1960s. Despite the dominance of 'pro-business' Conservative governments and the absence of a strong popular radical press in most western countries, there has been – particularly since Watergate – a cult of *exposé machismo* in media circles that favours the making of programmes on abuse of power by businesspeople or politicians. Watergate; industrial accidents at Three Mile Island, Seveso, Karlskrona, and Bhopal; less serious radiation leaks at Sellafield in England; the 'Greenpeace affair' involving the sinking of the peace ship Rainbow Warrior by employees of the French Government operating from New Zealand; the 'Northgate' scandal involving the redistribution by senior US Administration figures of illicit arms sales income from Iran to the Contras in Nicaragua: these are just a few of the major news stories devoted to 'white-collar crime' in different parts of the world. (This is not evidence that the media have been taken over by communism, however: the leak of radiation from the Soviet nuclear reactor at Chernobyl in 1986 was given enormous coverage in the western media, who treated it as a symbol of communist secretiveness and inefficiency, and of the low value attached by communism to human safety.) In addition to specialist financial media and investment advisers – who have an interest in gaining kudos by protecting their readers from fraudulent investments – there is a strong and sophisticated muckraking element in parts of the British press (particularly *Private Eye*, *The Observer*, and, since 1985, the *Financial Times*); in the French press (*Le Canard Enchaîné*); and in the Australian press (*The Age*). However, although serious fraud reportage cannot exist without institutional support, this activism depends substantially on individual reporters: for example, the departure of Barbara Conway in 1986 – to become Press Officer for the British securities watchdog, the Securities and Investments Board (SIB) – led to the almost complete disintegration of the *Daily Telegraph* coverage of fraud, at least until British and American insider dealing scandals enthused it and all the other media at the end of 1986.

Upperworld malpractices do not receive high coverage in all countries, and exposé journalism on British television and radio has suffered setbacks with the closure in 1985 of *Checkpoint, Watchdog*, and, for a time, *Rough Justice*. However, the British and American television viewer or the reader of the 'quality' or even of some of the 'tabloid' national press might find ample daily evidence to refute the assertion – still repeated in many key criminological texts (Box, 1983) – that because of the 24-hour news cycle and the fact they they are owned by 'big business', white-collar crime receives little or no attention in the media. This was an over-simplification even when Box wrote it, but despite the growing concentration of ownership of the press, it is even less true in the mid–1980s. During 1985, for example, there were few hotter press stories in Britain than the rescue of Johnson Matthey Bankers by the Bank of England at the taxpayer's expense, and the ensuing political scandal over alleged cover-ups. Nor has the Lloyd's insurance market been lacking in critical public scrutiny (Hodgson, 1986). The media and political outcry over these events have not been matched by the prosecution of those who have been, in the nice phrase of Clarke (1981), 'anathematized' (i.e. condemned), but it can hardly be claimed that this is due to a lack of pressure for such prosecutions. In November 1986, revelations of wholesale insider dealing by American financier Ivan Boesky – discussed later in the book – hit the newspaper and television headlines in the US and Britain, as did alleged smaller-scale insider dealing by some Britons (which *did* result in prosecution).

It is correct to observe that the media do not present the malefactions of the powerful as endemic, structural features of capitalism (Box, 1983): but, except in the sense that the pressures towards profit and/or low cost production in capitalist societies do not provide sufficient disincentives to prevent *all* pollution, industrial accidents, and consumer fraud, are they actually endemic? And if they are, are they not endemic to existing socialist societies too? There are assumptions here about the incidence and causation of corporate and governmental crime that require careful examination.

The examples given above reveal no clear link between the general political line of a newspaper or periodical and its propensity to publish financial and political scandal, and it is mistaken to view 'the media' as a coherent 'institution'. Except at the most general policy level (such as opposition to communism), capitalism is a competitive form of economic activity. The few magnates who remain – though ironically, the newspaper technology that has destroyed the power of the print unions means cheaper start-up costs for independent and/or radical campaigning newspapers – are only too happy to see their competitors under attack for malpractice, and scandal sells newspapers. Personal and commercial vendettas may also play a part: the enthusiasm of the *Observer* during the period 1984–87 for stories examining alleged links between the Prime Minister's son, Mark Thatcher, and Omani and Brunei commercial developments, and for delving into the background of the Al Fayed family – who took over Harrods in 1985 – may owe something to the fact that 'Tiny' Rowland, whose company Lonrho owns the *Observer*, was frustrated consistently by the Thatcher administration in *his* attempts to gain control of Harrods. (This is not without a certain irony, for in the 1970s, Lonrho's activities were branded by Conservative Prime Minister Heath as being 'the unacceptable face of capitalism'.) It would be false to infer that this wholly explains that newspaper's interest – it has long had a tradition of commercial exposés – but it does show what can happen when members of élites fall out. Financial scandal in high places generally receives much less daily attention than other sorts of crimes – not to mention 'tits and bums' – but it is more expensive, time-consuming, and libel-prone to work up 'white-collar' than other types of stories.

Business crime stories – like scoops of all kinds – also suffer from a relatively short news-stand life, which means that the investment of time to reward is comparatively high. With the possible exception of the less news-dominated and more analytic newspapers such as the *Financial Times* and the *Guardian* in Britain, or the *Wall St. Journal*, the *Washington Post*, and the *New York Times* (in the US), if one cannot get a scoop or write a new angle on a story, it is unlikely to get published at all, at least in Britain. One of the structural problems in television and radio reportage of fraud is not only that it is easier for the media to live on a diet of crime-pap fed by the police and the courts, nor even that Britain does not have a Freedom of Information Act which makes investigative journalism easier in the United States: it is that pin-striped blood does not show up very easily on the walls.

This is *not* to deny that most crime news is working-class (or 'underclass') crime news, nor that there is a generally conservative ideological bias in the media, nor that business and political scandals are not covered up as a result of political influence, economic interests (say, from advertising revenue), fears of losing a cheap and ready supply of news items from government departments or the police, and fears of being sued for defamation. The latter is a particular problem within the framework of UK legislation: to demonstrate the lack of simple unity between the state and commercial élites (discussed further in Chapter four), we should note that in 1985, a defamation writ was taken out against the Chancellor of the Exchequer by accountants Arthur Young in relation to statements made by him to the media about their alleged negligence in their role as auditors to Johnson Matthey Bankers. *Commercial* television has some excellent investigative documentaries, such as *World in Action*, and consumer programmes such as *4 What It's Worth*. But the enthusiasm of the BBC for investigative journalism was certainly dampened by the £75,000 damages and about £1 million costs it had to pay out in 1985, after the popular television programme *That's Life* branded a Harley Street slimming expert 'a profiteering, unscrupulous quack'. (Two doctors who had assisted the programme had to pay £25,000 also.) In 1986, it had to pay some £500,000 in out-of-court damages and costs to two Conservative MPs whom it had accused of being fascists. Books are sometimes withdrawn and their authors and publishers required to pay damages: this happened – temporarily – to the study of political corruption in the North East of England by Milne (1976) and to the study of Lloyd's of London by Hodgson (1984, now updated in 1986). The upperworld is not the only source of defamation actions, but damages (understandably) are likely to be higher where the 'victim' is someone of high status; and the wealthy can afford better lawyers, which is important in a legal system like that in Britain where there are no contingency fees (i.e. where it is a breach of professional rules for a lawyer to charge a fee proportionate to the sum obtained). For some earlier discussion of influences on publication of corruption in the British media, see Doig (1983) and Murphy (1983).

In liberal democracies, the perceived public acceptability of business, governmental, and police malpractice stories can change over time. It may be that until the Iranian arms deals, under Reagan – though not in 1985 or 1986 under Thatcher – the revival of patriotism and support for business as central cultural themes made exposé less popular among the media. However, unless the scandal concerns the direct owner or editor of the newspaper or television station (whether financially or in terms of a hoped-for title in the Honours List), or unless his actual or prospective business partners are affected, the *general* relative media neglect of business crime compared with other forms of crime is explicable more by laziness, investigative cost, the invisible nature of the crime and the deviousness of its progenitors, and by the difficulty of presenting it simply in the human terms expected by mass audiences, than by any élite conspiracy to suppress it. The exception to this is those societies –

capitalist and communist – where there is censorship or where the media are controlled directly by the government.

Fraud and the criminal justice system

The official picture of crime and offenders that is generated by criminal statistics shows that crime is primarily an activity conducted by working-class juveniles against motor vehicles, households, and shops. In England and Wales in 1985, fraud and forgery constituted only 3.7 per cent of notifiable offences, 5.7 per cent of convictions for indictable offences, and 1.3 per cent of all convictions (including summary and triable-either-way offences). Those imprisoned for fraud and forgery comprised only 11.8 per cent of those who received unsuspended or partially suspended sentences for indictable offences: (9.3 per cent if we include suspended sentences). Most of these offences are relatively minor value cheque frauds rather than major crimes requiring intensive investigative effort and vast trial costs. During the 1980s, expenditure on the criminal justice system in the United Kingdom has boomed, from about £2 billion in 1979–80 to about £4 billion in 1985–86. The police, the courts, the probation service, and the prison service have been expanded to cope with the rise in 'criminal business' (but not of busines crime!) There are no detailed sub-totals for particular forms of crime, but very little of this extra expenditure has been devoted to dealing with fraud or business regulatory offences, which comprise a tiny proportion of convicted offenders and criminal justice resources. Pending the establishment of the Serious Fraud Office – see Chapter 8 – the most expensive parts of the system are the Fraud Investigation Group – a task force which deals with the most complex frauds – which costs £1.5 million annually, and the Metropolitan Police Company Fraud Department, which costs under £5 million annually. (As a point of comparison, in 1984–85, gross expenditure on the Metropolitan Police totalled £866 million, though there are no separate figures for the CID.)

I will review in later chapters some possible ways of accounting for the relatively low position occupied by commercial fraud in the official crime problem. The political agenda within which fraud may be viewed has changed dramatically, at least during the mid–1980s, in the light of political scandal surrounding Johnson Matthey Bankers, Lloyd's, and insider dealing, but there is nothing unique to fraud about the fact that crime policies are influenced by political pressures. Despite the change of political attitude, the priority that fraud receives is indicated by the fact that in 1985, out of 120,116 police officers in England and Wales, only 588 were allocated to Fraud Squads (though this excludes the fact that many CID officers spend some of their time dealing with relatively minor frauds on division).

Street crime and household crime have understandably dominated criminological as well as political debate, and even on the political left, policy arguments have concentrated on these types of crime rather than on business crime, which has been disregarded as being irrelevant to the alleged drift into a 'law and order society' (Lea and Young, 1984; Norton, 1984). However, commercial crime remains interesting not only because of its 'objective' social and economic significance but also precisely because of the ambiguity in whether or not it is or should be part of 'the crime problem'. Particularly in the realm of investor protection, there is continuing debate about whether commercial malpractice is a proper subject for public law – the police and the courts – or whether it should be left to be dealt with principally by private law – civil redress for those wronged – or by 'self-regulatory' bodies of businesspeople and professionals with the unusual constitutional status of being licensed by the state to police crime. Although these are issues that must be resolved through moral and political debate (and action) rather than by empirical research, the chapters that follow will seek to systematize and review both knowledge and thinking on these topics, so that we can comprehend better the impact of commercial fraud upon different sectors of the population and how current methods of controlling it have come about.

Sutherland (1983, originally 1949) argues that white-collar crime *is* organized crime. Nevertheless, as he noted and as has become conventional wisdom in criminological circles, the control mechanisms for corporate and for organized crime are different (1) in terms of the social standing of the suspects and (2) in terms of the comparative immunity of 'white-collar crimes' both from police surveillance and from the 'normal' stimulus-response mechanism of crime-prosecution which – corruption apart – we observe in the handling of street crime and organized crime. However, one important change in this demarcation, which has not yet been appreciated sufficiently in Britain, is that the growing involvement of 'professional' and 'organized' criminals in sophisticated fraud, and the increasing use of financial institutions to launder vast quantities of money from fraud (as well as from so-called 'victimless' crimes such as narcotics, gambling, pornography, and prostitution), is bringing official attitudes to regulating 'the upperworld' closer to those of regulating 'the underworld'. (See, for example, the recommendations of the President's Commission on Organized Crime, 1986b.) This American trend has spread to Britain in the mid-1980s, and has been given impetus by the ease with which those who melted down and resold the £26.5 million gold bullion stolen in the Brinks-Mat robbery – the largest every robbery in Britain – were able to take from their accounts millions of pounds in notes from over the counter without any questions being asked by the bankers. When the local branch of Barclays ran out of £50 notes, the Bank of England rushed some more to them, again without query. The demands for American-style currency deposit reporting requirements upon banks are reinforced by the siphoning of funds overseas through British banks, allegedly to finance drug deals as a highly profitable form of re-investment (the *Daily Telegraph*, 25 July, 1986). After all, despite falls in the inflation rate during 1985 and 1986, the rational criminal capitalist still needs to make his money work for him!

The strategic role of financial institutions in facilitating international terrorism and the drugs trade (Adams, 1986; Arlacchi, 1986; Shipman, forthcoming) has brought in its wake a level of law enforcement interest in commerce that is beginning to prise open banking secrecy and increasingly will bring commercial fraud under police surveillance. This, combined with other social changes discussed in later chapters, means that *some* of the activities of commercial élites are now liable to greater official and social scrutiny than they have been hitherto, particularly in the United States. This observation about upperworld vulnerability to law enforcement does not apply to areas of corporate criminality such as health and safety at work offences, whose investigation has been hived off to non-police regulatory agencies. Moreover, there are powerful counter-pressures from financial institutions and other interested parties (such as arms dealers) who are concerned about the intrusions of government into 'private' commercial transactions and about the implications of this for their profits. (The concern about profits is left implicit or is made altruistic by talking about 'the damage to the balance of payments'.) But gangster involvement in money-laundering, in the illegal dumping of toxic waste, and in financial fraud is slowly altering the focus of policing, widening the aperture of its lens so that it brings into view at least those parts of the upperworld which intersect with the activities of organized crime groups. In Britain, as we shall see, in 1986, despite a gradual growth in Fraud Squad manpower, very few state policing resources were devoted to disciplining the upperworld, but developments in the organization of crime (including, but not restricted to, fraud) will make such an extension of policing seem necessary.

For conservatives and non-conservatives alike, it is not self-evident that rigorous crime control is always 'a good thing': extending and enforcing the ambit of law always involves costs to some sections of society, though if we ourselves are likely to suffer a reduction in liberty or profit, it generally makes a difference to our level of support for firmer action. Despite counter-attacks from tough-minded retributivists, there has been much talk in the 1970s and 1980s about the virtues of diversion from the courts, whether out of humanity, whether from the belief that labelling people as 'offenders' makes them behave worse rather than deterring them, whether to alleviate the fiscal crisis of the state, or – most likely – from a contribution of all three. (See Cohen, 1985; Garland, 1985; and Scull, 1982, for more general discussion of these themes.) Historically, the social problem of fraud has been the very obverse of the usual penal problem, for the difficulty has been to get fraudsters into the criminal justice system, not to divert them from it: when penal reformers or the Home Office have cause to complain about fraudsters overloading the prisons, we shall know that the nature of policing has changed quite fundamentally. The remainder of this book will flesh out the regulatory tensions and the crime control assumptions that lie behind this particular form of community policing.

2 The impact of commercial fraud

The scale of losses or injuries does not determine how we will react to any given type of conduct. If it did, we should pay more attention to industrial and road traffic accidents, and less to mugging and intentional homicide, as sources of limb damage and trauma. All sorts of things affect the way we view and react to 'social harms'. Apart from the physical and financial impact, among these factors are the perceived intent of the person who is seen as 'causing' the harm, and this in turn is related to our perceptions of the 'sort of people' who commit the acts: otherwise, why would it make a difference whether 'organized criminals' were involved in a particular form of crime?

Statistics are often deployed as a form of propaganda: those who doubt this need only ask themselves what would have been the consequences if, in the 1950s, Senator Joe McCarthy had said only that there were *two* (rather than hundreds or thousands of) communists working for the US State Department. In 1979, the US Internal Revenue Service (IRS) estimated that illegal drugs generated $16.5 billion in unreported income. However, this figure came as unwelcome news to the Senate Permanent Subcommittee on investigations (1980) who, in their 1979 hearings, attacked the IRS Commissioner's data. The Chairman plumped instead for Drug Enforcement Administration (DEA) figures which estimated the size of illegal narcotics profits as being in the range $44–63 billion. This substantially higher figure was a happy marriage between the self-interest of the DEA and that of Senators anxious to raise the level of public concern about drugs: it is possible that the higher figure was the more accurate one, but it strains our credulity to believe that it was chosen for that reason alone.

The President's Commission on Organized Crime (1986a) similarly makes great play of the profits (as well as the malevolence) of 'organized crime'. Estimating these profits is a rather hazy process, not least because for self-protective reasons, syndicates do not appear to keep books or other records of how much they have earned. There are no external audit requirements for criminal corporations! As former Los

Angeles Mafia Boss Jimmy (The Weasel) Fratianno observed to the Commission:

> 'Well, no, you don't keep track. You just put people there that you can trust, members of the family or sometimes you use front men, but you don't keep records. That was proven when they found that slip with Frank Costello. . . . They [the police] found a slip in his pocket with some earnings from the Tropicana and they lost millions of dollars, they had to sell the place. So, actually, they don't keep no records.'
>
> (President's Commission on Organized Crime, 1986a:30)

Sometimes, however, Commissions of Enquiry do not get what they want to hear. Later, Fratianno was asked about how he and other Mafia bosses might shield illegal money from the IRS. His reply suggests a somewhat less than impressive portrait of a multinational criminal corporation, and one which is markedly at odds with the world of effortless money-movers depicted in works on the international arms and narcotics trade (Adams, 1986; Arlacchi, 1986; Di Fonzo, 1983; Shipman, forthcoming):

> 'I can't do it. They more or less hide it. . . . They found one in New York where they had it in the attic in shoe boxes, a million dollars. One of the bosses in Buffalo, they found, I think five, $600,000. . . . They don't – I never heard of them laundering the money through banks. I have heard of only one person that had money in banks in Switzerland, a guy by the name of Joe Adamo and Meyer Lansky, that's a few years ago.'
>
> (President's Commission on Organized Crime, 1986a:44–5)

On the assumption that he was telling the truth as he saw it, and not lying to put agents off the trail of his own wealth, perhaps this commercial naivety was a reflection of Fratianno's assertion that the Mafia (though not necessarily individual Mafiosi acting for themselves) stayed out of the narcotics business, where money-laundering is most crucial. Even if it was true of the Los Angeles Mafia in the late 1970s, his account cannot be true of the Mafia generally: it is so inconsistent with other evidence given to the Presidential Commission and with almost all studies of Italian involvement in organized crime. However, his 'under the mattress' account of where the money went is an important qualification to the popular image of Mafia coherence and sophistication (or would have been had the Commission not ignored it). His testimony does not show that money-laundering does not exist, but it does show that it is not universal and/or is a comparatively recent phenomenon.

The Chief Investigator to the Commission, Manuel Gonzales, was asked to estimate the amount of money organized crime was making. He replied that 'there is presently no available estimate of organized crime income that could bear close scrutiny' (1986a:12). Under further questioning from the Commission, he continued:

'In 1979, Jack Key, Staff investigator for the Permanent Subcommittee on Investigations, using only information publicly available, concluded that income from illegal sources ranged from $121 billion to $168 billion annually. Mr. Key was astute enough to recognise that these figures were "subject to debate" because the way in which the underlying data was collected was unknown and not verifiable. Key also pointed out that his computations were incomplete because they did not take into account criminal activity such as auto theft, loansharking, hijacking and labor racketeering in all its forms.

Using Key's low estimate of $121 billion and even reducing that by 30 per cent as an arbitrary margin for error $84 billion as income generated by organized crime and comparing it to several industries and the GNP of several countries, the economic potential of organized crime becomes apparent. . . .

The staff of the Commission cannot accept Mr. Key's approximation of the income from illegal sources any more than he could. However, assuming the correctness of his estimate and that the figure used today of $84 billion were subject to an income tax of 50 per cent, the $42 billion thereby collected as income tax would dwarf the Department of Justice budget, fiscal year, 1985, $3.86 billion and that of the City of New York, fiscal year for 1983 and 1984, $18.3 billion.'

(1986a:14)

Gonzales produces figures to show that the (partly disowned but oft-repeated) estimate of the income of 'organized crime' is greater than that of General Motors and the GNPs of Austria, Denmark, and Greece. This itself is intriguing, for implicitly, 'organized crime' has become a monolith rather than an oligopoly or a competitive series of 'disorganized' criminal networks as argued by Reuter (1983). It is almost as if one had added up the turnover of all US corporations and referred to the total as the income of 'American business'. Even if the estimates of total organized crime income – gross of expenditures – were correct, why would we want to present the data in this way? One reason for doing so is revealed in his testimony:

'The extent of the economic influence of organized crime also may be valuable to policy makers. What might otherwise be viewed as extraordinary measures to prevent the distribution of the proceeds of narcotics trafficking could be warranted by the magnitude of the problem presented.'

(1986a:16)

In other words, impact data play a key role in the political process. If we can show that the problem is large enough, we can get greater powers and more resources from politicians and the public, who become more alarmed as the figures soar. Similar sorts of fears informed (or misinformed) discussions which led up to the passage of the Drug Trafficking Offences Act (1986) in Britain and will doubtless do so in the future. To expose statistical manipulations is not to belittle the seriousness of the drug problem, but the important sociological point here is that by contrast, with the exception of discussions of the 'black economy', no government department or even Chief Constable has sought to play up the cost of commercial fraud (though media enthusiasm for large figures remains unabated). We shall review in later chapters some reasons why this might be so. However, it is as well to look sceptically at cost of crime figures generally, particularly since the media are so fond of quoting them uncritically, and they later become 'true' by dint of repetition.

The cost of fraud

In spite of the qualifications expressed above to the practice of crime statistics, it is an important starting-point for social policy to comprehend the effects of fraud upon the social fabric (including the economy), for the question 'How much of a problem is fraud?' must be addressed partially through data on its cost. Estimating the extent of commercial fraud is a task that presents far greater problems than is the case in other types of crime. Indeed, these problems even extend to *official* statistics on fraud, whose very patchiness tells us something about the priority with which fraud – both by and against business – has traditionally been regarded.

The nineteenth-century philosopher and social commentator Jeremy Bentham saw criminal statistics as a way of representing the extent of morality (or rather, immorality) within the nation. From this viewpoint, it does appear that the forms of social pathology that are of interest to administrators, the police, and the courts, are property crimes engaged in by the working and non-working poorer classes rather than the property crimes committed by those with more control over the means of production. (This is not necessarily class bias: as we shall see, it relates partly to the visibility and reportability of the different crimes which tend to be characteristic of different classes.)

Thus, although the annual publication of *Criminal Statistics in England and Wales* imparts information about losses from burglary, robbery, and theft, nothing is communicated regarding the losses from fraud. The other major state agency responsible for the control of fraud – the Department of Trade and Industry – similarly neither publishes nor collects data on its cost. Only the Inland Revenue and Customs and Excise departments provide data on fraud costs (1) in relation to the prosecutions they undertake and (2) as estimates of the size of the 'black economy'. The Metropolitan and the City of London police forces present a very basic amount of data on numbers of cases investigated by their Fraud Squads and, usually, on the amounts of money involved 'at risk'. However, no other police forces give as much information as this. Consequently, even at the most basic level of presenting the 'official picture of fraud', criminologists face unusual difficulties.

Those data that are available show that in purely financial terms, losses from fraud dwarf all other types of property crime. During 1985, the Metropolitan Police section of the Metropolitan and City Police Company Fraud Branch undertook 791 new enquiries. The 446 cases still under investigation at the end of 1985 involved £867 million 'at risk'. At the end of 1985, the City of London Police had 109 cases under investigation, involving £446.2 million in sterling, plus overseas frauds totalling $52.4 million: an increase of 59.6 per cent over 1984. If we include those investigations that were completed before the year's end, the new enquiries undertaken by the City of London Police Company Fraud Department totalled £541.7 million. (Additionally, the Cheque Fraud Squad dealt with £1 million of fraud, plus one attempted deception of £9.2 million.) The City of London Fraud Squad recorded 613 new cases of fraud during 1985, and at the year end, 55 further cases were still outstanding from previous years, 2 of which had been first recorded in 1978! Such bald statements of cost data are misleading, however, for they do not illuminate the interaction between the stocks and flows of fraud cases. Particularly where businesses do not keep or destroy their records, the length of time that elapses before reporting and, after reporting, for all creditors to be contacted by the police or realize that they have been defrauded, means that it is less meaningful to produce annual fraud cost or case figures than is the case for other types of crime. Furthermore, giving a figure for the cost of frauds under investigation at a particular point in time is by no means as useful as giving a figure for the total of frauds dealt with during the year: what if a fraud was cleared up between the end of one year and the end of the next?

The costs of fraud do fluctuate, but as *Table 3* indicates, they have almost tripled since 1980 and have quintupled since 1974, when the cost of fraud in London was £223 million. Even if calculating the costs of 'fraud currently under investigation' on an 'at risk' basis is an inaccurate reflection of fraud in any given year (and may even involve double-counting the sums if, as often happens, an investigation continues over several years), this does not cast doubt upon the fact that fraud consistently recorded on this basis has grown dramatically. We should note that these figures *exclude* the costs of public-sector corruption cases, which are not collated either centrally or by individual forces.

It is instructive to compare the fraud data with losses from other types of recorded property crime. In doing so, we should note that it is not uncommon for householders and commercial victims of burglary to

Table 3   *The amount of fraud dealt with by London Fraud Squads in £m.*

	City of London Fraud Squad	Metropolitan Police Fraud Squad	combined total
1970			36
1980	54	400	450
1981	54	208	262
1982	100	294	394
1983	115	264	379
1984	302	617	919
1985	482	867	1 349

Source: Metropolitan and City of London Police

inflate their losses to defraud and/or to 'compensate' for expected reduction of their claims by the insurance company: it is so nice to be able to replace that old Kodak Instamatic with a nice new Minolta 7000! In the Metropolitan Police area in 1985, the costs of residential burglary were £75.7 million; non-residential burglary, £41.2 million; robbery, over £17.4 million; theft (excluding theft of vehicles), £74.9 million; and thefts of and from motor vehicles, over £113.1 million. (Recorded theft by employees amounted to a mere £5.5 million of this figure.) This burglary, robbery, and theft figure totals £322.3 million, almost 40 per cent of the total amount of money at risk in those frauds dealt with by the Fraud Squad which, it should be noted, excludes the very substantial number of less *individually* costly frauds dealt with by the CID on division. In the City of London Police area, in 1985, the losses from robbery were £661,986; from burglary in a dwelling, £46,225; from other burglaries £618,357; and from thefts £3,162,865. The total for burglary, robbery, and theft is £4,489,433: 0.9 per cent of the Fraud Squad total at risk at the year's end.

In short, in 1985, commercial fraud recorded by the Metropolitan and City Police Commercial Fraud Department represented four times the total cost of all other property crimes in London. (In 1984, it was just under three times the total cost of these crimes.) To this picture, we should add £814.4 million, which is the total for fraud and corruption recorded by Fraud Squads outside London, compared with £757.2 million of theft, burglary, and robbery outside London. (Unlike the London figures, the fraud cost data were derived from the cases actually completed during the year.) This gives a total of £1084 million for theft, burglary and robbery combined, and a total of £2113 million for Fraud Squad recorded fraud (including attempts). Further work is needed on the validity of the fraud cost statistics, but it appears that *the total cost of police-recorded fraud in England and Wales is approximately twice that of theft, burglary, and robbery.*

In addition, there are 'frauds' that are dealt with by non-state regulatory agencies such as Lloyd's, The Stock Exchange, and the Securities and Investments Board (SIB), though these may not be reported as crimes or, if reported, no prosecutions may ensue. To give one illustration of the potential scale of such cases, at Lloyd's, one insurance syndicate alone – the PCW syndicate, consisting of 1525 members – has lost some £80 million from frauds perpetrated by its managers, and Lloyd's has set aside a sum of £225 million from its reserve fund to cover the estimated collateral costs that are alleged to have arisen out of these frauds. But this is not (or not yet) a recorded crime. Finally, there are 'frauds' that are dealt with by the Department of Trade and by the tax authorities. Loss of revenue from Value-Added Tax evasion has been estimated by the Secretary of State at £300–500 million in 1986, and the Inland Revenue estimates the size of the 'black economy' to be £5000 million, which is considered conservative by many economists: estimates range up to £28,000 million! (What proportion of 'black economy' activity can be counted as 'tax evasion', however, is more difficult, since this depends upon making certain assumptions about the mental element required to demonstrate criminal culpability.) The scale of losses to the state therefore is considerable, even though some of the undeclared economic activity would not take place if the income was expected to be taxed. (The breakdown of frauds experienced by large companies is given later on in this chapter.)

Calculating the *net* loss to victims (after taking into account the property recovered and insurance payments) is more difficult. The 1984 British Crime Survey estimated the net losses from both reported and unreported non-fraud property crime in England and Wales to be as follows: from car thefts, £160 million; from burglary, £110 million; from thefts from vehicles, £100 million; from vandalism, £100 million; and from robberies and snatch thefts, £13 million (Hough and Mayhew, 1985:28–29). This totals £483 million. Metropolitan Police figures for 1984 reveal that without taking into account insurance payments, approximately three-fifths by value was recovered by the Metropolitan Police from thefts of and from motor vehicles, though comparatively little from other crimes. Discounting the money and property recovered, this made the net cost of non-fraud property crime total just over a quarter of the cost of Fraud Squad recorded fraud in the Metropolitan Police District in 1984.

However, except in the sense in which commercial losses can be treated as tax write-offs (for which there are no insurance premiums!) and in the special fields of fidelity insurance for employees, export credits, and indemnity for (and against) professional persons, fraud insurance is a relatively underdeveloped field. (The rise in negligence claims – particularly against auditors – in Britain and North America is making insurance cover extremely expensive if not unobtainable, and in the mid–1980s, the market has been contracting rather than expanding.) Since insurance requirements are a prime motive for reporting crime generally (Hough and Mayhew, 1985), the growth of the fraud insurance market could become a major factor in increasing fraud reporting rates in the future. For example, after 1986, it will become compulsory for all suppliers of financial services in the UK to take out professional indemnity insurance if they wish to obtain the authorization they will need to be able to trade legitimately. But whereas losses from break-ins cannot be redefined as accidents – they are either crimes or no loss at all – the failure of some financial services institutions can occur through commercial misfortune rather than malpractice, so the rate of fraud reporting may not rise in line with the amount of 'real' fraud.

One can look at these cost-of-crime data in yet another way. In England and Wales in 1985, in 22.7 per cent of *recorded* cases of burglary, the value of property stolen was nil. In those cases where something *was* stolen, the average value was £615 for burglaries in dwellings and £535 for non-domestic burglaries. The average cost of a robbery was £1256 or, if one excludes the sixth of robberies in which nothing was stolen, £1283. In the Metropolitan Police District, in 1985, the average cost of robbery was £1152, and the median value was less than £1000; in domestic burglary, the average cost was £778, and the median was less than £500; and in burglary other than in a dwelling, the average cost was £725, and the median under £100. By contrast, no statistics are available for frauds dealt with on division – which would reduce the average figure – but in 1985, the *average* fraud dealt with by the Metropolitan Police Company Fraud Branch involved £1,944,000 at risk – double the figure 1984 and that by the City of London Police Fraud Squad £4,422,000 at risk – also double the figure for 1984. In 1985, the *average* cost of frauds reported by banks to and under investigation by the City of London Police Fraud Squad involved £6,507,400 'at risk': the total cost of reported banking frauds (excluding those where no evidence of fraud had been found) that year was over £200 million.

The dark figure of unrecorded fraud

Crime surveys have undermined academic and governmental confidence in the validity of official crime statistics: see, for example, the British Crime Surveys conducted for the Home Office (Hough and

Mayhew, 1983 and 1985). Some of them have also demonstrated *how* the process of attrition in crime statistics works (see Sparks, 1982, for a review). These surveys conclude that although most unreported crime is not serious (either in objective terms of amount taken/injuries sustained, or in subjective terms as evaluated by victims), many 'serious crimes' are not reported to the police or, if reported, are not recorded by them as crimes. However, it is acknowledged that such surveys provide an only partial view of the 'dark figure' of crime, for they exclude crimes committed by and against organizations. In the absence of any reliable business crime victimization surveys with which to compare crime statistics, it is therefore not known with any degree of confidence how much changes in official figures for fraud reflect 'real' changes in fraudulent activity or changes in willingness (1) to report fraud, (2) of the police to record those frauds that *are* reported, and/or (3) to prosecute frauds. In any event, there would be severe theoretical as well as practical obstacles to such an enterprise. Not only are there no reliable 'body-counts' of unrecorded business crime: with the exception of one US study of securities regulation (Shapiro, 1983), very little is known about what factors influence the non-recording of commercial fraud.

Although there are no hard data on unrecorded frauds, it seems implausible that the average and total costs of fraud should be as low as in unrecorded crime generally. For example, according to the 1984 British Crime Survey, 81 per cent of burglaries in a dwelling over £100 and 71 per cent of burglaries under £100 were recorded by the police (Home Office, 1985:23). Therefore, the total cost of unrecorded burglaries was fairly small. Yet there is no reason to suppose that large frauds will be reported to the same extent as large burglaries. Fidelity insurance is not normally available to cover fraud by directors of the company insured. The larger the fraud, the greater the embarrassment, and in the absence of a clear insurance or compensation benefit from reporting, or legislative requirements or company policy to disclose (discussed in Chapter 5), there is no correspondence between fraud seriousness and reporting. Shapiro observes that 'the relationship of both the total economic cost of a securities offence and the per capita cost of victimization to investor disclosure is generally random', (1983:88).

One British study of companies (Consensus Research, 1985) ended its telephone survey with the question, 'Finally, how much money do you think your company loses through fraud of any kind, e.g. employee and customer fraud, in any given year?' Fraud, we should note, is defined in the Consensus Research survey as 'any act of deceit made with the intention of financial gain', which is rather wider than the offence of criminal fraud and would include civil torts. The 249 respondents estimated that their average loss was £6156. Of these companies, slightly more than half estimated that they lose under £1000 per year through fraud, including one in eight who stated that they did not lose any money at all. Seven companies stated that they thought they lost £60,000 per annum, five of whom estimated their losses at £100,000. (The *median* sum estimated to be lost was not referred to in the text, but it was in the cost band £1000–1999. This is probably more useful than the average, being less subject to the distortions of high value frauds.) Unfortunately, we are not told anything about the distribution of costs by company size, but we might expect larger companies to suffer more. When the report was published, this figure was grossed up in the press – presumably by multiplying the number in the sample by the number of companies in Britain – to conclude that British companies lost £3 billion annually from fraud. (This figure has been used in the media subsequently: *The Economist*, 4 October, 1986, used it – without source attribution – when supporting the government's anti-fraud initiative.) However, pleasant though it might be to believe that we have now uncovered the true figure of reported and unreported fraud – the companies were not asked what amounts they had reported to the police or any other body – some scepticism may be evinced on this score. Among these doubts must be (1) the validity of data from interviews with companies whose anonymity was not assured methodologically by the interviewers' not knowing who they were; (2) the level of honesty of respondents in a very complex and sensitive questionnaire, despite the fact that 'Interviews were conducted by experienced telephone interviewers working from a supervised central telephone unit' (Consensus Research, 1985:2). (We are not told how long the follow-up interviews were, but the first ones lasted an average of ten minutes!); and (3) the instruction to interviewers: 'If don't know push for rough estimate – suggest bands'. Hardly surprising, then, that there were only three companies in the no answer/don't know category (1985:24). To obtain an answer is not the same as obtaining a valid answer: there is clearly more work still to be done on the dark figure of unreported fraud.

With the possible exception of car theft, no crimes are fully reported and recorded. However, fraud does present some special problems, because it offers the possibility of inducing into the victim an erroneous interpretation of what has happened. The victim may believe that he or she has been unfortunate or has made a commercial misjudgment: capitalism, after all, is taking risks and profiting or losing by one's risk-taking. Victims may even remain unaware that they had lost money at all. How does a commodities investor or member of Lloyd's know that the best risks have been siphoned off into the dealer's own account or the re-insurance channelled to a firm beneficially owned by the underwriter? This can happen whether or not the primary investors actually *lose* any capital: the result may be merely that they fail to make as much money as they would have done had they not been defrauded. Similarly with 'insider dealing' which may be unnoticed by anyone except the conspirators. How do the victims of what the person carrying it out knows to be an insolvency fraud know that they have not lost money to just another legitimate failed business (see Levi, 1981)? The point about fraud is that the offenders can manipulate the victims' perceptions of 'what happened' so that it may never even occur to them that they have been victimized improperly or criminally. There are other crimes – such as violence, particularly within the family, and rape – in which the victims may be induced to blame themselves, but except for espionage, pickpocketing, and the special case of 'victimless crimes' such as narcotics use, there are no others where the victim is not aware that harm has been deliberately or recklessly caused to him or her.

Furthermore, even if one does identify a business failure to have been a fraudulent one, estimating the amount of fraud is theoretically and practically extremely problematic. What proportion of a 'bust' company's loss can one attribute to criminally reckless or deliberate trading whilst insolvent (which are both included in the legal definition of 'fraudulent trading' under the Companies Act (1985)), rather than to lawful incompetence? In 1984, the excess of liabilities over assets for individuals and unincorporated businesses that went into bankruptcy in England and Wales totalled approximately £458 million, of which one debtor alone accounted for £140 million (Department of Trade and Industry, 1985). What proportion of this total was fraud? In practice, the police may use the amount of the deficiency (i.e. net liability) as their measure, but this is not necessarily accurate.

From a theoretical viewpoint, the 'at risk' estimates are even worse. In some cases, the sums are readily justifiable: if a gang of forgers is caught with £300 million in well-forged bankers' drafts, or a banking operative is caught on his way to collect £10 million that he has transferred illegally by the Electronic Funds Transfer System to his account in Zurich. But in other cases, there are greater difficulties. Assuming that there had been some kind of fraud at Johnson Matthey Bankers – the small bank whose rescue was organized by the Bank of England in 1984 after a major portion of its lending turned out not to be realizable, generating a serious liquidity crisis – how much was at risk: the entire assets of the bank? (In fact, prior to the decision of the Director of Public Prosecutions that no further action should be taken against the principal suspects, the size of fraud at Johnson Matthey Bankers had been put down officially as a very low figure compared with media 'guesstimates'.)

If a solicitor, with or without total success, puts money from some clients' accounts into legitimate investments (rather than into consumption at gaming tables, etc.), does one put down that the entire sums on deposit with him/her were at risk? If there is an advance fee fraud, where prospective borrowers – often impoverished Third World governments – are promised loans in exchange for an advance payment, is the amount 'at risk' the size of the loan promised by the fraudsters or, as surely is more reasonable, the sum of money they have demanded 'upfront' in advance from those who want the loan? The number of cases in which overestimates occur probably is not large, for the corporations who are the primary clients (by amounts lost and by volume of cases reported) of the Fraud Squads usually have well-defined losses. But the resolution of these issues makes a critical difference to the fraud figures, because multi-million pound sums discussed in advance fee frauds make a sizeable difference to the total fraud costs dealt with by the police: one advance fee fraud alone, in 1985, was estimated at $242.5 million.

In addition, there are the costs of public-sector corruption, where not even the costs known about are collated by the police. How could one set about costing the economic and physical impact of corruption? It may bear no relation to the value of any bribes involved, for a bribe of a few hundred pounds may cover the failure to insert vital structural supports that may cause a building to collapse (or risk collapse under circumstances not as yet encountered). This has been alleged to have happened in many earthquake-prone areas, such as Italy and Mexico, as well as in some major industrial accidents in the west and in the Third World. (It may be difficult to work out whether this is corruption or is a consequence of the almost universally very low level of safety regulation that exists in most capitalist and at least some communist societies.) There are also collateral costs, such as the possible losses to other sorts of businesses – or even, perhaps, starvation of the public – if British or British-based overseas-owned banks are used to 'launder' money via false documentation intended to deceive exchange control regulations in Third World countries.

In *some* corruption cases, it may be argued that there is no damage at all, and even a possible *benefit*. Let us consider the case of a building contractor who bribes an official – in the public or the private sector – to let him know what the competition has bid for a contract. He then bids below the lowest offer. It is perfectly possible that the person or company awarded the contract might have put in a higher tender than the next lowest bid, and therefore the awarders of the contract have ended up paying less than they would otherwise have done. The only loser here is the company that would have received the contract at a higher price. (It seems fair to guess that this relatively benign hypothetical case represents a very small proportion of corruption cases, particularly in countries that do not have adequate rules regarding open tenders, or adequate enforcement of them, and/or fixed price contracts that cannot be adjusted dramatically upwards after the award of the contract. We should note also that one effect of the requirement to take out 'performance bonds' is to reduce competition from new entrants, thereby creating the possibility for greater oligopoly profit than might otherwise have arisen under more perfect competition.) At the opposite extreme are cases where due to corruption or inadequate supervision, inadequate structural supports are provided, though they were paid for, and the price-fixing cartels that have been found in businesses such as concrete supply (in Britain), where the work is shared out between the conspirators, each of whom makes much more profit than they would have done without the cartel.

The problems of cost estimation have been exacerbated by changes in policing and case-handling practices. Prior to the 1980s, the Fraud Squad used to investigate extensively the cases it handled, to build up as complete a picture as possible of the entire network of fraudulent practice. As a by-product (rather than central purpose) of that, it would pursue all avenues to discover the extent and ramifications of a fraud. Since the focus on winnowing fraud cases down to their bare essentials, however, and the charging of sample 'specimen counts' rather than broad canvas conspiracies – a process encouraged by the Fraud Investigation Group – that approach has been abandoned as being too wasteful of scarce investigative resources. Therefore, the police do not trouble to contact all possible creditors and – except in the rare Fraud Squad cases below the Criminal Bankruptcy Order limit of £15,000 – there will be an organizational tendency to *under*state the total of the fraud, for since the object of an investigation is to bring the offender before the court and obtain a conviction, extensive cost data serve no organizational purpose and only a very limited personal purpose for investigators: to show that they have dealt with an important case.

Given that 'fraud' generally requires some mental element of culpability – even if only that enormously difficult concept of 'recklessness' – the extent of fraud cannot be revealed simply by totalling the losses sustained to 'victims': otherwise one might end up including all commercial losses as 'fraud'. The mental element problem does occur in other areas of property crime – did I lose my wallet or was my pocket picked? Was there an attempted burglary if there is no evidence of an actual break-in? – and, as in rape, the victim's perception that a crime occurred cannot be taken as definitive in a legal sense. But resolving the mental element probably makes a larger difference to the cost-of-crime estimate range in fraud than in any other area of criminal behaviour.

International estimates of the costs of fraud and economic crime

The high cost of fraud also applies internationally, though, particularly because of insurance cost attribution problems, it is not possible to disaggregate the data to learn what proportion of the costs arose in the UK. For example, in August 1985, the international air transport body, IATA, calculated that $500 million – half the profits made by the air industry worldwide – had been lost through fraud. In 1984, the London-based International Maritime Bureau dealt with 109 cases of maritime frauds involving $262 million. From its inception in 1981 to 1986, the Commonwealth Fraud Office – a section of the Commonwealth Secretariat – dealt with 900 cases involving an estimated $21 *billion* 'at risk' throughout the Commonwealth. However, quite apart from the serious difficulties involved in evaluating cost estimates, different denotations of economic crime – the term used on the continent – make comparisons more hazardous still. Moreover, much of the following relates to tax evasion, whose estimation is particularly problematic because the data are based not on cases recorded by the police but on theoretical assumptions regarding the way the 'black economy' relates to the volume of large denomination bills, etc. (For a good overview of tax evasion estimates, see Walter, 1985.) Money from narcotics sales also affects the level of tax fraud as well as other regulatory reporting offences: it is not without interest that in 1983, the Organisation for Economic Co-operation and Development (OECD) found that the world's reported payments exceeded receipts by over $100 billion, thus indicating at least part of the international money flow that evades normal economic scrutiny. Finally, we should bear in mind the impact of inflation upon estimates of cost derived from studies in earlier periods.

WEST GERMANY

In West Germany, since 1974, the majority of public prosecutors have been invited to report all 'grave' cases of economic crime that they handle. Nevertheless, despite the fabled reputation of the Germans for administrative thoroughness, Tiedemann observes that:

> 'Due to the inner restrictions of this system of notification, it covers not more than 15 per cent of the known (!) cases of economic offences pending in the ordinary courts, thus excluding all minor and medium sized economic crimes and all special procedures of specialized agencies (as in most tax, anti-trust,

and black labour cases). On the basis of these more or less uniform, but personal, estimations of public prosecutors at the beginning of criminal procedures, we know that just this selected group of heavy economic offences causes a physical damage of several billion German Marks per year.'

(Tiedemann, 1985:101)

He goes on to 'guesstimate' that including the 'dark figure', economic crime in West Germany costs 50 billion DM (£15 billion sterling). Even less information is available for other European countries, but I include below what data I have been able to obtain on costs internationally.

CANADA

I have no figures for Canada generally, but one regulatory official informed me that insurance fraud alone cost $860 million in 1985.

CHINA

The Central Disciplinary Commission of the Chinese Communist Party has stated that in 1984, the Government lost about £1 billion because of 'irregularities' in state departments and enterprises. £450 million was lost because of 'excessive operation costs, unreported or concealed profits, fake losses, tax evasion, and bribes' (Niang, 1986).

FRANCE

In 1975, offences against the exchequer, representing a substantial proportion of economic crime (smuggling, tax evasion, and other costs to the state), were estimated by the French government to cost 35–40 billion francs (about £4 billion sterling): approximately 15–17 per cent of state budget expenditure. To express this more graphically, this was twice the size of the budgets of the Ministries of the Interior, Justice, and Health combined. No other data on commercial crime in France appear to exist.

HONG KONG

During the first half of 1985, the Hong Kong Commercial Crime Bureau was investigating 300 alleged frauds over £50,000, including one where suspected losses exceeded £20 million: the total cost of alleged frauds in 1985 was HK $2,462,365,000, more than double the figure for 1980.

ITALY

In Italy, the 'underground economy' is reputed to account for 30 per cent of GNP (Mattera, 985:84). This is the largest figure for any developed country, and reflects important features of the Italian economic structure. In Italy, in 1984, shopowners reported to the tax authorities average annual incomes of $3579 compared with $5694 for shop *assistants*, and higher incomes still for factory workers. (This suggests some inequality in the ability to evade taxes, based around control over the means of production and account-giving.) No data are available on the costs of non-tax fraud.

SCANDINAVIA

Scandinavian research focuses upon tax evasion, which is a critical economic and political problem for economies with a large public sector welfare system. The governmental need to reinforce public sentiments of morality (and maximize income) in the taxation area means that tax evasion is to them what social-security and welfare fraud are to the British and United States governments. One Norwegian estimate (Strom, 1985) is that the hidden economy constituted 6.3 per cent of the Norwegian GNP and cost NOK 14.5 billion (£1.4 billion) in 1978. In 1977, a Swedish working group against organized crime found that *detected* systematic tax evasion by businesspeople cost SEK 500–1000 million per annum (about £45–100 million). Subsequent intensive research suggests that approximately 5–6 per cent of Swedish GNP, including income from non-tax crime, is not declared (though part of this may be due to forgetfulness and other lawful excuses), totalling SEK 24–48 billion (£2.3–4.5 billion) in 1983 (Svensson, 1985).

UNITED STATES

In the United States, tax evasion estimates range from 3.9 per cent to 33.1 per cent of the GNP (Tanzi, 1982), though the latter figure includes illegal income from 'organized' (or, as Reuter, 1983, argues, *dis*organized) crime. Gartner and Wenig (1985) suggest that a figure in the range of 5–7 per cent of GNP is more plausible. Whatever the case, it is clearly a substantial amount of money! Analysis of the costs of non-tax business crime in America is little more advanced than it is in Britain. The US President's Commission on Law Enforcement and the Administration of Justice gives the general flavour of the cost debate:

'It is estimated that the cost to the public annually of securities frauds, while impossible to quantify with any certainty, is probably in the $500 million to

$1 billion range. A conservative estimate is that nearly $500 million is spent annually on worthless or extravagantly misrepresented drugs and therapeutic devices. Fraudulent and deceptive practices in the home repair and improvement field are said to result in $500 million to $1 billion annually; and in the automobile repair field alone, fraudulent practices have been estimated to cost $100 million annually.'

(President's Commission on Law Enforcement and the Administration of
Justice, 1967:103–04)

Reiman, as part of his indictment of the hypocrisy of the US criminal justice system, enthusiastically quotes articles from *Newsweek* and the *US News and World Report* in 1979 and 1982, which assert that corporate crime (including pollution, tax evasion, corruption, and price-fixing) totals 'as much as $200 billion a year' (Reiman, 1984:86). He then takes the US Chamber of Commerce's guesstimate in its 1974 *Handbook on White-Collar Crime* that white-collar crime cost $41.78 billion, indexes it to allow for inflation and the growth in the *total* US population, and concludes that in 1980, the cost was over $75 billion. This total comprises $0.14 billion for bankruptcy fraud; $5.4 billion for bribery, kickbacks and payoffs; $0.18 billion for computer-related crime; $37.8 billion for consumer fraud, illegal competition, and deceptive practices; $1.98 billion for credit and cheque-card fraud; $12.6 billion for embezzlement and staff pilferage; $3.6 billion insurance fraud; $6.3 billion receiving stolen property; and $7.2 billion for securities thefts and frauds. Reiman sums up with the observation that

'This is certainly a conservative estimate in the light of the estimates quoted earlier, but large enough for our purposes. For example, it is over 3000 times larger than the total amount taken in all bank robberies in the United States in 1980, and nearly nine times the total amount taken in all thefts reported in the FBI Uniform Crime Reports for that year.'

(Reiman, 1984:86)

By moral entrepreneurial contrast, Shapiro (1983) is rather more cautious in analysing the cost of securities violations registered by SEC. She states:

'For 42 per cent of the cases in the sample, it was impossible or inappropriate to estimate the amount of money involved. For the remaining cases, estimates were based on such data as loss to victims, profits to offenders, and amount of money involved in illegal transactions (regardless of their consequences). This variable is therefore of questionable reliability. . . . The median cost of offences in the sample is $100,000. Two violations cost less than $100, two others more than $35,000,000. Those offences netting the greatest amount of money involved stock manipulation, self-dealing, and boiler-room activities.'

(Shapiro, 1983:31–2)

Because of the greater ease of costing clear-cut embezzlements compared with the more complex schemes, leading to the placing of more of the latter than the former into her 'missing data' costing category, it seems likely that the median figures here are underestimates. However, even if the method of calculation does not bias the data against the higher-value frauds, they show typical costs to be much higher in the securities fraud field than in any other area of non-fraudulent crime (except, perhaps, racketeering and so-called 'victimless crimes' whose costing is problematic: see Reuter, 1983).

It may be helpful, as well as dramatic, to summarize by noting that over roughly the same period in the United States, the average robbery costs $338 (Sykes, 1978:94), while the average convicted federal white-collar felony costs over $300,000 (Wheeler and Rothman, 1982:1414), and the average offence investigated by SEC costs $400,000 (Shapiro, 1983:9).

PLACING CRIME COSTS IN PERSPECTIVE

Raw economic costs are by no means the only salient features of property crime. Compared with the total volume of business transactions, losses from fraud are only a relatively small proportion: credit-card fraud, where in 1985, Barclaycard/Visa lost 0.25 per cent and Access/Master Charge lost 0.14 per cent of turnover to fraud, is an example. Although Access losses from fraud rose from £6.6 million in 1984–85 to £7.9 million in 1985–86, the rise in turnover meant that percentage losses dropped from 0.15 per cent to 0.14 per cent of Access transactions. However, if we are to be consistent, the same logic should apply to other kinds of crime: burglary is smaller than fraud as a proportion of the amount of property in existence! Autocrime – the primary form of recorded crime in Britain – cost about £100 million to British Insurance Association members in 1984, but this was a small proportion of total motor insurance claims – £1,600 million – let alone of the total value of vehicles on the road.

Anxiety about crime and perceptions of the seriousness of different crimes have symbolic and emotional dimensions as well as an economic one, as we shall explore later. If we are to argue the pragmatic line that losses from fraud are just one more form of economic cost, could we not state this equally of shoplifting and vandalism? If it is scarcely reassuring for a burgled householder to be told that most homes are not burgled in any one year, why should this sort of statement reassure a fraud victim, or the state representing taxpayers or the interests of fraud victims as a class? The interaction between costs, risks, experience, and fear of crime is extremely complex (Hough and Mayhew, 1985; Maxfield, 1984). Indeed, the whole field of risk analysis requires the most careful consideration when we seek to place crime in context.

The notion of cost can present interesting conceptual questions. Although I propose to ignore them here, the redistributive effects of crime (including tax evasion) are intriguing to examine: it would be a strange economist who only looked at the impact of taxation on those taxed, without looking at what the money was spent on! Normally, when we look at the cost of a crime, we take it for granted that this cost is something that ought in principle to be prevented: to think otherwise would be to call into question the legitimacy of the criminal law. However, the desirability of protecting some sorts of property interests is less strongly ingrained – and the undesirability of crime thus less 'self-evident' – in some areas of social and economic life than in others. Cheating the tax authorities might be taken as one public sector example. In the private sector, action against product counterfeiting has become a major area of pressure-group activity within the UK, and the Anti-Counterfeiting Group wants to see it made a specific, imprisonable criminal offence. The merits of protecting 'intellectual property' – and, if so, for what period? – by the *criminal* law are a fascinating issue in themselves: even those who are not normally opposed to the extraction of 'surplus value' by capital from labour believe that some patent protections are an unfair monopolistic practice. What is a cost to the companies and to this author, however, may not be a cost to the wider community, if they are able to obtain products of the quality they want at a much lower price than they otherwise would have had to pay. Many counterfeit books – being badly reproduced – do not meet all these criteria; many counterfeit goods are sold at roughly the same price as the genuine articles, thus defrauding the consumer as well as the original producer, and pharmaceutical copies – whether legally obtainable drugs or illegal ones such as heroin and LSD – are sometimes extremely dangerous, since quality control is poor or non-existent. (The pharmaceuticals manufacturer may even be subjected to a product liability writ when, in fact, the drugs that caused the damage were counterfeit.)

Nevertheless, if the genuine and lawful goods were too expensive to be available to them in any form, some consumers *may* have benefited from even the inferior counterfeits: one's status 'on the street' is enhanced even by a fake Patek Phillippe watch, though those who pay full price would be justly annoyed if they found that theirs was a fake or if their friends bought good counterfeits cheaply (or, perhaps worst of all, thought that their own genuine article was a cheap fake). The damage done to future generations by the squeeze on the profits of the lawful producers and distributors may be serious, but the short-term purchasers do not see it thus. In this way, 'crime' is rationalized, just as it is in the distribution and purchase of goods stolen from the workplace

(Ditton, 1977a; Henry, 1978) and, in the face of clearer disapproval from the majority of the public, by burglars and robbers. Attitudes towards fraud will be reviewed in the next chapter. Bearing in mind that net social costs may differ from the losses occasioned to victims, let us now examine the costs to their victims of particular types of fraud, focusing upon Britain but including international data where available.

Computer fraud

Computer fraud occupies a special place in the criminal lexicon. Popularized by massive 'scams' such as the Equity Funding Corporation of America and used as the medium for unorthodox transactions in films such as *War Games* and *Superman III*, the computer occupies a folk devil role in crime as it does in social change generally. The social definition of 'computer fraud' has itself aroused some controversy. For some, particularly the media, it constitutes one of a growing number of 'new' technocrimes, and there is an obsession about 'hacking' into computer systems and obtaining information or manipulating data (whether for fun or for money). For others, including many respondents to the fraud surveys conducted for the Home Office (Levi, 1986a) and by Consensus Research (1985), it is little more than old-fashioned accounts manipulations by means of computers. The banks are certainly keen to emphasize this, since they want to allay public fears about the safety of their money and the confidentiality of financial details in their possession. The Audit Commission also supports the sceptical view by noting that 'It is evident that as with the 1981 survey none of the cases appeared to demonstrate any ingenious application of technological skills: indeed the majority took advantage of inherent weaknesses in particular procedures,' (Audit Commission, 1985:2). However, from both perspectives, computer fraud has the added subversive glamour that it can be perpetrated by schoolchildren who have no job at all and by people with relatively minor positions within a company. Thus, even more than the major swindles alleged to have been committed by high-status persons that have occupied much media space in 1985, 1986, and 1987, it contains an element of the unexpected: the status gap between formal role and size of crime. An added *frisson* is caused by the fact that computer fraud – perhaps tautologically – reflects a failure in supervision by those in high positions. This may be a temporary phenomenon arising from what is basically a generation gap between those brought up in a pre-computer era and those being educated today. However, this makes computer fraud into a kind of Chaplinesque morality play in which the little man humiliates and triumphs over those in authority.

It is important to note that fraud is only one form of business risk to which computer users may be exposed. Other losses can occur due to fire, flood, sabotage, blackmail, industrial espionage, and unauthorized usage for profit or for play. Nevertheless, although its sampling procedures remain somewhat obscure, the European Community Information Technology Task Force (1984) suggests that fraud comes a close second to fire damage as the most costly form of loss in regard to computer installations in Europe.

Before we can discuss the extent of computer fraud, it is necessary to define what is meant by this term. The Audit Commission rejects the argument that a fraud is a computer fraud only if it could not have occurred but for the presence of a computer, and opts for the following: 'any fraudulent behaviour connected with computerisation by which someone intends to gain dishonest advantage' (1985:9). By this definition, the amount of computer fraud as a by-product of the increasing use of computers should grow, unless computer security manages to eliminate traditional frauds committed by or through accounts staff. The link between crime and increased opportunity has analogies with the relationship between autocrime and the increased ownership of motor cars. Newly available microcomputers and personal computers are gradually increasing as a medium for the perpetration of computer fraud, to supplement the mainframe computer frauds that have dominated the field in the past (Institute of Chartered Accountants, 1987).

THE SCALE OF COMPUTER FRAUD

The scale of computer fraud, like all 'crimes' about whose existence even victims may remain ignorant, is impossible to estimate with confidence. In the US, where it is compulsory for all financial institutions (though not all businesses) to report incidents of fraud committed against them to SEC, the data are more reliable, but even these data assume awareness on the part of victims. Nevertheless, as in the case of the Mafia, the absence of hard evidence reinforces beliefs in the dangerousness of the beast, and alarmist comments frequently appear in the media. For example, *Which Computer* (August 1985:58) states that

> 'Foul play on the computer is all too often swept under the corporate carpet. . . . Computer crime has hit the banks hard. Security analysts believe that the Big Four have had to put aside £85 million to cover their losses from fraud this year. Worldwide estimates are in the region of $145 to 730 million.'

There are good grounds for believing that one major UK clearing bank lost £6 million in July 1984. The perpetrator, a data processor working for the bank, intercepted and changed computerized messages during 'front end processing'. Ten payments were intercepted, were directed to his own account and thence (with him) to Switzerland. The European Community Information Technology Task Force (1984) discovered 40 cases of theft or embezzlement via computers, most of them relatively simple input frauds. Eleven of these cases originated in the UK; 9 in France; 7 in West Germany; 6 in Belgium; 4 in Italy; and 3 in Switzerland. In Europe as a whole – over what period is unclear – out of 23 frauds for which figures were known, there were 2 major banking frauds (excluding the one referred to above) which cost over £5 million each; 13 cases costing an average of £500,000; and 8 cases averaging over £20,000. An unpublished study for the American Bar Association in 1984 noted that in the previous 12 months, over 25 per cent of those responding had sustained known verifiable losses totalling $145 million from computer crime.

But one of the irritating tendencies in much writing about computer fraud – apart from there being no discussion of its sampling frame, the Wong and Farquhar (1987) survey is a refreshing exception here – is the absence of any proper time or distribution scale in the analyses: for example, despite the views expressed by the Audit Commission (1985), there do appear to be some large computer frauds, but how frequent are they? A sceptic might well consider that rather than being an example of 'error and omission', high cost estimates are buttressed by the interests of the computer security industry in sustaining a market for security services.

Published official data suggest that there is no great cause for alarm. The Audit Commission state that out of 943 institutions surveyed, there were 77 frauds reported to them, of which 13 involved no financial loss. The total reported loss was £1,133,487, compared with £905,149 in 1981 (Audit Commission, 1985:1). Though the Metropolitan Police found that none of the 67 cases reported to the Audit Commission in 1981 had been reported to them, the above data are hardly the stuff of major moral or financial panics. Indeed, the Commission pours some cold water on the moral entrepreneurs in this field when it observes that

'Statements which purport to specify the precise size of undiscovered fraud must be treated with scepticism. Regrettably "authoritative" statements of the size of UK losses sustained through computer fraud are frequently quoted but the evidence to support such estimates is less readily available.'
(Audit Commission, 1985:7)

However, laudable though this demystification process is in principle, the Commission's own sampling methodology leaves a great deal to be desired. The 1985 report states that

'Individual invitations were extended to local authorities in England, Wales, and Scotland, to health authorities; to a number of government departments; and to all who participated in the 1981 survey. In addition, the list of commercial organisations was increased and a number of accountancy firms were asked to bring the Survey to the notice of their clients. . . . The Institute of Internal Auditors kindly agreed to distribute information to all of its members as did the National Computing Centre to its Security Awareness Scheme members.'

(Audit Commission, 1985:10)

After all this, the response rate was calculated at 55 per cent, though it is impossible to disaggregate sector response rates. (It may be, too, that since the commercial firms sampled belonged to the Security Awareness Scheme, they were more computer-literate than average.)

The results, therefore, are weighted against the 'authoritative' data the Commission seek to provide. Only 209 out of 943 respondents were private-sector institutions. The survey data thus grossly underestimate the private-sector risks because their public-sector sources handle less money and less exchange of goods, particularly since they include a high proportion of institutions such as universities where few such frauds are likely to occur. Furthermore, the importance of audit and the compulsory reporting of fraud detected by auditors has long been a feature of the public sector. By contrast, the private sector is where one would expect the main action to be in the realm of computer (and other forms of) fraud. (It is not without interest that the 1976 Report of the US Comptroller General on computer-related crimes in federal programmes found only 69 cases involving a little over $2 million. This is not a large sum compared with the vast frauds in the private sector such as Equity Funding and the Wells Fargo Bank.)

Computer services consultants Wong and Farquhar (1987) list some 190 examples of computer fraud in the UK since 1959, some of which were never made public. They state that most large frauds involved Electronic Funds Transfers – usually ending in Switzerland – and that the average amount stolen by computer fraud rose from £31,000 in 1983 to £262,000 in 1986. Over the same period, the maximum loss recorded increased from £500,000 to £10 million. (We should note that this one large fraud makes a significant contribution to the high average fraud cost figure for 1986: though not stated in the text, their Figure 1 suggests that the more useful median figure in both years was £20,000.) A 1986 report by one of the largest UK insurers, Hogg Robinson, takes a measured look at computer fraud on the basis of the claims experience of itself and other businesses, and puts the UK annual total at approximately £40 million.

In short, despite constant media 'hype', fuelled by the space-filling requirements of computer magazines, the computer fraud figures do not seem to be particularly high compared with non-fraud computer losses and compared with the vast frauds committed by 'insiders' in senior positions in the insurance and securities markets in Britain and America. This is not to say that computer fraud is trivial, nor that there is not great potential for its growth. Electronic Funds Transfer Systems enable very large sums to be embezzled in 'one-off' transactions, which was much more difficult in the past, where computer frauds tended to be 'slow-drip'. As the European Community Task Force observes: 'Some embezzlers ... would make use of their detailed knowledge of the system to manipulate the programs and data records. This type of elaborate fraud is rarer although it has grave consequences and appears to be growing in popularity' (European Information Technology Task Force, 1984:7). Nevertheless, it is equally significant that only 4 out of 40 cases of theft and embezzlement were of this type. What, then, are we to make of the alleged growth in popularity of elaborate fraud? The rarity of such frauds – as far as we know – does not mean that we should be tolerant of them or that they do not represent a serious problem for businesspeople anxious to protect themselves. How would we react if we were told that there were 'only' four armed robberies, or (perhaps more comparably) burglaries of banks under cover of darkness? What this analysis of computer fraud may illustrate is the need to examine critically *all* claims about the growth of any type of crime. The data also suggest that a more risk-based rather than actual crime-based approach to computer losses is appropriate: for an example of this, see Hogg Robinson (1986).

Both the interviews with senior executives and the questionnaire responses suggested that computer fraud was the area where businesspeople feel most *worried*, probably because it is the area of business that they feel they least understand. Yet computer fraud cropped up only twice when respondents were asked for details of the most recently reported case of fraud, and few stated in interview that they had experienced one (Levi, 1986a). When asked in the telephone survey of 401 companies by Consensus Research (1985) which areas of their company were most vulnerable to fraud, only 31 companies mentioned computer fraud and of these, only 13 considered this to be different from stock/stores or bank-account/petty-cash fraud. It may be, then, that as some have asserted about official views on the Mafia (Hawkins, 1969; Reuter, 1983), 'computer fraud' is a commercial bogey-man whose psychological significance is enhanced rather than diminished by the lack of hard evidence that it exists!

Maritime Fraud

At an international level, maritime fraud plainly is an expensive form of crime. The operations manager of Lloyd's Shipping Information Services has estimated that fraud through forged documents costs £4 billion per annum worldwide, though the basis on which that figure has been constructed is difficult to ascertain. The International Maritime Bureau estimates – on what basis it is uncertain – that it is only aware of 2 per cent of the losses from fraud that arise in world trade. Yet even its own statistics reveal very large costs. In 1984, in addition to normal day-to-day enquiries on behalf of members, it investigated 109 cases, broken down as shown in *Table 4*:

Table 4   *The costs of international maritime fraud, 1984*

type of fraud	no. cases	amount involved $m.
documentary frauds	15	105.0
charter party frauds/disputes	13	25.0
scuttling vessels	2	2.5
deviation of goods/vessels	15	12.0
insurance frauds	23	110.0
voyage/container monitoring	6	–
negotiations of bills	2	1.5
others	33	6.0
total		262.0

Source: I.C.C. International Maritime Bureau

Credit- and cheque-card fraud

Although the criminal statistics are not broken down with sufficient subtlety to confirm this, informed sources state that credit- and cheque-card fraud account for the majority of fraud prosecutions in England and Wales. However, here we witness yet again the disparity between prosecution and cost figures, for the costs involved, though large, are small as a proportion of fraud in general. The total cost of cheque fraud to all clearing banks in the UK was approximately £26 million in 1985. Access has estimated the total of 'plastic' card fraud in the UK to be £50 million in 1985. Barclaycard losses to fraud rose from £2.6 million in 1980 to £5.4 million in 1985, though the rate of increase in costs has declined. Access losses from fraud rose from £1.89 million in 1980 to £7.9 million in 1985–86. Yet we must place these costs in perspective: from 1982 to 1986, as a proportion of turnover – which has been rising rapidly – frauds (which exclude those 'bad debts' that are *not* deemed fraudulent) on Barclaycard have declined from 0.35 per cent to 0.15 per cent and those on Access have declined from 0.18 per cent to 0.14 per cent. (Caminer notes that in the United States, the cost of credit-card fraud was $1 billion in 1982 and 'soon could reach two billion dollars', but asserts that fraud has been rising *faster* than turnover there (Caminer, 1985:747).) This ratio is important when we come to consider the question of fraud prevention and criminal policy. The willingness of companies (and individuals) to take up crime prevention devices is related to a *corporate* rather than *social* cost-benefit analysis. The salience of fraud is dictated more by the proportion of turnover than by the absolute sums involved, particularly where turnover (and thus profit) might be reduced by taking the crime prevention measures. In cases where the company decides – rightly or wrongly, but almost certainly based on inadequate data – that the internal cost-benefit equation does not justify taking stronger prevention measures, some of the costs arising from this are passed on to the taxpayer in the form of policing, prosecution, and penal costs. Paradoxically, the higher the visibility of the fraud and the preparedness of the organization to take action against detected fraudsters, the higher the expenses from these externalities become: more concretely, in 1985, some 4200 persons were imprisoned for Barclaycard fraud and theft offences alone. There is scope for further prevention measures, but the constant *technological* war between banks and criminals, the varying of the methods by which cards are distributed to customers, and the rewards offered to shopkeepers who spot stolen credit cards, have all cut the amount of credit-card fraud from its peak in 1984.

Counterfeiting

The cost of product counterfeiting to commercial organizations is incalculable at the present time, partly because the reporting rate is so low as a proportion of offences: how many people complain to the authorities or to the market trader (or shop) if the Levi – no relation! – jeans they bought happen to fall to pieces a month after purchase? However, the UK Anti-Piracy Group (1986) have calculated that piracy – defined as the reproduction and sale of copyright material without the consent of author or publisher – of books, tapes, videos, and computer software in Singapore, Taiwan, Korea, Malaysia, Indonesia, Pakistan, and Nigeria cost the UK book publishing and music industries alone at least £158 million in 1985–86. British Trading Standards officials – who deal with many but not all prosecutions for counterfeiting – seized over £2 million of counterfeit goods from the 13,948 convicted persons and companies they had convicted between November 1982 and June 1984:

over half of that total was made up of counterfeit video and audio tapes (Murphy and Carratu, 1986). Motor vehicle component manufacturers estimate that they lose £100 million a year from sales of counterfeit products.

In the United States, the Intellectual Property Alliance – which represents the major US copyrighted industries – has estimated that in the ten most active counterfeiting nations, piracy costs the US economy $1.3 billion. The January 1984 Report of the US International Trade Commission put the losses suffered by US companies as a result of product counterfeiting at $6–8 billion annually. An article in the *Financial Times* (1 September, 1986) asserts that North American vehicle component manufacturers lose $2.7 billion annually from counterfeiting and that one in four of the two billion records and cassettes sold around the world is a fake. It also quotes estimates that Americans have lost as many as 250,000 jobs and the British 100,000 jobs.

The basis upon which these figures are calculated is difficult to discern : as with the relationship between tax evaded and benefits lost to the tax authorities, we ought to allow for a gap between the value of the counterfeit goods sold and the amount which the lawful producers would have obtained from their sales. There is doubtless an element of propaganda by manufacturers aimed at getting governments to act against counterfeiters overseas. Moreover, good quality counterfeiting can sometimes be a long-term benefit in publicizing brand names, which in turn encourages legitimate purchases of market leaders. But we should accept that whatever the short-term benefits to the consumer, these activities are damaging to the overall opportunities for authors and musicians. (They can, however, act as a useful psychological cushion to authors whose books are selling badly: the brilliance of one's work means that there are undoubtedly vast counterfeit sales!)

Some 1985 British survey findings on costs of fraud against large companies

For reasons of delicacy, and to avoid prejudicing the rest of the questionnaire, those executives who were not interviewed were only asked for details about those frauds that they *had* reported within the previous decade (Levi, 1986a). Even on that basis, there was a high level of victimization (though one should bear in mind that given the size of the companies surveyed, this is not altogether surprising).

The results of the survey show reporting in the expected direction. Fewer companies had reported cheque and credit-card frauds than other frauds, and the average value of the cheque and credit-card frauds

Table 5 *Reported fraud (other than cheque and credit card)*

	no. of times reported (% companies)			
size of fraud	never	once or twice	3–10 times	>10 times
less than £1,000	47.5	15.0	10.0	27.5
£1,000 to £4,999	47.5	22.5	12.5	17.5
£5,000 to £50,000	36.6	36.6	19.5	7.3
more than £50,000	61.5	25.6	7.7	5.1

Table 6 *Reported cheque and credit-card fraud*

	no. of times reported (% companies)			
size of fraud	never	once or twice	3–10 times	>10 times
less than £1,000	70.2	10.6	6.4	12.8
£1,000 to £4,999	75.6	9.8	2.4	7.3
£5,000 to £50,000	82.1	10.3	2.6	5.1
more than £50,000	94.3	5.7	0.0	0.0

was lower. The larger the sum involved, the smaller the proportion of companies who have reported frauds. (Despite the 'dark figure', it is unlikely that this *ratio* of large to small frauds would alter dramatically.) On the other hand, it is interesting that almost 40 per cent of the companies had *reported* at least one fraud costing over £50,000: 5.1 per cent of them over 10 times.

When asked the nature of the fraud that they had reported most recently, the largest single category was cheque/credit-card fraud (23.8 per cent), followed by embezzlement/expenses frauds (19 per cent). Internal frauds of various kinds were popular. These were concentrated around customer accounts and goods received, with false invoicing being the most common method, sometimes in collusion with suppliers. Both money and goods were taken, often by 'teeming and lading' – shuffling various accounts around – or simply not putting transactions through the books. After that, forgery of a bank paying in stamp, insurance (obtaining premiums for non-existent cover), hire purchase, commodities, investment (by a trustee of a fraudulent unit trust), liquidation, and computer fraud (against payments to pensioners) were mentioned by one or two people each. The sums ranged from less than £100 to over £100,000. The most common was the £10–50,000 range (35 per cent of those reporting). Next came the £5–10,000 range (20 per cent reporting); and a surprising 17.5 per cent in the £100,000 plus range. The average sum involved was £89,537, and the median sum was £15,000. One fraud involved £2 million, which boosted the average figure. However, even the median sum is quite high, particularly when compared with other crime figures.

It is important to distinguish between the average cost of a particular kind of fraud and its total costs. It is possible that the average computer fraud might be more costly than any other type of fraud, but that securities, insurance, or insolvency fraud may each entail a higher total cost. Similarly, although there may be many more cheque and credit-card frauds than any other type of fraud – this is probably the case in most western countries, at least when one looks at the *recorded* fraud figures – the total costs of such frauds may not be high compared with others. Social and political costs are a separate question still, and we will now turn to examine these.

The social and political impact of fraud

Another important dimension of fraud is more difficult to quantify: its impact upon social values and sense of well-being. Certainly, this has economic ramifications. All commerce, and even the acceptability of a national currency, depends upon *some* degree of trust and confidence. An early example of the consequences of such a collapse of confidence was the Wall Street Crash of 1929. More recently, during the 1980s, the failures of the Carrian and Pan-Electric corporate groups in Hong Kong, Malaysia, and Singapore, accompanied by proven allegations of widespread fraud, had disastrous short-term effects upon their national economies: stock market values plunged 20 per cent overnight. (In April 1986, Singapore and Malaysia share price indices dropped to their 1979 level, though part of this was due to the collapse of the tin market and the International Tin Council, though allegations of fraud there were hotly disputed.) Confidence in Malaysian banking institutions was undermined temporarily also by the huge losses among Deposit-Taking Co-operatives in 1986, due partly to the large number of loans advanced to directors and their families. During 1986, serious political as well as commercial concern was caused in Portugal, by the failure of a 'bank' run by a 'little old lady', Donna Branca, who was called (before her arrest) 'The People's Banker'; and in Argentina, by an alleged £76 million fraud by its senior management upon the aptly named Banco Alas which, the State Prosecutor claimed, involved high-ranking politicians and nominees of President Alfonsin.

In the case of fraud affecting financial institutions, or the diversion of funds from governmental or non-governmental aid agencies, the effects are measurable, but may well extend far beyond the money stolen: to the death of thousands from malnutrition, for example. But in other instances, where governmental officials take bribes from narcotics traffickers, the negative effects may be more external than internal. If, as was alleged to the 1984 Royal Commission of Enquiry into the Bahamas, Prime Minister Pindling had accepted $2.8 million in gifts and loans between 1977 and 1983, what damage was caused? Perhaps, if he had been accepting drugs money – of which he was cleared by the Commission – this would have been less harmful *domestically* than if the money had come from local or foreign businesspeople seeking favours or contracts? But the external political costs of the disfavour of the US are considerable, if hard to quantify, particularly when this falls short of an aid and/or trade embargo (as in Cuba) or an invasion (as in Grenada). This unorthodox way of looking at costs does, unfortunately, have its weaknesses, for quite apart from the fact that narcotics use tends to spread to the citizens of the producer or transit nation, those who take bribes from organized crime syndicates are not known to be especially virtuous regarding bribe-taking for internal activities. This was true, for example, of some senior ministers in the British dependency of the Turks and Caicos Islands, where corruption became so endemic that an enquiry in 1986 by Louis Blom-Cooper QC led to the return to direct rule by the Governor as the only feasible response to complaints of trafficking and money-laundering. The effects of fraud and corruption – including exchange control violations which are responsible for much of the capital flight from those countries – are probably greatest in the Third World, where the marginal value of the money lost is much more significant to people who have so little to start with, and in new securities markets, where patterns of trading are not yet secure and credibility as a deposit for funds has yet to be established. This is one reason for the concern in the Far East about securities frauds.

Despite scandals in some of Britain's financial markets, Britain has not yet experienced a loss of market confidence of the magnitude experienced overseas: despite the continuing controversy attached to the morality of some of its senior figures – past and present – Lloyd's managed to attract a record number of new members in 1985. This is an important qualification to the heady political rhetoric about the importance of trust to the conduct of commercial life, for if trust were so essential and so prevalent, commercial and contract lawyers would have far less to do and would be much poorer than they are! Certainly, trust is *preferable*, but in the commercial world – as in the world of politics, the family, and even of the university – much business is done between parties who distrust their partners or opposite numbers. Skill in risk-assessment is considered to be an important quality in commerce. In games of skill (as well as those of chance), the risk of being cheated is only one risk among many. For instance, trading in the commodities and financial futures markets has an appeal to gamblers, in the west as well as in the Far East, in spite of the fact that – whether due to fraud or not – so few actually make money. (Naturally, insider dealers and those who just take the money and run do better than the average!)

There are some occasions on which despite the political tremors they create in high places, exposés of the fraudulent activities of major securities dealers may yield national economic benefits: the settlement of insider-dealing allegations by SEC against major securities dealer Dennis Levine not only led to his paying a fine of $11.5 million but, from information supplied by him as part of the plea-bargain, to a $100 million settlement with top trader Ivan Boesky in November 1986. Boesky in turn, as part of the plea-bargain, informed on malpractices by *his* top level associates. It is likely that this will lead not only to more penalties in relation to insider dealing – making the SEC cost-effective – but also to a diminution of the activities of *arbitrageurs*, who take huge financial positions in the shares of actual or potential take-over companies, in expectation of profiting from the difference between the final price and what they pay. This in turn may benefit the stability of the stock market and enable corporate directors to spend less time worrying about mergers and take-overs and more time running their businesses. If, as is unlikely, the reduction of opportunities for making vast amounts of money quickly diminishes the popularity of finance rather than industry as a career for the bright and talented, the scandals may even produce a structural benefit for economic development.

It was perhaps fortunate for The Stock Exchange in London and for the British Government's espousal of the virtues of self-regulation that the Boesky settlement was revealed in the same week that very much more modest insider-dealing allegations involving £15,000 and £800 respectively hit the British media: until the Guinness share support operations were exposed at the end of 1986, Britons could not compete with the Americans even in financial scandals! The longer-term effects of falls in investor confidence are not readily calculable, yet there is some unknown and, perhaps, unknowable point at which the escalation of costs begins and may become irreversible, and this, along with *party* political reasons discussed later in the book, is why scandal in the City of London generates so much political concern.

Readers should note that I have now begun to write not just about fraud and corruption but about economic and political scandal. It may cause more political damage if commercial conduct that is defined *socially* as immoral is lawful or is not covered effectively by the criminal law (in statute and common law as well as in enforcement practice), than if people of high standing are prosecuted. For despite the potential for allegations of 'politically motivated prosecutions', there is a sense in which the use of the mystique of the criminal law may defuse scandal by taking it out of the political arena. On the other hand, as Szasz (1986) has argued, the long-term political effects of scandal are rather modest, even when they are as well publicized as Watergate and as Sewergate, the alleged misappropriation of funds and conflicts of interest within the US Environmental Protection Agency that were exposed in 1983.

Arguments over resources for and methods of policing commercial fraud are not a simple question of right-wing versus left-wing politics. Some Conservatives plainly fear that if they do not agree to set up a buffer between investors and the public along the lines of the SEC, the City will be handing a major political gift to the left on a plate. Similar arguments (which also cut across conventional political lines) may be found in the debates over the desirability of independent investigation and adjudication of complaints against the police, lawyers, and accountants. Irrespective of whether law enforcement agencies will actually be able to control the securities market more effectively than would be the case under a system of self-regulation (or, as some prefer to call it, statute-backed practitioner-based regulation), the long-term interests of commerce may rest upon defusing the political time-bomb of fraud allegations. Media and political concern can lead to heavy pressure to institute prosecutions, such as those in Hong Kong following the £690 million collapse of the Carrian group of companies in 1984, and those in Singapore in 1986, following the collapse of the Pan-Electric group of companies, owing Singapore $400 million in debts and $150 million in forward trading obligations that it could not meet. We may conclude that the effectiveness of policing is in practice inseparable from its political legitimation.

In the *realpolitik* of crime control, concern about direct victims occupies a secondary role: apart from myself and those of my friends who might have been poisoned, who is actually worried about how I feel about the fact that my expensive bottles of Austrian 1981 Trockenbeerenauslese contain diethyl glycol, and would be safer circulating around my car coolant tank than in my kidneys? It is the secondary victims – the national economy and actual or potential political supporters – who form the underlying focus for political response. It is for reasons of political economy that support for a tough state policing and prosecution line is by no means confined to socialist critics and to those businesspeople who think the City is riddled with conflicts of interest that require external regulation. Precisely because the public are likely to fuse mistakenly all financial institutions and therefore blame 'the City' globally for anything that goes wrong in one sector of it, many who – like the Chairman of the Stock Exchange, Sir Nicholas Goodison, the former Chief Executive of Lloyd's, Ian Hay Davidson, and the chairman of Lazards (formerly Secretary of State for Trade), Sir John Nott – do not believe that fraud is endemic or even common in Britain's financial institutions can see a long-term commercial advantage in competent state policing. Irrespective of the 'actual' best methods of control, the political impact of *perceived* levels of control is considerable. The principal objective of some supporters of the transfer from self-regulation to state regulation is to restore confidence in the market rather than to police it in the most rigorous way 'feasible'.

The political dimension of upperworld malpractice cannot be overlooked. In some Third World and Comecon nations, fraud and corruption may be endemic, but beliefs about their prevalence are damaging not only for the personal standing of politicians but also because of their effect on economic motivation and social morale. These have been the expressed concerns of a succession of West and East African leaders, where many coups – examples include Nigeria in 1985 and Uganda in 1986 – are accompanied by a promise to eliminate racketeering. In May 1986, following the deposition of President Marcos and allegations of huge kickbacks (particularly from Japan) in the award of contracts by his regime, President Aquino of the Philippines set up an 'anti-graft and corrupt practices board' to liaise with the Presidential Commission on Good Government to investigate the means by which senior army officers obtained their wealth. The political significance of this issue is indicated by the regularity with which 'new broom' assertions are made by newly elected governments, for instance that of Rajiv Ghandi in India in 1985, as well as by military dictatorships such as that of President Ershad of Bangladesh in 1983. (Successful practice is a separate issue: cynics might see these claims about future integrity as symbolic rather than instrumental ones, though the difficulties faced by even the best-intentioned leaders in eliminating or reducing corruption make it hard to assess whether or not the promises of reform were honestly made in the first place.)

Morale is particularly important in economic systems that rely for their success (historically inevitable or not!) upon the inculcation of a 'socialized' rather than a selfish and individualized work ethic: hence the popular anti-corruption campaigns of Presidents Andropov and Gorbachev, and their corresponding drives in China. In the eastern block, these are often backed up by large-scale executions: in China, it has been estimated that there have been 10,000 executions for 'economic crime' in the mid-1980s (*Daily Telegraph*, 23 June, 1986). In the first six months of 1986, the Chinese authorities arrested 18,793 people for fraud and black marketeering – an increase of 236 per cent over the same period in 1985 – reflecting the campaign against economic crime which coincided with the switch to a market-orientated economy (*China Daily*, 30 July, 1986).

Of course, such campaigns are also an excellent method of getting rid of those against whom one has a personal or political vendetta, under the banner of promoting public morality, and the more cynical may interpret anti-corruption drives in the Soviet Union in the mid-1980s as having more to do with 'de-Brezhnevization' than with concern about corruption or a sense of justice. Although there is some truth in it, such an interpretation would, in my view, be oversimplified. These campaigns are also motivated by the view of some senior Russian and Chinese leaders that both corruption and economic failure are the result of the presence of 'rotten pockets' of inefficient bureaucrats (Harris, 1986). This theory is not necessarily correct. One alternative is that corruption is the result of the *intrinsic* tendency of planned economies to develop 'degenerate commandism' (Simis, 1982), since bureaucratic centralism combined with scarcity will always encourage parallel economies: price rationing through corruption rather than through the market. One can understand why this is not a theory that is favoured by the eastern block countries themselves.

In the west, upperworld crime traditionally has generated less concern about its cost than about its political dimensions; for example, the US President's Commission (1967) asserted that the failure to deal with white-collar crime was undermining the moral legitimacy of the criminal justice system as a whole. However, it is uncertain whether revelations of upperworld malfeasance cause or merely reflect pre-existing cynicism. In a 1987 British Gallup poll, 11 per cent (but only 3 per cent of Conservatives) stated that the publicity over Guinness made them less likely to vote Conservative; only 9 per cent thought that the behaviour of the Guinness directors was peculiar to that company; and 80 per cent believed that allegations of 'shady dealings', 'underhand goings on', 'corruption', and 'cover-ups' applied to many City companies. The poll found that only 33 per cent had confidence in City institutions, compared with 41 per cent who had confidence in Parliament, 46 per cent in major companies, 47 per cent in the legal system, and 82 per cent in the police (*Daily Telegraph*, 26 January, 1987). Even prior to the spate of media attention to fraud in the City after mid-1985, a Gallup poll found that 50 per cent of the English public (compared to 35 per cent in 1969) believe that the courts favour the rich and influential (*Daily Telegraph*, 13 March, 1985). How such views as these are formed is unknown but superficially, they may appear to be supported by the low number of convicted fraudsters in Table 7 which, if one ignores the fact that detected tax frauds may lead to civil, administratively imposed penalties more severe in their economic impact than many court-imposed sanctions, might be read as 'there is one law for the rich and another for the poor'.

Table 7   *The costs of crimes and numbers dealt with for them, England and Wales, 1985*

type of crime	costs of crime £	no. convicted or cautioned
burglary in dwelling	221 338 000	26 500[1]
burglary other than dwelling	157 313 000	53 420[1]
robbery	28 781 000	4 607
autotheft	443 030 000	33 757
shoplifting	11 648 000	147 338
theft by employees	16 349 000	6 869
police-recorded frauds	2 113 000 000	27 574[2]
income-tax fraud (1984–85)	5 000 000 000	242[3]
VAT evasion (1984–85)	500 000 000	169[3]

Note: [1]Includes aggravated burglaries.
[2]The majority of fraudsters convicted and cautioned have committed offences whose cost is not included in the above Fraud Squad total, since they are dealt with by divisional CID officers.
[3]The cost figures for tax evasion are estimates of total fraud, and unlike the other data, are not confined to those cases formally recorded as crimes.
The above statistics do not include *all* offences for which businesspeople were convicted. In some cases involving 'regulatory' offences such as pollution, health and safety at work, and fair trading offences, no costs are calculated and/or available.
Sources: Home Office (1986d) and information collected by the author

Table 8   *Statistics for the Metropolitan Police District, 1985*

type of crime	costs of crime £m.	no. summonsed/arrested
(Fraud Squad) fraud	817.0	240
burglary	116.9	13 458
robbery	17.4	2 474
theft and handling	188.0	59 318

Note: There were 7962 people arrested in the MPD for fraud and forgery, but cost data are available only for the Fraud Squad.
Source: Home Office (1986a)

The financial damage due to loss of confidence may be confined to an individual market rather than to the economy as a whole, but even so, it can be severe: the 80 per cent drop in Austrian wine industry exports caused by the diethyl glycol adulteration scandals in 1985 is a case in point, and the Italian wine trade – honest and dishonest producers alike – was similarly damaged by deaths from the adulteration of cheap wine with methyl alcohol in 1986. (By April 1986, the latter had led to 23 deaths: it is expected to lead to a drop of 75 per cent in exports during the latter half of the 1980s, costing at least £400 million net in wine exports and in valuable foreign exchange.)

Given the central importance to the British economy of invisible earnings from the service sector – and the dependence of economic growth policy upon that broad sector – the repercussions of failure to think through criminal policy on fraud could be both economically and politically disastrous. During 1985, half the new jobs in the British economy were related to the financial-services sector, particularly the City of London. In 1985, the financial services industry employed some 1,890,000 people; it contributes £37 billion to the British Gross Domestic Product; and produced *net* overseas earnings of £7584 million in 1985, compared with £2019 million in 1979, when exchange controls were removed, and £1029 million in 1975. In 1985, the largest contribution to these earnings was made by the insurance industry (such as Lloyd's, whose net earnings from underwriting and portfolio investment were a massive £1208 million, the largest single institutional contribution), followed in descending order by banks, pension funds, commodity trading, and brokerage (including The Stock Exchange). Moreover, the spread of share ownership – a sample survey carried out for the Treasury in 1986 estimated that there were 6 million adult share owners in England and Wales, and that around half of these were in the (lower) social classes C, D, and E – means that what happens on the stock market has direct implications for a fairly broad spectrum of people. (The distribution data are slightly spurious, even if the estimate is correct, because even in relation to their incomes, those above the average income own a much greater average *number* of shares.) The de-industrialization of Britain and the global and highly competitive nature of financial markets means that unless there is a radical economic policy shift, ensuring the continued viability of the City is a central strategic issue for the British economy.

Searching questions might be asked about the distribution of benefits from the financial services sector: how much of a 'trickle-down effect' is there for those who are not employed in that sector or who do not sell goods or services direct to them? However, its economic importance should generate considerable thought among all except those within the revolutionary left who believe that there is nothing to lose that is worth having. Brian Sedgemore, the Labour MP who has become the *bête noire* of the City of London, observes that

'For a Conservative government, fraud is serious because it is mainly done by their supporters. The spectacle of rich men with villas, yachts, and jet planes cocking a snook at the Fraud Squad, and slipping off to Miami, Hong Kong and sunkissed islands in the Southern hemisphere with millions of pounds of stolen money, is bad news for them. At a time when they wish to put law – and order – high on the political agenda, it's a disaster which Labour ought to exploit. The public is not slow to ridicule a government which chases the most minor social security cheats, but at the same time refuses to put more police on the big fraud beat. . . . But, in the end, no institutional changes will put fraud out of business. The *ideology* that fuels it must be challenged at a political level. In a country where making money is more important than making things – and is itself the one sign of success – fraud is bound to flourish. Labour's front-bench must. . . . confront the ideology of greed head-on.   (Sedgemore, 1986:34–5)

Yet unless we are to have socialism Sedgemore-style – and what would happen to the balance of payments if those 'invisible exports' actually vanished? – has this type of scandalizing harmed or helped the British people in the short or the long run? (This would require us to define what this help or harm constitutes, and what groups benefit or are harmed.) Just as most academic writing from the left has dealt with crime in the suites only parenthetically, to illustrate the hypocrisy of the ideology of criminal justice, so too was there an almost total neglect of upperworld crime in the 'law and order' platforms of all the major parties prior to 1986: see the discussions of these in Downes (1983) and Norton (1984). Although it may be argued that all responses to crime by politicians are concerned more with politics than with the victims *per se*, issues as central as confidence to the economy are too important to be examined only at the level of political rhetoric and the Long March of Slogans.

Radical critics who argue that the police and independent prosecution system are a mere façade for the perpetuation of ruling-class interests might ask themselves why, if this is the case, City figures have not espoused state 'regulation' with enthusiasm, as giving them the best of both worlds. Indeed, there is a paradox in the way many of the political left view business crime (just as there is over violence against women). Many who are only too anxious to expose the way in which the state and the media create moral panics about crimes committed by the working class and the *lumpenproletariat* repeat uncritically as gospel truth the in many ways more problematic 'guesstimates' of the incidence and impact of 'white-collar crime' (Box, 1983; Clinard and Yeager, 1980; Conklin, 1977; Reiman, 1984), often accompanying them with remarks that the 'true figure' may be even greater! A popular figure is the estimate by the US Chamber of Commerce in 1974 that 'white-collar crime' – that is, fraud *against* business – cost $44 billion compared with $4 billion for theft, burglary, and robbery. This may be added by less pro-business groups to the hypothetical costs of pollution, consumer fraud, and injuries caused by unsafe products and preventable accidents at work or on the street. Reiman asserts that in the United States, in 1980, 'there was one property crime arrest for $4600 stolen, and one embezzlement arrest for every $635,000 "misappropriated" ' (Reiman, 1984:90). Crime statistics may be used for ideological purposes by those groups whose interests they serve but, even if one does not accept that any facts or theories are value-free, not everything is *equally* 'true' or 'false'.

There is an intriguing harmony of interest here between radical criminologists, on the one hand, and private security and self-regulatory organizations (SROs), on the other, who are equally anxious to play up the costs and significance of business crime. For example, in July 1986, the chairman of the Chicago Board of Trade claimed at Federal Trade Commission hearings that American investors have lost $2 billion in the past two years due to fraud, misrepresentation, and bankruptcy in futures trading. He urged a crackdown on futures and options trading carried out by dealers outside recognized exchanges, arguing that investors would otherwise continue to be duped (the *Daily Telegraph*, 28 July, 1986). I happen to agree that on balance, people would be better advised to trade on a recognized exchange. And for all I know, the figure may be as correct as any figure could be. But his estimate may have been influenced, however slightly, by his interest in maintaining the position of the Chicago futures exchange: granted that compensation may be available there, but one may note the absence of an estimate of how much was fraudulently lost from trading *on* recognized exchanges! And note again the magic power of numbers. However, although they might agree on the figures, whereas Reiman (1984) might claim that the frauds were committed by the élite insiders, the private-sector organizations (and, on the basis of her SEC case files, Shapiro, 1983) would point the finger at fringe operators. We will return to this empirical and ideological conflict in later chapters.

There are a number of ways in which Conservatives may seek to defuse the impact of fraud in high places. One is to assert that it is the inevitable result of the occasional 'bad apple' creeping into the barrel: self-regulatory monitoring by 'insiders' and controls over the entry of 'fit and proper persons' into commerce should reduce the risk of this happening, and the Financial Services Act 1986 will change everything. A different sort of approach is to subsume it under the general lament of Golden-Ageism taken up by the Conservative Party Chairman, Norman Tebbit, in his 1985 Disraeli Lecture, where 'permissiveness' is blamed for the rise in corruption as well as other forms of anti-social behaviour. This 'theory' of the causes of corruption is another example of authoritarian populism, used to reinforce prevailing beliefs that crime is the product of laxity in family and school (Jones and Levi, 1987). It is echoed partially in the survey by Levi (1986a), in which a number of executives stated that fraud had expanded in every part of the economy, due to increased opportunities combined with a 'get rich quick' social ethos, tolerance of expenses fiddles, and observation of large-scale malpractice escaping unpunished.

The permissiveness theme raises some interesting questions: what aberration from Victorian values produced the spate of corruption in local government, particularly, during the nineteenth century? (See Doig, 1984; Fennell, 1983.) Considering the history of fraud, corruption, and white-collar crime generally in the United States (Noonan, 1985; Sutherland, 1983), it is hard to sustain the implication that we can lay all blame upon Dr Spock's permissive child-rearing techniques, unless time does indeed travel backwards! Despite the correctness of the observation that there has always been a twenty-year cycle of moral panic regarding 'the young' (Pearson, 1983), there is evidence that juvenile crime has actually increased in recent years, though the relative contributions of increased numbers of juveniles, opportunity, and 'permissiveness' – such as being allowed out on one's own? – are a matter for debate. However, with the exception of a few computer whizz-kids, fraudsters are older than juvenile delinquents: did those responsible for City scandals really grow up in the Swinging Sixties, or was it in the Fast-living Fifties, the Flighty Forties, the Teeming Thirties, or even the Tawdry Twenties? Or is it Living under The Shadow of The Bomb that is 'the cause' of this alleged decline in commercial morality? (Perhaps, *pace* Max Weber, for older generations, 'making a bomb' was a sign that one had been Saved?)

There is some criminological evidence to support the view that 'permissiveness' contributes to juvenile delinquency (Riley and Shaw, 1985; Rutter and Giller, 1983), but 'lax supervision' can be taken in the context of current rather than simply juvenile activities. So if it *is* 'the cause' of the growth in commercial fraud, both the 'situational opportunity' and the 'make the family responsible' approaches to crime control – observable also in the Criminal Justice Act (1982) – may require us to tighten up levels of supervision. Bentham's Panopticon was not designed to observe the City of London, but we do need some kind of equivalent monitoring process to reduce the chances of fraud occurring and escaping undetected. As we shall see in Chapter 5 this costs money, unless the Government can shift the regulatory burden onto commercial institutions (with the attendant political risks mentioned by some City figures quoted earlier). In short, although the *precise* costs of commercial fraud are impossible to ascertain even in principle, the economic costs are greater than those of other forms of property crime, and the political costs also are beginning to loom large. Let us now examine how seriously this issue is regarded by the public in Britain and in the United States.

3 Attitudes to commercial crime

The seriousness of crimes: a general introduction

In political debate, the law is often treated as a unitary phenomenon. Thus, when people break the law and claim some special justification for so doing, others may seek to refute their claim by citing, for example, the general legitimacy of the process by which the law was promulgated. However, despite the use of such devices for and against, *inter alia*, those who claim 'political' status for their crimes, it is the case that few people treat *all* crimes as if they were the same. We would regard someone who stated that dropping litter was as bad as murder as having a rather peculiar set of moral standards. In practice, then, even if we regard all law as legitimate and subscribe to the view that law and order ought to be enforced in the most global sense, we tend to give crimes different ratings of seriousness. There is thus a tension: on the one hand, politicians sometimes treat law and order as if it were a coherent body of moral regulations of equal weight; on the other, they sometimes seek special justification for treating some particular crime or category of crime differently, whether more harshly or more leniently. Examples of such attempts during the 1980s include the leaking of Official Secrets, the prosecution of police officers for corruption or violence, riot charges against miners, Sunday trading by shopkeepers, and narcotics offences.

Appeals to 'public opinion' are an important aspect of criminal policy, and such opinion is used to justify particular policing strategies (including manpower distributions), prosecution policies, and (as we shall see in a later chapter) sentencing levels. In practice, few people feel bound by empirical evidence of what 'the public' think. If we try hard enough, we can always find reasons for not following public opinion: the public are insufficiently informed about the matter; the media have misled the public; public views are too volatile; this is a matter of professional or clinical judgment; the independence of the judiciary must be preserved; and so on. We can also usually find technical objections to the methodology employed in any survey with whose conclusions we disagree.

Public opinion, in other words, is used selectively to support views held on other grounds. This is not the prerogative of the right: for some on the left, the non-revolutionary working class are suffering from 'the hegemony of bourgeois ideology' or, in older variants of the same theme, 'false consciousness' of their 'true class interests'. Actual public opinion can thus be discredited and replaced by 'real' public opinion, that is, what people would believe if only they were as wise as oneself. It is therefore a natural successor to the Idealist notion of 'the general will' in political theory.

Crime policy by opinion poll clearly has its dangers, even to the most dedicated authoritarian populist. Their academic manifestation, crime seriousness surveys, have often been used as a rationale for tougher law-and-order policies, particularly when they come up with the desired answers. However, there is no denying their popularity among academic researchers, ever since Sellin and Wolfgang published their classic, *The Measurement of Delinquency*, in 1964. The reasons for this take-off into sustained growth are discussed elsewhere (Levi and Jones, 1985), but contrary to initial preconceptions on the part of conflict theorists, the results of seriousness surveys tend to show a high degree of consensus in the ratings of property and violent offences among people of different social classes. Miethe (1984) has called these findings into question, arguing that there is much greater agreement on the relative seriousness of different crimes than on exactly how bad any particular crime is, and that by contrast with offences involving violence, narcotics, drink, and public order, there is a great deal of disagreement on the judged seriousness of property and white-collar crimes. Yet the standard deviation figures and area comparisons in British (and much American) research shows that when we examine the average seriousness ratings of different offences, no great disparities appear among different sections of the public, except in relation to so-called 'victimless' offences involving under-age sex and drug use. (See Sparks, Genn, and Dodd, 1977, and Levi and Jones, 1985, for example.)

Critics of the use to which these consensus findings are put might counter that 'public opinion' does not arrive by magic, but is constructed during social interaction. Thus, although there are no large sample surveys of perceptions of crime seriousness before the First World War, reviews of the development of attitudes towards policing and crime over a longer time scale do show the ways in which these perspectives were moulded (Gatrell, 1987; Reiner, 1985). The influence of capitalism and business interests in this process is a matter of great dispute (and is reviewed in the context of law-making in the next chapter). However, it is a valid criticism that crime seriousness surveys are ahistorical in their explanatory approach and generally neglect the problem of how views about crime are formed. This aspect cannot be resolved simply by looking at time-series data which find (or may find) stability over quite lengthy periods, for this may simply reflect underlying continuities in the influences upon public views.

Attitudes towards commercial crime

Let us consider further attitudes to the seriousness of commercial crime. Even in the uncut version of his classic *White-Collar Crime*, Sutherland (1983, first published in 1949) did not address the question of public attitudes towards white-collar compared with other crimes. He appears to have assumed that the public thought it was wrong but were simply too badly organized and badly represented to do anything about it. His concern was focused primarily on how businesspeople used their social standing, money, and political influence to evade the imposition of criminal sanctions. In the past decade, greater interest has been displayed in public sentiments on white-collar crime. Carroll *et al.* (1974) found that students regarded only crimes involving direct personal threat as being more serious than Watergate-type offences. Schrager and Short re-analysed an earlier study by Rossi *et al.* (1974) and concluded that public evaluations of seriousness depended primarily upon the perceived *impact* of the crime:

> 'Individuals not only consider organizational crimes with physical impact to be far more serious than those with economic impact, but they also rate physical organizational crimes as equal in seriousness to a range of crimes . . . consider[ed] central to the "crime problem".'
>
> (Schrager and Short, 1980:26)

Likewise, 'purely economic' business offences were considered by the public to be as serious as non-violent property crimes with similar impact. They went on to reiterate (in the context of Watergate) the points made by Sutherland about the great 'objective' harmfulness of white-collar crime in damaging the social fabric.

In *The National Survey of Crime Severity*, Wolfgang *et al.* (1985) confirm that white-collar crimes involving physical damage are viewed extremely seriously by the public. For example, one of the most serious of all crimes – worse than rape and the stabbing to death of non-family victims – was 'A factory knowingly gets rid of its waste in a way that pollutes the water supply of a city. As a result, 20 people die'. This offence was rated the seventh most serious of 204 offences in the national survey of 60,000 respondents. Even where the actual human damage is less, deliberate toxic water-pollution is regarded as very bad: worse than smuggling heroin into the country or robbery at gunpoint. Another example of white-collar crime is 'Knowing that a shipment of cooking oil is bad, a store owner decides to sell it anyway. Only one bottle is sold and the purchaser dies'. This is rated marginally more seriously than 'A person, armed with a gun, robs a bank of $100,000 during business hours. No-one is physically hurt'. (However, the latter offence in turn is rated far more seriously than the sale of bad cooking oil after which no-one is hospitalized.)

The public do seem to be strongly influenced in their ratings of crime seriousness by the amount of damage – physical or economic – *actually* rather than potentially sustained. This is humanly understandable, though not, in my view, theoretically defensible. The survey by Wolfgang *et al.* (1985) also found that legislators who take a $10,000 bribe for passing laws favouring companies are viewed more seriously than someone who robs someone of $1000 and hurts them so that they have to go to hospital. Indeed, fraud by professional people (such as doctors), corruption and interference with the course of justice by the powerful are seen as very significant indeed: worse than any burglary.

The combination of the Schrager and Short (1980) findings discussed above and growing radicalism among US criminologists gave impetus to enthusiasm for such studies as a means of demonstrating that conservative politicians and criminologists such as Wilson (1975) were wrong to focus upon street crimes in their campaigns for law and order. (Though consciously or not, studies focusing upon white-collar crime often neglected the fact that at least some street and household crimes *were* rated very seriously by the public.) Cullen *et al.* (1982, 1983, 1985) revealed higher public ratings of white-collar crime seriousness in the post- than in the pre-Watergate period. However their results, though plausible, are not wholly conclusive, since their population base is very different from the metropolitan area surveyed by Rossi *et al.* (1974) which is taken as their point of comparison. US findings generally also show a public preference for tougher treatment of white-collar criminals than the courts generally impose (Cullen *et al.*, 1983; Newman, 1957).

Crimes such as embezzlement are not 'crimes of the powerful' in the same sense that price-fixing, pollution, and bribery to influence legislation are. According to some marxists (Pearce, 1976), this should make the former more likely to be prosecuted than the latter. We will review the evidence in this respect in the next chapters. However, whatever the priorities of law *enforcement*, it is certainly the case that in terms of public attitudes, crimes *by* corporations are viewed more seriously than crimes *against* corporations. This does not mean that frauds are not viewed seriously: it has been a consistent feature of crime seriousness surveys in the United States that frauds by employees and by outsiders against consumers and corporation alike *are* regarded more seriously than more 'common crimes'. The national survey by Wolfgang *et al.* (1985) found that 'A person signs someone else's name to a check and cashes it' was rated marginally higher than 'A person, armed with a lead pipe, robs a victim of $10. The victim is injured and requires treatment by a doctor but not hospitalization'. 'An employee embezzles $1000 from his employer' is rated as being twice as serious as 'A person breaks into a home and steals property worth $10' (though the latter is viewed considerably more seriously than the embezzlement of $10).

Less extensive research into commercial crime has been carried out in Britain. Tax fraud is examined later, but the public appear to view fraudulent activities such as embezzlement fairly seriously. In the first British study, Durant, Thomas, and Wilcock (1972) asked a sample of 1904 adults whether each of eighteen offences was serious or not serious. Sixty-four per cent thought that 'fraud' (that is, obtaining money by false pretences) was serious: a higher proportion than any other property crime including housebreaking (61 per cent) and breaking into a factory (46 per cent). Indeed, Sparks, Genn, and Dodd (1977) found that Londoners rated 'The offender sets up a bogus company and through it fraudulently obtains £1000 from a big manufacturer' more seriously than *any* other non-violent property offences including 'The offender breaks into a person's house and steals property worth £10'. The cashing of £100 in forged cheques and the embezzlement of £100 by the company accountant were also rated more seriously than any theft offence, though less seriously than burglary.

In a survey of 965 members of the public in two English police force areas, covering rural, small-town, and inner urban populations, Levi and Jones (1985) found that the public rated the bogus company offence above (uprated to £2000 to allow for inflation) less seriously than a mail-order fraud in which £1000 is lost to a number of private individuals. However, both these substantial fraud offences are rated more seriously than a domestic burglary in which £20 is taken. Despite the media and political fuss regarding 'social-security scroungers', the car-dealer who turns back the 'clock' on a car is rated more seriously than the £20 social-security fraudster, though less seriously than the burglar (*see Table 9*).

At the most modest possible interpretation, these surveys reveal that the public is highly intolerant of commercial frauds of the kind examined. On a stronger interpretation, they may imply that frauds involving large sums are seen as being morally worse than burglaries of small sums. Is this an attribute of differences between the moral blameworthiness of the offences themselves, or more of differences between the sums involved?

There is some reason to believe that monetary losses are important to judgments of seriousness. This was discovered not only by Walker

Table 9   *Public ratings of the seriousness of crimes*

offence		mean[1]	rank
the offender attacks a victim with a knife or another sharp weapon and the victim dies		10.65	1
	sd[2]	1.23	
the offender, a policeman who discovers a burglary in a shop, steals £20 worth of goods from the store		9.42	2
	sd	2.16	
the offender, using physical force, robs a victim of £50 – the victim is injured but is not sent to hospital		8.87	3
	sd	2.22	
the offender assaults a police officer with his fists – the police officer is injured and sent to hospital		8.83	4
	sd	2.41	
the offender sets up a bogus mail-order company and through it fraudulently obtains £1,000 from a number of private individuals		8.31	5
	sd	2.47	
the offender drives recklessly, causing £200 damage to another person's property		7.91	6
	sd	2.46	
the offender sells marijuana to an adult		7.85	7
	sd	3.18	
the offender steals £20 from another person's wallet or bag		7.49	8
	sd	2.79	
the offender sets up a bogus company and through it fraudulently obtains £2,000 from a big manufacturer		7.44	9
	sd	2.78	
the offender breaks into a person's house and steals property worth £20		7.13	10
	sd	2.92	
the offender, a 25 year-old man, has sexual intercourse with a 15 year-old girl, with her consent		7.09	11
	sd	3.24	
the offender, a car dealer, turns the mileometer back by 20,000 miles on a car he is selling		6.76	12
	sd	2.94	
the offender dishonestly obtains social security benefits to the value of £20		6.19	13
	sd	3.12	
the offender, a 14 year-old boy, has sexual intercourse with a 14 year-old girl		5.87	14
	sd	3.25	

Notes: [1]Respondents were asked to rate each offence separately on a scale from 1 (least serious) to 11 (most serious)
[2]sd = Standard Deviation.
Source: Levi and Jones (1985)

(1978) and Sparks, Genn, and Dodd (1977) but also in the 1984 British Crime Survey (Pease, forthcoming), which found that victims rated domestic burglary resulting in loss significantly more seriously than domestic burglary involving no loss, and criminal damage to both homes and cars to a value of £20 or more, significantly more seriously than, criminal damage of lesser sums. Research in the United States by Gottfredson, Young, and Laufer (1980) found that the amount of money involved had little effect on the seriousness ratings for violent offences such as robbery, but had most effect on the judged seriousness of cheque frauds. A possible explanation is that the impact of money taken is greater where the sums obtained are foreseeable in advance of the crime, and one might expect foreseeability to be slightly greater for fraud than for burglary. We deduce from the study by Sparks, Genn, and Dodd (1977) that pound-for-pound, burglary is seen as being more serious than embezzlement or cheque fraud. This is true of the United States also (Wolfgang *et al.*, 1985).

It is intuitively plausible that as one moves up the offence seriousness scale, the sums of money involved will make less incremental difference to judgments about offence seriousness: for example, the emotions surrounding robbery would tend to inhibit the effects of the small size of the haul in a way that one would not expect for shoplifting. One also suspects that the sums involved rather than the greater intolerance of fraud *per se* explain the rating differences between fraud and burglary in the studies by Sparks, Genn, and Dodd (1977) and Levi and Jones (1985). However, it is dangerous to treat fraud as a homogeneous category: in the survey of senior executives by Levi (1986a) which standardized the property crime losses – *see Table 11* (p.69) – executives rated a professional man defrauding £1000 from a client's account as being more serious than a burglary of a private home in which £1000 was stolen. Yet all other fraud offences of the same value were rated lower than the burglary. One possible hypothesis to account for the high disapproval ratings for fraud is the psychological need for the public to adopt a 'just world' perspective whereby everyone gets rewarded according to their efforts. Deliberate fraud (including consumer fraud) disrupts this sense of 'natural order' and therefore is a target for severe condemnation (tinged, at times, with envy and admiration). Such a world view may be intensified by the psychological distress occasioned by social change and a declining economy. However, it is not dependent upon such a decline, for American ratings and rankings of fraud seriousness have been consistently high over time. The need for security and just deserts in turn acts as an emotional foundation for the authoritarian populism which has been a key feature of the law-and-order debate, along with other aspects of 'permissiveness' condemned by the Conservative Party Chairman Norman Tebbit in his 1985 Disraeli Lecture.

Attitudes towards corruption and to 'the black economy'

A rather different aspect of the moral order relates to corruption. As part of a more general survey of British social attitudes, a sample of the population were asked how wrong they thought a number of acts in the public and private sector were. The survey found that there was a fairly general hierarchy of morality: soliciting gifts was worse than fiddling expenses, which in turn was worse than accepting gifts. Least serious of all was accepting entertainment. Higher standards were demanded of public-sector officials than of private-sector managers (Johnston and Wood, 1985).

Unlike the executives in the current survey – discussed later – the public were fairly tolerant of private-sector managers being given regular entertainment by suppliers of goods: though 6 out of 10 thought it wrong, only 6 per cent though it seriously wrong. However, three-quarters saw something wrong in council (municipal) officials being entertained regularly by suppliers, and 13 per cent said that this was seriously wrong. It is possible that the explanation for this is that people may regard themselves as being more affected *personally* by council official misdemeanours than by those of company officers. But why should there be different standards in the public and private sectors for the same sort of potentially corrupting influence?

The research further asked how people would judge the acceptance of Christmas presents worth £50 from suppliers. Again, there was much more tolerance of company managers than of council officials: no fewer than 85 per cent saw something wrong with the council official accepting the gift, compared with 59 per cent for the company manager. (No fewer than 28 per cent though it was *seriously* wrong for a council official to accept the Christmas presents, compared with only 7 per cent for the company manager to do so.) The fiddling of expenses claims was condemned more heavily and more evenly in both the private and public sectors, perhaps because the role of the fiddler is seen as being more *active* than in the previous cases, thereby increasing moral blameworthiness. Over three-quarters thought it wrong or seriously wrong for the company manager to fiddle £50 in expenses over a period, and 85 per cent took this view about the council official doing the same thing. Worst of all was the active soliciting of £50 gifts: only 2 per cent of people saw nothing wrong in it.

A representative quota sample survey of 2058 adults aged 15 and over, conducted by MORI in 1985, though somewhat cruder in scope, finds similar diversity of attitudes towards 'the informal economy'. *Table 10* summarizes some relevant data from this survey. There appear to be two distinct broad offence bands: tax fraud and frauds (including those of time) upon employers. The latter, with the exception of the widely condoned (though not by one company in my survey) activity of using an employer's telephone without permission – technically a fraud both on employer and on tax authorities! – are regarded seriously by the majority; the former, tolerantly by the majority. Earning undeclared income while on social security was regarded as morally wrong by almost twice as many people as not declaring income to the taxman. The MORI survey found a rather interesting difference in attitude to Value-Added

Table 10   *Attitudes to earning money 'on the side'*

offence	thinking morally wrong %	thinking generally acceptable to most people %	knowing someone else doing %	admitting having done themselves %
paying someone in cash who doesn't charge VAT	30	49	25	14
accepting cash for some work in order to keep earnings free of VAT or income tax	35	37	20	7
using an employer's telephone without permission	36	35	26	20
paying cash to someone if you suspect he or she isn't paying income tax	41	33	20	8
taking time off when you're supposed to be at work	66	21	28	11
people on the dole earning some money without telling the social-security office	67	24	32	3
claiming expenses from an employer to which you are not entitled	70	16	18	4
taking home things from work without paying for them	72	19	25	10
none of these	4	9	16	36
all eight of these	16	4	8	1

Source: Adapted from MORI poll, conducted for the *Sunday Times*, October 1985.

Tax and to income-tax fraud, perhaps reflecting the fact that non-payment of VAT by the trader benefits the direct consumer, whereas the non-payment of income tax appears to benefit only the evader. To adapt from Oscar Wilde, morality is simply the attitude one adopts towards people who do not benefit oneself!

The 1984 British Crime Survey (Pease, forthcoming) also found that 'someone fiddling their income tax' was rated relatively mildly, though the majority thought it was serious. Only 19 per cent of the population regarded it as very serious; 39 per cent as serious; 29 per cent as not very serious; and 12 per cent as trivial. The theft of £5 worth of goods from a shop was regarded as less serious. What the above surveys do *not* do is to specify the sums involved. This may be a weakness, for most seriousness surveys show far less tolerance of frauds involving large sums than of those involving small sums. It is interesting that a study by Walker (1978) in Sheffield found that pound-for-pound, income-tax evasion was rated less seriously than other property crimes, but the evasion of £100 in income tax was more serious than the theft of £1.

Class and group differences in attitudes to fraud and corruption

A priori, one would expect groups from which offenders come to be more tolerant of crime than those not in a position to commit any given crime. Consequently, one would expect the relatively wealthy to be less tolerant of burglary and more tolerant of fraud than the relatively poor. However, as we have discussed already, the poor rate common property offences more seriously than the rich. Partly because they are less likely to be insured, losses from crime may hit the poor harder than the rich, but another important reason for the poor to give higher seriousness ratings for crimes may be that although they contain more offenders, they also contain more victims (see Hough and Mayhew, 1985; Kinsey, 1985; Jones, Maclean and Young, 1986). By analogy (and depending on what particular sort of fraud we are examining), this is as true of the rich and fraud as it is of the poor and burglary/mugging. As anyone who has witnessed the reactions of a burglar who is burgled will testify, there is no simple inverse relationship between thinking a crime serious and committing it oneself. As I observe later, when criticizing the view that social reaction to crime is a function of class interests, the determination of interests is a complex matter in fraud as in other types of crime.

One of the earlier white-collar crime studies to look at opinion was Aubert's (1952) study of the attitudes of Norwegian businessmen towards price and rationing regulation violations. Aubert found that they did condemn such violations. However, his work implicitly raises problems for the *operational* meaning of such attitudinal data, since it reveals that justifications or rationalizations were often developed in particular instances. As Szasz has observed, 'men are often more interested in better justifying themselves, than in better behaving themselves'! (Szasz, 1973:29). Are businessmen typical in holding regulation violations to be serious? Clinard showed that the public were more intolerant than businesspeople of pricing violations (Clinard, 1952:333–34).

Since Aubert's study, there has been a marked paucity of research on the attitudes of businesspeople to business crime, possibly reflecting the scepticism of researchers towards attitudinal analysis. Bologna surveyed forty members of the Toledo Personnnel Management Association in the United States (Bologna, 1984:105). It is impossible to work out how the rank order of offences is related to seriousness, frequency of occurrence, and index weight (whatever the latter means), but the bribery of political leaders and padding the bill on government contracts came out joint top; employee theft, fraud, and embezzlement came third; and management fraud came much lower down the list. It may be useful to see what was ranked very low: falsifying company statements (17th), bribing *foreign* officials (19th), price-fixing (22nd), and falsifying profitability reports (23rd). Given the frequent use of profit-related management pay schemes, the tolerance of these practices is intriguing.

A more interesting study by Cole (1983) surveyed 100 executives in Adelaide, Australia. The principal focus of his work was upon attitudes to corporate environmental offences, and he found that offences involving actual injury or serious risk of injury (such as people dying following building collapses because contractors did not observe building regulations, and coach firms failing to maintain brakes as required by law) were rated most seriously. On the other hand, it was considered relatively non-serious for a 20 year-old woman to use a bank card fraudulently to obtain $100 or $1000 of clothes. Although there are no sample comparisons, the general results suggest that the executives were not all that dissimilar from the way one might expect the general population to react.

Unfortunately, Wolfgang *et al.* (1985) did not analyse judgments about the seriousness of frauds separately, so no light can be thrown upon the relationship between this and socio-economic status in the US national survey. Miethe, who re-analysed yet again the orginal Rossi survey of Baltimore, found that there were some important differences within the public (Miethe, 1984:41). White-collar crimes involving consumers were considered slightly more serious by blacks, while whites considered crimes against business (such as embezzlement and illegal interest rates) to be more serious than did blacks. (This corresponds broadly to a 'potential offender self-interest' hypothesis, but to test it properly, one would want more data on intra-white class differences.)

With regard to fraud in Britain, Walker (1978) found that the upper socio-economic groups were far more tolerant than the poor of the evasion of £100 in income tax. In the study by Sparks, Genn, and Dodd (1977), the lower-class groups rated the embezzlement of £100 by the accountant more seriously than the upper groups, but the differences were not statistically significant. There were significant differences (in the same direction) in the rating of the cashing of a £100 forged cheque and the fraud by a bogus firm upon a large manufacturer. However, like the general data on crime seriousness judgments, this lends no unambiguous support to the hypothesis that potential victims rate offences more seriously and potential offenders rate them less seriously. For although higher social groups are more likely to be accountants, they may be less likely than lower groups to cash forged cheques or to set up bogus companies. They surely are more likely to be the victims of these offences than are social classes 3b, 4, and 5. So although the higher social-class respondents were more tolerant of fraud, it is difficult to account for this in terms of self-interest.

In the survey by Johnston and Wood (1985), private-sector workers were more tolerant than public-sector ones in their attitudes towards all 'malpractices', particularly those involving company managers. On the other hand, the only major area where social class was important to judgments was in the solicitation of bribes, which social classes 1 and 2 judged *more* severely than social class 3, who in turn were less tolerant than classes 4 and 5. The 1985 MORI survey found that newspaper readership – a rough measure of social class – was highly correlated with tough-mindedness towards the informal economy. Of *Financial Times* readers, 57 per cent think it is wrong to pay in cash to someone you suspect is avoiding VAT, whereas of *Mail on Sunday* readers, a mere 21 per cent took this view. Ninety-two per cent of *Financial Times* readers, compared with only 56 per cent of *Sun* readers, thought it was wrong to take 'time off when you're supposed to be at work'. This may be a reflection of the managerial roles of *Financial Times* readers and of their greater ability to pay full price for goods. (Non-payment of £n in taxes is a greater saving in real terms to the poor than to the rich.) It seems plausible to this author that views about 'fiddling' are distinguishable from views about the seriousness of 'fraud proper', precisely because their occupational context and/or the absence of any identifiable victim makes them seem different. If that is so, the question of whether these social-class differences in attitudes to 'fiddles' extend to fraud generally remains an open one.

THE ATTITUDES OF SENIOR EXECUTIVES TOWARDS FRAUD

The broad theme of the tough-mindedness of social classes 1 and 2 towards fraud is reflected in the current survey of fifty-six senior executives from large companies. The seriousness ratings and rankings of offences are expressed in *Table 11*. The respondents were asked to rate each offence on a 0–20 scale, where 0 would represent the least serious offence – such as theft of a milkbottle – and 20 the most serious offence – murder. They were asked to imagine that £1000 was the sum involved in *all* offences where money or goods were obtained. The specific sum was used to help guard against the danger that the seriousness ratings of the commercial fraud offences might be inflated artificially if they were viewed as involving much larger sums. (It should be realized that this monetary equalization *does* distort the comparisons, but *against* fraud, since as we saw in Chapter 2, the average and median sums involved in fraud are much greater than in non-fraud offences.)

Table 11 *Senior executives' ratings of crime seriousness*

offence	mean	median	rank
someone being mugged and money taken	15.8	15	1
a professional man taking money from a client's account	13.64	14	2
a private home or property being damaged by vandals	13.14	14	3
a home being broken into and something stolen	12.77	12	4
someone taking money from mail-order purchasers without sending them goods in return	12.02	12	5
an employee taking money from his employers	11.8	11.5	6
someone making profits from insider trading	10.5	10	7
someone fiddling social security	10	10	8
someone overclaiming on insurance after a commercial burglary	9.39	10	9
someone fiddling their income tax	8.89	10	10
a car being stolen for a joy ride	8.86	9.5	11
someone smoking cannabis	5.76	5	12

Source: Levi (1986a)

The findings are consistent with the general trends from other surveys, inasmuch as violent crime is rated significantly higher than other crimes; at least one type of fraud – in this case a professional man defrauding his clients – is rated more highly than burglary or vandalism; and frauds by the wealthy against the less wealthy are rated more seriously than frauds against the relatively wealthy. Again, this provides no unambiguous support for the view that seriousness ratings reflect self-interest, though it is arguable that executives may find themselves at risk from professional men and may believe that mail-order frauds have a general depressing effect on the legitimate sectors of the trade. The high rating of insider trading is of interest: here again, respondents could see themselves as beneficiaries or as the victims of this, but it runs counter to the often-expressed view that statutes creating 'new' offences in the sphere of fraud and business regulation are regarded tolerantly as *mala prohibita* rather than *mala in se* (see Hadden, 1983; Levi, 1984a).

Although the survey sought to make finer rating distinctions than and incorporated extra fraud offences from the 1984 British Crime Survey, it is interesting to compare the ordering of offences with those of the general public. Offences that both surveys had in common were mugging, vandalism, burglary, social-security fraud, income-tax fraud, joy riding, and smoking cannabis (*see Table 12*). The wording of offence descriptions was the same, except that the executives were oriented towards regarding each property crime as being of equivalent cost by the express reference to a sum of £1000, whereas the public were left to fill in their own mental sums. The ratings of and the interval levels between offences may have been very different, but it is apparent that the executives viewed social-security and income-tax fraud relatively more seriously and cannabis smoking and joy riding relatively less seriously than did the public.

Table 12   *Public and executive crime seriousness rankings*

	public rank	*executive rank*
mugging	1	1
burglary	2	3
vandalism of home	3	2
joy riding	4	6
social-security fraud	5	4
smoking cannabis	6	7
income-tax fraud	7	5

Source: Levi (1986a)

AGE AND ATTITUDES TO FRAUD

An important dimension in attitudes to crime (and in attitudes towards the police) is age. This has some operational implications, for example in relation to jury selection, which is discussed in Chapter 8. Jones and Levi (1983a) found that with the sole exception of a £2000 fraud on a large manufacturer, older people judged frauds (as they did most other offences) significantly more seriously than did the young (*see Table 13*).

Table 13 *Age and attitudes to fraud*

offence	age group		
	14–24 *N=157* *average*	*25–54* *N=424* *average*	*55+* *N=372* *average*
a bogus mail-order company obtains £1000 from private individuals	7.37	8.18	8.85
a bogus company obtains £2000 in goods from a large manufacturer	6.94	7.20	7.94
a car dealer 'clocks' a car by 20,000 miles	5.33	6.32	7.84
dishonestly obtaining £20 social security	5.03	5.74	7.18

Note: Respondents were asked to rate offence seriousness on a scale from 1 (least serious) to 11 (most serious). For complete offence descriptions, see *Table 9* earlier.
Source: Jones and Levi (1983a)

The 1985 MORI poll also found considerable age-related differences in attitudes to 'fiddling'. For example, only 6 per cent of 15–24 year olds, compared with 28 per cent of people over 64, thought that all eight activities (*see Table 10*) were morally wrong. On the other hand, the over–64s also provided the largest proportion of those who thought that none of the eight activities were morally wrong. So old age appears to lead to extremism.

Johnston and Wood (1985) and the MORI survey (1985) came to similar conclusions in their analyses of attitudes to corruption and the 'informal economy'. We should bear in mind that there is by no means a perfect correspondence between attitudes towards offences and willingness to commit them (or, for that matter, opportunities to commit them). However, Johnston and Wood (1985) found that younger people were also much more likely to state they they would themselves *commit* minor acts of fraud and corruption (*see Table 14*).

Table 14 *Willingness to commit minor fraud or corruption*

might do it	18–24 %	25–34 %	35–54 %	55+ %
evade VAT on repair	80	80	73	50
bribe dustmen to take away rubbish	70	65	63	45
pocket extra change from shop	40	27	17	6

Source: Johnston and Wood (1985)

Conclusions

These survey findings are important indicators of the state of public sentiments and the degree of consensus that exists about the seriousness of different crimes. However, I have argued elsewhere (Levi and Jones, 1985) that we should be cautious in operationalizing their results into the criminal justice sphere. Subsequent usage of the US survey data comparing white-collar and 'common' crimes (for example by Box, 1983; Kramer, 1984) has tended to infer – usually implicitly – that all corporate harms will be held to be deliberate and therefore fall within the category of severely condemned acts. Yet such questions of intentionality and culpability – individual and corporate – often bedevil criminal trials. Much to the distress of radical criminologists (who persist in labelling these as examples of 'corporate crime'), even in instances where the media and the public have 'anathematized' corporations, juries nevertheless have acquitted those charged with criminal violations: the classic example of this is the trial of Ford for manufacturing the exploding Pinto motor car. It may be argued that such acquittals – rare examples of the ideal-typical 'due process' model in action – are due to restrictive evidentiary rules and resource imbalances between prosecutors and corporations (see Cullen, Maakestad, and Cavender, 1984; Mann, 1985; Swigert and Farrell, 1981) and as we shall see later, this is an important advantage that corporations possess over most other defendants. But to show that corporations have smart lawyers is not to show that culpability judgments are easy in corporate crime cases, however much the behaviour itself may be condemned in the abstract.

In the area of jury selection, it may be quite mistaken to infer willingness to convict or acquit from crime seriousness judgments. For example, Jones and Levi (1983a) found that older people rated the theft of £200 by a police officer from the scene of a burglary significantly more seriously than did younger age groups. (See also Johnston and Wood, 1985, who found that intolerance of fraud increased with the age of those surveyed.) Does this mean that a police officer on trial for this offence should aim for a young jury? Not necessarily, because if surveyed, it seems likely that we would find that older people are more likely to believe the account of the police officer on trial, perhaps because they do not want to believe that police officers can commit offences like that.

Similarly, the high ratings of fraud seriousness by senior executives are interesting, important, and intelligible. Yet would this lead them to be prone to convict businessmen on trial for alleged offences of insider trading? Again, not necessarily, for particularly in corporate crime cases where individual blameworthiness may be hard to identify, judgments about credibility and culpability are different from judgments about crime seriousness. The policy issue of jury trials will be explored in Chapters 6 and 8 but paradoxically, it is possible that unless one is unsympathetic to the 'sort of defendant' on trial, the more serious the offence, the harder it is to find a high-status person guilty of it: jurors will be sensitized to the severe consequences of the fall from grace and, perhaps unconsciously, they may be induced to look for reasons to acquit rather than reasons to convict.

As regards arguments about whether or not there is social consensus in attitudes to offences, more attention needs to be paid to differences in culpability, to the relationships between offenders and victims (as in victim-precipitation), and to the impact of the offence. What constitutes provocation and excusability, for example, may vary considerably by race and class, and testing this requires more elaborate vignettes than have often been used, particlarly in America. (For a good discussion, see Rossi, Simpson, and Miller 1985; Wilkins, 1984.)

Finally, what are the policing and sentencing policy consequences of seriousness studies? Because people regard an offence as more serious than another, does this mean they they want it to be more heavily policed? Or more heavily sentenced? Bryant, Chambers, and Falcon (1968) found that police judgments about the value of preventing or detecting a crime were the same as judgments about its seriousness. But there is an imperfect correlation between executives' rankings of crime seriousness and their rankings of policing priorities: *see Tables 11* and *16*. Rossi, Simpson, and Miller (1985) also cast doubt upon the correlation between seriousness ratings and punishment preferences, which Braithwaite (1982b) assumes are more or less the same thing. Indeed, sometimes, the possibility of heavy punishments may deter prosecutions (and/or jury convictions) even for offences that are regarded as being very serious: Beattie has shown that although forgery and coinage offences were viewed very gravely by the legislature during the seventeenth and eighteenth centuries, prosecutions for them were very rare, largely because being 'non-clergyable' offences, there was no alternative to the death penalty for them and, particularly in the light of the social standing of many offenders, there was a reluctance to see them hanged (Beattie, 1986:191–92).

By focusing – as retributivists also do – upon the characteristics of 'the crime' rather than placing 'the offender' and his conduct in its social context, crime seriousness surveys leave out some complex aspects of prejudice which we know to be important to social judgments. For example, as attribution theorists have shown in social psychological research (and as ordinary people know!) 'attractiveness' is significant not only in influencing jury verdicts (Hans and Vidmar, 1986) but also in social relations generally. People who commit fraud benefit not only from the criminal justice procedures discussed in later chapters but also because they may be more charming (as their tradecraft requires), and because they may provide employment, come from 'good homes', give money to charity, or confer other social benefits such as letting friends have goods 'cheap'. Severe punishment is easier to impose not only when the offence is serious but when we – and in particular, sentencers – do not empathize with the offender. This is not restricted to inhabitants of the upperworld: those who commit workplace 'fiddles' also benefit. Just as in our social relationships, we willingly allow people who are more 'fun' to exploit us, so we are more tolerant of criminals who display *panache*. In short, we may contextualize fraudulent behaviour (which in the abstract we condemn) within an overall *gestalt* or 'social typification' in such a way that it becomes less malign or even romantic. (At least until *we* become, or become aware that we already *are*, its victims.) As I shall argue in Chapter 7, this undoubtedly affects sentencing practice, and forms a counterweight to the popular perception that fraud itself may be a very serious crime.

Nevertheless, despite these reservations, research data on public attitudes towards crime and punishment are both interesting and useful. British research, for example, shows that although the public want 'tougher sentencing' as a global preference, they in fact underestimate the sentences that actually are imposed and they want the levels of sentences that currently exist! (See Hough and Moxon, 1985.) Thus, in a concrete sense, they can be a useful corrective to popular mythology and to moral entrepreneurship. However, liberals have reason to fear the setting of retributive punishment by popular acclamation. In the United States, populist justice has led to harsher sentencing policies that have been restrained only by the fiscal costs of tougher penalties. One suspects that many white-collar crime writers who utilize seriousness survey findings to call for tougher policing and sentencing of white-collar 'criminals' would be very much less happy to embrace public support for corporal or capital punishment for offenders coming from more deprived environments. So the cry of *Vox Populi Suprema Lex* can turn out to be a hydra-headed monster, and those academics who are captivated by the notion that white-collar crime is high on the gravity list should beware of worshipping false and powerful gods.

4 Economic interests, law, and the politics of fraud control

Capitalism, the state, and the legal process

In the previous two chapters we have examined critically what is known about the impact of frauds and attitudes towards different sorts of fraud. Yet social problems do not just exist 'out there': they are constructed and managed, both by private-sector individuals and organizations, and by public-sector agencies that develop a responsibility for dealing with them. And one of the ways in which they are constructed is by the mobilization of concern, which may be aimed at introducing or revising (1) substantive legislation (for example, banning the counterfeiting of branded commercial products such as videos or aircraft parts), or (2) procedural legislation (such as police powers of surveillance, search, and seizure), or which may be aimed at increasing the resources of the police. Public concern can be enhanced principally by emphasizing the social harm done by the conduct and/or the nastiness of the people who are involved in it, and lobbying may take place in the media and in political circles to organize tougher responses to the phenomenon in question.

Given the domain assumptions or value context of any particular society at a particular moment in time, some behaviours lend themselves more easily than others to the mobilization of concern (or to that much over-used phrase, moral panic). In most western nations, 'terrorism', 'organized crime', and 'drugs' (along with other 'rebellious youth' themes) are comparatively easy issues on which stronger crime control measures can be generated; the dropping of litter, racial attacks and, to a decreasing extent, spousal violence, are harder targets for organized legislative (and enforcement) concern. Moreover, quite apart from any questions of contributions to party funds, people who are considered to be 'sound' and who control powerful organizations are more likely than others to be listened to or even to be consulted in advance by civil servants and legislators who, quite rationally, want to find out what the consequences of regulatory proposals are likely to be: insurance companies lobbying on the Financial Services Bill (1985) were able to effect changes in the legislation (and probably would have influenced a Labour government); social-security claimants are somewhat less likely to be consulted in advance of legislation on social-security provisions. It is important to stress that state intervention does not necessarily mean *criminal* law intervention taken by the police; it can just as well entail administrative procedures, as in the case of antitrust (anti-monopoly) and insider dealing in securities in the United States.

The legal framework is important for both symbolic and practical reasons. Legal relations – whether by criminal law or by taxation and social security – define the distribution of property rights between those who benefit greatly from the economic system and those who do less well (or, in some countries, gain nothing at all) from it; and specific legal *forms* (such as the separate legal identity of the corporation and the powers conferred upon a debenture-holder) have a huge impact upon the rights of the parties involved. As Poggi observes,

> 'One can visualise the state as a legally arranged set of organs for the framing, application, and enforcement of laws . . . within the system of rule the law is the state's standard mode of expression, its very language, the essential mode of its activity.'
>
> (Poggi, 1979: 102)

Whether or not we believe in the legitimacy of all law and/or that law embodies the customs of the majority, it is beyond argument that the content and form of law are determined by political actions. However, the political significance of new laws differs from that of existing ones. Except in rare cases where there is unanimity of viewpoint, new laws generally result from some kind of interest-group struggle in which economic, cultural, and ideological appeals, as well as political trade-offs, may be made. On the other hand, old laws – which in turn are the product of some earlier political struggle – may remain 'on the books' not because there is a conscious decision that they are appropriate but because no-one in a position of power has sufficient motivation to change them: decriminalization proposals would normally lead to some objections, and thus to political difficulties, and even if there were near unanimity of opinion, the sheer physical constraints of a crowded parliamentary timetable militate against decriminalization. That is one reason why for all the talk among legal academics of 'the crisis of overcriminalization', so few laws are repealed.

Those laws that *are* repealed tend to be completely non-controversial, such as the abolition in 1986 of the Dog Licence, which cost four times as much to enforce than it brought in in revenue. However, this is not always the case: the Wages Act (1986) is an example of controversial decriminalization. This Act retained but emasculated Wages Councils – industry-wide bodies given a statutory power by Winston Churchill's *Conservative* administration to set minimum wages in areas like clothing manufacture and catering where weak unionization was acknowledged to have resulted in widespread exploitation – and was passed in the face of strong opposition by the Labour movement. Like the demise of the Occupational Safety and Health Act in the United States (Calavita, 1983), the changes in the Wages Act (1986) can be understood as a symbolic gesture on the part of a Conservative government: in this case one of support for the view that too many workers were 'pricing themselves out of jobs'. The answer to unemployment is lower wages! More generally, the reluctance to decriminalize does not mean that all laws continue to be enforced: it is comparatively easy to allow a law to become irrelevant by not providing resources to implement it. But the point is that except in a tautological sense, we should not 'read' the statute book – still less the common law – as a simple reflection of the *current* balance of power in society: political inertia is important too.

Much law relating to fraud has grown up not as the product of a coherent set of intellectual or moral concepts but piecemeal, in response to particular economic and political crises. It is also scattered about in a multiplicity of statutory and common-law provisions. At the time of writing, a non-exhaustive list of legislation that is relevant to commercial fraud includes (alphabetically) the Banking Act (1979); Bankruptcy Act (1914); Bankruptcy (Amendment) Act (1926); Bills of Exchange Act (1882); Building Societies Act (1986); Car Tax Act (1983); Companies Act (1985); Company Directors Disqualification Act (1986); Company Securities (Insider Dealing) Act (1985); Consumer Credit Act (1974); Copyright Act (1956); Copyright (Amendment) Act (1983); Criminal Law Act (1977); Customs and Excise Management Act (1979); Fair Trading Act (1973); Finance Act (1985); Financial Services Act (1986); Forgery and Counterfeiting Act (1981); Insolvency Act (1986); Prevention of Corruption Act (1906); Prevention of Corruption Act (1916); Taxes Management Act (1970); Theft Act (1968); and the Theft Act (1978). Given this panoply of legislation, incoherences are likely to arise from the different and historically specific power relations that existed at the time of each law's enactment. This is exacerbated by the fact that in Britain, the regulation of fraud is largely bound up with general company legislation which embodies particular views on how business can best be encouraged: ever since the introduction of the Limited Liability Act (1856), the scandals or perceived abuses that tend to occur prior to these enactments have affected the general balance of the legislation, but fraud prevention has never been treated as superordinate to economic growth. Proposals to legislate against fraud often produce more cautious responses from politicians than is the case with anti-crime legislation generally, for they are concerned with the way in which important sectors of the economy are able to make money. Notwithstanding this generalization, given the heightened political profile of fraud, scandal and allegations of conflicts of interest have played a much more prominent role in influencing the provisions of the Financial Services Act (1986) than they did the Companies Act (1948), or even the Lloyd's Act (1982), which set out the regulatory framework for the Lloyd's insurance market. (On the latter, see Hodgson, 1986, Chs 10 and 11 and Neill, 1987.) 'Consolidating legislation' such as the Companies Act 1985 merely brings together in the same place some of the existing diffuse measures found in company law: see Arlidge and Parry (1985) for a good technical discussion of this potpourri.

A detailed sociological analysis of company law remains to be written. I will not examine legislation against frauds in its entirety, because that would consume the remainder of this book. Instead, I will review some of the key arguments concerning the importance of class and economic interests to law-making generally, and then relate these to some case studies of fraud legislation.

It is self-evident that although law *can* take away existing property rights, capitalist societies have legal frameworks that are generally conducive to the reproduction of capitalism. After all, if they did not, they would soon cease to be capitalist societies! But when analysing the relationship between law-making and pressure-group politics, there is a need to think rigorously about whether we are discussing the interests of capitalism, capitalists, or merely some capitalists. Some argue that the form and content of the criminal process are determined by the interests of capitalism (Pearce, 1976). Certainly, this proposition does force us to focus upon the question often neglected by lawyers of whose interests *are* served by a particular piece of legislation or set of enforcement practices. However, how illuminating is it when applied to the area of business crime? Capitalism (and, for that matter, any non-capitalist system) requires an element of trust and confidence in its capital and trading markets. Therefore from one perspective, any commercial malpractice that undermines that trust, whether committed by high-status businesspeople or not, is a danger to the fabric of a capitalist economy. Labour MP Brian Sedgemore (1986) has asserted that support for a free enterprise system automatically entails leniency towards fraud because it is committed by Conservative-Party supporters. However, though it may be true that fraudsters – like many other criminals – do vote Conservative, to express the issue in this way is both intellectually and politically simplistic, for businesspeople and investors who might be expected to be supporters of the Conservative Party are also City of London fraud's usual victims. Lloyd's of London and The Stock Exchange are not particularly fertile recruiting grounds for Labour-Party activists!

This is not to deny that there are many frauds on consumers, or that those of the poor who are not tapped into 'hidden economy' networks do not pay over the odds for goods and credit: but normally, what W.C. Fields would have termed 'the regrettable absence of spondulicks' insulates the very poor from becoming *direct* victims of the sorts of frauds which cause political scandal. The slightly less poor, however, are more vulnerable, as was found during the pyramid selling scandals of the 1970s, where on the 'chain letter' principle, people were encouraged to believe that they could make great fortunes from selling to their friends and neighbours franchises to sell goods. As a result, many lost their homes, for they had taken out 'second mortgages' to finance these wonderful investments.

A priori, it is not always apparent what concrete measures in relation to fraud would best preserve 'capitalist interests'. The rational capitalist who had no vested interest in a particular sort of fraudulent practice might state that 'action against fraud should be at the level which optimizes the balance between enterprise and fraud prevention'. But what is this optimum, and how will we know when we have reached it? This is a problem that taxed the Government and SROs in the City of London during the debate over the Financial Services Act (1986), just as it has always taxed SEC in the United States. Conservative governments in the United States and western Europe during the 1980s have all leaned strongly towards the *laissez-faire*, and this – along with their heavy funding and lobbying by business interests – has influenced their stance on commercial regulation and on the resources they are prepared to devote to it. However, as we have noted elsewhere in this book, there is so much money and national interest involved that the problem of balance is not a simple political cosmetic one. Presumably, if the interests of capitalists were so homogeneous and easy to discern, they would have little trouble in arriving at a policy on fraud that best served them, yet their difficulties persist. Consequently, both substantive and procedural laws regulating fraud are likely to remain the object of continuing political conflicts based around both the narrow economic self-interest of particular groups and genuine disagreements about the likely practical consequences of different approaches to legal regulation.

There are substantial inequalities of power and influence in all existing societies. The history of crime is largely the history of how relatively wealthy people used the criminal (as well as the civil) law to discipline their social and economic inferiors, and the area of 'crimes of the powerful' is interesting to some radicals as a way of highlighting the inequalities in the way the criminal justice system treats different sorts of law-breakers: hence the excellent title, *The Rich Get Richer and the Poor Get Prison* (Reiman, 1984). Businesspeople will generally be in a better position to defend the encroachment of the criminal law upon the terrain of private law than were English peasants during the Enclosure movement and in the middle ages generally (Hay, 1975; Thompson, 1975), or than youths who enjoy going to football matches carrying steel combs and wearing studded belts, whose enthusiasms are intended to be curbed by the provisions of the Public Order Act (1986). There is some sophisticated economic analysis which can be applied to argue that insider trading benefits or at least does not significantly harm securities markets (Posner and Scott, 1980, Ch. 5), but although many employers would accept the 'necessity' of engaging in tax fraud on behalf of their *employees* or of tolerating embezzlement in order to retain particular employees or to avoid industrial disruption, the argument that workplace appropriation is morally neutral or positively justifiable would meet with little official support. (I am not claiming that 'insider trading' and 'workplace theft' are equivalent.) However, although it is important to examine the structural origins of such inequalities in the treatment of different 'crime issues', there are enough variations within capitalist societies in crime control – including commercial crime control – methods to cast doubt upon the usefulness of 'capitalism' *per se* as an explanatory tool. It is precisely for this reason that without comparative research, we would be wise to avoid generalization about the way 'crime control' operates under 'capitalism' and 'socialism'. (See Clinard, 1978, for an absorbing comparative study of crime in Sweden and Switzerland; and Rider and Leigh Ffrench, 1979, for an early – if technically dated in parts now – comparative survey of insider trading legislation.)

In early Marxist work (Pearce, 1976) on the relationship between class interests and social reaction to different crimes, there was a fairly crude relationship between the economic base of 'ruling-class interests' on the one hand, and the political and legal superstructures of law, politicians, the police and the judiciary, on the other. However, this has largely been replaced by a much more subtle and fluid approach based on the 'class hegemony' views of the Italian Marxist, Gramsci, where much greater importance is given to the independent role played by ideology and to the complexity of interest-groups. Authors in this Marxist tradition insert the study of human agency (and intention) into the more traditional Marxist emphasis on structure. Good general illustrations of this sort of approach may be found in the work of Hall and Scraton (1981) and Hunt (1981); for concrete applications in the area of organized crime, see particularly Block and Chambliss (1981), Chambliss (1978), and Brady (1983).

To ascertain how helpful the hegemony approach might be in providing insight into the relationship between capitalism and the social control of fraud, let us examine a thoughtful introduction to the policing of the British coal miners' dispute of 1984–85 which, though drawn from a different context, articulates this position as well as it can be articulated:

> 'The law does not simply correspond to the needs or demands of economic relations, but through the interventions of its institutions it is essentially educative: it "manages" consent, "organises" domination, and secures "hegemony". . . . In this process the state and its legal institutions are sites of the class struggle while also being essential to the anticipation and resolution of such struggles. . . . In fact the state comprises a series of relations which exist at different levels. It is its very complexity, encompassing contradictory elements, which both enables opposition to emerge within the state while defending established positions through internal alliances. It does matter that senior personnel share educational backgrounds and contemporary world-views. . . . While each confrontation, internally or externally, develops and changes the state – policy makers and policy advisers do learn from their experiences – its shifts are more likely to be protective of social relations laid down in the economy than they are to be antagonistic. Advanced capitalism, with the added complexity of managerial relations and class fractions, is served, serviced but rarely confronted by the state's institutions who share its ends, if not always its means, in a common ideology. It is at this level that the function of institutions, exemplified by the rule of law, tutors and guides the broad membership of society. . . . If consensus cannot be forged, however, it will be forced.' (Scraton, 1985a: 262–63)

As we can see from this brief synopsis, one advantage hegemony has over the rather static approach of both traditional criminology and, in a less ahistorical way, traditional marxism, is its focus on the dynamics of change in crime and, more particularly, in crime control. Unfortunately, attempts at the 'periodization' of these changes in line with supposed shifts in state and economy are usually artificial and unsatisfactory: see, for example, the devastating critique by Styles (1983) of the attempts of Ditton (1977b) to explain the historical development of control over pilferage as an attack on the 'customary rights' of factory workers. Moreover, the notion that the state in capitalist societies is the arena for the playing out of 'contradictions' may be a fruitful *method* of analysing social forces but, in common with other 'explanations' in the field of the sociology of law, it does not tell us what the result of a particular intergroup or intragroup struggle is going to be.

There is nothing uniquely marxist about the view that family life, the education system, and involvement in crime are shaped by the economic structure. Nor would it surprise many people – whatever their political beliefs – to read that politicians and businesspeople seek to manipulate public opinion into supporting their specific policies and general ideological perspective. Self-styled 'non-partisan' conflict theorists such as Turk (1980) argue that the class determination of crime control is so remote that it is illusory to assert that it exists at all. (See, more generally, Parkin, 1979.) I will not seek to resolve these conflicts of analytic perspective here. Suffice it to observe that the more complex the linkages between class interests and crime control, the harder it is to arbitrate empirically between marxist and non-marxist accounts of the control process as an arena in which competing interest groups of unequal prestige and wealth vie for influence over legislation and enforcement practice.

Historically, many marxist accounts of law (like those of the Welfare State) discredited any improvements brought about by labour-supported governments as mere mystificatory window-dressing. Now, faced with cutbacks in welfare and labour protections, they are more inclined to note that some benefits accrued, and that the provisions opened up 'arenas for struggle' which the working-class movement could have made use of had they not been wrenched from their grasp. However, there is continuing criticism from some on the left that the 'left realism' of Kinsey, Lea, and Young (1986) is supportive of capitalism because it uses the conceptual categories (such as 'crime') from which capitalist social control methods draw their ideological strength (see also Downes, 1979). These sorts of perspectival conflicts occur throughout sociological accounts of law and its enforcement, and readers will doubtless have their own preferences as to how social control should be 'read'. I will pursue here the more modest goal of seeking 'to illuminate things formerly obscure' (Becker, 1973). What counts as 'illumination' may be the product of indoctrination (and not only in capitalist societies), but what people often want from an explanation is some plausible account of why things turned out as they did rather than in some other way. This, as we shall see, is a hard enough goal to achieve.

Legislation against fraud

Although the distinction between 'honest' and 'dishonest' money is not one that many fraudsters find convincing (see Levi, 1981) – a cynicism nicely encapsulated in Al Capone's view of the business and the law as 'the legitimate rackets' – it would be wrong to see it as just a mystificatory ploy invented by businesspeople to induce false consciousness into 'the punters' among the general public. Most businesspeople and professionals do have a notion of unethical behaviour – sometimes a corporate or professional code – which they use to delimit how far they are prepared to go and against which they judge others, whether convicted or not. Cases in which sham businesses are set up with the intention of cheating others are defined by business and professional élites as improper (though they may not be prosecuted), but except for these and clear instances of embezzlement, fraud victims knowingly engage in voluntary commercial transactions with the accused and transfer property rights to the accused in exchange for an anticipated consideration. This, combined with the often intricate nature of transactions between different companies and the transformations of property rights and liabilities that accompany them, makes fraud allegations intrinsically harder to justify than allegations of burglary or shoplifting, where the ownership of legal title is not in doubt.

With respect to fraud, many individuals and groups have internal conflicts of interest which makes it hard for them to decide what selfish line to take: the desire to protect public confidence in the legitimacy of the system is countered by the fear of damaging the volume of trade and of putting themselves and their colleagues at risk of being convicted of criminal offences; and many groups have conflicting short-term and long-term interests which are not resolvable in a self-evident way. Furthermore, there are conflicts between the 'respectable' and 'rough' business sectors which emerge, for example, in the building trade, where the Building Employers' Confederation and Federation of Master Builders – representing the larger firms and better-established small firms – support clamp-downs by the Revenue departments on the 'unskilled cowboys' who are not registered for VAT and who are able therefore to undercut the prices of their members. To some extent, this is true also of investment businesses: considerable opposition to last-minute proposals in the Financial Services Bill (1985) to establish an industry-wide compensation scheme for fraud victims came from firms on The Stock Exchange. These objections were not to the principle of a compensation scheme – The Stock Exchange has long had one – but to the fact that they would have to pay higher premiums if they were mixed in with investment business who were members of less well-established SROs such as FIMBRA (formerly NASDIM), and who would be rated by insurers as worse risks than themselves. This theme that it is unfair or even immoral to require 'the good' and 'the efficient' to cross-subsidize incompetence or lower regulatory standards is a well-worked one in the commercial crime area, even if it does not extend to the refusal to offset commercial losses against taxation! SIB soon responded by promising further consultation and by suggesting a compromise measure whereby each SRO would be responsible for its own compensation fund, but there would be effectively what insurers term a 'stop-loss' facility: other SROs would be involved only if a particular SRO found itself with such a bad experience of claims that it believed that its members would be unable to pay them. In such a case, the SRO would apply to a central Compensation Board for a grant, and if that body and SIB was convinced that the claim was necessary, a grant would be paid and recovered by a levy spread across the rest of the industry.

Bearing in mind that these are not typical cases of law-making and that they represent more complex interests than may be found in many laws (see Chambliss and Seidman, 1982), let us examine some examples of commercial conflicts at work in the British legislative process. I have selected these three because they are the most recent laws which have a significant bearing upon the control of fraud. However, it should be borne in mind that like most such legislation – the anti-fraud provisions of the Theft Acts (1968 and 1978) are the exception to this – the laws were formulated not just to deal with fraud but to provide a (though not necessarily *the*) regulatory framework within which commerce could function profitably. First, the making of the Insolvency Act (1985), which deals with corporate bankruptcies.

THE INSOLVENCY ACT (1985)

For many years, disquiet had been expressed by the media – via weekly exposés on popular radio programmes like *Checkpoint* and television programmes such as *That's Life* – by the Consumers Association, and by other professional groups such as liquidators, about the abuse of the corporate form to escape personal liability following behaviour that was at best reckless but which had not been subjected to criminal proceedings. (Under the Companies Act (1948), directors could be made personally liable but only if they were convicted of offences of fraud under the Act: as we shall see later, such prosecutions were and are very rare.) Moreover, though slightly less significant in this context, there had been a drift towards the involvement in fraud of 'professional criminals', exploiting the anonymity as well as the freedom from personal liability of the corporate form (Levi, 1981). These anxieties (along with a host of other problems of insolvency legislation, which had grown *ad hoc* over a century) led to the formation in 1977 of a Committee headed by Sir Kenneth Cork – former Lord Mayor of London and senior partner in the leading firm of insolvency practitioners, Cork Gully – which reported in 1982 (Cork Committee, 1982). Many proposals – including one reducing the preferential status of the Crown as a creditor, which means that if any taxes are owed, the Revenue departments get first bite at what is left in a liquidation before unsecured 'ordinary' trade creditors can get anything at all – were rejected by the Government from the start. But a White Paper in 1984, followed by the Insolvency Bill in 1985, did eventually arise from the ashes of the Cork Report. Among many contentious issues were the proposals to disqualify the directors of 'failed' (or oftentimes, from the directors' viewpoint, successful) companies.

The White Paper (Department of Trade and Industry, 1984)

proposed that the directors of companies that were wound up compulsorily – normally those that are suspected of malpractice and/or where there are thought to be few assets left to pay a liquidator and creditor – *ipso facto* should be deemed 'unfit' and should be disqualified *automatically* for three years from the management of any other company. In all liquidations, the court making the winding up order was to be given the discretion to disqualify for up to fifteen years after even *one* liquidation (compared with two under the Insolvency Act (1976)), and liquidators would have the right to apply to the court for such an order. Disqualified directors would have to apply to the court for permission to act in management: if they did so without permission, they would have committed an offence punishable by a maximum of two years' imprisonment, as well as become personally liable for all corporate debts incurred. These proposals were embodied more or less intact in the Insolvency Bill, though, after hostile comment from commerce and the professions, directors were to be given twenty–eight days to lodge an appeal against disqualification.

The provisions that were enacted are discussed in Chapter 7, but there was enormous resistance in the House of Lords, and an impressive lobby was organized by the Institute of Directors and representatives of merchant banks, who argued that the provisions for imposing personal liability and disqualification upon any director who failed to take *every step* he ought to have taken to minimize loss to creditors *from the moment he knew or ought to have known that there was no reasonable prospect of the company avoiding insolvent liquidation* would deter company rescues by making outsiders unwilling to serve on the boards of companies in difficulties. In the end, a compromise was accepted whereby the provisions of s.12 of the Insolvency Act (1985) – now s.214(3) of the Insolvency Act (1986) taken with s.10 of the Company Directors Disqualification Act (1986) – were made less draconian than was envisaged, but Parliament specifically rejected the proposal of Lord Denning to insert 'reasonable' before 'every step'. There was almost no resistance, however, to the requirement that liquidators must be members of professional bodies, since this had no wider implications for venture capital and since the major interest-groups such as the Insolvency Practitioners Association stood to gain (and certainly would not lose) by the enhanced professionalization of their role: for insiders, one beneficial consequence of the establishment of professional entry control is to interfere with market forces and thereby to create the possibility of imposing higher charges. This brief account is a good example of a political struggle over fraud prevention legislation which involved an interplay between different interest groups and a genuine dispute over what is best for the functioning of a capitalist economy.

THE LLOYD'S ACT (1982)

Like the Financial Services Act (1986), discussed next, the Lloyd's Act (1982) was devised in the shadow of the fear of more draconian governmental intervention. Scandals over fraud, threats from American insurance interests, and bad publicity over the management of Lloyd's had made reforms of some kind politically and economically necessary by the late 1970s. The official process of the reform of Lloyd's began in 1979 with an enquiry chaired by Sir Henry Fisher – a distinguished former High Court judge and merchant banker who went on to become Master of Wolfson College, Oxford – into how self-regulation should be managed, consistent with the overall economic dynamism and profitability of Lloyd's. As Hodgson acutely observes, it 'was from the start an enquiry into *self-regulation at Lloyd's* – not an enquiry into how best Lloyd's ought ideally to be regulated' (Hodgson, 1986: 290). This ties in neatly with notions of the 'non-decision-making process' in political theory, whereby certain possibilities are automatically ruled out of the political agenda.

The effect of the Fisher Report of 1980 was to move the responsibility for the regulation of Lloyd's from the mass democracy of the General Meeting of all 20,000 members to the representative democracy of a Council. However, representation on the Council was not based upon the mass constituency alone: the Report recommended a Council comprising 'working members' (for instance, those who carry out the underwriting of risks on behalf of Lloyd's members), 'non-working members' (those who hope to make lots of money by putting their wealth at theoretical risk in exchange for backing the insurance decisions of the working members), and lay members nominated by the Council with the approval of the Bank of England. The Council was to include a Disciplinary Committee, and it was proposed that it should have legal immunity against lawsuits arising out of acts and omissions carried out in the course of their duties, including immunity against being sued for negligence by members who had sustained underwriting losses.

The great majority of the Council – 16 out of 28 – were to be working members, and they in turn were dominated (in terms of volume of underwriting) by the eight large firms of broker-underwriters. Given the dominance of these eight, it was slightly surprising that the Report identified as a central issue the potential conflict of interest between brokers, representing those seeking insurance, and underwriters, representing those taking the financial risks. This undoubted conflict – realized or merely potential – arose because brokers might put pressure upon underwriters *inter alia* to take a risk for a client at a premium that ought to be higher, to settle claims that were 'dodgy', or to take extra people ('Names') into insurance syndicates in order to increase the volume of business that they could insure. The recommendation was that there should be compulsory divestment of broking from underwriting interests by some unspecific future date – perhaps in five years' time – to the extent that they should not be able to hold shares in each other. These provisions were approved by the great majority of the membership and a draft private Bill – one not sponsored directly by any MP – which became the Lloyd's Act (1982) was submitted to Parliament to put them into effect. Hodgson (1986, Chs 10, 11) has discussed the tactical ploys adopted by the parties to further their ends, but the result of attention to the conflict of interest issue was that Lloyd's was forced to accept the compulsory divestment between brokers and underwriters by July 1987, the period of grace being needed to unwind them with minimum disruption and loss.

Despite the objections of some Lloyd's members and members of both Houses of Parliament that it would give Lloyd's Council a licence to be negligent in regulating fraud, s.11 of the Act also granted the Council immunity against lawsuits from members (though not from the general public or policyholders) that it demanded. (Though legal actions still unresolved in 1987, pursued by Names who lost money to fraudulent underwriters before the passage of the Act, suggest that the legal drafting has proved not to be as watertight as had been hoped by the Council.) Lloyd's successfully campaigned against its being included within the provisions of the Financial Services Act (1986), arguing that no major scandals have arisen from business *transacted* after 1982: it is just that fraud scandals take a long time to resolve! An enquiry ordered by the Government praised the progress achieved at Lloyd's but criticized the inadequacy of action taken to prevent conflicts of interest like managing agents or underwriters favouring those insurance syndicates on which they and their friends were represented over others for which they were responsible (Neill, 1987). Reforms proposed by Sir Patrick Neill QC include more disclosure (for instance on charges and profit records), better complaints procedures, and to ensure fairer contracts and fewer conflicts of interest, the replacement on the Council of some working members by outsiders approved by the Governor of the Bank of England (though still nominated by Lloyd's). Lloyd's promised the speedy implementation of some of those proposals (within 2 years)!

THE FINANCIAL SERVICES ACT (1986)

Another very important piece of legislation which combines civil and criminal anti-fraud provisions is the Financial Services Act (1986), which provoked acrimonious debates in both Houses of Parliament during the ten-months gestation period before its passage into the outside world. So complex and controversial was this legislation – much of which comes into effect only in the latter part of 1987 – that after it had been passed by the House of Commons and had been discussed in detail in committee in the House of Lords, there were tabled no fewer than 380 government and some 200 non-government amendments, to be debated in just three days. The 212 clauses and 17 schedules agreed by the Lords were then hurriedly passed by the Commons to meet the end-of-session deadline: otherwise, the Bill would have lapsed in its entirety. In the light of political, media, and academic criticism of both state regulation and private-sector (or 'self') regulation in Britain in the 1970s and early 1980s, it was generally agreed that new investor protection legislation was required. However, the urgency of the legislative revisions was given further impetus by the need to cope with the extra risks to investors predicted in the aftermath of the deregulatory 'Big Bang' in financial services in October 1986 and of the contemporaneous internationalization of securities trading (see Glossary).

The Financial Services Act (1986) *inter alia* provided the statutory framework for the creation of a new entity – the Securities and Investments Board (SIB) – which, though funded by the private sector and possessing the legal status of a mere private company limited by guarantee, was given delegated power by the Secretary of State for Trade and Industry to act as the Designated Agency for investor protection: to licence investment businesses and SROs under which they were grouped; and to draft detailed rules to govern the conduct of different forms of investment business which, if violated (and detected), might lead to de-authorization. If the banned person, firm, or company thereafter continued to deal with investments, this could lead to criminal prosecution for carrying on an investment business without authorization, *plus* prosecution for any substantive fraud offences that might have been committed. Moreover, the unauthorized business will normally (without court permission) be unable to enforce its contracts (s.5), and the Secretary of State will be able to apply (s.6) for a court injunction to prevent a person from carrying on business without authorization and for a restitution order to require it to disgorge for the benefit of investors any profits it has made and to meet any losses it has produced.

Special-interest lobbying was the keynote of the long run up to the passage of the Act. By April 1986, political obsession with the allegations of fraud at Johnson Matthey Bankers – see Chapter 2 and Clarke (1986) and Moran (1986) – had waned, and this diminution of anxiety continued until the Act was passed. (It immediately rose again following some insider dealing scandals discussed later.) Investor protection, though important, became less salient, and preserving (or creating) London's pre-eminence as an international financial trading centre became the central concern not only of financial entrepreneurs but also of a British Government faced with declining world markets and the possibility of generating new jobs. Frequent attempts were made – particularly in the House of Lords where the Government has less control – to bounce Government into not prejudicing the volume of trade and the much-vaunted 'flexibility' of the City by passing rules that 'on balance' were 'unnecessarily protective'. A survey of fifty-nine executives from leading international securities and investment houses, commissioned by accountants Deloitte, Haskins, and Sells (1986), revealed a general City complaint that the legislation was 'designed for the Aunt Agathas and not the professional investors', and would not do a great deal for either group. These findings were used to press for looser regulation, but were countered by the Chief Executive of SIB who stated that the protection of Aunt Agathas was both morally appropriate and in the interests of the industry itself (SIB press release, 31 July 1986). Indeed, as we shall see, many (though not all) of the investor protection proposals that *were* abandoned were those in which interest-groups were able to argue that those affected were 'professionals' who did not need the higher standards of protection afforded to others. This supports the line of argument employed by Frank (1983) in her study of health and safety legislation in the United States, inasmuch as appeals to principle as well as interest coalitions play a significant role in the legislative process, particularly where there is media interest and political opposition.

Some of the draft rules issued by SIB are aimed at prohibiting oppressive practices such as 'cold-calling' individuals to persuade them to invest. (S.56 of the Act does not make it a criminal offence to make a personal visit or oral communication without express permission: subject to any de-authorization or other sanctions, the remedy is simply that the contract is unenforceable and damages sustained may be recoverable.) However, Aunt Agatha does not benefit as much as she might have done. Life assurance and unit trust companies are required by the new provisions to base their illustrations of future benefits not on their own fantasies but on assumptions prescribed by SIB or the relevant approved SRO. But in July 1986, after the Bill had been passed by the House of Commons, SIB rejected as 'technically impossible' the proposal that insurance companies should be required to state their charges or expenses as a simple proportion of the premiums paid, and this drew the wrath of the Consumers Association as well as that of some Conservative MPs who had withdrawn earlier amendments to the Bill on the assurance by the Minister that this information *would* be disclosed. The issue here is principally that initially, an extremely large commission – in 1985 averaging around 120 per cent of five-year premiums – is paid by insurance companies to motivate sales, and it is feared that if known, this might lead consumers to believe that they are not getting value for money in life assurance. Though there is a short (14-day) 'cooling-off' period during which the investor can change his (or, less frequently in the UK, her) mind, purchasers normally will be *legally* entitled to discover what commission the insurance advisor has received for selling the insurance only if they write to the insurance company *after* they have signed the contract. Moreover, because of SIB rules approved by the Secretary of State, life assurance is now the only area of investment sales where unsolicited calls on the doorstep or on the telephone can lawfully be made.

The sympathetic understanding of the arguments put forward by the insurers may have been facilitated by the presence of Mark Weinberg as Deputy Chairman of SIB: Weinberg had set up (and sold) two large life assurance businesses and, at the time that the rules were approved by SIB, was a substantial shareholder in and director of financial conglomerate Allied Dunbar, to whom he had sold Hambro Life. Despite its influence on SIB, 'the insurance industry' itself is not homogeneous: there were (and are) conflicts between different sectors over what should be the scale of standardized commissions, and the two 'consumer representatives' on LAUTRO – the SRO concerned – exerted pressure for greater disclosure and lower commissions.

It is almost certain that had there not been so much public and media concern, some of the consumer protection measures put forward in the Act and in the draft rules of SIB might not have been introduced at all. Some of the enhanced powers of the SROs were the result not of governmental but of back-bench initiatives: cross-party tactical alliances in the Commons standing committee between two Conservative backbench MPs and the then Labour trade spokesperson, Bryan Gould, led to government acceptance of amendments that strengthened SIB by giving it immunity against negligence suits, giving it the power to institute prosecutions, and enabling it to require an SRO to change its rule book if the latter gave insufficient protection to investors. The sensitivity of the Government to City scandal in a post-Big Bang and pre-election period is illustrated by the rapidity with which it brought forward – from 1 January 1987 to 15 November 1986 – the date of coming into force of enhanced powers of insider-dealing investigation granted to inspectors appointed by the Department of Trade and Industry (s.177), in response to media revelations – particularly in the *Financial Times* – of the background to the resignation of the head of the securities department of bankers Morgan Grenfell for violating house rules to conduct personal dealings only through approved channels.

(Their investigations were carried out in record time and resulted in the issue of a summons against the person concerned.) Quite apart from any desire to see wrong-doing allegations investigated thoroughly, coming in a week in which The Stock Exchange warned Members that they faced up to fourteen years in prison for offences under the Drug Trafficking Offences Act (1986) if they helped drug dealers to launder the proceeds of narcotics, the Government could not afford to be seen as casual in its approach to fraud.

It is possible that if media and consumer scrutiny subsides, some of the regulators will be 'captured' by the suppliers of services more than they are at present. But – as may be confirmed from the protests about their compliance costs from many commercial organizations who sell investments – there seems little doubt that despite the watering-down of some proposals as a result of pressure from interest-groups such as the insurance industry, the rules are generally consumerist in their motivation. Whether their *enforcement* (and that of the SROs generally) will match this initial motivation is an open question, and one that will remain open: enforcement, though relatively autonomous, is influenced by the political climate, and this may vary depending upon the relative salience of (1) City scandal, and (2) pressure from the vendors of financial services not to lose 'Britain' (and themselves!) business by making regulations that are tougher than those prevailing in competing financial centres.

There is no doubting that business interests do try to influence legislation and discretionary decisions (such as references to the Monopolies and Mergers Commission) in their own favour. But even when they succeed, the *ideological* implications are not as clear-cut as they may appear. Not *all* self-interested attempts by businesspeople to change legislation are aimed at advancing their interests and diminishing, in some zero-sum way, the interests of workers and/or consumers. Let us take as an example traders in Eurobonds, interest-bearing stocks issued by foreign governments, companies, and international syndicates in currencies of major trading nations, and which are traded outside national stock exchanges. In 1986, British dealers on the vast secondary Eurobond market – which had a turnover of £1460 *billion* in 1985, over three-quarters of which went through London – succeeded in changing clauses in the Financial Services Bill (1985) which would have required lengthy vetting of telexes: the principal method of selling new issues. The effect of these fraud prevention requirements would have been to make London slower and more expensive than other commercial centres such as Luxembourg for the sale of Eurobonds, and modest protection for British investors – nearly all of them professional dealers – would have been obtained at the expense of driving a considerable part of the market to less protected climes elsewhere. Although this is clearly an example of commercial pressure-group politics, it is difficult to see it meaningfully as *class* legislation, except in the tautological sense that all legislation maintaining the position of capitalists (and British invisible exports) is class legislation, or in the sense that because of their social and economic position, some groups are in a better position than others to have their claims listened to and implemented.

Another illustration from the area of financial services is the successful attempt of SROs and their mega-regulator, SIB, to obtain legal immunity against civil lawsuits for decisions taken in pursuit of their regulatory functions. (See the Lloyd's Act, 1982 and the Financial Services Act, 1986.) Does one interpret this as a way of evading responsibility (including, significantly, civil liability for negligence) to investors for *failure* to act against members, or as a way of facilitating fearless 'incapacitation' of suspected fraudulent traders? The correct answer is probably 'both'. The clinching argument in the granting of immunity – which initially was opposed by the Department of Trade and Industry – was that senior figures from commerce and industry would not sit on SROs if they risked personal lawsuits as a result: note the parallels with the Insolvency Bill argument that merchant bankers would not rescue ailing companies if they risked disqualification and personal liability for corporate losses. But one (undiscussed, and probably unintended) consequence is that provided that it cannot be proven that they acted in bad faith, the immunity from liability of regulatory bodies also gives them greater latitude to ban individuals against whom they have commercial or political grudges: the courts may be very reluctant to interfere with their administrative discretion. Again, one should beware of too ready an 'Establishment conspiracy theory': despite considerable political and media lobbying, the Government rejected the demand of the professional law and accountancy bodies to obtain blanket legal immunity against being sued in performance (or for non-performance) of their regulatory duties, even when their members are dispensing investment advice.

Issues of pressure-group politics become more complex still when the internationalization of markets brings different national legislation and self-regulatory rules into conflict, particularly where powerful pressure groups such as ISRO become involved. This has occurred increasingly in the attempts of the United States to apply domestic legislation to purchasers abroad (such as the ban on exports of 'strategic goods' including computer components to communist countries). However, it also affects the sale of securities. For example, s.47 of the Financial Services Act (1986) makes it a criminal offence – punishable by up to seven years' imprisonment and/or an unlimited fine on conviction on indictment – knowingly or recklessly to make a false or misleading statement with the intention of inducing someone to enter into an investment agreement or for anyone to engage in any act or course of conduct which creates a false or misleading impression of the price or value of an investment. But to what range of markets should this apply? It is a common technique that when a Eurobond is issued, the price is 'stabilized' by the issuing banks supporting its price in the initial stages, thus creating order in the market. Almost all dealers in Eurobonds are professionals who are aware that this happens, and the Department of Trade and Industry readily agreed to exclude Eurobonds from this part of the Act: s.47(2) applies only if the act is done or the course of conduct is engaged in, or if the false or misleading impression is created in the UK. Moreover, it is a defence under s.47(3) 'for him to prove that his act or conduct would not create an impression that was false or misleading'.

However, dealings in shares create different principles, because particularly with the Government's espousal of the notion of a share-owning democracy, many amateurs have come into the market, and it is a consistent feature of the dealing rules that they should receive greater protection than professionals, who are deemed capable of looking after themselves. One form of devious practice is that where an issuer of new shares has difficulty in finding buyers, it may instruct intermediaries – possibly using false names – to telephone a 'target' bank and state that they wish to buy the new securities. As a result, the bank agrees to buy shares from the main issuer, which it sells to the pseudo-purchasers, who pass it back to the original issuer, who can then claim that the issue has been a great success (though in fact, the great majority of the shares may still be in his hands). If the market 'buys' this story, the shares will rise and the issuer will be able to offload the surplus stock without anyone else knowing. This is known – somewhat euphemistically – as 'price stabilization'. It is far from clear what the justification is for this practice, but it does occur in the hitherto unregulated Euro-equity market, which handled $3.2 billion of issues in the first half of 1986 alone (*Financial Times*, 18 July 1986).

Broadly supported by The Stock Exchange, ISRO – which later merged with The Stock Exchange to become The International Stock Exchange – succeeded in obtaining some degree of exemption from this clause for new issues and for so-called Euro-equities, arguing that if this was not granted, many US share issues could not be sold in London, nor British shares sold in the US, because prices stabilization as described above is common in Wall Street and is lawful in the United States. Complete exemption was opposed (1) by those international banks who are not issuing houses, who argued that it is a harmful form of manipulation which will hurt small investors particularly, and (2) by the Department of Trade and Industry, who argued that if issuers disclosed in writing that they might stabilize the market by making bids after the initial issue, they would have a valid defence to a charge under s.47.

In the end, a compromise was found by SIB (draft rules, 13 October 1986) whereby stabilization of international securities would be permitted provided, *inter alia*, that (1) any firm wishing to carry out stabilizing transactions disclosed this fact; (2) other investment businesses took reasonable steps to determine if an investment was likely to be stabilized and to ensure that its own customers understood the implications of buying such an investment; and (3) the investments were dealt with on a recognized, or designated, investment exchange. Consequently, 'open stabilizers' have nothing to fear, but some regulation was considered necessary to prevent real abuses in the market. So again, the Government had to perform a balancing act: here, the risks to investors were weighed against the fact that commission income was at risk. Are these protections real, or mere lip-service? Though at present, the Euro-equity market is comparatively small, it may grow rapidly, and unless the Government can generate agreement internationally with its own rules of protection, British invisible exports in an important strategic economic field will suffer. We see here the way in which the state seeks to balance competing commercial interests. At a general level, during the 1970s and 1980s, finance capital interests have predominated over industrial capital interests (Gamble, 1985; Moran, 1986). However, there are many competing interests within the financial services world, and estimating the impact of particular measures is often uncertain, so the state has a very difficult job in arbitrating between them and in defining for its own and for public consumption what the overall 'public interest' demands.

One further point should be borne in mind when thinking about law-making in fraud (and in other spheres also). Although there may be some instances in which a clear, planned strategy is achieved without great difficulty, much legislation is conceived, drafted, and revised under considerable pressure. The Lloyd's Act (1982) was needed urgently to reassure the financial community that something was being done to prevent future abuses on the insurance market; the legislative timetable for the Insolvency Act (1985) allowed only six weeks between the publication of the 1984 White Paper and the drafting of the Insolvency Bill; the Financial Services Act (1986) was passed in the belief that untold chaos might ensue if securities markets were freed from major restraints in October 1986 without there being any half-way plausible regulatory structure in place (though in fact, neither the Act nor many parts of the regulatory structure were in force until many months later). Given the general pressures upon the parliamentary timetable, masses of amendments and objections can threaten these important Bills altogether: as the Insolvency Act (1985) went through Parliament, over 1200 amendments were tabled.

Government departments which sponsor legislation – in this field, normally the Department of Trade and Industry – have learned to consult those commercial interests that are affected, but those interests do not always respond rapidly, nor are they always united or consistent in their responses over time. This leads to complaints from the business and/or professional groups (such as accountants) that they are not given enough time to formulate a response, and from the government department that the groups are dragging their heels: in September 1986, the Department of Trade and Industry complained bitterly about the lateness of the Confederation of British Industry in submitting their comments on the Financial Services Bill, which was then reaching its final stages, and it even allowed the Association of Corporate Treasurers to draft itself (subject to official approval) *government* amendments to the Bill in areas where it had received criticism from the Association, leading to the exemption of most investment activity carried out by corporate treasurers from the Financial Services Act or from its formal authorization procedures (schedule 1 of the Act). This pressure of time – for once lost, a Bill is very difficult to revive – creates its own momentum for compromise and becomes part of the legislative tactics.

In the United States, the role of special interest lobbyists has long caused controversy, though concern has intensified during the period of the Reagan administration. The comparative independence of the Congress from subservience to the political party to which the Senator or Representative belongs – particularly in the powerful committees which are underpinned by the seniority system rather than by party patronage – makes for a large number of pressure points at which interest-groups can aim. In Britain, by contrast, prime-ministerial government has generally been the keynote, and those interest-groups that are unable to persuade the government of their case traditionally have been weak. However, in the legislation discussed above, the unelected Members of the House of Lords have played a major role in undermining that generalization. The results have not been ideologically consistent. On the one hand, those representing the interests of finance capital succeeded in restricting the scope of disqualifications in the Insolvency Act (1985); on the other, the Government sustained a defeat when members from a number of parties supported a Labour amendment to the Financial Services Bill enhancing the independent element in SRO governing boards. This amended schedule 2(1) requires that as a condition for their approval, the arrangements for rule-making and rule-enforcing in all SROs

> 'must be such as to secure a proper balance –
> (a) between the interests of the different members of the organisation; and
> (b) between the interests of the organisation or its members and the interests of the public.'

This strengthened what previously had been largely a rhetorical government commitment to consumer representation. The unstable attendance in the House of Lords and the comparatively small amount of government patronage that can be exerted over its permanent, unelected members makes it easier to organize an anti-government coalition on a particular issue there than in the Commons. Although the House of Lords has the power only to delay – not to reject altogether – the passage of Bills that can command majority support in the House of Commons, the pressure of business means that the Government can sometimes be induced to compromise on concrete issues that are not central to its programme.

It is hardly surprising, then, that major commercial and company law reforms end up in such a mess, and that the Insolvency Act (1986) had to be passed to revise yet again some criticized provisions in the Insolvency Act (1985) and to consolidate its receivership and liquidations provisions with that of the Companies Act (1985). The Insolvency Act (1986) in turn was to be supplemented at some unspecified future date by a substantial amount of secondary legislation (e.g. Statutory Instruments implementing regulations, rules and orders). Similarly, the Financial Services Act (1986) underwent a series of metamorphoses. Initially, Department of Trade and Industry adviser Professor Gower wanted a regulatory system broadly along the lines of SEC but the Conservative Government was opposed – on grounds both of cost and ideology – to such an interventionist stance, so the revised proposals (Department of Trade and Industry, 1985) were intended to provide a low-cost regulatory system with the minimum of governmental or legal interference. Opponents of direct state regulation argued that a government watchdog would be too rule-bound and that government salaries would be too low to attract regulators of sufficient calibre: one prominent advocate of 'statute backed, practitioner-based regulation', SIB Chairman Sir Kenneth Berrill was appointed at a salary of £100,000 per annum, over a quarter more than that of the Head of the Civil Service.

However, faced with the internationalization of securities markets, it was soon apparent that the notion of regulation without extensive law was unworkable: armies of American and Japanese corporate lawyers simply would not stand for it and would apply for (though not necessarily receive) judicial review of regulatory decisions. Litigiousness soon spread to the domestic front: in November 1986, advisers to the losers in two take-over bids allowed to go through by the informal self-regulatory agency, The City Take-Over Panel, applied for judicial review of its decisions. In *Prudential Bache* v. *City Takeover Panel* (*Financial Times*, 6 December, 1986), the Court of Appeal upheld the merits of the Take-Over Panel's decision, but held that notwithstanding the non-statutory basis of its powers, because its role was approved by the Department of Trade and Industry and by The Stock Exchange and because of its effects in the public domain, the Panel *was* subject to judicial review. However, it ruled that unlike other spheres of judicial review, the Panel's findings should be accepted and pursued as valid and binding unless and until overturned by the court. Moreover, the Master of the Rolls stated that the court should intervene only if the Panel's interpretation of the take-over rules might mislead an ordinary user of the market, and would quash a decision only if the Panel acted unfairly and in breach of the rules of natural justice. Judicial review might relieve individuals of the disciplinary consequences of any erroneous finding of breach of the rules: in my view, this could be vital because shares can be de-listed from The Stock Exchange for breach of the take-over rules. But except *in extremis*, lest this render SROs ineffective, the courts would stay out of being sucked into playing an active role in deciding the merits of take-over bids.

In other spheres, such as the Conduct of Business Rules for investment dealers, self-regulation was under attack: the Committee of London Clearing Bankers (as well as Scottish banks and the Building Societies Association) was incensed by the attempts of SIB – backed by Department of Trade and Industry officials – to impose upon them its concept of 'polarization', under which bank branches – like any other dealers in investment business – would have to choose between (1) acting as fully independent intermediaries, advising on products from a range of companies, and (2) company representatives selling only their own products. A corollary of this rule was that banks acting as investment advisers would not be allowed to sell the bank's *own* unit trust unless the latter was 'demonstrably better' than competitors – which none of them at the time could be shown to be.

The Committee responded by proposing in the House of Lords an amendment to the Financial Services Bill that would have de-authorized SIB if its rules were anti-competitive: this amendment, which would have generated enormous legal uncertainty before the competition issues were decided, was withdrawn after SIB agreed to further discussions with them. The motive for bankers' opposition was profit:

they have a semi-captive market in their customers, who can be sold in-house products in the belief that they are receiving impartial advice that these are the best ones available, whether they are or not. The purpose of the SIB proposal was to make it impossible for the banks to trade upon the image of impartiality unless they could demonstrate that they would have no conflict of interest: the latter could be attained only by preventing them from promoting their own products. But this conflict opened up a key 'can of worms' in the area of competition policy: under what conditions can restrictions on competition be justified as being 'in the public interest'?

Overruling most of the objections from the Office of Fair Trading, the Secretary of State for Trade and Industry approved the SIB rule book in April 1987. Despite the intensive lobbying to which it was subjected, SIB offered the banks and building societies only a modest degree of compromise under which, *inter alia*:

1 independent intermediaries within a banking or other conglomerate will *not* be allowed to recommend the group's in-house life assurance or unit trust products unless failure to do so would disadvantage the customer;
2 whichever way they 'polarize', bank officials and others may give 'generic' investment advice (e.g. 'advice to a customer about the appropriate broad distribution of a lump sum');
3 if the branch advisers choose to sell only their own group products, but find that they have no suitable investment for their client, they will be able to refer him to an independent intermediary, including one within their group, though they will have to relinquish any role in advising further the customer whom they refer on;
4 because they are selected for their investment management expertise and not for their value as a genuine independent intermediary, portfolio managers working for banking conglomerates can put a client's money into their in-house unti trust (but maybe *not* life insurance products) provided that they have the client's explicit permission in the customer agreement and that this conforms with their general obligation to act in the best interests of the customer.

As a consequence of these actual or incipient challenges to self-regulatory authority, extremely complex and detailed legislation had to be formulated rapidly to deal with a large variety of present problems and possible future contingencies. This in turn generated hasty and anxious responses from traders who themselves had not previously had to worry about detailed legal compliance and, encouraged by the success of Eurobond traders and insurance companies in wringing concessions from the Department of Trade and Industry and from SIB, the amendments spiralled. Despite the central importance of victim compensation schemes to the political justification for permitting self-regulation, neither the general outlines nor concrete details of highly problematic insurance arrangements in the professional indemnity market – from which many underwriters had retreated with long tails between their legs after sustaining heavy losses – were considered fully until the last minute. Perhaps it was assumed that professional indemnity insurance would be as easy to arrange as auto insurance for the over-21s, but the difficulties of finding insurance had a profound effect in determining the system of compensation that was eventually decided. Little wonder that government competence and commitment to investor protection was attacked in the City and in Parliament.

Financial services regulation is something of a special case in the area of 'crimes of the powerful', inasmuch as the 'reputation of the industry' is necessary to investor confidence and hence to profitability. Indeed, Coleman asserts that 'The success of the SEC can be attributed to the fact that unlike most of the other [regulatory] agencies . . . it enjoys strong business support' (J. Coleman, 1985a:172). Furthermore, many – though, as we shall see, by no means all – securities offences that are reported to or detected by the authorities are committed by persons outside élite circles. Unlike laws such as those which impose strict liability on manufacturers for the safety of their products, it is in the overall economic interest of *any* securities industry in the world to have sound investor protection regulation (or the appearance of it), even though particular individuals and firms may lose out as a result of their misconduct being exposed. Overall, these case studies of legislation in the field of fraud regulation reveal that although economic interests shape the content of the laws in important ways, the pressure of unanticipated external events plays an equally vital role in the legislative process. Neither the visible nor invisible hands are always competent at planning commercial surgery!

The judiciary, case law, and commercial fraud

The role of the judiciary in relation to commercial fraud depends upon those cases which are brought to court. Expressed in this way, this has the appearance of a trivial, self-evident proposition, but in fact, it points us towards the crucial role played not only by self-regulatory and state policing agencies but also by victims. Given the overlap between civil and criminal laws relating to fraud, to the extent that victims choose to pursue their remedies through the civil courts or through informal complaint, the role of the *criminal* courts will be comparatively limited. I will not seek to review here the role of lawyers and judges in relation to civil fraud, but it *is* significant: see Coffee (1986), Hermann (1983), Mann (1985), Sealy (1984), and Tunc (1986) for some relevant discussion.

Historically, one may note a marked lack of judicial activism in extending the scope of the fraudulent obtaining of goods (Levi, 1981, Ch. VII). On the other hand, the outer boundaries of the activities covered by the common-law 'conspiracy to defraud' traditionally have been extremely ill-defined and broad in their potential. In *Scott* v. *Commissioner of Police for the Metropolis* [1974] 3 All E.R. 1032, Viscount Dilhorne said that the common law conspiracy did not necessarily have to involve deceit, and

> 'an agreement by two or more by dishonesty to deprive a person of something which is his or to which he is or would be or might be entitled and an agreement by two or more by dishonesty to injure some proprietary right of his, suffices to constitute the offence of conspiracy to defraud.' (1039)

The Criminal Law Act (1977) (as amended by the Criminal Attempts Act, 1981), sought to put some order into the law of conspiracy: for a discussion, see Arlidge and Parry (1985). The wording of the statute, the principles which underlay this reform of conspiracy legislation, and widespread concern among the senior judiciary to narrow down fraud charges in order – they hoped – to increase certainty in the law, led in the 1980s to the rejection of the common law conspiracy to defraud in favour of charges of conspiracies to commit more specific offences, usually under the Theft Acts. In *Ayres* (1984) 78 Cr. App. R. 232; (1984) AC 447, the House of Lords held that the prosecution could charge conspiracy to defraud only where there were *no* specific statutory conspiracy charges that could be laid in relation to the conduct in question: this appeared to leave the common-law offence as a residual category for 'frauds' which were not covered, in whole *or in part*, by any substantive statutory offence. As the Lord Chief Justice observed in *Grant* (1986) 81 Cr. App. R. 324, the principle adopted in *Ayres* created great difficulties for prosecutors, and in *Cooke* [1986] 2 All E.R. 985, HL, the House of Lords further refined *Ayres*, holding that the Crown could after all charge common-law conspiracy to defraud as well as statutory conspiracy (for example, to obtain property by deception or false accounting), if there was *separate* evidence that might found a non-statutory conspiracy charge.

This still left unresolved the ambit of conspiracy to defraud, and partly in response to judicial comments in *Cooke* that legislative clarification was necessary, clause 12(1) of the Criminal Justice Bill (1986) heralds a possible return towards the earlier, broader conception of conspiracy to defraud when it states that if '(a) a person agrees with any other person or persons that a course of conduct shall be pursued; and

(b) that course of conduct will necessarily amount to or involve the commission of any offence or offences by one or more of the parties to the agreement if the agreement is carried out in accordance with their intentions,

the fact that it will do so shall not preclude a charge of conspiracy to defraud being brought against any of them in respect of the agreement.'

Although the *effect* of *Ayres* was to help businesspeople to avoid conviction for fraud, it would be mistaken to think that the House of Lords deliberately sought to grant immunity to any capitalist élite: my view is supported by their self-criticisms and call for legislation in *Cooke*. What the cases show is that judges seldom strain legal concepts to convict businesspeople whose activities are not 'plainly criminal': any judicial temptations towards moral entrepreneurialism against 'unsavoury' business practices are constrained by convention and by the rules of statutory interpretation in criminal law.

This self-denying judicial ordinance should not be construed as simple bias in favour of the powerful. In some of the above cases, it assisted professional criminals who defrauded large companies and holiday timeshare investors, though the proviso to s.2(1) of the Criminal Appeal Act (1986) which allows the appellate court to sustain the conviction where it is convinced that no properly directed 'reasonable jury' would have failed to convict the accused and/or where there is a charge left 'on the file' which *would* have been appropriate, has meant that some of the 'successful' appellants have gone to jail just the same: no doubt their legal triumphs will have consoled them greatly as they contemplate them from their prison cells! In other cases, appellate courts have sought to stem the tendency to treat breaches of contract as if they entailed fraud or theft. For instance, in *Navvabi* [1986] 3 All E.R. 102, the Court of Appeal considered a situation in which the defendant opened accounts with two banks and a building society in false names and with false references and, without obtaining permission for an overdraft, drew cheques on these accounts far in excess of the balance, to pay for gaming chips. The court took the view that the issue of the cheque did no more than give the casino a contractual right against the bank and was not therefore an assumption of the rights of an owner and not an 'appropriation' under s.1(1) of the Theft Act (1968). The appellate courts have also held that a salaried manager of a public house does not commit theft against his employer – merely a breach of contract – when despite a contractual obligation to buy only from his employer, he secretly buys beer from a wholesaler which he intends to resell in order to make a profit which he thereby denies to his employer:

Attorney-General's Reference No.1 of 1985 [1986] 2 All E.R. 219. There are, in addition, a series of cases lucidly reviewed in *Cooke* [1986] 2 All E.R. 985, HL, where doubt is expressed as to whether those British Rail stewards who bring their own food and drink to sell to passengers can be convicted of Theft Act offences: since they did not alter any invoices or accounting records – they merely did not sell British Rail produce they were paid to sell – there was no offence of false accounting; and since there was no evidence that passengers would have refused to purchase the produce had they known that British Rail was being 'cheated', a conviction for 'going equipped to cheat' could not be sustained either. Lord Mackay stated (997–98) that if there had been an agreement 'dishonestly' to retain moneys that they were obliged to hand over to British Rail, a conviction for conspiracy to defraud at common law would have been warranted: but the jury had acquitted all co-defendants, so there was no conspiracy.

Judicial views do not always work *against* the use of powers to combat fraud committed by high-status professionals: I will discuss later the verdict of the House of Lords that upheld – albeit reluctantly – the legality of the Inland Revenue raid against the Rossminster tax avoidance schemes. But it will be interesting to see how, when they consider directors' conduct prior to liquidation in dealing with personal liability for corporate debts under the Insolvency Act (1986) and with applications to disqualify under the Company Directors Disqualification Act (1986), the courts apply the criteria that require directors to have taken 'every step' to minimize loss to creditors: will they re-instate in practice the limiting condition that requires only 'reasonable' steps?

Nevertheless, the willingness to be constrained by legal rules when trying many business frauds – which attitude, as judicial acquittals in fraud cases indicate, is still a feature of the criminal justice process (see Chapter 6) – may be contrasted with the much lesser reluctance to extend the ambit of the criminal law of encompass working-class claims to common or to private property outside the realm of 'ordinary' business transactions (Fletcher, 1978; Hall, 1952; Smithies, 1985). The preparedness of judges to bring credit-card abuses – which are committed principally by 'criminal types' rather than businesspeople or employees – within the law of criminal deception has attracted criticism from some legal commentators (A. Smith, 1982), who argue that such transactions are civil rather than criminal matters: is it truly 'deception' when stolen and/or forged credit cards are used to buy goods from salespeople unless there is evidence that the vendor actually cared about whether or not the purchaser was seeking to defraud the credit-card company? (Contrast with decisions in 'employee fraud' cases reviewed in *Cooke* [1986].) But such criticisms – like most from legal academics –

have not impressed the appellate courts, who take the pragmatic line that credit-card fraudsters are rogues who ought not to be allowed to get away with it.

It may well be the case that judges – like many other people – are brought up in such a way that they make a taken-for-granted differentiation between the 'dangerous classes' who threaten the governability of the nation and those whom they believe to be the creators of prosperity. To the extent that that is so, we would expect them to show more empathy with those (e.g. businesspeople) whom they see as making a useful contribution to society than with unions or rebellious youth whom they may see as being less useful and as the sources of 'public disorder'. (See Griffith, 1985, for an examination of judicial attitudes, though there is no mention of fraud in his work, which explores areas of law where there is class conflict.) But even if Griffith's account of the influences upon judicial decisions is correct, does this mean that criminal law is created and interpreted by 'the powerful' in their own interests (even 'in the last instance')? Or is it more the case that legislators and, in a different way, judges are concerned about the impact of legal rules on an enterprise economy? The two propositions are not incompatible, but they embody major differences regarding both methods of interpretation and levels of explanation.

In capitalist societies, both civil and criminal law do favour 'the wealthy' and, to a lesser extent, 'the respectable poor' against those who openly resist bourgeois values. Conservatives must accept the radical critique that the law has this function, even though they may consider it to be a justifiable one. But since there are many laws that are (or appear to be) irrelevant to interclass struggles (Cotterrell, 1984; Greenberg, 1981; Sparks, 1980), and great difficulties in determining whether there are coherent interests among 'the powerful' and, if so, what they are (as in the Insolvency Act (1985) discussed above), it seems doubtful that any one theory or theoretical paradigm could *explain* the content of all law. For example, one would not wish to read too much about the state of the struggle between capitalists and workers into the abolition of the Dog Licence or the defeat of the Shops (HL) Bill (1986), which would have legalized general commercial trading on a Sunday. The latter was achieved by a coalition of Ulster Unionists, Conservative back-bench MPs, and opposition parties, representing the varied interests of small businesses, all the Churches, and shop assistants' unions, plus the desire to punish the Government for supporting a political accord with Eire over the future of Northern Ireland!

Many neo-marxists would be happy to acknowledge that much legislation – civil or criminal – has no *direct* relation to the economic substructure or the class struggle, and that a law controlling the freedom of businesspeople will be allowed to go through and even be enforced provided that it does not threaten the basis of the capitalist system as a whole. But this does not help us either to predict or to illuminate much of the content of legislation, particularly in the area of intercapitalist conflicts. The more mundane models used by political scientists focus rather upon the methods by which these abstract interests work their way into the legislative process, whether behind the scenes, in the political lobbying undertaken by many pressure-groups including specific business ones, or more openly during parliamentary debates. If we wish to build up a more complete picture of the relationship between commerce and government, we also need to look for those cases in which commercial pressures and representations to government have *not* yielded fruit: for example, although the penalties for video and audio piracy were increased in the Copyright (Amendment) Act (1983) (as they were in the United States also), the Department of Trade and Industry has so far resisted the attempts of the British Anti-Counterfeiting Group to make product counterfeiting a general criminal offence.

Moreover, in addition to the multiplicity of business and professional groups seeking to advance their interests, governmental (or quasi-governmental private-sector bodies such as SIB) bureaucracies have some autonomy in promoting administrative 'solutions' to commercial abuses, particularly where they are not the captives of the groups they are supposed to regulate (see Chapter 5). This is quite independent of the interests of the state itself in raising money to pay for its expenditures, whether these be on defence, criminal justice, or social security. Even here, there are ambiguities: prestigious economic groups – who may also be generous contributors to party funds – seek tax relief on the grounds that taxation is inhibiting entrepreneurial activities; tolerance of tax evasion by the poor (including those drawing social security) may dampen down the pressures to riot or to organize revolution. In short, it would be mistaken to argue that in any one area such as fraud legislation there are no patterns in the mosaic of control, but we must not understate the significance of 'class fractions' (i.e. conflicts of interest not just between but *among* business, governmental, professional, and employee representatives) in influencing laws regulating commercial life.

In the quasi-criminal sphere of 'business regulatory offences' (Levi, 1984a), there is simultaneously pressure to decriminalize offences and to toughen sanctions against unfair trading. Thus, following the recommendations of the Keith Committee (1983), those who are late with their VAT returns are no longer hauled before the criminal courts: criminal penalties – which were generally trivial – have been replaced by sliding-scale administrative fines. Decriminalization may look like a victory for capitalists, but its practical impact on business will probably be greater than the criminal provisions that preceded it. As for fair trading, the review of UK competition policy in 1986/7 has to consider the view of the Director-General of Fair Trading that there are far too many loopholes in the law relating to price-fixing and market-sharing agreements, that there ought to be prohibition of all restrictive trading agreements unless they can be justified, and that there is too lenient treatment of those who fail to register them. He observed, 'What is indisputable is that an effective means of controlling trade agreements, wherever they are found, is a *sine qua non* for an effective competition policy and therefore for an efficiently functioning market economy' (*Financial Times*, 12 March, 1986). In the introduction to his Report for 1985 he expressed the regulatory ambivalence thus in his comments on his future role in regulating the competition aspects of the securities industry:

> 'I recognise that investor confidence and investor protection require some regulation of financial markets. But it is important to keep a balance between protection and restriction, to ensure that restrictions on competition are the minimum necessary. There must be no return to the cosy world of yesterday if the financial markets of the United Kingdom are to grasp the opportunities of tomorrow.'   (Department of Trade and Industry, 1986b:11)

These examples reinforce the point about the difficulties in pinning down what is or is not in 'the average interests of the ruling class'. It can be argued that large monopolistic or oligopolistic conglomerates dominate modern capitalist societies, and that competition policy is merely a façade to present the appearance of fair trading. That is an empirical matter, though variations in competition policy between capitalist countries – for example, between rules that apply to trade between members of the European Economic Community (including Britain) and those imposed by Britain on non-EEC trade – suggest that 'capitalism' *per se* is not a *sufficient* explanation. The existence of institutions such as the Office of Fair Trading and the Monopolies and Mergers Commission enables the government of the day to defuse political pressure by arguing that an independent body is examining the issues, while preserving their powers to reverse the verdicts of those bodies (as the Conservative Government did over restrictive practices on The Stock Exchange). Political lobbying may influence decisions on such matters, though hard evidence is difficult to find. However, it is surely the case that in a mixed capitalist economy – even one on the extreme fringes of *laissez-faire* – governments have an interest in obtaining revenue, in reducing inflation by maximizing competition, in encouraging investment and wider share ownership, and in promoting their country as a secure financial services market. How those goals can be achieved is a matter of delicate judgment, and we will examine the extent to which current policies among the different 'institutions' are compatible with them. But it is not surprising that the results of such debates are not essentially antagonistic to capitalism!

FRAUD AND THE CIVIL LAW

We have noted that in the criminal sphere, the relationship between fraud and the complex set of agencies which regulate different aspects of it is ambiguous and is in a state of flux. In the civil sphere, also, the willingness of the courts to interfere by looking behind the form to the substance of commercial transactions has increased. Two rather different areas of civil law will illustrate this point. Since the late 1970s, the judiciary have become far less tolerant of tax avoidance, at least when it has no underlying commercial rationale. Although judges always have to find *legal* justifications for such changes, they may have been influenced by the feeling that tax avoidance was becoming such a widespread activity that it was imperilling the entire tax base and undermining the moral basis for the fight against tax evasion. The wealthy and their armies of accountants continue to struggle to find legal loopholes for avoidance schemes, but this indicates that like criminal law, tax planning law is not simply the handmaiden of the rich. (See Tutt, 1985, for an absorbing analysis of the background to these policy shifts in tax cases, which argues that there was little ethical justification for the clamp-down on tax avoidance schemes). Indeed, in a broader context, tax avoidance is an important arena of struggle between the business sector and government, which is interested in maximizing its revenue without damaging business enterprise and/or driving businesses into more welcoming commercial homes overseas. To emphasize the financial aspects of this conflict, in 1986, Lloyd's paid the Inland Revenue £43.5 million in exchange for dropping further investigation and legal action over re-insurance activities by its members that may have been unlawful (though this does not mean that they were criminal).

Another important development in civil law which has affected commercial malpractice is the *Mareva* pre-trial injunction, which enables the freezing of assets that are in danger of being dissipated out of the reach of the plaintiffs. Such injunctions are allowed only if the plaintiff (or counter-claiming defendant) is able to show a good arguable case that he will succeed at the trial. Judicial perceptions of 'the breakdown of commercial community' have made them willing to entertain radical changes to protect the meaningfulness and integrity of the legal process. For example, the early case of *Nippon Yusen Kaisha* v. *Karageorgis* [1975] 2 Lloyd's Rep. 137, CA, was described with typically modest understatement by Lord Denning as follows: 'a case came before us which started off the greatest piece of judicial law reform in my time' (Denning, 1980:134). Hoyle accounts for these reforms in the following functionalist terms:

> 'The answer must be in the rapid change in commercial and banking practice since the Second World War, and the increasing anonymity of international businesses and traders. It is no longer possible to rely on personal knowledge of the parties to transactions, still less to vouch for them to others, and the great competition that there is in the shipping and international trade world, together with the profits to be made in carefully constructed deals, present many opportunities for contracts to be broken or debts unpaid. The recovery of damages or debts is made more difficult by the ease with which an unscrupulous litigant can remove his funds from country to country, often in secret.'   (Hoyle, 1985, 11–13)

In other words, both outright fraudsters and smart but unethical businesspeople can flout national judgments by transferring their assets out of the jurisdiction: indeed, they may even lead plaintiffs to drop cases because they realize that the payment of litigation fees would be throwing good money after bad, since there would be no assets within the reach of the plaintiff judgment creditor. The *Mareva* is important not only in the enforcement of civil liabilities: it has been used also in cases of suspected fraud, civil and criminal. In *Chief Constable of Kent* v. *V and another* [1983] 1 QB 34, the majority of the Court of Appeal held that the police did have standing to freeze the accounts of a defendant charged with forgery and theft. However, the police have to be able to show that the assets to be frozen are the proceeds of crime: see *Chief Constable of Hampshire* v. *A Ltd. and others* [1984] 79 Cr.App.R. 30, CA. This aspect of civil law is becoming increasingly important in the fight against narcotics traffickers and organized criminals generally, as we may see from the provisions of the Drug Trafficking Offences Act (1986), particularly s.7 and 8, which confirm the power to freeze assets via 'restraint orders'. It can be an important accompaniment to regulatory action against suspected frauds on investors. Indeed, the *Mareva* focus on the control of assets of those accused of fraud has now been supplemented with a revived focus on controlling the personal movements of suspects who have failed to provide security for debts that they are alleged to owe. In *Al Nahkel for Contracting and Trading Ltd.* v. *Lowe* [1986] 1 All E.R. 729, the injunction of *ne exeat regno*, the ancient prohibition on leaving the realm, was enforced against Lowe, who was alleged to have stolen £14,000 from his Saudi employer and was known to be in London in transit for Manila. The court held that this restraint on travel was justified in extreme circumstances to ensure that a *Mareva* injunction was not frustrated: see also *Felton* v. *Callis* [1968] 3 All E.R. 673. (It should be noted that leaving the jurisdiction in contemplation of bankruptcy was a specific offence of Act of Bankruptcy under legislation from the sixteenth century onwards.)

The civil courts have also developed the use of *Anton Piller* orders, which sometimes are used in conjunction with *Mareva* injunctions: see *Anton Piller KG* v. *Manufacturing Processes Ltd.* [1976] 1 All E.R. 779. In cases where plaintiffs have strong grounds to believe that the defendant in a civil action is likely to destroy or dispose of evidence vital to the proof of the case, *and* that the plaintiffs are likely to suffer serious damage as a result, they can apply *ex parte* (without the defendant's presence) for a mandatory injunction to allow the plaintiff's solicitor to inspect documents and goods on the defendant's premises, and to take photographs or copies of them. Such orders are frequently used to deal with counterfeiting of goods, including video piracy, and with industrial espionage. If the solicitor is refused entry, he cannot use force but must apply to have the defendant dealt with for contempt of court. It has been held that *Anton Piller* orders can be used also to ensure that defendants do not spirit away anything that might frustrate the execution of a judgment debt: *Distributori Automatici Italio SpA* v. *Holford General Trading Co. Ltd. and another* [1985] 3 All E.R. 750.

The significance of these legal changes is the willingness of the courts to intervene at an early stage to prevent civil or criminal defendants from frustrating future judgments that may be made against them, despite the stigmatization of the defendants that is entailed by the granting of the injunctions. Unlike the tax avoidance measures discussed earlier, *Mareva* and *Anton Piller* orders are not aimed principally at infringing the privileges of the wealthy: indeed, insofar as the main victims of counterfeiting are large multinationals, they aim to preserve the property rights of the powerful. Whether anyone other than the 'rogue company' defendants suffer from these orders is a moot point. (Does the working class benefit from counterfeiting, for example?) But the justifying rhetoric behind the injunctions is that of preserving the fairness and value of the legal process, and it is this which is properly viewed as the motivation of the judges who make the legal decisions in such cases.

Fraudsters and the criminal justice process: a summary outline

In relation to commercial fraud (and, in essence, of *all* crime for gain), the social control system involves a succession of stages through which people must pass before they become defined as convicted 'offenders'. Given that the conduct is punishable by the criminal law – a problematic issue in fraud – the first set of stages relate to crime commission, and take the form of barriers to entry: moral, social, technological and, particularly in the case of the more elaborate frauds, intellectual/imaginative. As the discussion in Chapter 1 indicated, these barriers are not immutable: they can and do change over time and from place to place. Consequently, we should try to account for variations in opportunities to defraud: as defined both subjectively and objectively in different social strata.

Those potential offenders who cross the initial barriers of technique and morality and who consider participating in fraud are influenced in their decision to go ahead or not by their subjective perceptions of the risk from the criminal justice system and by the salience to them of the expected consequences of involvement in crime, for them personally and for the people to whom they may be attached (such as their families). To the extent that they anticipate a risk of being caught at all, one dimension of this – discussed in Chapter 8 – is how painful they expect the sanctions to be for the sort of fraud that they are contemplating. (The 'reckless' or thoughtless involvement of people in, for example, trading whilst insolvent, presents some special problems for deterrability that have been discussed elsewhere: see Levi, 1981.) Those who fail to be deterred (or succeed in not being deterred!) may find that they enter the second set of stages: the actual (rather than just expected) processing of cases through the criminal justice system.

The labelling of an act as 'a crime' and a person (including a corporation, which has a separate legal identity from those who run it) as 'a criminal' is the product of whether the official agencies with the formal competence to impose the labels actually do so. This is a universal principle that applies to all 'crimes'. Before an act becomes a recorded fraud, the following processes have to be undergone:

1 The legal framework within which the social problem will be managed has to be negotiated, which usually entails refining the 'nature of the problem' in such a way that rules can be formulated, either very broadly or very narrowly.
2 The act has to be prohibited, either by the judiciary alone (in common law) or (in the case of statute law) by both the established law-making body/bodies (the Queen-in-Parliament or President and Congress) and the judiciary (in their subsequent interpretative work in case law).
3 The victim of a 'fraud' (or, in some relatively rare cases, a regulatory agency representing investors or consumers as a class) has to define his/her experience as an example of (1) a 'rip-off', and (2) an illegal act.
4 The victim has to decide to report the matter to the criminal

authorities (such as the police) rather than, say, putting it down to experience or treating it solely as a civil debt.

5 The police (or other regulatory agency such as the Department of Trade and Industry) have to concur with the victim's interpretation that 'what happened' was a crime (rather than, say, 'a civil matter' or, in police parlance, an 'unsatisfactory business transaction').

In addition, for someone to become a convicted fraudster, there has to be:

6 a police investigation;
7 a decision to prosecute;
8 a conviction.

The analytic perspective that will be adopted here is that these legislative and criminal justice stages are social and organizational processes, and that they result both from current political pressures and from the historical development of particular institutions in any given society. The creation, enforcement, and publicization of different crimes are profoundly influenced both by specific business interests and by the more amorphous cultural climate of materialism which creates (and destroys) both profits and jobs. We saw, in my discussion of the Insolvency Act (1985) and the Financial Services Act (1986) how commercial interests succeeded in watering down some – through by no means all – 'consumerist' provisions by convincing the government that they would have bad consequences for the balance of payments or by lobbying pro-business members in the House of Lords. However, there are also elements of theatre and vicarious personal fear in many crimes that attract media, political, and police attention, such as burglary, violence, sex, and civil disorder, which are absent from many frauds.

The enforcement of criminal law as a symbolic gesture

I will now introduce some ideas about the enforcement of law which will be examined in detail in the next two chapters. One should not underestimate the difficulties of analysing the intentions and strategies of different sets of actors in formulating and applying legislation on 'crimes of the powerful'. McCormick (1979) has discussed in detail the political manoeuvres by which Republican Congressmen with strong business constituencies in the eastern United States watered down the more radical anti-trust proposals emanating from Republican agrarian constituencies in the west. He has also shown how, contrary to the initial intentions of legislators, the Sherman Anti-trust Act was used primarily against union leaders and barely at all against business. Other work on enforcement reveals that in 1911, the Supreme Court upheld a lower-court decision that Standard Oil should be dissolved, and ordered this along the lines recommended by the prosecutor, which led to a situation in which the same group who owned Standard Oil originally ended up controlling each of the constituent companies into which it was dissolved! Was any corruption involved? Did the prosecutors share the same interests as Standard Oil? It is impossible to be sure, but Bringhurst implies that the prosecutors simply did not give enough practical thought to what should happen to the oil business: the prosecutors 'were more interested in winning a politically important case than in restoring competition to the industry' (Bringhurst, 1979:147). Coleman concludes his review of anti-trust law in the petroleum industry by stating that the picture 'is certainly one of a serious struggle for control of the legal apparatus, but not a struggle between equals' (Coleman, 1985b:273). (For a good overview of these regulatory themes, see Snider, forthcoming.)

Some conflict theorists and Marxists take the argument that legislation against 'crimes of the powerful' is merely symbolic one stage further. They suggest that where businesspeople *are* prosecuted, it is either pure symbolism or a way of getting rid of unwelcome opponents: see Box (1983), Chambliss and Seidman (1982), and Pearce (1976). This too is an example of a broad functionalist 'explanation' that needs to be rooted in some harder empirical evidence or, at the very least, in plausible particularized connections. It may be true of *some* prosecutions in Third World' countries (as in Clarke, 1983), in self-proclaimed Marxist societies such as the Soviet Union (Lampert, 1985), and in the United States (Chambliss, 1978; Noonan, 1985).

Certainly, 'political conspiracy' is a claim frequently made by those in high positions who are accused of commercial crime. Examples including the following cases drawn from different countries. In May 1986, Edwin Edwards, the three-times Democrat Governor of Louisiana, was acquitted of obtaining £1.3 million by using his influence to get building contracts granted for hospitals and private clinics in which he and associates had a private interest: he accused the prosecutor, a Republican appointee, of using the trial to harass the Democrat Government of the State. Ruiz Mateos, the former head of the vast Spanish Rumasa chain (from financial conglomerate to sherry producer) who was charged with serious offences of fraud and sued by the Spanish Government for £31 million allegedly transferred by fraud, claimed in 1986 that he was the victim of a conspiracy by the élite Catholic group *Opus Dei* and by senior politicians. Former West German Cabinet Minister Count Otto Lambsdorff, acquitted by the

German District Court in 1986 of unlawfully accepting money on behalf of the Free Democratic Party from the giant Flick corporation in exchange for tax favours, claimed that he was the victim of a political conspiracy by the state prosecutors (appointed by the Social Democratic Party). In 1983, thirteen directors and managers from the cement business owned by the Tsatsos family were accused of false invoicing to transfer over $100 million illegally out of Greece, and claimed that they were being punished for having supported the Greek military junta.

Indeed, whether or not a claim of political persecution is made, and irrespective of the guilt of the accused, political reasons may underlie the decision to prosecute. For example, US commodities trader Marc Rich was prosecuted in 1983–84 for tax evasion and other frauds involving about $150 million, plus secretly buying Iranian oil after the 1977 US trade ban. He did, in the end, plead guilty to some charges, but sceptics might ask themselves whether the prosecution would have occurred had he not traded with the enemy. However, does this prove that behind *every* white-collar prosecution lies the hand of class or ruling-group interest? Surely, the truth of this proposition depends upon the relative autonomy of police and prosecution institutions from the executive or, in cases where there is *formal* autonomy, upon the extent to which senior decision-makers within the various institutions involved in crime control have a shared way of looking at the world which involves not undermining the *status quo*. By contrast with the cases mentioned above, it is hard to see any clear political or power-élite interest in the prosecution of Antonio Gebauer, a former senior vice-president of the prestigious Morgan Guaranty bank and, later, employee of the important New York investment bank Drexel Burnham Lambert, who in October 1986 pleaded guilty to bank fraud, tax evasion, and making false bank statements in the course of looting money from the (illicit) dollar accounts of Brazilian businessmen at Morgan Guaranty.

None of this is incompatible with a 'hegemony' perspective on social reaction to crime, but even if we were to accept that the low prosecution rate of businesspeople harms the interests of the working class, decisions to prosecute or not to prosecute powerful people are not explicable simply in terms of class solidarity or conflict. For example, prosecuting large corporations may enhance the political ambitions of some individuals, who may not care what the collective interest of capitalism may be; prosecutors may even be influenced by a sense of fairness and desire to show that all are equal before the law. These arguments may be evaluated further against the data presented in the following two chapters.

Whatever their conflicts over the origin and functions of the legal process, Conservatives and marxists alike would agree that the delimitation of 'fraud' is a highly charged matter in a society where central importance is given to the profit motive and where the word 'criminal' has very negative moral connotations. To have one's conduct labelled 'fraudulent' is to undergo a sharp status transition, particularly if one lives among people who value their standing as 'law-abiding individuals'. (Indeed, as we shall see, those who are convicted may suffer considerable commercial disabilities as a secondary consequence.) The dilemma this produces has led to criticism that the English Director of Public Prosecutions is excessively keen not to prejudice the reputations of the police and businesspeople by taking them to court (Williams, 1985). It is expressed nicely (if unconsciously) by Brett LJ in the unreported case of *Wilson* v. *Clinch* (1879): 'I must confess to having such an abhorrence of fraud in business that I am always most reluctant to come to the conclusion that fraud has been committed.'

When Sutherland (1983) first began writing about white-collar crime in the 1930s, the essence of his critique of conventional criminological theory (and political practice) was that it was through official policy rather than corporate virtue that so few white-collar violations led to conviction in the criminal courts. However, whatever explanatory line we take, we ought not to assume that the control (or non-control!) of white-collar crime is a static phenomenon. In respect both of 'business regulatory offences' and commercial fraud – a difficult line to draw at times, for instance as regards the 'failure' to keep proper books of accounts or to file annual accounts – there have been significant changes over the past decade and a half. In the United States, for example, the policing of 'white-collar crime' moved into a much more active phase during the 1970s, partly because it was seen to be personally and politically advantageous to be seen to fight 'big business' successfully (Katz, 1980). These changes have not been without their critics from all sides of the political spectrum. As may be seen from the Abscam case of 1980 – in which FBI agents posed as Arab oil sheikhs and offered bribes to politicians in the form of cash for them and jobs for their constitutents – and subsequent 'Sting' operations such as that after which John De Lorean was tried and acquitted of narcotics dealing in 1984, the 'proactive' policing tactics adopted by the FBI arouse much controversy, particularly when they are applied to 'upperworld' crime and to high-status suspects rather than to burglars, credit-card fraudsters, and 'fences' (Bok, 1982; Caminer, 1985; Klockars, 1980).

Since the 1970s, the West Germans have taken 'economic crime' – from fraud and corruption to anti-competitive behaviour – very seriously (Tiedemann, 1985). Likewise, the Dutch have become more active in the fight against white-collar crime in the 1980s. Not only have they passed new legislation – the Securities Transactions Act (1986) – to counteract 'boiler-room' companies – often run by Canadians with convictions for securities fraud – who sold speculative and downright fraudulent shares by aggressive telephone and personal 'cold-calling', usually to persons overseas (Bax, 1986); they have also begun to act more vigorously against other forms of white-collar crime. The Social and Cultural Planning Office (1986) expresses the mood of the Dutch Government somewhat ambiguously in its report on 1984:

'The apprehension, prosecution, and punishment of offenders guilty of abuse of welfare facilities, tax evasion, company fraud, environmental offences, and other attacks on the technological welfare state has only become large scale in the last few years. . . . Some saw this leniency as a sign that the judicial authorities were concentrating selectively on criminals on the bottom rung of society. Criticisms of this kind no longer have much foundation; this is at present an area that provides clear examples of codification and criminalisation. Not only have there recently been cases against entrepreneurs who would previously have been styled 'white-collar criminals', but the interest of the judiciary in their activities has also been growing. The fight against fraud has been given high priority within prosecution policy as a whole. . . . The penalties for such offences have been increased and are expected to become still harsher. . . . Using criminal law to combat undesirable behaviour on the part of the very powerful, as urged by writers on 'white-collar crime', could do greater damage to the law than to the offenders. Fines are of little use where large amounts of money are at stake; only prison sentences have any deterrent effect. Consequently, the prisons can soon be expected to deal with another growing group of criminals with backgrounds different from the customary ones.'

(Social and Cultural Planning Office, 1986:234)

The Dutch experience cannot readily be generalized elsewhere, though to varying extents, most western countries have caught the anti white-collar crime 'bug'. It is self-evidently true that capitalism affects the forms that fraud takes: not even the most ingenious fraudster could commit securities frauds on the Moscow Stock Exchange, because no such institution exists! (Though in 1986, Shanghai companies were allowed to raise capital by issuing shares and the Jinjiang Trust Company was authorized to make a market in them.) But to account for the control of fraud, we need to incorporate into our analytic framework variations in national economic activities, in policing traditions, and in the way that those who determine the extent and allocation of fraud regulatory resources perceive their task.

We need also to understand the ways in which victims – particularly institutional victims – make use of the criminal law rather than deal with 'fraud' and with other forms of occupational deviance informally. This will be discussed further in the next chapter, but neither the criminal nor the civil law can be activated without a decision being taken by someone – whether it be an individual or corporate victim, or the police or some other regulatory agency acting on their own initiative – to initiate investigative and/or prosecutorial action. It is only when the regulators take up a report and transform it into an active investigation that the issue of police powers becomes directly relevant, though initial police views about whether the case is likely to yield 'a result' (i.e. a conviction) influence whether or not they will investigate or even record it.

It will be argued that except in totalitarian societies – including some self-proclaimed Marxist ones – where power is highly concentrated, the relative neglect of 'white-collar crime' by state agencies is not explicable *satisfactorily* in terms of a power-élite thesis. First, it is an analytical leap of faith rather than a demonstration of fact to jump from showing that a particular policy serves the interests of particular groups to the view that this fact explains why the policy came about. And second, in liberal democracies, there are sufficient conflicts of interest between powerful groups that even if one could identify a selection of people as constituting a ruling class, it would often be difficult for insiders and outsiders alike to define what its 'average interests' were. This problem of identifying and enforcing 'common interest' has become more acute as modern capitalism breaks down the commonality of background which has been an important feature of the British commercial and political élite.

Greenberg (1981) pungently observes that critical criminologists generally assume a degree of omniscience among the ruling class that is not possessed even by those armed with the most powerful tools of scientific socialism. As I have noted earlier, most Marxists would argue not that there is any identifiable conspiracy between élites but rather than there exists a vaguer process of ideological hegemony which acts to reinforce the interests of businesspeople. However, in relation to fraud, it is not clear that we need the abstruse intellectual and literary apparatus of neo-Marxism to enable us to comprehend this process, nor that using this apparatus refreshes parts that other theories cannot reach.

Gusfield (1962) has distinguished between the 'symbolic' and the 'instrumental' approach to legislation. One of the most intriguing aspects of the debate about policing the City (and policing commercial fraud generally) is the introduction of sophisticated social cost-benefit analysis considerations which are absent from the more emotive terms in which we normally discuss what to do about crime. (The Scarman Report and the Home Office 'situational crime prevention' approach are important exceptions to the latter generalization.) This cost-benefit theme is captured nicely in the White Paper on Financial Services which forms the basis for the much-amended Financial Services Act (1986):

'This does not mean excessive regulation. That would impose unnecessary monitoring and enforcement costs; and would stop or delay new services and products being developed in response to market opportunities. The Government therefore intend that the regulation of the financial services industry should be no more than the minimum necessary to protect the investor. This will be in the interests of the customers of the industry as much as the industry itself.'   (Department of Trade and Industry, 1985a:1)

Movements to 'do something about crime' – whether justified by 'objective' harms and changes in crime rates or not – have their own control momentum. Scandals in the police force (Cox, Shirley, and Short, 1977; Punch, 1985; Sherman, 1978) and in politics (Block, 1980; Clarke, 1983) may bring about personnel or organizational changes for symbolic reasons, independent not only of any real increase in the offending behaviour but also of the effectiveness of those changes that actually are made. Crime control rhetoric always contains an element of propaganda, whether we are discussing 'public order' (or rather disorder!) or what is to be done about commercial fraud. Teenagers on the street or who seek to enter football grounds may be treated as if they are plotting, and were about to achieve, the downfall of civilization as we know it. Those contemplating fraud may find it somewhat less morally and technically forbidding when they are confronted by language and control systems involving the avoidance of 'excessive regulation' and rules which are the 'minimum necessary to protect the investor', although in 1987, City scandals led the Government to replace this with the language of law and order.

The stages through which conduct has to pass before it can be defined as 'fraud' under the criminal law may be divided into three sub-headings: negotiating the law; negotiating the police; and negotiating the trial. I have focused in this chapter upon the first of these stages. Having attempted to elucidate some of the difficulties entailed for theories linking legislation to the generalized abstract interests of 'capitalism', let us now review the way in which that part of 'the fraud problem' visible to the public through the media and the courts is constructed, and how those agencies entrusted with enforcing the criminal law against frauds actually go about their business. Bearing in mind that – at least in terms of volume of cases, if not in terms of average or total sums involved – fraud in the City (i.e. in the financial-services sector) is only a small proportion of the official fraud problem outside London, let us first examine the reporting and policing of commercial fraud.

5 The reporting and policing of commercial fraud

When we think of dealing with crime, we normally think of the role of the police as *the* official crime control agency. This is not to deny the existence of a considerable amount of community self-policing, not only in the passive sense of non-reporting of crime but also in the active sense of dealing with crime informally, without police intervention. In relation to fraud, however, it is important to note that the police have by no means a monopoly of control. Consumer frauds (including restrictive trade practices) may be dealt with by Trading Standards officers or by the Office of Fair Trading; bankruptcy, liquidation, banking, and investment frauds are within the remit of the Department of Trade and Industry; and tax frauds are dealt with by the Inland Revenue or Customs and Excise departments.

I shall not be dealing here with consumer issues, although one such issue – the fixed commission on share transactions – has had a dramatic effect: precipitating, via the court action by the Office of Fair Trading against The Stock Exchange for alleged restrictive practices, the end of 'single capacity' – the system whereby the same firm could not act both as broker and jobber of stocks and shares. However, it is as well to bear in mind the multi-agency involvement in the control of commercial fraud for, as in other spheres such as narcotics, demarcation disputes are the source of some rivalry and confusion in the battle against business crime. This inter-agency competition and divergence of approach may be fuelled by conflicts of personality or by bureaucratic empire-building, but it is only rarely explicable solely in these terms.

Despite the popularity of 'police bias' as a criminal justice topic – for a good review, see Reiner, 1985 – there has been a comparative neglect of differences between the police and non-police regulatory agencies, and an almost total lack of awareness of the work of Fraud Squads, in the 'police studies' literature. It is almost as if they were parallel policing universes which operated independently of each other's existence. Yet contrasts are instructive. Unlike the police (and HM Customs and Excise, whose historic role against smuggling may have influenced their approach to fraud), agencies in the 'regulatory' sphere have always adopted a future-oriented reformative rather than a backward-looking retributive approach to 'violations': this is one reason for their low prosecution rate, discussed in Chapter 6.

In fact, the policing of pollution, of the cleanliness of eating establishments, and of health and safety at work is not *purely* correctionalist in its orientation, though agency officers may believe that it is. Even where there seems little chance of reformation, companies seen to be particularly recalcitrant in their refusal to improve their practices may be prosecuted as punishment and/or as a symbolic gesture *pour encourager les autres*. However, the reluctance to prosecute – partly because of the perception that it would damage regulator/client relationships and partly because preparing cases for prosecution creates disproportionate demands upon very scarce personnel resources – stands in marked contrast to the focus on retribution characteristic of 'the police', who seldom consider what is the purpose of taking adult suspects to court.

Nevertheless, neither sphere of policing is immutable. The role of the state in dealing with unlawful behaviour is most commonly challenged in the areas of 'political crime' (such as terrorism and industrial disputes) and 'victimless crimes' (such as consensual sexual behaviour and narcotics use), normally on the grounds that these activities are not the criminal law's business. However, as we have seen in Chapter 2, the 1970s (in the United States) and the 1980s (in Britain) have seen the converse sort of attack on state agencies for alleged bias in the *under*-policing of fraud and white-collar crime in business. As the theoretical discussion in Chapter 4 revealed, this is not a simple class issue, for it is by no means clear that a low policing profile on fraud is best for companies. Furthermore, some Conservatives who think that there is no case for a highly formalized and bureaucratic American model of securities regulation either in principle or in terms of regulatory effectiveness nevertheless support such a model on the grounds of political expediency. Although Americans are less coy in acknowledging the existence of and risks from commercial fraud, concerns have been expressed there over the impact of the well-staffed statutory SEC in the prevention and prosecution of investor fraud in the United States (Karmel, 1982; Posner and Scott, 1980; Shapiro, 1983).

There is a substantial amount of spurious argument in the debate over regulation of securities markets, but it is too simple to view these divergences of perspective as conflicts of interest masquerading as conflicts of principle. It is true that self-regulation *can* be just a façade to permit firms to do what they want, and that members of institutions like Lloyd's have increasingly brought expensive counsel with them when facing disciplinary enquiries: Ian Posgate's defence against charges at Lloyd's is estimated to have cost him over £130,000. Whether we are analysing conflicts in the financial services or the 'sports' sectors, the age of regulation without law (and, *a fortiori*, without *lawyers*) seems to be over, particularly where overseas legal jurisdictions are involved. But there is something in the argument that state bodies – bound as they are by the 'despotism of legality' – are too slow and inflexible to fine-tune their control activities. (This is the upperworld equivalent of the arguments in favour of using neighbourhood police officers rather than paramilitary squads to control public disorder.)

The police role in dealing with fraud

The police role in relation to fraud is not a novel one. In England, during the nineteenth century, the London police were sometimes involved in lengthy investigations, including tracking suspects overseas, though what level of financial expertise they were able to bring to such tasks is a matter for speculation (Levi, 1981, Ch.2). In particularly complex cases such as the collapse of the moneylenders Overend and Gurney, they could call – if they could afford it – upon the services of solicitors and accountants.

Until the end of the Second World War, the pursuit of fraud depended largely on the chance availability of detectives with both an interest in and time for it (see Jackson, 1967; Millen, 1972; Thorp, 1954). In 1946, however, alarm at the fraudulent opportunities offered by demobilized troops from both sides of the Atlantic precipitated the formation of a Company Fraud Department within both the Metropolitan and City of London police forces, which had been discussed before the war but had not been put into effect. As a political compromise, operational control was to be separate, vested in the hands of the respective Commissioners, but there was to be better communication than was normally to be found between independent police forces at that time. The head of the Metropolitan Police side – who has the rank of Commander – has always been the titular head of the joint squad, but there is no constitutional reason why an officer from the City of London force cannot head the squad. Gradually, with encouragement from the Home Squad and HM Inspectorate of Constabulary, Fraud Squads have been formed in all British police forces, though some contain as few as two officers. Like other British specialist squads with the possible exception of Scenes of Crime (forensic) officers, CID officers are assigned to fraud work on a temporary basis: they normally spend from two to five years in this area of work and, as in other spheres of policing, are almost invariably transferred on promotion.

The police have to provide a range of services for the public. These include not only crime investigation but also traffic, public order, and an array of activities best described under the umbrella of the 'service role'. As is true of many other public services – the National Health Service, for example – the public-initiated demand for these services is, if not infinite, certainly much greater than can be satisfied. Like other professionals, police chiefs (and operational detective and beat officers) have considerable scope for interpretation of public needs and demands. The setting of policing priorities is a delicate, quasi-political (though not, it is argued in Britain, *party* political) judgment, and in allocating resources to fraud investigation, fraud must take its place alongside other demands upon the police.

In principle, the police can adopt two different sorts of approach to their role (Reiss and Bordua, 1967). The first is primarily *proactive* (as in the stronger forms of community policing), where policing resources and strategies are police-initiated, albeit perhaps in response to general public requests for action (such as clearing the streets of prostitutes after non-prostitute residents complain of the nuisance to them). The second is primarily *reactive*, where police activity is initiated by a specific complaint from a victim or bystander. Traditionally, criminologists have viewed the policing of business crime as proactive policing, largely because the imagery of control is drawn from the inspectorial role of the state in relation to activities such as pollution or health and safety at work. There is a trend in Britain and the United States for the primary responsibility for the policing of Standard Operating Procedures regarding criminal law governed spheres such as health and safety at work to be devolved upon 'responsibile companies'. However, it is generally acknowledged that because violations may not be visible to third parties such as water users (in the case of pollution), or because workers may not be in a position to enforce safety rules (or may not care enough about them), the regulatory agency must seek out violations rather than rely solely upon confessions by the offender. In this sense, the dominant policing method for business regulatory offences remains proactive.

However, although the American Federal police – the FBI – may have moved along the proactive road in the control of commercial fraud and corruption, the British police have remained in a highly reactive mode. This does not mean that they do not work very professionally and conscientiously, but unlike other 'regulatory' agencies – such as the Health and Safety Executive – involved in the policing of commerce, they wait for complaints to arrive rather than seek out fraud among the 'symbolic locations' in commercial areas (to borrow the phrase used by Metropolitan Police Commissioner Sir Kenneth Newman to describe the inner-city areas where it is vital to maintain a police presence). Even on this basis, there is more than enough to keep them occupied. In

London, each Fraud Squad officer deals with an average of over £5 million of fraud 'at risk' annually.

Where proactive policing of fraud does occur, it is more commonly among the SROs such as the Surveillance Division of The Stock Exchange, which act as the primary filters for the criminal justice process. From 1987, there will be a secondary filtering stage in the shape of SIB: the overall supervisory body for the securities industry, though how active its investigative role will be remains unresolved. The principal governmental agency with a proactive role in relation to fraud is the Department of Trade and Industry, which monitors a wide variety of activities including the registration of companies and of unlimited liability businesses trading in names other than those of their owners, and the filing of company accounts on time. There will be more discussion of Department of Trade and Industry officials later but in practice they, like the police, operate reactively and are so overwhelmed by the routine processing of cases that the scope for deducing the existence of serious criminal violations from non-compliance with regulatory legislation is almost non-existent.

The rationale for 'proactive' policing is that where victims are weak and disorganized, and/or may find it difficult to know whether or not an offence has occurred (as is the case with the adulteration of food, drugs, and, most recently, wine), the state must intervene to detect offences in order to prevent harm as well as to 'do justice'. In reality, however, even regulatory agencies that might be classified as 'proactive' – such as the Office of Fair Trading and local-authority Trading Standards officers – largely operate in reaction to complaints rather than on their own initiative. Where it is difficult to predict the occurrence of crime, and staffing is very limited, this is a way of rationing scarce investigative resources. My point is not that the way the police deal with commerce is unique but that it is important to be aware of how dependent Fraud Squad officers are upon complaints from victims or professional persons as a determinant not only of how many but also of what kinds of frauds they get to investigate. The scope for Fraud Squad officers to indulge in strategic planning – to spend a large amount of time in abstract contemplation of where fraud might occur – is extremely limited, though despite the absence of extra resources, the Metropolitan and City Police Fraud Squad altered the distribution of their squads to adapt to the expected changes arising from the so-called 'Big Bang' on The Stock Exchange.

Given the reactive mode of operation in the policing of fraud by the police and by the Department of Trade and Industry, it is clear that although it is important to study the role of the police as gatekeepers of the criminal justice system, consumers and businesspeople (in their role as victims) and professionals such as accountants and corporate lawyers play a primary role as initiators of action via their decisions to report fraud or not. From time to time, the police in London complain in the media (and to the author) about the lack of co-operation they receive from business not only in the investigation of fraud but also in the initial reporting of it. Little is known about the criteria that companies or individual victims and consumers use when calling the police or other regulatory agencies to deal with allegations of fraud. Let us examine some aspects of reporting in greater detail.

The reporting of financial transactions

There are several sorts of requirements of commercial organizations to report their transactions. In Britain, businesses are required to register for VAT once their turnover reaches a certain legally prescribed level; companies are required to file accounts annually with the Registrar of Companies; and public companies have to have their accounts audited independently. These are not requirements to report fraud, but in principle, they may deter fraud: without overstating the objectivity of accounting standards and evaluations, one has only to imagine how difficult commercial transactions such as the purchase of a company would be if there were no accounts that were even vaguely reliable as a 'true and fair view' of a company's trading position.

There may also be requirements to inform the government – or, in countries which have exchange controls, seek permission from government – about cash deposits and/or transfers of funds abroad. In the United States, the Banking Secrecy Act (1970) requires banks to file a Currency Transfer Form 4789 whenever an individual seeks to exchange $10,000 or more in cash. Moreover, the banker has to file a form 4790 whenever currency or a negotiable instrument such as a bearer cheque is brought into or leaves the United States in a denomination of $5000 or more. Yet these provisions are easily evaded (1) through the frequent depositing or transfer of slightly smaller sums; (2) through the use of nominees or even false names; and (3) through the placing of a firm on a bank exemption list, whereby firms that regularly deal in large amounts of cash have their transactions recorded and retained by the bank, but the details are not forwarded to the US Treasury.

This may entail corruption of bank officials: one undercover agent working (with permission) as a Citibank official in New York was offered a 0.1 per cent commission on all laundered funds deposited, which deposits totalled $151 million in this case (President's Commission on Organized Crime, 1986a:90). But it may be done simply to improve the firm's profitability rather than for direct personal benefit. In the narcotics laundering case mentioned above, $97 million of the money went through a US banking firm named Deak-Perrera. Between 1969 and 1975, Deak-Perrera acted for Lockheed Aircraft Corporation in paying bribes to Japanese business and government officials. In fifteen transactions, they transferred $8.3 million from Los Angeles to Hong Kong, where it was changed into Yen and presented in cash to Lockheed's bagman, who flew with it to Tokyo to present to the Japanese. They also knowingly laundered funds for Filipino businesspeople involved in exchange control violations (and a Vice-President of the company was convicted of currency reporting violations in this respect). A US Vice-President of Deak-Perrera told undercover Drug Enforcement Agency Officials: 'Deak-Perrera puts financial accounts into whatever name people tell us they want. You make up a name, we give you your account and we give you a key code number to access the account' (President's Commission on Organized Crime, 1986a:136).

So we see here how the worlds of political corruption, organized crime, and white-collar crime intersect, and how the 'legitimate sector' of the economy can utilize its immunity from routine law enforcement surveillance to provide services for large corporations, fraudsters, and drug traffickers alike. Because there is a legal obligation to report currency deposits, the non-reporting is a crime, though if the firm is put on the bank exemption list, the activities may be concealed and unless there is an active investigation, no-one in authority will ever know. Hence the value of legitimate fronts which do genuine (or apparently genuine) business. In England and Wales, there are currently no such currency deposit requirements and, since the abolition of exchange control in 1979, there is no need to obtain permission (or to evade such a request) to transfer funds overseas. This may be one reason for the growth of invisible earnings in the City since 1979, but it also means that there is less surveillance of routine transactions than occurs in the US, even allowing for the evasion of those regulations by many American financial institutions, mob-run or not. The prospects for developing further routine reporting requirements will be examined in Chapter 8. Let us now look at the issue of *fraud* reporting.

The reporting of fraud to the police and other statutory bodies

Before an act is reported to the police as a fraud, it normally goes through a filtering process by which an individual or group, acting on their own behalf or on behalf of an organization, has to make a symbolic statement that 'something should be done' by the state rather than by suing for the debt in the civil courts or 'putting it down to experience'. (There are some rare exceptions to this: a complaint or, more usually, the threat of a complaint, may be made to the police or to liquidators as a way of putting pressure on suspects to provide compensation.)

Organizations – in shoplifting and employee theft as well as fraud – often perform some kind of cost-benefit analysis before making the decision to report, though if their calculations were purely economic, it is not certain that they would report anything at all. (Particularly if all the costs were 'internal' and were not 'externalities' in the form of taxpayers' and ratepayers' contributions to policing, criminal justice, and penal costs.) Discretion in the use of formal justice is an important feature of all commercial organizations, which predominantly use informal methods of dealing with disputes, from time-keeping to workplace theft (Henry, 1978, 1983; Shearing and Stenning, 1981, 1983). However, it is crucial to understand that the use of informal discipline is influenced by the background of civil and criminal sanctions that *could* be applied (and/or that workers *believe* could be applied). Thus, formal and informal justice are complementary/overlapping rather than isolated spheres of regulation.

The decision to report a fraud is commonly a reflective choice rather than an emotional or habitual response to loss: it may even involve very difficult legal decisions by third parties such as auditors, who may have to face lawsuits from companies if they do report a fraud. Let us first look at the theory of fraud reporting. Do victims have a duty to report crime? It is arguable that if the distinguishing feature of the criminal law is that it preserves the interests of the people as a whole rather than simply the parties involved, then there is an obligation to report. However, with some rare exceptions such as the duty to report some road traffic accidents, there appears to be no legal duty to report: otherwise, a non-reporting nineteenth-century victim might have found himself in the dock for compounding a felony committed against himself! If there is any kind of duty upon victims to report a crime, it does not appear to be a duty for whose breach there is any remedy.

Do any other citizens have a duty to report crime? This is a more difficult question. Company liquidators have an obligation under s.218 of the Insolvency Act (1986) to report to the Official Receiver – an official of the Department of Trade and Industry – and/or to the Director of Public Prosecutions in every case where it appears to them that a criminal offence has been committed by any past or present officer or member of a company they are winding up. However, those liquidators to whom I have spoken have expressed considerable dissatisfaction with the results of doing so – i.e. with the absence of prosecutions – and have indicated that they soon learn not to allow the suspicion of company offences to 'appear'!

In some countries, of which the best known is Switzerland, it may actually be a criminal offence to disclose banking or any other financial or trading secrets. Plainly, there *can* be statutory requirements to disclose fraud, but it appears that the primary duty of an accountant or a banker is towards his or her client, and that except where allowed for by statute (such as the Drug Trafficking Offences Act, 1986), the reporting of fraud without prior permission from the client is a breach of confidentiality which is a violation both of professional ethics and of the civil law. (Given the boom in litigation for negligence by auditors – who are unlimited partnerships in the UK – and the explosion of insurance premiums consequent upon the success of some of that litigation, their concern has an economic as well as an ethical base.) Auditors, for example, are in a curious position. They have a long-established statutory duty to report fraud in the public sector. However, in the private sector, the accountant owes a civil duty of care towards the party with whom he or she has a contract. Who is this party? It is not the state, not the employees, not the shareholders, not even the directors, but that artificial, independent legal entity 'the company'. For it is the company that provides the 'consideration' which forms the basis for the contract with auditors. (See, more generally, Woolf, 1985.)

As a matter of practice, the auditors would generally report their suspicions of fraud to the director they considered most appropriate. The guidelines to auditors issued by the Consultative Committee of Accountancy Bodies state:

> 'The auditor should report to the management of an enterprise when the audit has brought to light any frauds or other irregularities. He should ensure that management are informed promptly and that, in the case of a company, a report is made to the board of directors or, if appropriate, the audit committee. It is particularly important that the auditor reports to a suitably senior level within the enterprise if he suspects that management may be involved in, or are condoning irregularities. Legal advice may be required if he believes that his report may not be acted upon or if he is unsure as to the person to whom he may report.'
>
> (Auditing Practices Committee, 1985: para 31)

If the fraud or (more coyly) 'other irregularities' led to the 'material' failure of the company's financial statements to give a true and fair view of its trading – a heated issue upon which professionals might come to very different conclusions – then the auditor should qualify the accounts. If the auditors were dissatisfied by the action taken by management, they might decide to pursue the matter further. Prior to 1976, auditors were in an absurd position: they could refuse reappointment but not resign before the expiry of their contract. The Companies

Act (1976) allowed auditors to resign during their spell in office, but s.16 of the Act nullified any such resignation unless the auditors stated in full any circumstances connected with the resignation that they thought should be drawn to the attention of shareholders or creditors (or else stated that there were no such circumstances). Under s.17 of the Act, the auditor might require the directors to convene an extraordinary general meeting to consider the circumstances of his resignation. (See, now, s.388, 390, and 391 of the Companies Act, 1985.) However, short of and prior to resignation, the obligation of confidentiality exists. We shall consider in the final chapter whether there *ought* to be an obligation to disclose, but pending the passage of the Banking Bill (1986), which – in keeping with the provisions of the Financial Services Act (1986) – grants auditors qualified privilege against being sued by their client in respect of information they *choose* to pass to the Bank of England, it is legally dangerous for an auditor to discuss a client's business with anyone. This is partly what lies behind the controversy over whether Johnson Matthey Bankers' auditors ought to have discussed the state of the bank's loan accounts with the Bank of England when they suspected that the bank would encounter problems in collecting its debts. The auditors could have resigned and expressed their concerns then, but it is doubtful that they had any right, still less a legal duty, to report anything to the Bank of England or to the police. In practice, this forbidding outline of the legal position may be more apparent than real: informants state that in the few cases where auditors suspect serious fraud by management, they would normally find some way of reporting the matter.

The December 1985 Auditing Practices Committee draft guideline on fraud is less than clear in its suggestions on what auditors should do in relation to reporting to third parties (such as the police, the Bank of England, or the Department of Trade and Industry). It states:

'36. In the course of his audit the auditor may discover a fraud or other irregularity perpetrated by his client. Normally the auditor's duty of confidentiality debars him from reporting any matters to third parties without his client's permission. He should therefore have regard to his own reporting responsibilities, and to the contents of any guidance issued by his accountancy body, and obtain legal advice as to whether this duty of confidentiality should be disregarded and the information disclosed as a 'public duty' to the appropriate authorities.

37. A public duty arises where an auditor possesses information of any intended criminal offence, or a serious criminal offence, civil wrong or breach of statutory duty, even it if has already been committed, *if it is likely to cause serious harm to an individual or if it may affect a large number of people.*'

(Auditing Practices Committee, 1985; my emphasis)

It is not self-evident how we would define the term 'serious harm' (though the Police and Criminal Evidence Act (1984) and the criteria for incapacitating 'dangerous offenders' suffer from similar vagueness of definition, so the objection clearly is not fatal). There are also problems – as there would be if reporting frauds were to be made compulsory – in deciding when something becomes 'a fraud'. Most interesting, however, in my view is that the possibility of a 'public duty' appears to arise only if the harms have not been completed but rest at least partly in the future. Is it intended that persons should be covered who continue to suffer from past fraudulent injuries, though the *actus reus* is long since spent? And if so, how are auditors to know that victims suffer still? If not, what is the rationale for restricting the coverage to incomplete frauds? It does seem clear that in such a restricted category of 'public-duty' cases, except where there is a legal duty to disclose (e.g. a 'true and fair view' requires it; it is a material fraud in the public sector; or a court or authorized official requires it), or where the professional accountancy body requires disclosure (which subject to revisions in the light of the Banking Bill, 1986, to the best of my knowledge, none does), the onus rests upon the auditor to consult his legal adviser as to where his duty lies. In a rare case where the auditor, as a company officer, might commit an offence himself by not disclosing, the advice might be to report the alleged fraud. But in cases where the auditor is not a party to fraud?

In my opinion, this view of legal obligations relates to cases where there are no reasonable grounds to believe that the *client* is guilty of fraud. (In the United States, attorneys have a duty of non-disclosure even where they know their clients are committing fraud.) In *Gartside* v. *Outram* (1856), 26 L.J. Ch. 113, Wood VC stated:

> 'The true doctrine is that there is no confidence as to the disclosure of iniquity. You cannot make me the confidant of any crime or a fraud, and be entitled to close up my lips upon any secret which you have the audacity to disclose to me relating to any fraudulent intention on your part: such a confidence cannot exist.'
>
> (114)

It may well make a difference whether the alleged fraud was committed by or against the party to whom there was a duty of confidentiality. The courts might hold that there was no duty of confidence towards a client who was committing a crime, but that there was a duty not to reveal a crime against a client without his permission. An example of the former is *Weld-Blundell* v. *Stephens* (1919), 1 KB 520.

Responding to a claim that an accountant owed a duty of confidentiality to a communication from his client, Bankes LJ stated:

> 'There may no doubt be cases to which the rule laid down by the learned

judge may be applied, as for instance confidential communications to a professional adviser as to the proposed commission of a crime, or as to the proposed commission of a civil wrong upon an individual. A contract to keep such a communication secret may well be considered as an illegal contract, and the duty to the public to disclose the criminal or illegal intention may properly be held to override the private duty to respect and protect the client's confidence.'

(526)

In that case, Warrington LJ commented upon *Gartside* v. *Outram* (1856) in the following terms: 'The fraud there alleged was a systematic fraud pursued by the plaintiffs in the course of their business, and the disclosure of the evidence in the defendant's possession would tend to prevent such frauds in the future' (534). Scruton LJ, added:

'The clients there had committed frauds, which their confidential clerk had known as such confidential clerk. The Court refused to restrain him from disclosing them. The acts were fraudulent and clearly criminal, and there was no public policy, such as the importance of defence by solicitors, to enforce the agreement; the frauds were not committed in pursuit of any aim supposed to be of public advantage.'

(548)

In *Initial Services Ltd* v. *Putterill and another* (1967) All E.R. 145, Lord Denning appeared to develop this theme further when commenting upon exceptions to the general duty of servants to respect confidences obtained in the course of their employment. He stated:

'Suppose a master tells his servant: "I am going to falsify these sale notes and deceive the customers. You are not to say anything about it to anyone." If the master thereafter falsifies the sale notes, the servant is entitled to say: "I am not going to stay any longer in the service of a man who does such a thing. I will leave him and report it to the customers." It was so held in the case of *Gartside* v. *Outram*. Counsel suggested that this exception was confined to cases where the master has been "guilty of a crime or a fraud"; but I do not think that it is so limited. It extends to any misconduct of such a nature that it ought in the public interest to be disclosed . . . The disclosure must, I should think, be to one who has a proper interest to receive the information. Thus it would be proper to disclose a crime to the police; or a breach of the Restrictive Practices Act, 1956, to the Registrar. There may be cases where the misdeed is of such a character that the public interest may demand, or at least excuse, publication on a broader field, even to the press.'

(148)

There is ample scope for disagreement over what 'the public interest' is, but attempts have been made to apply this non-culpability principle to the leaking of secrets regarding the conduct of the Falklands War to a parliamentary Select Committee (Ponting, 1984) and of details of price-fixing by Hoffmann LaRoche to the EEC (Adams, 1984).

One of the serious policy problems is that reporting management fraud to management is prone to conflicts of interest, which may explain the enthusiasm of some directors to keep matters in their own hands! What do auditors do when they discover management fraud? The first time that they discover a possible tax fraud, they may give the company the benefit of the doubt – mistakes are always possible – and give some strong advice on proper procedures (possibly including going to the Inland Revenue and admitting past errors), but if it re-occurs, they may then resign and inform the Inland Revenue – without specific comment – that they are resigning. Given that no-one gives up audit-fee income enthusiastically, the Inland Revenue will respond appropriately to the signals that are thus transmitted!

In the case of non-tax frauds, the present Rules for Guidance issued by the Council of the Institute of Chartered Accountants state that the only time that accountants are obliged to disclose a crime is when that crime is treason. It has been agreed in discussions on the Drug Trafficking Offences Act (1986) that bankers and accountants who disclose to the police transactions by suspected narcotics dealers will have immunity from being sued by their clients. But bankers and accountants have been less than bold in their whistle-blowing efforts to date. (See my earlier discussion of problems in enforcing the filing of currency transfer forms in the United States.)

The 1985 professional guidelines from accountancy bodies might reasonably be described as a minimalist strategy which will do little to meet the mounting criticism from the police and from the Director of Public Prosecutions, who observe that none of the major cases currently being dealt with by the Fraud Investigation Group resulted from reporting by auditors. Yet this criticism of evasion of responsibility rests upon the assumption that auditors do actually know a great deal about fraud in large companies. Is this the case? Of course, the low detection and awareness rate is itself the focus of criticism of auditors and of vast lawsuits for negligence, particularly in the United States. But my interviews suggest that although experiences may differ among firms – depending partly on their client group – major firms of auditors can expect to detect a 'serious fraud' in only 0.2 per cent of the companies they audit in a twelve-month period: a yield of 2–4 extra cases annually per audit firm. In a few more cases, the auditors might learn that a client had experienced a serious fraud within the past twelve months.

In short, it seems that professionals such as accountants and lawyers who are not corporate employees relatively seldom know about non-tax fraud, which makes it less surprising that few such frauds actually are reported by them. In the United States, where corporate lawyers generally play a prominent role, the position may be rather different (see Mann, 1985 and Spangler, 1986). We know very little about the impact of salaried lawyers and accountants in formulating corporate policy on fraud reporting in Britain, though my unsystematic observations would suggest that their influence on corporate or tax planning is modest. There are rare occasions when firms specializing in 'criminal work' are employed by British companies who are under investigation for possible criminal offences: at the end of 1986, the chairman of Guinness employed Sir David Napley rather than the firm's normal commercial solicitors to handle the response to the investigation by outside inspectors appointed by the Department of Trade and Industry, although Kingsley Napley's services were dispensed with when the chairman was sacked in January 1987. (He also employed the Prime Minister's former public relations adviser to help Guinness with its corporate image problem.)

Current methods of dealing with fraud in large companies

Having discussed the legal theory behind the obligation to report, let us now examine what is known about the *practice* of fraud reporting. One thing that emerged from the interviews with senior executives (Levi, 1986a) was the widespread variation in attitudes to fraud and in what was done when fraud was discovered. It was noticeable that companies with an American connection had a much tougher line on the reporting of fraud than did the British companies. Indeed, one large bank which dealt with countries on both sides of the Atlantic stated that attitudes varied even *within* the bank: 'in the United States and Europe there is an attitude of prosecute and be damned; in the UK the attitude is rather different and there is a much more dainty attitude towards prosecuting.' This may be because of a less genteel tradition in the way they view fraud and deterrence – the Americans are less prone than Britons to believe that if they went to school with a chap, he must be honest! – and also because American corporations have become more habituated to reporting requirements under, for example, the Foreign and Corrupt Practices Act.

A number of companies – including some for which interviewees had worked previously – had a general rule that frauds would be prosecuted, and required specific high-level authority for a decision not to prosecute. For example, one textiles company required a strong justification to the Executive Vice-Chairman from his junior if someone was to be allowed to escape prosecution. In large companies, there is sometimes a chain of reporting: the larger the sum, the higher up the chain it has to be reported. In fact, even in the American-based companies, none of the companies reported every fraud they had experienced in Britain and, to the extent that they did not do so, this often reflected uncertainty as to the consequences of reporting it – they did not want to be sued for defamation – as well as lack of confidence in the police and the Department of Trade and Industry. On the other hand, some of the rise in prosecutions appears to be attributable to the wish to have independent evidence of 'good cause' to dismiss an employee: a response to the civil laws against unfair dismissal. A small number of executives preferred to rely solely on normal management controls to minimize the risks of fraud: one referred to calling the police as 'opening Pandora's box' because once they are in an organization, 'there is no telling where they will end up and what they will uncover'. For this very reason, some commercial organizations who do not have large internal squads or who want an outside verdict employ specialist fraud investigators, for they then retain control over the direction of investigations.

The interviews produced a good deal of insight into the way executives saw the police, and this was particularly important because all of the eighteen interviewed had had contact with the police over fraud. The general view seemed to be that it was worthwhile reporting fraud to the police provided (1) it was not very complicated, and (2) you had done a very thorough internal investigation first, so that you could present the police with a clear picture of what had happened. Where these conditions did not apply, there was less satisfaction with and confidence in the police. The major role played by the police appeared to be that of expert and legally authoritative statement-takers and of prosecution-handlers. Indeed, only one interviewee expressed very positive views about the police *investigative* contribution to a fraud case in which he had been complainant. One man in the international transportation business stated that in this country, the problem is that the police are not very good at keeping things quiet. A second opined that 'the ability of the police is very low' and a third, a senior provincial stockbroker, stated that 'the police would not have a clue in looking at a fraud in the Stock Exchange or in a stockbroker's office'. He added that the whole form of organization and systems for settlement were so complicated that the police would never understand them and would never be able to get to a successful prosecution. This had the consequence that the police would be unlikely to be called to deal with any stock-market fraud. Furthermore, the disastrous effects that calling in the police would be likely to have upon the firm's general trading position would increase his inhibitions against reporting.

Another, with a large consumer credit business, complained that the courts and the police in different parts of the country look at questions of fraud in very different ways, and he would like to see more consistency. On frauds against the company by outsiders, his view was that the police were getting there, but very slowly; it was difficult to get in touch with them and with the relevant people. He added – a common theme among those interviewed – 'If we didn't push the police wouldn't respond. . . . It is hard for them to be up to date on fraud, including computer matters. . . . The situation is always that we take the case to the police and then that we have to wait for them to do something.' The willingness to use the police, then, was only partly related to belief in their efficiency.

One American conglomerate executive took a very tough line on what should be done about fraud but a fairly sanguine view of its policing. He stated that 'we are thorough, complaining witnesses'. His company is willing to invest the management time and effort that is required to obtain a successful prosecution where the evidence sustains it. In liaison with the corporate legal department, a substantial fifteen-man internal investigation department headed by a former police officer conducts the initial investigation with a view to the legal requirements of proof of fraud in court. The company expects the issues to be complicated and does not expect the police to be familiar with the systems and issues concerned. In those cases where they do report to the police, the police listened carefully and listened hard: 'in one complex case we had to lead the police through the case time and time again. We have to help the policeman to ensure that he is able to stand up to cross-examination.' The Fraud Squad were described as 'nice guys', but the company recognized that they had to put in the legwork and the expense, and assemble the greater part of the case. It was not clear what investigative work the police actually did, though clearly, they were seen as having a critical role as gatekeepers of the criminal justice system. He did not complain about lack of motivation, and the alleged police lack of ability was attributed principally to lack of inside knowledge of the way his particular business operated.

Several respondents seemed to be treating fraud as a problem for private policing: when the company was satisfied that there was enough evidence to establish at least a *prima facie* case, it *might* – depending on corporate policy and the particular position of the suspect within the company – call in the police. At that stage, the state could take over the expense of prosecuting, though some costs (in management time) would continue to be borne by the company. This is ironic in view of the political controversy over self-regulation in the City: commercial firms are already practising a considerable degree of self-regulation, though this is in their capacity as victims, where there is less suspicion of conflicts of interest than might occur among City financial institutions, where the victims might be investors from outside the market rather than corporate or individual 'insiders'.

The usage of the police was generally part of an overall implicit or explicit corporate policy profile on fraud. (American corporations and/or multinationals were more likely to have explicit policies.) The chairman of one British company stated that the police should always be called in on fraud cases, no matter what the short-term pressures might be. He put it as follows in his comments upon one tortuous case in which he had been involved as a principal complainant:

> 'I believe in discouraging others. . . . The police were very good. I would certainly do it again. Many companies think that it is better not to lift the paving stones for fear of what they might find underneath them, but the trouble with these people [fraudsters] is that they go on and on. I believe the law about Directors is right. They must have clear personal accountability for these matters and be held responsible for them.'

This theme of reporting to discourage re-offending and for both retributive and general deterrent purposes was an important part of the reasons given by some executives for reporting frauds. Indeed, given the frequency with which interviewees mentioned repeat 'offenders' not as a hypothetical problem but as part of their actual experience, the importance of this aspect of policy should not be underestimated.

These findings supplement existing research on the definition and reporting of workplace theft, which concludes that most employees are 'on the fiddle' to some extent, but that there are norms among the workers themselves that separate 'permissible' from 'impermissible' crime (Ditton, 1977a; Henry, 1978, 1983; Mars, 1982), usually based around the notion of abstaining from being 'too greedy'. Those who overstep the mark will be shunned by their work group and may even be reported to management. (Cynics might choose to view these norms as related to the increased risk of damage to their entire fiddling system as thefts escalate, rather than their being the product of moral views about the fairness of taking small amounts: perhaps the two are related!) Likewise, if the management catch them (or if they are seen as disruptive, for instance by organizing other employees into active unions), action may be taken against them, either by dismissal or by prosecution. As Henry observes, in cases of employee theft, 'whether public court action is taken or not depends on the degree of rapport that can be anticipated or built up between the local courts and the company' (Henry, 1983:109). In handling employee theft, the company, as a 'repeat player', can become a participant in the construction of routinized justice, as its procedures, personnel and reliability become taken for granted by the local magistracy. On the other hand, fraud is more likely to be taken to the Crown Court, where trial before 'one-shot' players – the jury – has less predictable outcomes. (The protection of workers afforded by civil legislation may have encouraged management to take workers to court, to minimize the risk of a successful claim for unfair dismissal.) More generally, I would suggest that suspect/victim relations are a central factor in the activation of the criminal justice process: many companies who know that they are being cheated regularly and deliberately by their suppliers (including the owners as well as the employee-distributors) refrain from doing anything about it because they do not wish (or cannot afford) to disrupt a long-standing pattern of economic and social interaction, especially when they think that they may need the supplier at some future date.

In the financial services sector, structural changes in the aftermath of the Financial Services Act (1986) are likely to affect the reporting of fraud. Under the Act, all authorized investment businesses are required to ensure that they have adequate means of compliance with its investor protection aspects, such as maintaining 'Chinese Walls' to prevent insider dealing by the corporation on its own account when another part of the company is advising clients on takeover bids. To the extent that in practice – whatever the rule book states – compliance officers employed by the company are independent of management and employees alike, and report *direct* to the appropriate SRO and/or to the non-executive directors or to a special audit committee of their company, this may raise the level of reporting considerably. However, even if – responding to government signals – statutory prosecution agencies show greater interest than they have done hitherto, it is far from certain that breaches of company rules will lead to referral for prosecution rather than to dismissal or resignation. Let us take as an example the case of Geoffrey Collier, then head of securities at bankers Morgan Grenfell, who in 1986, minutes prior to the announcement of the takeover bid for AE engineering by a corporate client of Morgan Grenfell, purchased 50,000 shares in AE via another market-maker, Scrimgeour Vickers. The shares were sold by Chase Manhattan Securities. A former colleague, a Los Angeles associate of Scrimgeour, placed the order for Collier in the name of a Cayman Islands company actually owned by him. Scrimgeour and Chase may have lost money, because they were both trading in the shares as principals and were not expecting the sudden substantial price rise. The companies investigated and traced the purchaser back to Morgan Grenfell, whom they informed. Collier confessed that he had breached the house rules – which clearly stated that all personal dealings must be made through Morgan Grenfell – and resigned, (as did the Los Angeles employee of Scrimgeour Vickers).

It is impossible to be certain that had it not been for the press interest or the involvement of other (competitive) firms who were aware of what had happened, the details of this breach would have been reported to The Stock Exchange and thence referred to the Department of Trade and Industry who prosecuted Collier for insider dealing. It may be significant also that both Scrimgeour Vickers – owned by Citibank – and Chase were American firms, used to a vigorous line taken on insider dealing in the United States. But now that stockbrokers have merged with jobbers, the former have less interest than they used to have in protecting their clients from insider-dealing investigations, particularly if the market-making firm itself has suffered a financial loss! It is dangerous to generalize from the particular circumstances of this case, but it may indicate the shape of reporting to come.

Let us now examine what fraud victims are likely to face if they do decide to report an unsatisfactory business transaction as a fraud, bearing in mind that research generally suggests that the police may not view the significance of victims' experiences in the same light as do the victims themselves (Jones and Levi, 1983a; Shapland, Willmore and Duff, 1985).

Fraud as a policing priority

There are all sorts of reasons why commercial fraud might not be seen as a key priority by police officers. The simplest is that it involves a high ratio of officer-hours to *number* of crimes cleared up, and in a system where the clear-up rate is regarded as a critical indicator of police performance, the allocation of officers to tasks with a low rate of numerical return is discouraged. Indeed, it is a curious paradox that if the average fraud was *less* time-consuming to investigate, senior officers might be inclined to devote more resources to fraud than they do at present! On the other hand, the effect on the clear-up rate is not a sufficient explanation. The weight of historic practice in a traditionalist organization; the perceived lack of public concern over fraud; cultural stereotypes shared by the police that all serious offenders – convicted or unconvicted – are 'villains' who form part of an underworld; and the relative absence of outcry (if not downright lack of interest) regarding fraud from the popular media, from public–police consultative committees (set up under s.106 of the Police and Criminal Evidence Act, 1984), and from the 'police authorities' to whom the police are formally accountable: all these factors play their part.

Episodic parliamentary attacks upon commercial malpractice – from Conservative Prime Minister Heath's condemnation of corporate asset-stripping as 'the unacceptable face of capitalism', through the scandals in the Lloyd's insurance market in the early 1980s, to the efforts in 1985 of Labour MP Brian Sedgemore to implicate the Bank of England and government ministers in the scandal over the losses at Johnson Matthey Bankers – do occur. In early 1987, the Labour Shadow Cabinet finally awoke to the political value of City scandal.

However, most 'Left-wingers' in Parliament and on Police Authorities – the statutory bodies to which the police are theoretically accountable (Jefferson and Grimshaw, 1984; Reiner, 1985) – are far more interested in the policing of the working-class city than in the policing of the City. Some may seek to 'explain' the policing (or non-policing) of commerce in terms of ruling-class interests, but as I have contended earlier, such an approach (1) provides a simplistic picture of 'capitalist interests', and (2) even if one were to accept that the non-policing of fraud was functional to capitalism, fails to do justice to the relative autonomy of state institutions. Let us consider the facts in more detail.

How seriously do the police regard fraud? There are a number of ways of addressing this question. One is to look at how many resources are devoted to combating it; another is to examine police attitudes towards fraud. 'The police' are not a homogeneous group, and we should beware of taking the views of any particular individuals as being representative of majority opinion. Chief Constables may have a very limited effect upon the actual policies pursued on the ground (Bradley, Walker and Wilkie, 1986; Reiner, 1985; Weatheritt, 1986). However, they do control the resources available to specialist squads such as Fraud Squads, and it is difficult to combat fraud if one has no troops! One fruitful initial source of police perceptions of social problems is the Annual Reports of Chief Constables. These are interesting both for what they state and for what they leave out. After all, whatever one's views regarding the extent of and need for 'police accountability', these (and the memoirs of police officers) give a good indication of what issues senior officers believe most interest and are of most concern to their Police Authorities, the media, and the public. Clearly, one expects some comments on the activities of Fraud Squads as part of a review of criminal investigations, but one should look to the general introductions in Annual Reports for insight into what senior officers think are the high priority issues of the day.

By contrast, the recent Annual Reports of the Commissioner of the City of London Police pay far more attention to fraud, both in terms of the space devoted to it and in the gravity with which the issue is discussed. No mention was made of it in the forewords to the 1980 and 1981 Reports, but both Sir Peter Marshall and Owen Kelly have commented on it in their forewords as well as making more detailed remarks in the substantive sections (City of London Police, 1983, 1985, 1986). The Report on 1985 included improved detection rates for 'large scale organized fraud' among the force objectives (City of London Police, 1986). The apparent difference in the seriousness with which the Commissioners of the Metropolis and of the City of London view fraud may partly reflect the relative absence of public order, organized crime, and street-crime problems in the Square Mile. However, it also results from the central importance of finance capital to the prosperity of the City of London. It is noteworthy here that even prior to the political scandal-mongering that has occurred since 1985, the City of London Commissioner repeatedly referred to the 'wide recognition' of the importance of fraud regulation and to 'public and governmental interest' in this 'crucial' area (City of London Police, 1983, 1985). Plainly, though the statistics suggest that fraud is a far greater total cost in the Metropolitan Police area – much greater than other crimes in London (see Chapter 2) – the political constituency there is much broader than in the City, where fraud is far more salient. It remains an interesting question, however, why perceptions of the degree and nature of public concern about fraud should differ so widely in the two London forces.

The low priority fraud receives from senior officers who deploy manpower resources is reflected in the number of personnel allocated to Fraud Squads: approximately 5 per cent of detective manpower and 0.5 per cent of overall police personnel nationally, totalling 588 in the UK as a whole. At the beginning of 1986, excluding officers dealing with cheque frauds, in the City of London Police, there were 52 Fraud Squad officers. In the Metropolitan Police, there were 127 Fraud Squad officers. In 1986, Fraud Squad officers comprised 1 per cent of the total police establishment and 5.5 per cent of the CID strength in the London forces combined (3.5 per cent of the Metropolitan Police and about 40 per cent of the small City of London Police CID). Indeed, subject to the results of Home Office suggestions in October 1986 that the Commissioner might devote to fraud work some of the extra officers that he was to be allocated, the number of Fraud Squad officers in the combined London force total devoted exclusively to company fraud and corruption has actually *declined* as a consequence of Sir Kenneth Newman's policy of reallocating officers from the centre to divisional street-crime and burglary work: in October 1978 it was 202; in October 1982 it was 211; and in October 1985, it was 190. (One might note that this does represent a historic rise: in 1946, there were 12 officers; in 1971 there were 99.)

In early 1986, West Midlands has the next highest number – 36 – and there are 27 in the West Yorkshire, 19 in the Greater Manchester, and 16 in the Merseyside forces. At the lower end, Cumbria, Gwent, and Wiltshire have 4, Northamptonshire has 3, and Dyfed-Powys and Surrey 2 Fraud Squad officers. The *actual* size of Fraud Squads at any given moment in time is likely to be lower than their formal levels: they may be taken off for a homicide enquiry or for any major incident. Indeed, Fraud Squads are generally regarded within the police as a spare support unit of detectives, who can always be made available when something 'important' comes along: after all, as the City of London Commissioner notes in his Report on 1985, fraud complainants are used to waiting a long time for a result. They are not active 'screamers' and so except in cases that attract high media profile – which few outside the City of London do – the police receive no real immediate aggravation for making them wait. So fraud complaints are just stockpiled until there is time to deal with them: little wonder that the reporting rate for fraud is low! Quite apart from any criticisms one might have of the subordination of service to organizational convenience, there is some ideological significance in this fact. Those who believe that the criminal justice system is mainly the handmaiden of capitalist institutions should note that the main fraud complainants are large corporations. Yet it is precisely these powerful victims who – particularly in some provincial forces – receive the most dilatory service.

Because of its demography – which is largely non-residential – the City of London force is a very unusual force, and even though only 5 per cent of its 2646 officers are in the Fraud Squad, all officers must find it difficult not to be aware of the importance of fraud to the City as well as to their Commissioner. The 127 Fraud Squad officers in the 26,844-strong Metropolitan Police constitute a smaller proportion of the total than in the City of London, and given the greater prevalence of non-fraud crime in the Metropolitan Police District, it seems plausible that Metropolitan Police officers overall might share the view of officers in the Northern and Southern forces studied by Jones and Levi (1983a) that fraud was relatively non-serious. *Table 15* contrasts the police's with the public's views on crime seriousness.

Table 15   *Police and public ratings[1] of the seriousness of crimes*

offence		public mean	public rank	police mean	police rank
the offender attacks a victim with a knife or another sharp weapon and the victim dies		10.65	1	10.94	1
	sd^2	1.23		0.39	
the offender, a policeman who discovers a burglary in a shop, steals £20 worth of goods from the store		9.62	2	10.10	2
	sd	2.16		1.20	
the offender, using physical force, robs the victim of £50; the victim is injured but is not sent to hospital		8.87	3	9.62	3
	sd	2.22		1.25	
the offender assaults a police officer with his fists; the police officer is injured and sent to hospital		8.83	4	8.99	4
	sd	2.41		1.65	

Table 15 *continued*

offence		public mean	rank	police mean	rank
the offender sets up a bogus mail-order company and through it fraudulently obtains £1000 from a number of private individuals		8.31	5	7.46	5
	sd	2.47		2.04	
the offender drives recklessly, causing £200 damage to another person's property		7.91	6	6.44	6
	sd	2.46		2.12	
the offender sells marijuana to an adult		7.85	7	5.95	10
	sd	3.18		2.64	
the offender steals £20 from another person's wallet or bag		7.49	8	6.91	7
	sd	2.79		2.26	
the offender sets up a bogus company and through it fraudulently obtains £2000 from a big manufacturer		7.44	9	6.32	9
	sd	2.78		2.83	
the offender breaks into a person's house and steals property worth £20		7.13	10	8.04	5
	sd	2.92		2.17	
the offender, a 25 year-old man, has sexual intercourse with a 15 year-old girl, with her consent		7.09	11	5.94	11
	sd	3.24		2.73	
the offender, a car dealer, turns the mileometer back by 20,000 miles on a car he is selling		6.76	12	5.33	13
	sd	2.94		2.28	
the offender dishonestly obtains social-security benefits to the value of £20		6.19	13	5.88	12
	sd	3.12		2.28	
the offender, a 14 year-old boy, has sexual intercourse with a 14 year-old girl		5.87	14	4.54	14
	sd	3.25		2.56	

Source: Levi and Jones (1985)
Notes: [1] Respondents were asked to rate each offence separately on a scale from 1 (least serious) to 11 (most serious).
[2] sd = standard deviation

It is interesting that Rossi, Simpson, and Miller (1985), in their smaller sample but methodologically sophisticated study in the United States, also found that the police rated business crimes less seriously than did the public. The low seriousness ratings for fraud may be a reflection of the 'action-oriented' motives that lead many to enter the police and that – despite the fact that the police actually spend most of their time on service functions and paperwork – are reinforced by 'the police sub-culture' not only in Britain (Holdaway, 1983; Policy Studies Institute, 1983; Reiner, 1985) but also in the United States (Klockars, 1985; Skolnick, 1966) and Canada (Ericson, 1981, 1982). My interviews with police officers suggest that their perceptions of offence seriousness are related to their beliefs about the prevalence and impact of each type of crime. Since the British police seldom encounter fraud, and since it receives little publicity in the popular media, it seems plausible that they would see it as less prevalent, less damaging, and thus less 'serious' than other offences (such as burglary and mugging) that do have 'real' victims. Moreover, 'feeling collars' is a central goal of CID work, and the very high ratio of investigation time to collars felt is not only demoralizing for fraud investigators but also lowers the desirability of the work in the eyes of other CID officers. The risk of being seen to be incompetent – of 'the wheel coming off' – is also higher in fraud work, particularly when one is faced with high-status suspects who are in a better position than most to have their complaints given credibility. Although rises in police pay may have placed the British police very high up the income distribution scale nationally, the more 'up-market' suspects are not only wealthier but also better educated and connected, and this contributes to the unease of many officers in dealing with them. Whereas the police in Britain may be positively attracted to pursuing and prosecuting those who drive Porsches, investigating fraud presents a different set of technical problems from the proof of motoring offences: for example, documentary access has to be negotiated, including documents from abroad. For all these reasons, postings to the Fraud Squad are viewed negatively by many police, even though the complexity of the work makes a judicial commendation more likely if it is handled competently, and this is good for career prospects.

Equally significantly, it is unlikely that anything will happen during a police officer's typical career that will transform this attitude to fraud. Unless he or she is in the Fraud Squad – which is unlikely for most officers – there is little experience of dealing with frauds (other than those involving cheque and credit cards) and of observing their impact. For similar reasons, there is little organizational incentive to develop an interest in fraud: rather the reverse, since so few opportunities are open within the small squads and one is almost compelled to be transferred – sometimes in the middle of a complicated job – if one wishes to be promoted. This is in marked contrast to the FBI or the SEC, where there are high rewards for expertise in and commitment to this field, internally or in terms of subsequent opportunities to work for oneself or for other firms in the private sector (Katz, 1980; Mann, 1985; Roth, 1978; Shapiro, 1983).

On the other hand, it is important not to make too much of the relative tolerance by the police of fraud. First, role theory implies that many people do a job efficiently even if they would not have chosen it in an ideal world, particularly if it makes a difference to their futures whether they do it well or badly. Second, Fraud Squad officers do receive some status because of their ability to handle a particularly complex world, and some envy because their work is more nine-to-five and involves occasional trips abroad. Although the senior police hierarchy are much more interested in public order and in high-drama offences, fraud may be viewed as more important now that media and political attention has become focused upon it (albeit principally in London). Lest this should seem too cynical for some, it is a general rule that careerists in politics, the civil service, law, policing, and even the groves of academe will seek out those areas in which they think they are most likely to be noticed by those in a position to promote them.

When discussing the organizational reward system within the police (or any other institution), there is a danger in adopting an over-deterministic perspective. There are often some individuals (from Police Constable to Chief Constable) who will pursue a particular hobby horse out of their personal beliefs and interests. However, such moral entrepreneurs will be unlikely to exercise a significant influence upon manpower distribution levels or upon force strategy as a whole. None of the few senior police officers – such as former Chief Inspector of Constabulary Sir James Crane – who have had a strong interest in and concern about fraud have made any significant impact upon the 'domain assumptions' that are prevalent within police forces about the gravity scale of crimes. These are deeply rooted in history, and the absence of a national police force makes the mobilization of change even more difficult than it would be under a centralized system. Nevertheless, despite the absence of explicit discussion in the Annual Reports of the Chief Inspector of Constabulary, there has been a slight shift in emphasis towards acknowledging the significance of fraud, partly due to the drift of 'villains' (professional criminals) into it and partly due to some Chief Officers' perceptions that fraud is one of the few specialist areas to which they can plausibly appeal for a small amount of extra manpower resources. The others are drugs and financial asset-tracing (in the aftermath of the Drug Trafficking Offences Act, 1986). Given the amount of money involved in fraud in the provinces, and the likely geographical spread of securities fraud after the 1986 deregulation and after enhanced public interest following the profits made from denationalized company share issues like British Telecom, one might think that attention to fraud outside London would be appropriate. But that does not mean that it will happen!

Though there are no studies of law enforcement official attitudes to business crime in the United States or Canada, it is arguable that much of the greater commitment to fraud policing there derives from the association between major fraud and organized crime figures rather than simply from a heightened post-Watergate moral sensibility regarding the defalcations of 'the upperworld'. (Similar observations could be made about Australia in the post-Costigan Report era of the mid-1980s.) Given Mafia and other 'organized crime group' involvement in fraud – which has spread to investment frauds carried out from mainland Britain and from the offshore tax havens of the Channel Islands and the Isle of Man – one would expect a tough-minded attitude from police at least to those frauds committed by 'outsiders'. Indeed, in March 1986, the Metropolitan Police set up a special squad to combat international organized fraud.

What does it matter if the police themselves do not attach great priority to fraud? It matters because in crimes like fraud that lack the 'habit' and insurance components that are very significant in the reporting of 'ordinary' property crimes (see Hough and Mayhew, 1985; Sparks, 1982) the level of police interest is a crucial determinant of the rate of recorded crime as well as the number of crimes cleared up. It is only by actively proselytizing reporters, or at least not encouraging them to regard what happened as 'a civil matter', that the official rate of fraud will more closely resemble its 'actual' incidence. Such a 'community policing' strategy is unlikely when small squads are overwhelmed by their existing case-load, and so the low police resources devoted to fraud serve to de-amplify rather than to amplify the scale of the officially defined 'fraud problem'.

The actual (rather than theoretical) process of objective-setting in the mid-1980s vogue for policing by objectives is shrouded in mystery, but logically, whether one sets one's objectives consciously or not, such a process clearly requires prioritization not only of cases *within* crime caseloads but also *across* categories of crime. In this sense, social cost-benefit analysis is inevitable in policing. Yet such analysis does not proceed by pure abstraction. The starting-point is normally the organization's existing tasks and case-load. Here, fraud is at a disadvantage because – as Sir Kenneth Newman's comments (Home Office, 1985b:100) imply – without a large Fraud Squad, one does not have a large fraud problem! It is hardly surprising (nor should it be seen as an indication of active support for either conservatism or commercial fraud) if Chief Constables take the view that they already have enough problems dealing with the crimes they do know about without finding more crimes to combat with the same number of personnel.

As we saw in Chapter 2, most 'crime' is not reported. The police could expand their workload in 'ordinary' forms of crime by tapping into the 'dark figure' of unrecorded crime. (Indeed, this is precisely the paradox of police-community liaison schemes, for the closer this liaison, the lower will be the 'dark figure' and the higher the official crime rate.) However, the general reason why most unreported 'ordinary' crimes are not reported is that the victims do not consider them to be sufficiently serious, whereas in fraud this is not the case. In fraud, it is not so much that what happened to non-reporters is regarded by them as trivial: motives of embarrassment or the cost-ineffectiveness of reporting predominate. There *is* a cost to the community at large, even if the direct victims do not wish to take further action regarding the frauds they suffer.

POLICING RESOURCES IN RELATION TO COMMERCIAL FRAUD

Having examined the attitudes of senior and general police officers towards fraud, let us review their resources in a different way. Cost and cost-effectiveness have become key features of the attempt to obtain value-for-money in the criminal justice system. Quite apart from any criticism that one might advance of whether the police have actually operated these efficiency and effectiveness criteria, there are serious objections of principle to the view that one can depoliticize the distribution of policing resources. Setting aside the problem that this crime-orientated approach may unjustly devalue the service functions of policing, how do we judge objectively the effectiveness of measures against fraud compared with those against vandalism, particularly given the dark figure of unrecorded offences?

The total strength of fraud squads throughout England and Wales has grown steadily, from 232 in 1971 to 427 in 1976 to 588 in 1986. In addition, there are regional crime squads and divisional CID officers, who spend an unknown amount of time investigating frauds – generally of smaller size and certainly of lesser complexity – as part of their general crime investigation remit. However, the police are not the only organization involved in fraud investigation.

In 1986, the Department of Trade and Industry had some 35 professional officers in the Companies Investigations Branch, though they do not devote all their time to fraud. They also had 7 support staff and 4 in-house lawyers to provide advice. In 1985, the most recent year for which information is available, they carried out 111 secret enquiries into companies under s.447 of the Companies Act (1985) (compared with 99 the previous year). The total cost of this department was £965,000 in 1985. There are also external inspectors appointed in major enquiries, at a cost of £772,000: a reduction of a quarter from 1984. (Between 1979 and 1983, there were 14 reports carried out by external inspectors, at an average cost of £463,000.) However, these are not solely fraud enquiries and, as the small number of prosecutions that arise out of them might suggest, they are seldom *defined* as fraud enquiries in the end. Enquiries into companies by the Companies Investigation Branch and external Inspectors resulted in just 5 successful prosecutions in 1984: in the light of the Guinness scandal, it is worth noting that only one of those related to a company providing financial assistance for the purchase of its own shares. (No figures are available for 1985.)

Additionally, there are 675 officials in the Department of Trade and Industry Insolvency Service (compared with 545 in 1979). Each Insolvency Examiner has an annual workload of 30-40 cases, but from these generally only one or two reports alleging fraud arise, partly because insufficient time is given to searching for it. There are some 24 investigators (ex-police officers) and 12 solicitors involved in investigating and prosecuting insolvency cases referred to them by the Insolvency Service. The staffing level of the Department of Trade and Industry was increased by 190 in 1986, partly to deal with fraud and partly to deal with the increased work resulting from the Insolvency Act (1986). A rough estimate is that about 10 per cent of Insolvency Service time is spent investigating malpractice, including the absence of proper record-keeping. Yet it is impossible without further detailed study to evaluate what proportion of that time is spent on fraud, even if we were to set aside the conceptual problems referred to in Chapter 2. An informed guesstimate would be that some 100 man-years per year are spent by the Insolvency Service on investigating fraud. If one takes into account the amount of money 'at risk' of being defrauded by directors of the 19,021 companies whose liquidations were notified in 1985, either in or prior to liquidation, this is a small amount of resources. Prosecutions for fraud are not self-generating: they require detailed investigation, case reports, and preparation for trial. It follows logically that as long as case-loads are high and staff resources low, few cases *can* be prosecuted, however high (or, as in this case, low) the level of agency motivation to take fraudsters to court. The need to demonstrate 'effectiveness' has encouraged more prosecutions but very few are for serious fraud.

The resources of the Department of Trade and Industry are supplemented by self-regulatory bodies such as The Stock Exchange. Indeed, one of the attractions to government of self-regulation is that it offers a way of shifting the costs of regulation onto the private sector direct rather than doing so via taxation. In the United States, SEC employs some 2000 people and costs over $100 million a year. In addition, the panoply of US SROs such as the New York Stock

Exchange are also expensive, though these are funded by members. By contrast, the securities regulation parts of the Department of Trade and Industry are extremely cheap, and in 1986, the combined cost of the regulatory sections of private-sector SROs was only £20 million approximately, to which should be added the cost of professional indemnity policies which are a form of regulatory cost.

SIB had a set-up and running cost of £6 million in 1986, and aims to have a central staff level of approximately 100, to formulate general rules for subsidiary bodies, vet applications for authorization to deal in securities, and take disciplinary actions against members. In 1985–86, The (London) Stock Exchange cost over £22 million to run. It had about 4500 Members grouped in about 200 firms. Prior to November 1984, when the Surveillance Division of The Stock Exchange was established, there were only 2 inspectors: by April 1986, this had risen to 5 teams of 4 people, so that each team was responsible for monitoring the compliance of 40 firms with the Rules of the Exchange. By October 1987, following the merger with ISRO, the number of compliance and surveillance staff in the new SRO, The Securities Association, had risen to 75, with a further 20 in the discipline and complaints section. Most firms are visited once annually, and the aim is to increase this to 2 visits per annum. The total surveillance budget for March 1986–87 was £1.75 million. In October 1986, Lloyd's brought together and expanded pre-existing control functions into a new General Review Department analogous to The Stock Exchange Surveillance Division: this started with approximately 15 staff, including several accountants. In fact, because of the overlap between routine administration, recruitment, political lobbying, and surveillance resources, it is very difficult to gauge the quantity of control personnel. However, if we ignore this significant problem, *The Economist* (9 August 1986) put the number of regulatory personnel at 25; the Association of Futures Brokers and Dealers (AFBD) at 12; the Financial Intermediaries, Managers, and Brokers Regulatory Organization (FIMBRA) at 50 (full-time and part-time), of whom about 18 are involved in fraud regulation; the Investment Management Regulatory Organization (IMRO) at 35; and the Life Assurance and Unit Trust Regulatory Organization (LAUTRO) at 10.

The effectiveness of the SROs is impossible currently to assess, not least because the measures of violation are wholly inadequate and because their aims are far from self-evident. Are they intended to cut out fraud and conflicts of interest? Or to hide them behind a smoke-screen of public relations? Moreover, as The Stock Exchange Chairman Sir Nicholas Goodison has observed (*The Times*, 16 January 1986), criticising the Director of Public Prosecutions, SROs cannot discipline non-members nor can they send anyone to prison.

The Inland Revenue and HM Customs and Excise also investigate commercial fraud. Unlike the Department of Trade and Industry, they can impose administrative penalties that may be viewed as an alternative to court sanctions. Four special Inland Revenue squads, with a total staff of 500, costing £21 million, investigate income-tax fraud. A study in 1980–81 found that because of resource pressure, only 3 per cent of self-employed traders' accounts and 0.6 per cent of companies accounts are examined in depth by the Inland Revenue (Keith Committee, 1983, Table 19). This low level of in-depth investigation exists despite a pilot survey where a random sample of 5500 'Schedule D' tax returns by the self-employed were given to District Inspectors, who considered that 1 in 5 accounts contained 'probable understatements' and a further 2 in 5 'possible understatements' of income (Keith Committee, 1983, para. 10.8.2). With such a reservoir of estimated undetected fraud (or taxpayer reporting 'errors'), it is little wonder that in-depth investigations are such high-yielding work in terms of the amount of tax that is recovered as a result of them! In 1984, there were some 100 staff in the Special Investigation Section, which deals with sophisticated artificial tax avoidance and evasion schemes; 140 in the Enquiry Branch, which deals with serious fraud in business accounts and cases where the honesty or competence of professional advisers is in doubt; 160 staff in Special Offices which handle other avoidance, evasion, and non-compliance cases that are too lengthy and complex for local district offices to deal with; and 100 in the Investigation Office which deals with frauds in the construction industry. In the past decade, despite staffing cutbacks, the Inland Revenue have mounted a concerted attack upon artificial tax avoidance schemes and upon organized evasion. Moreover, by 1988, it is scheduled to have 850 staff in its 'Black Economy Unit', an undercover squad targetted upon the lower end of the evading market.

The number of Customs and Excise officers engaged in anti-fraud measures is unknown, but there is a specialist Investigation Division with a staff of over 400, which deals with narcotics smuggling as well as with fraud. They have been particularly active against organized frauds involving the deliberate 'failure' of vendors of gold bullion that had been smuggled into the country to pass on to Customs and Excise the VAT paid to them by bullion dealers. Part of the difficulty in estimating the anti-fraud resources of the regulatory agencies is that it is hard to tell where routine regulation stops and anti-fraud measures begin. For the purpose of routine reporting/book-keeping legislation is to ensure that fraud is more difficult to perpetrate and escape undetected. However, it is not without interest that despite a 570.5 per cent growth between 1978–79 and 1984–85 in underdeclarations of tax discovered on routine control visits (from £61 million to £409 million), the total number of officers employed on fraud work and administration combined dropped from 6226 in 1978–79 to 5538 in 1984–85.

One area of immediate simple contrast with the Revenue departments – since it equally involves losses to the state rather than to any private or corporate victims – is the Department of Health and Social Security, which deals with welfare fraud. The special anti-fraud divisions had some 2000 staff at May 1986, when despite the importance of controlling civil service staffing levels – used to limit the growth of the Fraud Investigation Group, and the Department of Trade and Industry and Revenue fraud-fighting staff – the Government agreed to provide an additional 500 staff. As a further observation, it is not without interest that despite a 'law-in-books' increase – until recent administrations – in consumer and worker protections, from a 'law-in-action' perspective, far less has changed. The 'deterrence' rather than 'compliance' law-enforcement approach (Reiss, 1983) does not apply to the policing, and particularly not to the prosecution, of so-called 'business regulatory offences' such as pollution and health and safety at work in Britain (Carson, 1981; Hawkins, 1984; Hutter, 1986; Levi, 1984a; and Richardson, Ogus and Burrows, 1983) and in the United States and Australia (see Braithwaite, 1985b; Gunningham, 1985; Reiss, 1983). As Block and Scarpitti (1983, 1985) have shown in their incisive analysis of the US toxic waste disposal industry, the representation of such violations as a 'white-collar crime' rather than as an 'organized crime' problem leads to a genteel control strategy which is functional for the criminal prepetrators (including, in this case, corrupt officialdom). It is important to see investigative resources as a critical part of this process. In 1985, for example, the Office of Fair Trading, which has general oversight of consumer credit, trading standards, and competition policy, had only 315 staff, and a further 72 full-time and 876 part-time municipal employees were engaged in the enforcement of the Consumer Credit Act (1974). This is far from being a vast regulatory army!

Although staffing levels may alter over time, in tune with changes in government policy over the desirability of regulation and over cutting back the number of state employees, the general distribution of law enforcement personnel demonstrates that commercial fraud (and, *a fortiori*, regulatory offences such as industrial safety) commands a small amount of resources compared with matters more conventionally thought of as constituting 'the crime problem'. Whatever the views that readers may have about the origins and justifiability of this distribution of resources, given the obstacles which stand in the way of observing and collecting evidence against fraudsters, it is evident that the upperworld is a safer venue than the underworld for the commission of crime. Let us now examine how these anti-fraud resources are trained and deployed.

PREPARING FOR CONTROL: POLICE TRAINING AND COMMERCIAL FRAUD

It is important to understand the problems that specialized areas of sophisticated crime create for large multi-task bureaucracies such as the police. The police are orientated towards the competent disposal of their central functions of service assistance, emergencies, street and house-hold crime, and traffic. The routine administration of these jobs preoccupies management. Unless there is a crisis, other tasks remain submerged. Unfortunately, fraud cannot be dealt with efficiently within the routines of standard policing formulae. As an organization, the police are geared up to fairly short enquiry periods, though many officers may be drafted in to deal with a homicide or a rape (or a series of these). Personnel changes cause havoc in lengthy enquiries, and with the short-term nature of many Fraud Squad postings, these difficulties can be exacerbated. (This even occurs at senior levels, such as Commanders in the Metropolitan Police, who – despite the predetermined 'reactive' nature of much of the fraud case-load – can generate policy shifts over priorities.)

The small size of Fraud Squads, particularly in provincial forces, has important operational consequences, for if a substantial case involving fraud allegations should come along – such as the activities of one Warwickshire-based commodities trader – there are no senior officers and insufficient experienced officers available to deal with it. This can lead to difficulties of the kind criticized in homicide enquiries, with reluctance to call in police from outside forces who, anyway, may not have the spare resources for a lengthy enquiry. The small number of fraud investigators locks the police into a vicious circle, for it becomes more difficult to justify a high level of police training and specialization in fraud.

The extent and content of training reflects the perceived seriousness of an issue and the perceived problems that exist in dealing with it. By this criterion, fraud is not a problem. It does not form part of the mainstream courses for officers of intermediate and senior rank at the principal Police College, Bramshill, though a 'carousel' course in computer-related crimes was introduced there for a few selected officers in 1986. It *is* taught as part of specialist courses at Hendon, West Midlands, and Greater Manchester, but for Fraud Squad officers only. Since only a small proportion of CID officers, let alone officers in general, ever join the Fraud Squad, this means that few police officers of any given rank receive any education or training about fraud other than basic general criminal law taught in other courses they may have attended. Moreover, except perhaps for graduate police officers in the social studies, financial matters (other than personal finances) are not part of the routine discourse or reading of many officers, so they are unlikely to pick up much knowledge about business custom and practice unless they are actually posted to the Fraud Squad. The implication of this is that any officer on division faced with handling a complicated fraud comes to his task 'cold', without the background understanding that accompanies the policing of the sorts of crime that are more frequently encountered, and without much specialist training.

For Fraud Squad officers, most learning – as in other areas of policing – comes 'on the job', though the nature of what has to be learned – particularly the complex issues related to company law and international evidentiary regulations – is more difficult and extensive for fraud than for other types of criminal investigation. It is self-evident, then, that preparation for a (generally short) career in fraud investigation is conducted at a modest level in Britain compared with the extensive training programmes of the FBI and the Royal Canadian Mounted Police. (Indeed, approximately one-quarter of FBI recruits are graduate accountants, reflecting not only the growth in economic crime investigation but also the salience of asset tracing in organized crime enquiries.) It is true that police training in Britain – despite post-Scarman improvements – is very short compared with that overseas, but this placing in perspective does not help the Fraud Squad officer faced with a labyrinthine international fraud in which evidence has to be obtained from unhelpful overseas tax havens. This is one reason why the linkage between Fraud Squads and other agencies with (hopefully) greater specialized knowledge is significant.

POLICE SPECIALIZATION IN FRAUD WORK

Like other British specialist squads with the possible exception (in practice) of Scenes of Crime (forensic) officers, CID officers are assigned to fraud work on a temporary basis: they normally spend from two to five years in this area of work and, as in other spheres of policing, are almost invariably transferred on promotion. According to one informant, a senior prosecution official, when asked what he regarded as an experienced fraud investigator, replied 'someone who has served for longer than 18 months'.

Because of the small size of most Fraud Squads and the reluctance of senior officers to treat fraud as a special case, opportunities for internal promotion within Fraud Squads are limited, and since most competent people want promotion, the skills that they have acquired are largely wasted in other police work, while others have to take time to acquire (temporarily!) the skills that have been lost. There is strong internal resistance within the police hierarchy to doing anything about this, partly because of a low valuation of fraud and partly because it is difficult to accommodate it within the routine rank structure. Career specialization is not a *sufficient* condition for a motivated and successful workforce: able personnel have to be employed and their efforts sustained by good management and external reinforcement for good policing. However, without a career structure which contains greater possibilities for personal advancement, it is difficult to see why the most competent police officers would wish to take on fraud tasks for a long period. The Fraud Investigation Group – a team of lawyers and accountants who direct complex investigations – has not solved this, because the police are recruited from the available temporary pool. It may be the case that officers will specialize in fraud more in the future, given the career prospects in the financial services world and in the Serious Fraud Office which the Government announced in 1986. But to do so currently would entail sacrificing present promotion prospects for speculative future benefits. These issues are discussed further in the final chapter.

Police powers in relation to fraud

There has been a tendency in much recent literature on policing to discount the impact of law on the regulation of police actions in Britain. The latitude offered by the Judges' Rules on interrogation and the generosity of the courts towards the admissibility of evidence obtained in violation of them have become standard parts of the liberal/left critique that due process exists at a symbolic rather than at a substantive level. (See Baldwin and Kinsey, 1982; McBarnet, 1981; Scraton, 1985b.) Whether the Police and Criminal Evidence Act (1984) (implemented principally in 1986), will change this, and if so, in what direction, is and will remain an open question. (See, generally, Leigh, 1985; Reiner, 1985.) But there is widespread academic scepticism about the fears expressed by some police officers that policing in Britain suffers from over-regulation by the courts. One only has to contrast typical British cases with those in Third World countries such as Pakistan, where police evidence is not admissible at all without corroboration by (supposedly) independent witnesses, to see almost opposite legal approaches to controlling the police. However, whatever the formal legal frameworks for regulating routine police work, researchers in all countries where research has been conducted have been able to point to their ineffectiveness (albeit to different extents). The implication is that although western democracies may sustain the imagery and rituals of due process, in practice they have moved close to a crime control model in which the importance of 'doing something about crime' tends to override constitutional protections for suspects. Indeed, McBarnet (1981) implies that due process was nothing more than a metaphorical cover for the underlying repressive reality.

It is important to note that the analysis is derived principally from the study of what happens (or is alleged to happen) to those people living in poorer sections of metropolitan centres who are suspected mainly of street and household crime, including public order and narcotics offences. I will not review here all the research on the practice of police powers, but quite apart from the possibility that the way police powers are used may vary over time, the observations about the absence of due process and/or about police harassment may be less true of areas outside the inner cities where rightly or wrongly, both crime and offenders are believed to be less common: see Levi (1985).

By contrast with this portrait of the suspect as victim of police power, however, some types of commercial fraud present issues of a different order. In the United States, the more up-market suspects hire expensive private counsel (rather than Public Defenders whose principal *modus operandi* is to arrange guilty pleas). Counsel in turn employ a battery of accountants, and from their earliest involvement in the case, avail themselves of every conceivable legal device to restrict prosecution access to documentary evidence and potentially damaging witnesses (Mann, 1985). Ironically, one of the major obstacles to successful defences in white-collar cases is that the suspects delay going to criminal counsel because they psychologically resist the possibility that the label of 'criminal' might be pinned upon them, and because they do not want the social stigma of being known to be consulting counsel about a criminal investigation. Some of the activities of these defence counsel in coaching witnesses are so close to the role of criminal *consigliere* that they would be violations of professional codes in Britain, but the result is that white-collar criminals (and, though Mann does not discuss them, the higher echelons of 'organized crime') certainly do receive due process.

In England and Wales, compared with the United States, there are fewer legal protections for any suspects – irrespective of their wealth or social standing – to enjoy: for example, there is no Exclusionary Rule whereby the slightest violation of police search procedure can be used to render evidence – no matter how conclusive – inadmissible. However, people who commit commercial frauds are insulated from the legal system in a number of ways not open to thieves and burglars. First, their activities are relatively unlikely to enter the routines of criminal intelligence collation. The police are organized primarily to receive information about threats to public order and to physical premises such as homes and businesses, and cash in transit. The 'natural cover' afforded by the merging of fraud into the routines of ordinary commercial life is enhanced by the ability of 'offenders' to account for what they did in a non-criminal way: e.g. insolvency frauds get defined as ordinary business failures; by the low reporting rate of those victims who *do* realize that they have been defrauded; and by the latitude offered to commercial organizations in submitting their accounts and in being allowed by regulatory agencies such as the Department of Trade and Industry to delay submission of those accounts long after the legal deadline has passed. (At times during the 1980s, up to 40 per cent of companies in England and Wales have been in breach of their legal requirements to file annual accounts.) This is partly a resource issue, for the number of personnel available does affect the level at which more intensive examination by enforcement agencies is 'triggered'. As I have shown earlier in this chapter, these resources are generally very modest in the business regulatory arena.

Another critical part of the protection afforded to commercial fraudsters is the set of rules related to search and seizure of documents. Documentary or forensic evidence plays a very minor role in crime investigation generally, but except in those cases where the *absence* of documentation itself constitutes an offence – for example the offence of failing to keep proper books of account– successful investigations and prosecutions usually depend upon some kind of paper trail. Getting access to this paper trail is a major hurdle, because (1) the potentially damaging information usually is kept by the suspect himself or by organizations such as banks that owe a duty of care and confidence towards the suspect personally and/or companies connected with the suspect(s), and (2) overcoming the barriers of commercial privacy often requires the demonstration of a *prima facie* case that is difficult to establish clearly without the information that is being sought! This means that we must pay close attention to the legal rules governing access to documents and to the attitudes of regulators and judicial authorities towards the invasion of privacy.

It is extremely doubtful, for example, whether SEC would have been able to pursue successfully major cases in 1986 against foreign investors who traded on insider information in the shares of the Santa Fe International Corporation or against Dennis Levine (discussed in Chapter 7) if it had not been able to penetrate banking secrecy laws in the Bahamas and Switzerland to discover the identity of account-holders. (The key to the Levine case was his identification as a client of Bank Leu, a Nassau subsidiary of a major Swiss bank which later assisted the Guinness take-over of Distillers.) These cases resulted in the recovery of $7.8 million and over $11 million respectively. By contrast, the British authorities such as the Department of Trade and Industry have been proved far less effective in discovering the beneficial ownership of shares held abroad, though as we shall see, the powers in the Financial Services Act (1986) and those proposed in the Criminal Justice Bill (1986) will improve their success.

At present, powers are scattered around as the detritus of historical development of agencies and problems posed by frauds at various times. Powers have sometimes been rationalized at an intra-agency level, but inter-agency co-ordination has not received legislative priority hitherto, though the proposals of the Criminal Justice Bill (1986) may alter this. First, I shall review briefly the powers of the police inasmuch as they affect fraud. (For further discussion of police powers, see Leigh, 1985; Zander, 1985.)

Prior to the Police and Criminal Evidence Act (1984) (PACE), the police had no powers to search for evidence prior to charging a suspect (see Leigh, 1982; Levi, 1981). However, under s.8 of PACE (1984), a magistrate may issue the police with a warrant to search for evidence if he/she is satisfied (1) that there are reasonable grounds for believing that a serious arrestable offence has been committed, this being defined in s.116 as an offence which has led, or is intended or likely to lead, to substantial financial gain or loss to any person; (2) that there is material evidential value on the premises which, taken alone or in conjunction with other material, is likely to be of substantial value to the investigation of the offence; and (3) that it is not subject to special provisions under s.8 (1)(d) discussed below. Such warrants may be issued *ex parte*, without the proposed subject of the search being informed.

S.8(2) of PACE (1984) defines three further categories of material for which the police might wish to search: 'items subject to legal privilege', which cannot be subject to a search warrant from anyone at all; and 'excluded material' and 'special procedure material', for which warrants may be issued only by a circuit judge. It is important to note that a search warrant may be issued only for material that has evidentiary value in the legal sense. Thus, records of interviews between fraud suspects and journalists or accountants would not be admissible under the hearsay rule, and therefore cannot properly be the subject of a warrant to search for 'evidence'. Applications for warrants to circuit judges should normally be made *inter partes* (both parties represented), but where the court is satisfied that service of a notice for an application of an order may seriously prejudice an investigation, the application may be made *ex parte* (without the knowledge of the other party). This clearly is an area of considerable judicial discretion.

Excluded material includes 'journalistic material' and personal welfare records held in confidence by a third party (such as a doctor) who has acquired it in the course of any trade, business, or profession. The principal circumstances in relation to *fraud* in which the police might be interested in such records are (1) where a fraud suspect has consulted a psychiatrist or other doctor about his health with special pleading in mind; and (2) a journalist has information about a fraud suspect in relation to which there is an express or implied undertaking of confidence. However, much information in the latter category is in any event unlikely to be admissible, so a warrant to search for it would not be obtainable.

Special procedure material, however, is more germane to fraud investigations, since it includes other material held in confidence, such as financial information, share certificates, or company records held by accountants, solicitors, and bankers. The criteria that circuit judges must apply before issuing such warrants to search for special procedure material are (1) those applicable to magistrates' search warrants above; (2) other methods of obtaining the material either have been tried and failed or have not been tried because it appeared that they were bound to fail. Thus, if a banker or an accountant is unable to disclose information without a court order, this criterion would be met; and (3) the court must be satisfied that access to the material would be in the public interest, having regard to the benefit likely to accrue to the investigation if the material is obtained, and to the circumstances under which the person in possession of the material holds it. (Whatever the latter might mean!) To try to avoid the artificial construction of special procedure material by the devious, s.14 (3–5) provides that material acquired by employees from their employer or by a company from an associated company is special procedure material only if it was so immediately before it was acquired. Otherwise, employers could make their records subject to special procedures simply by instructing their employees that it was held in confidence.

However, no warrant may be issued to *anyone* to search for evidence which is legally privileged. Such material is defined in s.10(1) as covering communications between a professional legal adviser and his client or his client's representative made in connection with the giving of legal advice; communications made between the adviser and his client and any other person that have been made in connection with or in contemplation of legal proceedings; and items enclosed with or referred to in such communications and made in connection with the giving of legal advice. A legal adviser includes barristers, solicitors, and their clerks, and 'any other person' referred to might include an accountant asked to prepare a report 'in connection with' legal proceedings. S.10 (2) states that no privilege is attached to items held with the intention of furthering a criminal purpose, but this may be hard to establish without having access to the items first.

The interpretation of these issues in case law has yet to be decided, but even though commercial fraud has become highlighted as a 'real crime' issue during 1986, it is unlikely that the courts will allow the provisions to be used for evidentiary fishing expeditions, even if police supervisors were willing to put warrant applications forward on that basis. For example, in *R v Central Criminal Court ex parte Adegbesan and others* [1986] 3 All E.R. 113, the Divisional Court quashed the 'special procedure' order made by the Common Sergeant (a senior Old Bailey judge), stating that it was the duty of the police to set out a description of all the material that was to be produced. Failure to do so could result in the recipient of the notice unwittingly destroying the material, since it was impossible for him to know whether or not it was covered by the order. When the police did provide further particulars, the defendants appealed once more, on the grounds that the particulars were still inadequate. Again, we may be in the land of Catch-22: the police may not know precisely where they may be able to find documents which they suspect exist without inspecting them, but they cannot get an order requiring production until they know where the information can be found! This rule does not apply just for the benefit of 'the powerful': in *Adegbesan*, it protected blacks administering 'community funds' on the riot-hit Broadwater Farm Estate in London. Moreover, the Codes of Practice that accompany PACE (1984) state that searches for special procedure or excluded material must be carried out under the command of an officer of at least the rank of inspector, who has a duty to ensure that it is carried out with discretion and in such a manner as to cause the least possible disruption to business carried on at the premises (para 5.13). The failure to observe the Codes of Practice is a breach of the police discipline code, though it will not automatically render inadmissible any information that is obtained.

As regards the *seizure* of material during a search, this may occur if the officer reasonably believes it is evidence in relation to an offence that has been committed and/or he is investigating. He may not seize material that he reasonably believes to be subject to legal privilege, and if he 'unwittingly' does seize such material, it may well be rendered inadmissible at trial. Evidence that was not part of the original warrant may be seized. Before taking away property, the officer should listen to any representations made by the person from whom he is taking it. S.19(4) enables a police officer acting in pursuance of his powers to require information stored on a computer to be produced in a visible and legible form so that it can be taken away.

In relation to commercial fraud complaints, the question of how much selectivity should occur before seizure presents some difficulties, for it is often hard to know which documents will be relevant. This is not a problem that arises in other spheres of alleged crime, and thus suspected fraudsters enjoy a comparative advantage. Much criticism of the Inland Revenue and the police in the *Rossminster* tax raid arose from the apparent failure to examine all the documents in detail prior to carting them away. Children's scrapbooks were removed, and the average viewing time per file was 90 seconds: see *R* v. *IRC, ex parte Rossminster Ltd* [1980] 1 All E.R. 80, HL; and Tutt (1985). The Court of Appeal has held subsequently that in cases which involve a very large quantity of records, the police should be broadly selective, ruling out those documents that are 'clearly irrelevant' and taking away others that they reasonably believe to have evidential value: see *Reynolds* v. *Metropolitan Police Commissioner* [1985] 2 WLR 93, CA. It is evident that discretion has to be exercised, and the courts will not be slow to criticize the police for being too seizure-happy in fraud cases. This is quite apart from any lawsuits for civil damages that may be taken out by the subjects of searches who claim that there were no reasonable grounds for them: in 1987, a claim against the Metropolitan Police for £7 million is still being pursued by the former directors of the Rossminster 'tax planning' company.

Finally, as regards police powers, s.7 of the Bankers' Books Evidence Act allows any party to legal proceedings that have been commenced to apply to a magistrates' court or, more commonly, to the High Court, for a warrant to examine and take copies of entries in a banker's book for any purpose in connection with such proceedings. Schedule 6 of the Banking Act (1979) extended the definition of a banker's book to include all records used in the ordinary business of the bank, whether they be in written form or on microfilm, magnetic tape, or any other form of mechanical or electronic data retrieval mechanisms. The police sometimes do seek (and obtain) information unofficially from commercial institutions without exercising any of the powers discussed above (or in previous legislation). However, despite the presence of former police officers as directors or security advisers in many large commercial institutions, the Ways and Means Act – that directory of police powers that has not received formal statutory blessing – is very much more difficult to operate in the commercial sphere than it is on the streets. This is partly a question of business attitudes: as may be seen from their resistance to the demands for routine co-operation in the struggle to prevent 'the Drug Barons' from laundering their profits, banks, for example, do not like to police their clients unless the evidence is very strong. (It is a matter for speculation to what extent this concern is affected by the profits they obtain from unlawful behaviour.) The money-laundering sections of the President's Commission on Organized Crime (1986a, 1986b) show how even major, respectable US banks would alert their customers if the police displayed an interest in their accounts, and the reluctance to assist the police can shade over into corruption where bank employees are being paid off by the fraudsters or drug traffickers. The Drug Trafficking Offences Act (1986) made it a criminal offence to assist in laundering the proceeds of trafficking. But subject to the changes that have come about as a result of the specific lifting by that Act of the obligation of confidentiality, the traditional reluctance on the part of commercial organizations and professionals to get involved in policing is also strengthened by their fear of civil liabilities for breach of confidence, although unless news of the police interest became public and/or led to arrests, it is not clear what concrete damage their clients and customers would sustain from the handing over of information to the police.

The powers of the Department of Trade and Industry

The Department of Trade and Industry has a number of different sorts of powers. Some of these – now largely delegated to SIB and its constituent SROs under the Financial Services Act (1986) – relate to the *licensing* of certain classes of business such as 'licensed dealers in securities' and 'licensed deposit-takers', and have generated much public and media criticism because of the Department of Trade and Industry's reluctance to refuse the initial granting of licences or to revoke them once issued. Others include the power to institute winding-up proceedings, whether after insolvency or following complaints. Here, I will focus upon the powers – which in many ways are more extensive than those of the police – to investigate allegations of fraud and other corporate irregularities, which date from the mid-nineteenth century. (See, generally, Department of Trade and Industry, 1986a.)

First, I will set out the circumstances that are allowed to *trigger* an investigation by the Department, which arise under the consolidating Companies Act (1985):

1 S.431, which gives it a discretionary power to appoint inspectors to investigate the affairs of a company and to report on them, if a company or a prescribed proportion of its members request this *and* if the applicants can show that they have 'good reason' for requiring the investigation;

2 S.442, which enables it to investigate the beneficial ownership of shares in a company or the persons who control it. (This may be important if it is alleged that anyone has been buying shares in excess of the proportion that is legally allowed before he is required to make an open bid for all the company's shares: this is known as a 'concert

party'. It might be important also if it is feared that 'organized criminals' have gained secret control of a company);

3 S.446, which enables it to investigate the share dealings of directors and their close relatives. [The Department of Trade and Industry Handbook observes (1986a:2) that 'such enquiries being infrequent are not discussed in this publication'.]

4 S.432(1) which *requires* the Department of Trade and Industry to appoint inspectors when ordered to do so by the Court;

5 S.432(2), which gives the Secretary of State the power to appoint inspectors where it appears to him that there are circumstances suggesting that

  a the company's affairs are being or have been conducted 'with intent to defraud its creditors or the creditors of any other person or otherwise for a fraudulent or unlawful purpose or in a manner which is unfairly prejudicial to some part of its members';

  b 'any actual or proposed act or omission of the company (including an act or omission on its behalf) is or would be prejudicial or that it was formed for any fraudulent or unlawful purpose';

  c 'persons concerned with the company's formation or the management of its affairs have, in connection therewith, been guilty of fraud, misfeasance or other misconduct towards it or towards its members',

  d 'the company's members have not been given all the information with respect to its affairs which they might reasonably expect'.

The useful Handbook prepared by the Department of Trade and Industry rather misleadingly observes: 'In most cases, the Secretary of State appoints under Section 432(2) where it appears to him that there are circumstances suggesting' the irregularities referred to above (Department of Trade and Industry, 1986a:3). However, this does not illuminate the Department's activities greatly, since the level of usage of *any* of the above provisions is indicated by the fact that there were 6 such investigations in 1983 and 1 in 1984 (Department of Trade and Industry, 1985b:15). There was another one in 1985. All it tells us is that other sections are employed barely at all!

Except where the enquiry is requested by the company itself – often out of concern that there may be a 'concert party' between nominee shareholders as a prelude to a takeover bid – given the historic reluctance of the DTI to intervene, the mere announcement that a Department of Trade enquiry is taking place can itself prove extremely damaging to a company. In December 1986, the value of Guinness shares dropped dramatically when the DTI cryptically stated that it was undertaking a S 442 investigation into undefined allegations of misconduct. These actually related to suspicions of secret agreements between Guinness and supposedly independent US financiers during Guinness' successful but bitterly contested takeover bid for Distillers much earlier in the year. (Media interest was fuelled by the correct rumours that the investigation was linked to statements made to SEC by upperworld 'supergrass' Ivan Boesky.)

In practice, partly because of the fact that the publicity which follows the appointment of outside inspectors – who are normally a senior accountant and a Queen's Counsel, but may include a stockbroker – can itself prove highly damaging to the company, and partly because of the high cost and slowness of these (usually part-time) enquiries, most investigations are carried out without public announcement by the Department's own staff under s.447 of the Companies Act (1985). This gives the Secretary of State a power 'at any time' if he thinks that there is (undefined in law) 'good reason to do so' to require any company incorporated in Great Britain *or* that in the past or present has done business there, to produce books or papers, and for any past or present officer of the company to provide an explanation of them to an officer of the Department of Trade and Industry. All statements made are admissible in evidence. However, there is no general power to question officers of the company about matters not in the books, nor are employees or 'financial consultants' included within the category of people who are required to answer questions. The peak years for such internal investigations were the mid-1970s, but recent years have seen an increased use of them: there were 103 in 1983; 99 in 1984; and 111 in 1985. The extensive discretion used by the Department of Trade and Industry in agreeing or not agreeing to carry out inspections – setting aside any initial enquiries that may be turned away without formal recording – is revealed by the fact that only between 1 in 3 and 1 in 4 applications made under the foregoing sections of the Companies Act are granted: in 1984, 101 out of 449 applications were granted; in 1985, 116 out of 528 were approved. (For a more extensive though less contemporary discussion of the role of the Department of Trade and Industry in company inspections, see Leigh, 1982.)

The Financial Services Act (1986) extends the powers of the DTI and of 'competent authorities' (Schedule 13) – such as investigators from self-regulatory organizations – in relation to persons carrying on investment business. Apart from provisions applying to the managers and trustees of unit trusts or other collective investment schemes (s. 94), the major powers are granted under sections 105 and 177. S 105 gives the Secretary of State or a competent authority the power to require a person whose affairs are to be investigated to answer questions or furnish information 'with respect to any matter relevant to the investigation'. Likewise, documents (including computer-held data) must be produced if requested and, subject to legal professional privilege, 'the person producing them or any connected person' (extending as far as bankers, auditors, and solicitors) may be required to explain them. Evidence compulsorily obtained is admissible in subsequent criminal proceedings: failure to comply without reasonable excuse is a summary offence punishable by up to six months' imprisonment and/or a fine.

S 177 of the Financial Services Act (1986) relates to insider dealing and is more extensive than the other investigation powers, perhaps reflecting the Catch-22 difficulty of establishing without a full enquiry whether or not insider dealing has occurred. Sub-section (3) creates a duty for any person whom the inspectors consider is or may be able to give information:

(i)   to produce to them any documents in his possession or under his control relating to the company in relation to whose securities the contravention is suspected to have occurred or to its securities;
(ii) to attend before them; and
(iii) otherwise to give them all assistance in connection with the investigation which he is reasonably able to give.

As with sections 94 and 105 of the Act, statements obtained under compulsion are admissible in evidence and these informational requirements extend to bankers provided that the Secretary of State is satisfied – not necessarily 'reasonably', for that word is not contained in the text – that the disclosure or production is necessary to the investigation and that the bank customer 'is a person who the inspectors have reason to believe may be able to give information concerning a suspected contravention': see s. 177 (8).

Under s. 178, if anyone refuses to co-operate, the inspectors may certify this in writing and a court may enquire into the case. If, after hearing any witness produced by the offender and any statement made by the defence, the court is satisfied that the person had no reasonable excuse to refuse to give the information requested, it may punish him as for contempt of court or direct that the Secretary of State may exercise his powers to restrict or cancel the person's authorization to undertake investment business, either generally or in specific areas. This may be done even though the offender is not within the jurisdiction of the court, if the court is satisfied that he was notified of his right to appear before it and of the powers available to the court. S 178 (6) expressly states that it is *not* a reasonable excuse for non co-operation to claim

'in a case where the contravention or suspected contravention being investigated relates to dealing by him on the instructions or for the account of another person, by reason that at the time of the refusal

(a) he did not know the identity of that other person; or
(b) he was subject to the law of a country or territory outside the United
Kingdom which prohibited him from disclosing information relating to
the dealing without the consent of that other person, if he might have
obtained that consent or obtained exemption from that law.'

The Court of Appeal has yet to rule on the interpretation of these
provisions but in 1987, a High Court judge ruled that a journalist for
The Independent, Jeremy Warner, was not obliged to reveal to Department of Trade and Industry inspectors his sources for a story on alleged
insider dealing within the Office of Fair Trading, on the grounds that
his testimony was not so crucial that it overrode the public interest in
confidentiality.

Proposed with the active support of The Stock Exchange *before* major
British and American scandals involving insider dealing, this was
intended to be a fairly tough response to those who hide behind
professional and banking confidentiality relationships to perpetrate
breaches of confidence themselves. During the period 1980–86, some
50 investigations by The Stock Exchange or the DTI could not be
completed because they could not penetrate nominee accounts in
foreign banks and/or companies. Given these protections from state and
professional surveillance, it is scarcely surprising that in the first six
months of 1986, the share prices of 19 UK companies went up by over
20 per cent in the four weeks prior to the announcement that they were
to be the objects of a takeover bid: strategic judgment or insider dealing?
S 177 may be a useful deterrent by generating a more effective audit
trail and by discouraging banks and professionals in the Channel Islands
and the Isle of Man from allowing insider dealers to use them as a
conduit for funds. However, unless new international judicial assistance
treaties are negotiated (see Chapter 8), bankers and others in countries
such as Switzerland, Liechtenstein, and Panama which impose a legal
obligation of secrecy on banks will continue to fall outside the
provisions: their bankers could not 'have obtained exemption from that
law'. Nor is it yet certain how the phrase 'if he might have obtained that
consent' will be interpreted. Will it count as a reasonable excuse for the
banker if the person under investigation refuses to give his consent
though consent might lawfully have been given? There is still ample
scope for judicial interpretation and for argument by defence counsel.

In addition to powers to investigate companies while they are still
operating, there are more draconian powers to conduct inquisitorial
post-mortems on those that have ceased to trade and, in particular, on
unincorporated firms that have gone bankrupt (see Aris, 1985; Farrar,
1985; Leigh, 1980; Levi, 1981). These, like all police powers, are a
'resource' to be drawn upon when needed. Given the opportunities for

fraud afforded by the corporate veil, there is a certain irony in the fact that there is a higher level of susceptibility to interrogation in the case of personal bankrupts than in the case of those who manage companies that go bust. (This is largely the result of the later historical development of the corporate form, which arose when moral views about the inherent sinfulness of bankruptcy had begun already to subside.) However, the workload of Insolvency and Bankruptcy Examiners is such that in practice, few companies or unincorporated traders are subjected to serious inquisitions unless there is a formal complaint by a creditor. Except for the occasional incursion by an enthusiastic examiner, to carry out muck-raking expeditions into many of the 19,021 company liquidations – or even the 5761 compulsory liquidations – notified in 1985 or into the 7726 bankruptcies notified during 1984 would mean that the routine functions of the Department in dealing with the probate paperwork for these defunct businesses could not be performed.

The Insolvency Service, then, like the police and the Companies Investigation Branch, works largely on a reactive rather than on a proactive investigative model. It is important to set this fact in context. First, many complaints about corporate misconduct *are* legally ambiguous, in a way that most crime complaints are not: the law does not proscribe all cases of 'misconduct' that are defined as criminal by those who suffer from them, and some complaints may be motivated by the desire to put pressure on other parties to a civil dispute. Second, although there is relative autonomy of crime investigation units within the Department of Trade and Industry, the general role of that Department is to encourage trade, and this tends to make officials more sales-oriented than control-oriented. This sort of phenomenon has been noted by Carson (1981) when discussing the extreme reluctance of officials in the Department of Energy to concern themselves with health and safety violations in the North Sea oil business. It also finds its parallels in many companies, where sales are given primacy over credit control (Levi, 1981). But the functional ambiguity of some regulatory agencies sets them apart from the police, who may have problems in deciding whether to adopt a peace-keeping or a law-enforcement style but whose basic job is unambiguously to minimize law-breaking rather than, say, to encourage people to walk the streets.

The powers of the Revenue departments

The Inland Revenue and HM Customs and Excise are also involved in the policing of commercial fraud, the former via its role in collecting income tax payable by individuals and the latter via its role in collecting VAT. Indeed, unlike any other sphere of policing, the policing of revenue fraud offers some direct economic *benefit* to the Government rather than being a pure economic cost. There is no space here to review in detail all the powers of these departments (see Keith Committee, 1983; Levi, 1982; Tutt, 1985). Largely because of the organizational need to ensure that traders are registered for and are paying the correct amount of taxes, Customs and Excise officials do have greater powers than the police or the Department of Trade and Industry to require the production of information and documentation from traders. For example, under s.37(1) of the Finance Act (1972), they have a general power of entry to business premises to assess VAT 'at any reasonable time', without a prior warrant from the courts.

The Finance Act (1985) has made some important alterations to the powers of Customs and Excise officials. First, under s.12(6), officials now have a power of arrest for offences under s.12 relating, for example, to the furnishing, sending, or otherwise making use of a document which is false in a material particular with intent to deceive. Second, schedule 7 para. 3 extended the requirement to supply such information as officials may reasonably specify from suppliers of goods to (1) the suppliers of services; (2) the importers of goods in the course or furtherance of a business; and (3) any persons who may be involved in a supply or the receipt thereof. Third, schedule 7 para. 5 has restricted the issue of search warrants to the more serious VAT offences. Magistrates may now issue warrants where Customs and Excise have reasonable grounds for suspecting that 'a fraud offence which appears to be of a serious nature is being, has been, or is about to be, committed' (compared with the previous broader wording of 'an offence in connection with VAT is being, has been, or is about to be, committed'). Warrants may specify the number of officers allowed to execute the search, the times of day during which it may be conducted, and unless stated otherwise, searches under warrant must be made accompanied by a police officer in uniform. Moreover, the occupier of the premises or the person who appears to be in charge of them must be provided with a copy of the search warrant.

For non-fraud VAT offences, schedule 7 para. 6 enables magistrates to require information (including that held on computer) to be disclosed and, if considered necessary, removed. In all cases of removal, a record of items seized must be given and the person from whom they were seized has a right to take copies of them under supervision. The aim of these legislative changes was to clarify and codify the rights and obligations of traders, as a response to episodic criticism of abuse of powers in the media – usually in response to groups representing small businesspeople – and in keeping with revisions to police powers in the Police and Criminal Evidence Act (1984). The net effect was to restrict

Customs and Excise powers slightly and to bring them more in line with the powers of the Inland Revenue.

Perhaps more significantly, however, these information-requiring functions are exercised as part of the proactive operation of the department, whose role is to maximize governmental revenue subject to the legal obligations of traders: indeed, most fraud investigations commence from the dissatisfaction of a local VAT office with the state of a trader's affairs in the aftermath of a routine visit. In a sense, the fact that the victim is the abstract one of 'government' – rather than the individuals or companies who are the victims of other commercial frauds and who are thought to be in a position to complain if they wish to do so – means that there is no question of relying upon some kind of *laissez-faire* victim-activation of criminal investigations into revenue frauds. For if the tax inspector does not detect the fraud, it is unlikely that the authorities will get to know about its existence at all. (Informers account for only 5 per cent of recorded VAT frauds, though as in the case of other frauds, disgruntled wives or lovers are the downfall of many a tax fraudster, and underworld-connected VAT fraudsters are as susceptible to gossip and to target surveillance as are other suspected offenders.) Routine control visits are usually made by appointment with businesspeople, but 'investigation visits' – those made when fraud is suspected – are made unannounced in nine out of ten cases. The powers of Customs and Excise officials are a good example of the latitude with which governmental officials may intrude upon the lives of businesspeople without a great deal of control by the courts over conditions of access to information by search and interrogation. Yet they appear to exercise these powers with considerable restraint.

Under s.37(3) of the Finance Act (1972) – now amended by the Finance Act (1985) reviewed earlier – Customs and Excise officers could apply for a warrant from a magistrate to search premises when they believed a VAT offence had been committed. Between April 1976 and June 1980, such warrants were taken out 702 times. No warrants were refused during this period, but in spite of the apparent rubber-stamping by magistrates, the care taken in vetting applications before they are made is revealed by the fact that the 'success rate' of these warrants was very high: evidence of fraud was obtained in 94 per cent of cases. (This compares favourably with 40–50 per cent success in warrants taken out by the police: see Appendix 7 in the Law and Procedure volume of the Report of the Royal Commission on Criminal Procedure, 1981). The Keith Committee (1983) gave the exercise of these powers a clean bill of health, noting (para. 9.23) that in only 3 out of 14 complaints from 834 searches was there any ground for concern. What is equally intriguing, however, is the financial threshold that triggers off VAT fraud investigations. Departmental instructions state that a fraud investigation should not normally be commenced where less than £250 in arrears of tax is involved. However, the Keith Committee observes that

> 'because of pressure on resources in recent years, higher threshold levels prevail in practice, and vary from locality to locality and from office to office. ... Following staff cuts in control work and the increasing scale and complexity of investigation cases, few cases would now be subject to formal fraud investigation, even by non-specialist staff, if the suspected evasions were less than about £2,000 VAT ... and that the minimum limit for investigation by specialist staff was now more like £10,000 VAT, i.e. almost £70,000 under-declaration of turnover.'
>
> (Keith Committee, 1983: para. 9.1.5)

This pressure has not eased in subsequent years. The unofficial starting-point had risen to about £30,000 in 1986. Quite apart from any possible changes in business morality generally, the involvement of organized crime groups both in long-firm frauds and in smuggling gold into the UK on which VAT has not been paid, selling it to bullion dealers at a price which includes VAT, and pocketing the VAT themselves, has increased the regulatory burdens of Customs and Excise officers considerably, though in 1986, they revised the system so that VAT would be paid by the bullion dealers to the Treasury rather than being passed back through the vendors. Suspected under-declarations of turnover below £2000 may be dealt with by attempts to bargain traders upwards or by threats of close surveillance in the future, but serious investigations do not arise in such circumstances. The implication is not only that VAT control officers exercise some care in how they interpret 'reasonable suspicion' but also that they *start* a fraud investigation at a level of economic loss that would be a very major crime if it fell within the purview of the police.

The activities of the Inland Revenue – though important to the understanding of how it is that many rich people succeed in remaining rich – will not be discussed in detail here. Despite its reputation for being much milder than Customs and Excise in its resort to search powers under criminal statutes and to criminal prosecutions, the Inland Revenue has developed considerable expertise in redrafting legislation to take account of the highly sophisticated schemes devised by the army of 'tax planners' whose occupational lives are dedicated to minimizing the tax burdens of their clients. (This could be viewed as an up-market job creation scheme: in an infinite regression, these technical legislative changes give rise to further avoidance schemes to which the Inland Revenue responds, creating still further demands for expert legal and accounting advice among wealthy individuals and companies.)

Ordinary taxation matters are handled by local District Inspectors, who are kept more than busy dealing with their routine case-load and have little time for proactive investigation. In cases where they suspect the existence of 'serious' fraud, the matter will be referred upwards to the Enquiry Branch of the Inland Revenue, which comprises approximately 100 Inspectors of Taxes (who are much in demand by the private sector), divided into groups of 10, consisting of 1 group leader, 6 inspectors, and 3 accountants. Referrals from district account for some three-fifths of the criminal investigations made by the Enquiry Branch. 'Seriousness' is not defined officially, but entails any of the following criteria: over £20,000 is involved; the taxpayer is a professional tax adviser or is of special status (such as a Revenue Appeal Commissioner); where there is evidence that documents have been forged with intent to deceive; where there is a second offence or series of offences soon after an investigation into an earlier one; where the suspected fraud is particularly large or ingenious or involves a conspiracy; and where the taxpayer fails to own up to matters that the Inland Revenue know about already. However, apart from the problem of identifying such schemes – a task for which District officers are given no special training – only some of them are actually made the subject of intensive investigation when referred, though a high estimated assessment of tax may be made upon the taxpayer as a move in the negotiation game that taxation has become.

The Inland Revenue has developed special investigation units which target suspect businesspeople for civil as well as for criminal action. Sometimes, this intersects with other areas of alleged commercial fraud. For example, in 1986, special investigations were mounted against some former active underwriters suspected of involvement in defrauding members of Lloyd's by channelling favourable risks into so-called 'baby syndicates': re-insurance companies overseas that, unknown to most of the members of their underwriting syndicates, were beneficially owned by themselves and a few select friends (see Clarke, 1986; Hodgson, 1986). In other cases, the investigations may relate to people who are suspected of tax fraud but not of fraud against any party other than the government: an example is the Rossminster tax avoidance schemes, which were artificial devices aimed at minimizing (for a very large fee) the tax liabilities that would otherwise arise out of legitimate company and individual earnings (Tutt, 1985).

Prior to the passage of the Finance Act (1976), taxpayers had to be given notice of Inland Revenue requirements for information or for the handing over of documents. Generally, this produced no (known) problems, but sometimes evidence would be destroyed or the person would abscond. (For some United States analogies, see Mann, 1985.)

However, s.20c of the Taxes Management Act (1970), as implemented in the Finance Act (1976), spelled the symbolic end of the era in which taxpayers were to be treated always as gentlemen. Having obtained permission from at least two members of the (formally independent) Board of the Inland Revenue – normally including the Chairman – officials may apply for a warrant to search premises. To do this, they must satisfy a circuit judge – *not* a magistrate – that there are reasonable grounds for suspecting *some form* of tax fraud, and that evidence of it is to be found upon the suspect premises. (In other words, the subject of the search may not know what evidence under which precise statutory provision exists against him, though he would presumably know what fraudulent *behaviour* – if any – he had been engaged upon.) Moreover, except for documents in the possession of a lawyer for which a claim of privilege could be made (see the earlier discussion on PACE, 1984), the Inland Revenue has the right to remove from the premises anything which there is reasonable cause to believe may be needed as evidence in a criminal prosecution for tax fraud.

Between 1976 and October 1982, s.20c Taxes Management Act warrants were only used in just 15 cases (involving 83 different places of business), only one of which ended in acquittal in the courts: no figures are available for the subsequent period, but the pattern of low use has continued. To set this in context, during the period 1976–80, when warrants were issued in 13 cases, there were some 80,000 cases in which fraud was discovered and penalties imposed, and over 300,000 cases of a more minor nature where settlements were reached after understatements of income had been admitted.

It is possible that many of these settlements were reached because the taxpayer – who cannot obtain Legal Aid – decided that he could not afford to fight for his just cause. However, that is a question of some dispute. What is plain is that the powers are used extremely sparingly. That did not stop Lord Denning from asserting in the *Rossminster* case [1979] 3 All E.R. 385 that this was the worst intrusion of the state into individual liberty since the times of John Wilkes and of the Spanish Inquisition. In the judgment of the Court of Appeal, the search was held to have been unlawful and all the documents seized were ordered to be returned to their rightful owners. (Following the return of the documents, and much to the distress of the tax avoidance experts, a temporary secretary accidentally threw out an out-of-date diary which was believed to contain details of meetings that were crucial to the Inland Revenue's case against them, resulting in a small fine for contempt of court. The directors denied having had anything to do with the accidental loss.) In the end, the House of Lords [1980] 1 All E.R. 80, reluctantly upheld the validity of the search warrants. In June 1983, the Attorney-General announced that no criminal proceedings would be instituted, though the Inland Revenue continues to pursue claims for back tax and penalties against the two persons principally responsible for the schemes, while they counter-claim for civil damages.

In view of the hostile comments of Lord Denning regarding the seizure of apparently irrelevant material (such as children's books), it is interesting to note the observations of the Keith Committee:

> 'We noted that evidence of fraud had been found in a wide variety of places, including on the person of suspects . . . a concealed wall safe . . . the drains of a private house . . . in a book claimed to be a child's drawing book (evidence of the true takings of a business) and a book claimed to contain only devotional extracts from the Book of Leviticus.'
>
> (Keith Committee, 1983: para. 9.16.33)

Inland Revenue branches, like policing agencies, differentiate their investigative styles in accordance with their perceptions of the characters of the people with whom they deal. The Enquiry Branch follow to the letter the guidelines on the conduct of interviews that were in the Judges' Rules and are now in the PACE (1984) Codes of Practice, and – with the exception of the rare Rossminster-type raids – generally interview taxpayers in the presence of their professional advisers after making a prior appointment. By contrast, the Investigation Office, which deals with frauds by building subcontractors (who are always under suspicion of allowing building workers not to pay tax), adopts an investigative style more akin to that of the police. We should bear in mind that subcontractors do have a place of work at which they could be interviewed, and that there is less scope for the Inland Revenue than for the police to obtain direct evidence of crime (such as stolen goods or incriminating documents) at the home of a suspect. However, the differences in the rhetoric with which arguments over police powers are conducted in tax compared with theft or burglary cases is revealed in the following discussion by the Keith Committee:

> 'It was urged upon us on behalf of the subcontractors that investigation visits to the home were undesirable in principle because of the inconvenience and even distress which could be caused to their families; that evening visits at the end of a hard working day added to the pressure on the taxpayer; that interviews were sometimes unduly protracted, given the time of day, and that statements were normally taken towards the end; and that in contrast to the Enquiry Branch it was not usual either for the subcontractor to be informed of the possibility of having an adviser present or for him to be given a copy of his statement or other record of the interview.'
>
> (Keith Commitee, 1983: para. 9.12.3)

The Committee rejected these pleas, but the fact that they could be raised at all in this way is illuminating. The revenue-raising task of the department makes the motivation behind its activities different from the police, but in 1984, 91 per cent of all investigations mounted by tax offices and by the Enquiry Branch resulted in the payment of additional tax and 47 per cent of them yielded additional interest payments also: the 'success rate' of investigations has increased since 1979.

What this relatively brief summary of the principal powers of the Revenue departments and their use indicates is that in practice, the internal departmental controls and the media and political environment in which they operate act so as to constrain the abuse of any latitude that might be accorded by the technical drafting of the statutes. This relative restrictiveness (compared with the police) does not inhibit complaints alleging abuse of power on the part of the tax authorities – 'voluntary' compliance may be induced frequently by the threat of using formal powers – but as in other studies of police powers, it is important to look at the practice of powers 'on the ground' – the law in action – as well as at statutory provisions.

The powers of SROs

Finally, it is important to note that in addition to those agencies that have powers conferred upon them by statute or by common law, there are regulatory institutions which exercise power over their members by virtue of contract law. There is no particular consistent logic in this. Lloyd's insurance market, for example, has been governed by statutory provisions since the Lloyd's Act (1982), whereas subject to those changes brought about by the Financial Services Act (1986) and by the merger with ISRO in 1986–87, most of the powers of The Stock Exchange were not created by statute but as a contractual condition of membership.

Self-regulation by statute or contract produces advantages as well as limitations compared with governmental regulation. In October 1986, Lloyd's promulgated amendments to the Lloyd's Act (1982), establishing for the first time a Review Department to police the institution, and obliging members to provide information, documents, open their books, and to allow access to premises to check that they have complied with the rules. Inspections can be made without prior notice if authorized by the Chief Executive. These rules were modelled on those of The Stock Exchange, where Members are required to allow the Surveillance Division to examine any documents they consider relevant at any time. They have powers to scrutinize in detail all the firms' records and to investigate any suspicion of irregularity or malpractice. Moreover, where a possible breach of discipline by a Member is reported, the Chairman of The Stock Exchange will consider the appointment of an *ad hoc* Committee of Investigation: a sort of Grand Jury stage preliminary to the formulation of charges. Under Rule A10–6(b),

'Each Committee of Investigation shall have powers to take evidence and, in particular, may exercise the powers of the Council under Rule 20.1 to require Members and clerks to attend before them; such Members and clerks shall give the committee of Investigation such information as may be in their possession relative to the matters under investigation.'

So there are considerable powers to require the production of information, which can be triggered off without any requirement to show reasonable suspicion. On the other hand, prior to the passage of s.147 of the Financial Services Act (1986), which gave them powers equivalent to those of outside inspectors appointed by the Department of Trade and Industry, The Stock Exchange inspectors and Committees of Investigation had no powers to require information from anyone other than a Member or a clerk, so in this sense they were much more circumscribed than the police or governmental regulatory agencies. Since most cases of suspected insider dealing involve interviewing people who are not Members of The Stock Exchange, certain types of criminal violation as well as rule breaches were relatively immune from effective investigation by the Surveillance Division, though in theory, they could have been investigated by the Department of Trade and Industry. Henceforth, Department of Trade and Industry inspectors (including authorized self-regulatory investigators) who are frustrated in attempts to compel offshore intermediaries to co-operate in insider-dealing investigations will be able to ask the Secretary of State to restrict or even de-authorize business activities by, for example, overseas banks if they fail to disclose to the inspectors the identities of those traders whose identities they *could* know. This is a response to the increasing use of offshore facilities and nominees by professional insider dealers to evade the surveillance of The Stock Exchange.

The police: handling the fraud workload

Let us now return to the role of the police in dealing with fraud. The increase in recorded frauds, against a background of fairly constant staffing, has meant that the workload for Fraud Squads has been growing considerably over the past decade. Excluding frauds investigated on behalf of provincial and overseas police forces, and excluding cases that were 'no crimed', the number of *new* investigations into City frauds by the City of London Police rose from 54 in 1981 to 81 in 1985. In 1974, Fraud Squad officers in London had an average of seven cases each to investigate, some of which might take two years to complete. By 1984, this figure had risen to an average of 12 in the Metropolitan and 13.5 in the City of London Police Fraud Squads.

We have examined the views of the police generally – though not Fraud Squad officers in particular – about the seriousness of fraud. Here, we focus upon fraud work within the constraints imposed by overall resources. Total law enforcement is not a feasible goal, even if it were a desirable one. In the real world, decisions have to be taken about how to distribute resources. This necessarily entails setting priorities and assigning some cases less attention than one would like in an ideal world. It would be absurd to suppose that we are capable of generating an objective method of deciding these issues which would lead to results about which there would be certain consensus. Even in crimes such as burglary, which seldom involve any high political considerations, solvability is neither a necessary nor a sufficient criterion for deciding which cases to tackle and which to leave.

As I stated in my preface, 'commercial fraud' is not a homogeneous phenomenon. There are a great variety of frauds, and there is correspondingly great variety in the length and difficulty of the clear-up process. Many frauds, such as those involving credit and cheque cards, are almost self-detecting, in the sense that they are recorded usually only when someone is caught. Others, particularly with an international dimension, may be cleared up readily but be impossible to prosecute because the suspected offender has fled abroad beyond the jurisdiction of the courts. The time taken by enquiries is an important problem for resource allocation (and, also, for investigator satisfaction).

Normally, a fraud case begins with a complaint. Sometimes, a complainant speaking to a detective, usually by phone, will outline the nature of his grievance and, after hearing the summary, the officer will suggest that there are at present insufficient grounds for recording the matter as a crime. The complainant may be given advice to pursue his remedies in the civil courts or, particularly if it is a corporation, to investigate specific issues more thoroughly and to come back when this has been done. In other instances, a preliminary investigation may result in the complaint being written off as 'no crime', often by statements that raise minimal possibilities for their conclusion being queried by superior officers:

> 'The letter would appear to have been sent . . . as a means of putting pressure on [the complainee]. . . . All agree that this is a civil dispute.'

> 'It is believed that a certain amount of "sharp practice" has taken place by the above in running a competition called . . . but there is no evidence of criminal deception.'

'Allegation that [complainee] had obtained supplies . . . and failed to pay for them. The company has now ceased trading. No trace of liquidation, voluntary or otherwise. . . . This is unsatisfactory business transaction.'

Some of these 'no crimes' might have yielded evidence of crime had it been possible to investigate them in depth, but resources do not permit going beyond a *prima facie* judgment by the preliminary investigator. Indeed, the cut-back in Fraud Squad resources has reduced the number of cases in which time was spent on activities ending up with a 'no crime' decision. This brings me to the question: how are fraud investigation priorities decided? In fraud, some cases in the public eye cannot be left uninvestigated, however unpromising a preliminary cost-benefit analysis of policing resources may look. Despite all that has been written about the lack of police accountability in London, while questions are being asked in Parliament, and letters are written to the Prime Minister by senior figures in the City of London, major scandals such as alleged frauds by and against Lloyd's members and Johnson Matthey Bankers cannot be written off, at least officially, without an intensive investigation. (At the end of July 1986, following a major City of London police enquiry into a £1.5 million loan linked to Johnson Matthey Bankers, which tied up a substantial number of officers for several months, the Director of Public Prosecutions advised that 'no criminal activity has been demonstrated and no further enquiry by the police is necessary'. Nevertheless, in March 1987 two people were charged with false accounting and another with corruption.) In this sense, assessing the *political* importance of an allegation is an integral element of resource-allocation decisions in fraud work, as it is in other spheres of policing such as enquiries with a racial dimension.

Unless they are in control of prosecution decisions – and in constitutional theory, the police lost control over prosecutions in 1986 with the introduction of the independent Crown Prosecution Service under the supervision of the Director of Public Prosecutions – rational investigators will try to second-guess the future reactions of prosecutors to the cases they present. In fraud, the policy of the Director of Public Prosecutions is critical here. Much concern has been expressed over the issue of cost constraints in decisions not to prosecute for fraud – not least by the senior executives in my 1985 survey, who overwhelmingly thought that prosecutions where Britain's commercial reputation was at stake should be pursued whatever the cost – and over the policy of not prosecuting foreign fraudsters who use London as a base for their operations against other foreigners. (This too was a policy which aroused strong hostility among senior executives, who thought such people should be prosecuted.)

The maker of a BBC television Panorama programme, Will Hutton, expressed some outrage regarding the lack of priority given to complaints from overseas investors:

> 'For around four years, a German team ran one of Europe's biggest frauds out of some offices in London's Regent Street. It was a simple operation. Advertise in Germany the wonders of commodity investment . . . using glossy videos; wait for the cheques from Germany to come in; cash them and pocket the money . . . a total of £400 million was taken – a figure corroborated by independent sources. The German operators regarded London as an El Dorado. . . . Neither the Department of Trade nor the police seemed to take any notice; at least, not until four years had gone by.'
>
> (*Listener*, 7 November, 1985)

However, setting aside the question of whether the allegations of police lack of interest were well founded, it may be difficult to justify lengthy and expensive investigations – necessarily entailing the non-investigation of other cases – if police are aware that the Director of Public Prosecutions will not sanction prosecution when the report is submitted to him. Even if we believe that such frauds on overseas investors should command high police priority in relation to other sorts of fraud or to other sorts of crime, it is unfair to blame the police for responding rationally to the policy of the Director, though departmental policies do fluctuate – at least officially – over time.

Does cost of a particular investigation affect what is done about the allegation? Not in those domestic frauds where the police have investigative autonomy, except inasmuch as a 'minor fraud' – perhaps under £1 million! – might be shelved if it looks as if it will take up too much scarce manpower. Investigations are influenced more by a combination of perceived offence seriousness – which may be affected by public pressure as well as by the culpability and vulnerability of the victim – and anticipated pay-off in terms of case prosecutability. The task of senior allocating officers is to try to judge which cases are most likely to 'produce a result'. If anything, this produces pressure to neglect complicated enquiries in favour of work on minor cases which generate more 'nickings per man-hour'. In any event, the costing (in terms of investigator-hours) of individual fraud investigations presents considerable difficulties, because only special enquiries such as those involving the Property Services Agency or Johnson Matthey Bankers have officers working on them full-time. Much fraud work – like fraud research! – is spent waiting for people or documents to become available, and it is inefficient not to be able to 'partial out' time. (This is a problem in applying the Association of Chief Police Officers Major Enquiries staffing rules to fraud: it is not like investigating homicide or rape.) Activity time-sheets are possible, but have never been employed in fraud investigations in the past, and they are not always truthful. However, although cost is relatively insignificant in domestic frauds, it can assume greater direct or indirect importance in overseas enquiries, for permission for the necessary funding will be required to travel abroad on an investigation, and unless – Catch-22 – the investigator can show *both* that the fraud is particularly serious *and* that there is a good chance of 'a result', permission will almost certainly not be granted. (If this seems to be a less than clear-cut interpretation, it is because the criteria are less than clear.) Financial restrictions in the budgets of the police and the Director of Public Prosecutions have certainly inhibited the investigation of alleged international frauds. If the Fraud Squad salaries, including overheads, total £5 million and they investigate 500 cases, the average manpower cost per investigation per year is £10,000: lest this seem particularly high, it may be compared with the average sum 'at risk' of over £5 million and with the average trial cost at the London Central Criminal Court of over £100,000 in 1980–81 (Levi, 1984b).

Most detectives are engaged in investigating a number of crimes at the same time (though most of their time is spent on paperwork and at court rather than investigating). However, it may not be appreciated that this is true of fraud work also. Whereas we know what resources are available to Fraud Squads overall – even though it may be impossible to calculate retrospectively the cost of any particular investigation – we do not know how many people-hours investigating frauds are spent by divisional CID, and by non-fraud specialist staff of the Department of Trade and Industry, Customs and Excise, and Inland Revenue. The amount of work that frauds involve varies enormously. Some frauds arrive to the police with extensive preliminary analysis by internal accountants, independent auditors, or by firms such as Carratu International, a major British-based private-sector fraud investigation agency. Others arrive with no documentation other than a complaint that there has been a 'rip-off': frequently, such complainants are told that the case cannot be dealt with until there is more evidence of fraud to go on. Unless there has been a signed admission, even the former may require a great deal of time to be spent taking witness statements and writing reports for prosecution. One further disadvantage in fraud compared with other cases is that victims and witnesses tend to be spread throughout the country, if not overseas, and this consumes further time and manpower as well as travel costs. (Such widespread cases tend to be handled by Fraud Squads because divisional detectives do not have the free time to travel.) Unlike normal divisional detective work, it is more difficult to predict the amount of work that a fraud will require, and this presents problems for case allocation as well as inducing, on occasion, a state of temporal anomie on the part of investigators caught in the time-warp. For supervisors, a side-effect is to make it harder to control the work-rate of their junior staff. If there are few norms for jobs, how can one decide whether they are working fast enough?

Cost and personnel constraints, then, have a more diffuse effect than is often claimed. They lead to a shift of investigation time (and therefore cost) back onto corporate complainants, often prior to a complaint being recorded as a fraud; they may lead to the dropping of an international investigation whose fruitfulness is not transparent at the time a decision has to be made to send an officer overseas; and they have a more general effect on the extent and thoroughness of investigations, by encouraging the police (sometimes under prosecutorial direction) to look at narrow specimen counts rather than the whole picture of the suspected fraud. (An important additional dimension here is the police perception that 'doing a Rolls Royce job' of investigation is unlikely to result in any additional sentence for the perpetrators, because judges will not hand out long prison sentences whatever happens.) Manpower levels also affect the distribution of work between fraud squads and divisional CID: if the former had more personnel, cases that are currently farmed out to divisions to be dealt with (or not) would be handled internally by the fraud squad. As it is, fraud squads tend to deal with the more 'up-market' frauds and public sector corruption, while most of the cases handled on division are 'working-class frauds', such as financial fraud involving cheque and credit cards and Post Office giro cheques.

The resource burden of investigations – most notable in international cases – is a point repeatedly emphasized not only in my interviews with police officers but also in the Annual Reports of successive Commissioners of the Metropolitan Police (Home Office, 1976:16; 1983:53; 1985b:99; 1986a:45–6) and of the City of London Police (1986:14). This crisis of international fraud policing was one reason for the formation of the Fraud Trials Committee (1986) and of a lightly-staffed (currently there are *two* personnel) but extremely dedicated fraud investigation section of the Commonwealth Secretariat, based in London, which was set up in response to concerns expressed by the Commonwealth Law Ministers at their 1978 and 1980 meetings.

Coping with a rising tide of major fraud cases is a world-wide problem for the police. For example – and this applies also to the series of bank frauds investigated by the Hong Kong Independent Commission Against Corruption in 1987 – in July 1985, the Director of Public Prosecutions for Hong Kong complained about the impossible burden upon the Commercial Crimes Bureau there. He stated that no other country has ever had to handle so many and such large cases, and that whereas other countries would have up to 20 investigators on each case, the most Hong Kong could afford was 3, and sometimes only 1. This led to concentration on the key elements in the case, for otherwise it would take ten years to follow up all the lines of enquiry. The difficulties referred to are partly a reflection of the low visibility of fraud and of restrictive rules regarding police access to commercial records of activities that take place behind closed doors. However, they are related also to levels of policing resources – skills and manpower – that are allocated to the task.

The mid-1980s saw a gradual but marked increase in the professionalism with which the investigation and prosecution of fraud was conducted, a process that was given impetus by the criticisms in the Roskill Report (Fraud Trials Committee, 1986). In 1985, the method of setting up *ad hoc* task forces of lawyers and police to deal with individual frauds – which itself had originated only with the enquiry into the corrupt architect John Poulson in the early 1970s – was transformed into the Fraud Investigation Group (FIG). However, this much-trumpeted development was more cosmetic than substantive: police and non-police investigators still changed from case to case; the major difference was in the setting aside of the Director of Public Prosecution's staff to deal with fraud. In mid-1986, there were three specialist divisions of four lawyers, headed by an Assistant Director of Public Prosecutions, each with a back-up staff of accountants and secretaries. There were two FIG divisions, and within the general division, a further division which deals with smaller frauds. During 1985, the Fraud Investigation Group experienced a tripling in its workload: the number of fraud cases reported to the Director rose from 304 in 1983 to 408 in 1984 to 593 in 1985. In 1985–86, each professional officer in the three divisions had to deal with an average of 38 active serious cases: an increase from the original 30 cases-per-officer. Given the tremendous size of the files, it is self-evident that the number of personnel is very small. Prior to 1986, when an increase of 9 staff was approved (but, due to overspending by the Crown Prosecution Service, was not implemented!) there were just 15 lawyers and 3 accountants working for FIG. What this reveals is the depth of the problems involved in generating substantial organizational change without a major political push. Whether the investigative-cum-prosecution agency, the Serious Fraud Office, proposed in the Criminal Justice Bill (1986) will enable the war on fraud to be waged more effectively is a matter to be considered in the final chapter.

The 'consumer perspective': executives' views about the police

In a free market economy, consumer wants and satisfaction are supposed to determine the provision of services. Much research has been conducted into public attitides to and satisfaction with the police generally, though with one major exception (Jones and Levi, 1983a), there has been an unfortunate tendency to concentrate upon 'problem areas' of the inner city (Kinsey, 1985; Policy Studies Institute, 1983; Jones, MacLean and Young, 1986). However, nothing is known about public satisfaction with the investigation of fraud. Certainly, the cynicism of the public regarding the toughness with which businesspeople are dealt with by the law appears to be high. But as I observed in Chapters 1 and 2, it is the relatively wealthy who are the principal victims of non-consumer frauds: in 1985, banks, building societies, and insurance companies accounted for over 60 per cent of the costs of frauds dealt with by Fraud Squads outside London.

The study of senior executives' attitudes (Levi, 1986a) does throw some interesting light upon the levels of satisfaction among one sector of possible repeat victims and complainants, though their attitudes may not be typical: for one thing, people who are older and of higher social standing may be less likely than others to have a negative attitude towards the police generally, and such general attitudes may colour perceptions of police efficiency as well as the willingness to express negative views. On the other hand, senior executives in the private sector may have higher expectations of the police and of service personnel generally, so that may increase their annoyance when they encounter what they perceive to be a stonewalling or incompetent response. (Those interested in the ideology of crime control may want to think through two contradictory elements here: on the one hand, criminal law and its enforcement is thought to be directed mainly at serving the powerful – such as business executives who *want* the police to intervene – while on the other, it may be legitimated – not least in the eyes of the police themselves – by being aimed at assisting weak individuals, which corporate complainants certainly are not, so that would imply that the victims of mail-order type frauds would receive greater policing preference from Fraud Squads than would less 'deserving' victims. In my experience, the 'populist' perspective generally triumphs, though high politics may incline the police towards investigating frauds and corruption that are in the public eye – i.e. in media and politicians' eyes – more than the deserts of the victims might merit.)

The policing of fraud was an issue upon which there was considerable divergence of opinion among the seventy-four respondents. They were not asked if they had ever had any negative contacts with the police in a personal context, but research findings would lead one to expect general support for the police among this social group. The questions asked about policing were deliberately specific, so as to avoid vague expressions of confidence. In particular, since so much concern has been expressed about the policing of large frauds, a moderately substantial sum was selected as the baseline. When asked how much confidence they had that if they were to report to the police a fraud involving over £50,000, it would be dealt with *by them* in a competent manner, no-one expressed very little confidence and only 12.7 per cent expressed little confidence. However, at the other extreme, only 7.3 per cent had a great deal of confidence. Forty per cent had a lot of confidence and 38.2 per cent had neither a lot nor a little confidence. So although it is possible – particularly in the light of bad publicity for fraud policing subsequent to (but not caused by!) the survey – that this confidence might be lower in relation to some of the mammoth City frauds, just under half were positive in their attitudes towards the competence of the police in handling a major fraud. Contact with the police in this sphere did not produce very different responses: of the 12 people whose companies had actually reported to the police a fraud involving over £50,000, 2 expressed a great deal of confidence; 5 a lot of confidence; and 5 neither a lot nor a little confidence in police competence.

Considerably less confidence was expressed in the competence of the Department of Trade and Industry to deal with a fraud of the same size. There were 17 'don't knows', possibly reflecting the low profile of that Department and the fact that only 5 respondents had actually reported any fraud to it. However, of those asked no-one had a great deal of confidence; only 12.7 per cent had a lot; 38.2 per cent had neither a lot nor a little; 14.3 per cent expressed little confidence; and 3.6 per cent very little confidence. Perhaps the only positive feature is that despite the fact that the Department of Trade and Industry took no action in 3 out of the 5 cases reported to it, those who had reported did not express any abnormally low degree of confidence. In the interviews, one executive stated that the Department of Trade and Industry's resources and attitude to deal with fraud were 'pitiful and disgraceful' and cited his experience in reporting liquidation fraud. He believed that there was a lack of will in the Department to engage with the problem of fraud. Less extreme but allied sentiments were expressed by a senior provincial stockbroker, who also had sought to press a prosecution upon the Department of Trade and Industry.

A different aspect of attitudes towards the police is support for extra police powers and extra personnel. In principle, someone might regard the police as incompetent but regard that as a good thing. (This, indeed, appears to be the view of some advocates of extra police accountability!) Such a person would presumably not support measures that would improve the efficiency of police in the control of fraud. It is interesting, then, that in response to the proposition 'The police have too little power to investigate financial records prior to charge', less than one-quarter felt that the police did *not* have too little investigative power prior to charge. (This example was chosen deliberately because one might anticipate much greater commercial opposition to pre-charge than to post-charge powers, and because some radical critics claim that businesspeople want to keep the police out of commercial records, for fear that they discover too much.) There was also strong support for specialization among the police: 42.9 per cent strongly disagreed that fraud investigators should be ordinary trained detectives, not specialists; 48.2 per cent disagreed; 5.4 per cent were neutral; and 1.8 per cent agreed (with 1.8 per cent 'don't knows').

On manpower levels, only 3 people disagreed with the proposition that there should be a considerable expansion in the number of non-tax fraud investigators. Twelve-and-a-half per cent strongly agreed; 44.6 per cent agreed; and 23.2 per cent were neutral; the remainder being 'don't knows'. Again, the phrase 'very considerable' was employed to test the strength of support. (It should be noted that the research was conducted prior to the high points of media and political interest in policing fraud. It seems doubtful that respondents would have known that there was a reduction of 19 in Metropolitan Police Fraud Squad personnel in 1983.) The need for an increased level of staffing in Fraud Squads was an issue upon which strong views were expressed by some interviewees and in the 'general comments' section at the end of the questionnaire. *In short, there was a fairly high degree of support for increased levels of policing fraud; for specialization by police in fraud work; and for quite intrusive pre-charge police powers of access to financial records.*

On the interesting issue of overall policing priorities, the executives were asked to rank seven types of crime in order of preference. Some of these items were replicated from the crime seriousness section, to ascertain whether the ranking of policing priorities corresponded with that for crime seriousness. On a 1–7 scale, where 1 was the highest priority and 7 the lowest, the averages and ranks were as set out in *Table 16*:

Although theoretically, these priority rankings cannot be treated as interval-level data, it is noteworthy that there are large gaps in average rankings between the first three offences – mugging, domestic burglary, and mail-order fraud – and between the sixth and seventh offences – long-firm fraud and VAT fraud. Moreover, despite the preamble to the question which alerted respondents to the fact that they might want to treat police priority rankings differently from crime seriousness judgments, the two sets of responses are identical in their rank ordering of offences. The descriptions of offences in the two questions were slightly different, but where they were roughly in common, the rankings were in the following order: mugging, domestic burglary, mail-order

Table 16   *Executives' rankings of police priorities*

type of crime	rank	average ranking
muggings	1	1.39
(unarmed) domestic burglary	2	3.32
setting up a phoney mail-order firm to get money from a large number of private individuals without supplying goods	3	4.11
(unarmed) commercial burglary	4=	4.30
frauds that damage Britain's reputation as a respectable market (e.g. international insurance, banking, or investment frauds)	4=	4.31
setting up phoney businesses to get large quantities of goods from manufacturers without intending to pay for them	6	4.87
under-declaring large sums of VAT payable	7	5.79

Source: Levi (1986a)

fraud, and tax fraud (*see Table 11*). A question about income-tax rather than VAT fraud was asked in the crime seriousness section, to provide comparability with the 1984 British Crime Survey, so the tax fraud questions in the sections on seriousness and policing priorities may not be strictly comparable.

It is interesting to note the high priority given to mail-order fraud, from which executives are much less likely to suffer compared with commercial burglary or long-firm (insolvency) fraud. Narrow self-interest, then, does not seem to apply either to policing priority judgments or to judgments about the seriousness of different crimes. Moreover, the priority that executives wanted attached to some fraud offences was very high – higher than the burglary of commercial premises. To illustrate further the distribution of views within the sample, *Table 17* sets out the raw scores for the rankings of police priorities. It may be observed that frauds that damage Britain's reputation attract more extreme views than does commercial burglary, where opinions are clustered more around the mean.

Summary

This chapter has sought to throw some light upon an important area of police work that has been neglected by researchers and police alike. The overall paucity of policing resources devoted to fraud compared with its

Table 17 *Executives' raw scores in ranking police priorities*

type of offence	number given to each rank, N=56						
	1	*2*	*3*	*4*	*5*	*6*	*7*
mugging	44	6	1	2	1	1	0
domestic burglary	2	25	10	5	3	8	3
mail-order fraud	2	9	8	15	7	14	1
commercial burglary	1	4	18	10	7	9	7
frauds that damage Britain's reputation	5	9	6	8	5	15	7
long-firm fraud	0	3	9	8	17	10	9
VAT fraud	0	0	3	8	12	8	25

Source: Levi (1986a)

cost and public seriousness ratings has been attributed principally to the lack of organized public pressure for more fraud policing and the traditionalism of police perceptions of 'real crime'. Given limited resources, the police normally do not adopt a proactive intelligence-gathering strategy and they ration their priorities in relation to judgments about what enquiries are likely to lead to successful prosecution and the sorts of pressures they experience from senior officers, the public, and the media. The general consensus is that frauds upon 'the public' are the most serious types of fraud, but these may be the object of less high-profile 'public pressure' for clear-up than sensational and 'complex' City frauds.

6 The prosecution and trial of commercial fraud

Ever since Sutherland's pioneering work (1983), much emphasis has been laid upon the low prosecution rate of white-collar offences. All the 'business regulation' literature demonstrates that prosecution is the control method of the last resort, selected generally after other possibilities are exhausted or when some major symbolic point can be made only by using the criminal process. Shapiro's (1983) study of SEC observes that despite its reputation for being primarily a prosecutorial agency, less than half of its investigations result in legal proceedings and of these, only a quarter are criminal in nature. Mann's (1985) study of the preparation of defence cases against white-collar crime allegations reveals the lengthy processes of what Galanter (1985) has termed 'litigotiation' between defence and regulatory personnel at a variety of stages, from front-line investigators, through those who take the decision to refer an investigation to agency prosecutors, to those who actually take the decision to prosecute.

At each stage, depending on the evidence they believe the agency possesses – which in turn reflects defence actions in seeking to limit prosecution access to damaging documentation or witnesses – the defence counsel and their batteries of accountants and subsidiary personnel will seek to get the investigators/prosecutors to define the case either as 'no crime' or as a relatively minor violation that, without damage to the effectiveness of the regulatory agency or to public morality, could be disposed of by means other than prosecution. Sometimes, defence arguments rely upon implicit notions of resource prioritization within the regulatory agency: as I observed in the last chapter, it is more expensive in resource terms to take a case to prosecution than to deal with it informally by administrative penalties. If they cannot deny culpability altogether, counsel therefore argue that this case is not a particularly grave example of its general class of violations. Thus, many against whom there is a strong *prima facie* case of fraud negotiate their way out of the criminal justice process. The administrative penalties may be financially expensive, but they involve less publicity, less (if any) stigma, and no chances of imprisonment. (See also analogous observations by Coleman, 1985b and by Green, Moore, and

Wasserstein, 1972, on anti-trust delays, in the hope that so many prosecutorial resources will be consumed that the agency gives up, or that changes in political leadership will lead to the case being dropped or modified.)

This sort of negotiation between suspects and regulators does occur in Britain, though as far as I know, it is on a much more minor scale than in the United States. This is partly because the resources of regulatory agencies are so much lower to begin with, and therefore the chances of initial detection are negligible. However, it is also partly because administrative law is a less developed part of the regulatory process in Britain. Formal and informal administrative penalties are certainly the dominant method of disposal in tax cases (Keith Committee, 1983), except (1) where organized criminals – in the sense of people with underworld connections – are involved, or (2) where, as in the case of prominent tax-avoidance counsellors who threatened the general effectiveness of corporate taxation during the 1970s (Tutt, 1985), investigation and prosecution are undertaken (or, in these cases, are intended to be undertaken) for symbolic, general deterrent purposes. But except in the occasional case, such as the multi-million pound alleged gaming fraud in which on payment of a large compounded fine and agreement by the defence to publication of the settlement, HM Customs and Excise withdrew a criminal prosecution on the eve of its opening – 'Operation Nudger', 1981 – I am not aware of many Mann-type manoeuvres over the *prosecution* of tax frauds in Britain.

Indeed, Enquiry Branch officials generally decide broadly from the outset whether the case they are dealing with is to be taken along the criminal prosecution or settlement route. The taxpayer is normally interviewed by two members of the Branch who explain the nature of their work in outline. Before they put any questions to the taxpayer, they generally issue what is known as 'the Hansard Extract', a Parliamentary Question response (from 1944!) which sets out the Revenue's policy on prosecution in fraud cases. Although taxpayers are informed that s.105 of the Taxes Management Act (1970) does not preclude the admissibility in criminal proceedings of evidence given after they have been shown the Hansard Extract, it is the Board of the Inland Revenue's practice to be influenced by full disclosure. (In fact, it is the invariable practice that no criminal prosecution will be undertaken if the taxpayer subsequently makes a full and complete disclosure within the time available, and offers full co-operation.) Conversely, though he does not know precisely what the risk of prosecution is or what the Revenue already know, the taxpayer is led to understand that prosecution is very much *more* likely if, having been given the opportunity to 'make a clean breast of it', he prevaricates or misleads them. (In some instances, the taxpayer may be referred to particular accountants – usually the larger firms – who are considered honest and competent enough to re-arrange his tax affairs.) These principles do not require the Revenue to be bound by a promise made under false assumptions, as when it comes to learn about a taxpayer's undisclosed activities after it has written to the taxpayer telling him that it does not propose to inquire further into his affairs: see *Preston v. IRC* [1985] 2 All E.R. 327, HL. Normally, interviews take place at the commercial premises of the taxpayer or of his professional adviser, and the taxpayer is informed in advance of the questions that are to be put. Experienced accountants – often former Inspectors of Taxes who have left the Inland Revenue for more lucrative positions in the private sector – will not allow interviews with their clients where the 'Hansard warning' has not been given or even where questions have not been put in advance. The pressure to be cost-effective in the use of resources encourages settlement by the Revenue for less than is owed, so that they can move on to another case.

Much of the negotiation in tax cases arises in the context of assessments of how much tax is payable (and how much the Revenue will settle for) rather than in the context of criminal investigation. However, to observe this is not to state that there is no *potential* for 'buying out of prosecution' in tax cases. The evidentiary standard for compounding is the criminal one, as may be supported by the fact that all of the 44 persons who rejected offers by Customs and Excise in 1981–82 to settle were successfully prosecuted. The Keith Committee made the following observations about prosecution criteria:

> 'Customs and Excise told us that as respects VAT fraud . . . the balance of advantage lay in having some prosecutions for the serious offences, in order that the public might understand what serious VAT fraud could be. . . . Unless there were aggravating circumstances, where the alleged culpable arrears of tax were less than £10,000 the Department tended to regard the offer of a compounded settlement as the first option; above that figure the Department regarded prosecution as a first option. . . . We note that in 1981/2 as many as two thirds of VAT fraud offence cases with culpable arrears greater than £10,000 were in fact compounded, and of the 10 cases with culpable arrears in excess of £100,000 each, as many as five were compounded.'

(Keith Committee, 1983:350)

This was attributed largely to the pressure of investigatory resources, which also inhibits investigation, as mentioned in the previous chapter. In 1984–85, 445 cases were settled by compounding compared with 176 prosecutions for fraudulent evasion of VAT. In 1985–86, prosecutions were stepped up to 238, partly reflecting the view that more general deterrence was needed. Although no mention of this was made in the

Keith Committee report, I understand that the cost of prosecutions is also a significant factor: in some cases, an extra 'vote' of funds has had to be obtained from the Treasury because the money to pay for tax prosecutions has run out!

The Inland Revenue do not have the power to compound formally as an alternative to prosecution, though settlement serves a similar function. Within the past decade, the peak year for the number of persons prosecuted occurred in 1976–77, when there were 538 prosecutions. Since then, there has been a marked drop: in 1981–82, there were 385 prosecutions (of which there were 30 acquittals); in 1982–83, 345 prosecutions (with 11 acquittals); in 1983–84, 244 prosecutions (with 21 acquittals); and in 1984–85, 332 prosecutions (with 6 acquittals). In each year, the greater part of these prosecutions have been against builders who obtain exemption certificates from having their tax deducted at source and who subsequently 'fail' to pay the Inland Revenue, and for theft of payable orders and giro cheques: hardly the kinds of frauds committed by high-status professionals or businesspeople. The latter are more likely to be charged for making false claims: in 1984–85, there were 21 prosecutions (with 1 acquittal) for furnishing false accounts or returns of income, and 4 prosecutions for false claims to personal allowances, deductions for expenses, and repayments. The highest combined total for these categories in the past decade was 61 prosecutions (with 6 acquittals) in 1978–79.

We may note the fact that this sort of attrition rate occurs also in criminal tax investigations in the United States, and that there are strong variations over time in the number of cases initiated by the Internal Revenue Service there. In any given year, about one-third of cases initiated by the Criminal Investigation Department are recommended for prosecution. Of these, between 10 per cent and 50 per cent are not proceeded with because the Office of Chief Counsel states that they are 'unwarranted'. The net result is that of 9035 investigations initiated in 1976, 2037 were prosecuted; of 9780 investigations in 1979 (the peak year), 2515 were prosecuted; and of 6498 investigations in 1982, 1680 were prosecuted (Administrative Office, 1984).

The above are cases of fraud which the state has learned about, whether proactively or reactively. However, prosecutions are dependent upon the receipt of information or complaints, and to the extent that commercial firms and SROs deal with 'fraud' informally or through their formal disciplinary tribunals, it could be argued that offenders *can* buy their way out of prosecution. The extent to which this is so may depend upon how those who run schemes which indemnify investors or travellers against default see their task. In the period 1952–86, the Stock Exchange Compensation Fund paid out £7 million, recovering two-thirds from the estates of defaulters. Lloyd's, too, particularly since its powers (including qualified privilege against being sued in pursuit of regulatory action) were enhanced by the Lloyd's Act (1982), has been active in the disciplinary field, as we shall see in Chapter 7. In strict law, disciplinary and criminal proceedings are complementary, not mutually exclusive, but inasmuch as retribution may be satisfied by disciplinary sanctions (and the government is determined to minimize costs), it is arguable that members may have negotiated their way out of prosecution. In a different way, this may also be true of those who are required to make personal contributions to the debts of their company under the 'wrongful trading' provisions of s.214 of the Insolvency Act (1986). Ironically, in the future, the pressure on defendants to settle by paying damages to the plaintiffs may diminish, as conviction becomes less salient to the definition of the defendant as being *not* a 'fit and proper person', and thus to his or her being banned from the insurance or securities industries, or to being disqualified from the management of a company under s.6–11 of the Company Directors Disqualification Act (1986).

As we have seen, the criminal justice system is a loose-coupled set of organizations in which policies and resources of each feed back into the sorts of decisions that are made elsewhere, though not necessarily in a manner that produces a coherent set of control practices. The prosecution process, for example, affects and is affected by policing activities. Personnel and political changes can have a powerful effect: prior to 1985, there had been only 11 criminal prosecutions for insider dealing in New York; between the end of 1984 and mid-1986, there were 39. The difference was the aggressive approach taken on this issue by the new publicity-hungry US Attorney for Manhattan (and Republican Party political hopeful), Rudolph Giuliani. During the five years from 1981 to 1986 that John Shad headed SEC, it brought 90 actions: well over half the total number since it was set up during the New Deal to enforce the Securities Exchange Act (1934). (Though there were no prosecutions for insider dealing between 1981 and 1986, until an anonymous informant 'grassed' on Dennis Levine from Venezuela, leading to the snowballing of cases.) However, despite governmental concern to be seen to be doing something about fraud in the City of London and a (relative) rash of Department of Trade and Industry investigations at the close of 1986 which followed closely upon information provided by financier Ivan Boesky to SEC, there were no corresponding personal/political changes that generated any significant boom in upperworld prosecutions in England up to 1987.

Although the prosecution system in England and Wales adopted in 1986 roughly the system that has existed for a long time in Scotland

(Moody and Tombs, 1982), and all 'police prosecutions' are now undertaken by the Crown Prosecution Service under the direction of the Director of Public Prosecutions, there is no such thing as an overall prosecution body in England and Wales. Except for the large and complex cases within the remit of the Serious Fraud Office announced in the Criminal Justice Bill (1986), the regulatory agencies will continue to prosecute their own cases. This is partly because in its review of the fairness of the prosecution system, the Royal Commission on Criminal Procedure (1981) chose not to grasp the nettle of the wide disparities between the non-police agencies' prosecution policies. The Commission observed that to place non-police prosecutions under the aegis of the Crown Prosecutor would be impractical (1) because there were many more such prosecutions than were commonly supposed, raising resource implications, and (2) because there were a lot of those agencies and they operated differently. With an impressive mixture of pragmatism and conceptual inadequacy, the Report went on to observe:

> 'The very extent and nature of this variation might be thought to make the case for bringing some measure of uniformity. . . . That is particularly so if the standards that we have used in discussing police prosecutions are applied to prosecutions by other agencies. This variation does not, however, attract much specific criticism from our witnesses. Such as there is focuses on the disparity of policy between agencies; the zeal with which social security frauds are prosecuted being contrasted with the relatively limited extent to which income tax defaulters are prosecuted. That is a good example of different agencies having different functions and objectives; and it does raise the question of whether it is proper to use the criminal process to enforce revenue and regulatory laws which are the typical province of most of these non-police agencies. With the current pressure of criminal business on the courts this is surely a matter to which the Government should be giving attention.'
>
> (Royal Commission on Criminal Procedure, 1981:159)

Whether or not one agrees with the policy recommendations, the dismal level of reasoning in this paragraph is fairly self-evident (except, presumably, to those who wrote it). Why the fact that different agencies see themselves as having different functions and objectives should make them immune to critical argument may strike the outsider as rather puzzling: 'is' does not imply 'ought to be'! However, suffice it to observe that with the exception of the Keith Committee's (1983) proposals regarding policy harmonization between the Inland Revenue and HM Customs and Excise, there was no subsequent pressure either to make the prosecution policies of the non-police agencies more consistent or to subsume them under the aegis of the Crown Prosecution Service. (For confirmation of this point, see Samuels, 1986.)

All non-police agencies – whether they regulate the rich or the poor –

exercise more discretion than the police in *not* prosecuting cases of which there is *prima facie* evidence of crime, but the extent to which they do use prosecution varies between agencies and over time. The Health and Safety Executive have adopted a more active prosecution stance during the 1980s compared with earlier periods (for the latter, see Carson, 1970). But although convictions for indictable health and safety offences have increased from 555 in 1980 to 1036 in 1984, prosecutions have remained fairly static: there were 1301 in 1981 and 1267 in 1984. (The difference *may* be explicable in terms of lesser willingness to abandon the prosecution when – as often happens – the company rectifies the fault virtually on the eve of the case.) However, in addition to informal advice and warnings, there were roughly three cases of non-prosecutorial action – such as improvement and prohibition notices, and infraction letters – for every prosecution in 1985.

Over the same period – though on grounds of internal cost-effectiveness rather than moral principle or the desire to be more consistent with the Revenue departments – Supplementary Benefit welfare fraud prosecutions by the Department of Health and Social Security (DHSS) have dropped from 20,105 in 1980–81 to 9765 in 1985–86. In 1984–85, the DHSS considered 50,000 cases for prosecution and took some 7000 of these to court (with a 98 per cent conviction rate). Combining prosecutions for welfare fraud by the DHSS, the police, the Department of Employment, and the Post Office (who handle benefit payments made via the Giro system), the total in 1984–85 was 12,500: over 30 times the number of fraud prosecutions undertaken by the Inland Revenue and HM Customs and Excise combined. In the majority of cases of suspected welfare fraud, the DHSS prefers simply to cut off welfare payments, leaving it to the claimant to pursue any grievance through the complaints procedures or through intervention by social workers or by unofficial claimants unions. (This is equally the practice in relation to alleged welfare fraud in the United States: see Gardiner and Lyman, 1985.) Naturally, this raises questions of fairness in the use of administrative discretion, particularly where welfare claimants do not have the benefit of expert and/or professional advice: no Legal Aid is available for appeals against the termination of benefit. It is also not without interest that in late 1984, the DHSS ceased prosecuting *employers* who had gone into personal or corporate bankruptcy and had failed to pay on to the DHSS the National Insurance contributions that they had deducted from their employees. Prosecutions for this offence dropped from a peak of 1971 in 1983–84 to 1326 in 1984–85, and totalled 13 in 1985–86. (I have no information on whether this was replaced by civil proceedings for debt recovery, but this seems unlikely.)

Although breakdowns by social class are not given in the official criminal statistics reports, it is evident that the great majority of offenders taken to court are from the working class or the *lumpen-proletariat*. This is less true of those convicted in US District Courts, where almost one in three are convicted of fraud and other 'white-collar' crimes: however, that is largely an artefact of the coverage of federal statutes, most 'lower-class' crimes being dealt with in local or state courts. In any event, it is somewhat specious to treat the raw numbers prosecuted as an index of social favouritism, as Reiman (1984) does, because there are comparatively few people in senior positions, and thus fewer 'at risk' of prosecution for white-collar compared with 'common' crimes. Although it is impossible to ascertain whether those involved in 'bank embezzlement' or even 'securities and exchange' offences were senior executives or employees, it is noteworthy that there were few prosecutions under 'white-collar statutes': 23 for securities and exchange violations; 180 for anti-trust violations; and 97 under the Food and Drug Act in 1983. Even though it is misleading to compare *federal* 'common crimes' with white-collar ones, it is worth examining federal prosecutions in the latter category, for they give a breakdown of the types of violation that are prosecuted:

Table 18   *Prosecutions in US District Courts, 1983*

type of fraud	convictions	prosecutions
bank embezzlement	1131	1200
postal embezzlement	228	265
other embezzlement	602	672
income-tax fraud	1009	1163
lending institution fraud	498	598
postal fraud	1165	1756
veterans and allotments	17	21
securities and exchange	20	23
social security	273	315
false personation	37	46
nationality laws	124	140
passport fraud	78	93
false claims and statements	928	1143
other frauds	1449	1731
transport forged securities	250	295
postal forgery	167	211
other forgery	1174	1354
counterfeiting	774	892
bribery	160	192
anti-trust violations	144	180
Food and Drug Act	84	97

Source: Administrative Office (1984: 340–41)

This leads us to the question, is there a *class* bias in the prosecution process? Certainly, even setting aside police prosecutions – which primarily affect working-class juveniles and adults – there are far fewer prosecutions by non-police agencies which deal with offences committed by businesspeople than by those which handle matters such as non-payment of television licences and social-security fraud which are committed by the poor. Even within the DHSS, there is a much greater readiness to prosecute Supplementary Benefit frauds than the non-payment of National Insurance by employers (Lidstone, Hogg, and Sutcliffe, 1980; Smith, 1985; Uglow, 1984). However, to the extent that we conceive of 'class bias' as *intentional* discrimination against one group and in favour of another, the case remains to be made out: politicians undoubtedly can affect the prosecution process, partly by making decisions such as the increase in social-security fraud investigators by 1000 at a time in the early 1980s when the Health and Safety Executive and the tax authorities were being cut back. (Politicians can also increase commercial fraud regulation resources, as we saw in the last chapter, though even with the establishment of the Serious Fraud Office in 1987, this has been done at a comparatively modest level.) But where is the Leviathan that is co-ordinating class prosecution policy from on high? If, on the other hand, we are judging 'bias' not – as ordinary parlance would have it – by intent, but rather by *consequences*, the allegation of 'structural bias' is considerably more convincing.

Let us pursue this theme of disadvantage rather than discrimination. One of the reasons why social security fraudsters fare so badly – and we may also see this in the way they are sentenced – is that they have so few resources to bargain with and they are cursed with the social image (reinforced by the media) of people who contribute nothing to society. (Except, perhaps, to reduce the wage-bargaining power of those in work.) By contrast, employers are people who 'create jobs', whose prosecution might damage business, or closing down their places of work on health and safety grounds might not only hurt them but also those who work for them and even the national economy and balance of payments. Given that it is seldom the fault of the unemployed that they are not factory-owners, the *result* is unfair, but there is a pragmatic rationality in the decision-making process.

Instead of simply labelling the criminal justice process as discriminatory, it seems more enlightening to examine the way in which these results emanate from the regulatory agency philosophies and concrete control practices which tend (1) to be concerned with advising and encouraging businesspeople to adopt 'best practice' consistent with the economic realities as perceived by the regulators at any given moment in time, and (2) to entail the view that regulatory offences are not 'real' crimes. The same threads that run through policing, as discussed in Chapter 5, run also through the prosecution process. I shall merely outline the state of the non-police prosecution process in the mid-1980s as it relates to 'crimes of the powerful'. (For further discussion of policing by non-police agencies, see Hawkins, 1984; Hutter, 1986; Leigh, 1980; Levi, 1982, 1984a; Sanders, 1985; Smith, 1985; and Uglow, 1984.)

Most regulatory agencies take few of the 'offenders' they 'catch' to court, and they prosecute very few of the violations they detect that are committed even by those they *do* prosecute. For example, in 1985, 1534 convictions were obtained in England and Wales for health and safety at work violations: one third of the number of improvement and prohibition notices issued (Health and Safety Executive, 1986). The Health and Safety Executive (1985, p.28) observe that the policy is 'to prosecute where flagrant or repeated breaches of the law occur'. Sometimes, prosecutions are undertaken not because the offences are serious nor even because the offender has been 'defiant' in attitude towards regulations, but rather because there has been an accident that places the violation in the public eye (Richardson, Ogus, and Burrows, 1983). It should be emphasized that unlike the police, regulatory agencies see prosecution as an indication of their own failure. The regulatory perspective is almost a Fabian one of gradual improvement of standards, with the reluctant use of graduated sanctions for the recalcitrant commercial child. Sometimes, the child's conduct is so naughty that he or she has to be kept out of circulation, but this may be attempted by the use of extra-criminal sanctions (i.e. sanctions that may be imposed following conviction, but may also be imposed in the absence of criminal court proceedings), such as banning from conducting business under the Company Directors Disqualification Act (1986) or under the Fair Trading Act (1973): these are discussed in Chapters 7 and 8. Thus, the low number of prosecutions may not satisfy our retributive or fairness criteria but neither does it mean that nothing has been done about offenders.

There are differences in the sanctions available to different regulatory agencies. Those agencies such as the Department of Trade and Industry that have a joint fraud/business regulatory function generally opt to prosecute for easy-to-prove regulatory breaches rather than for more emotive frauds which are more likely to be contested. Whereas to the Health and Safety Executive, the alternative to prosecuting or closing down factories owned by unco-operative management may be doing nothing, the Revenue departments may take the money and run rather than prosecute. Which is more fair (or less unfair) compared with the policing of 'ordinary' crime: to extract a large civil administrative penalty from a tax evader, or to prosecute him and obtain a lesser penalty from the judge or magistrate? If one examines closely the sentencing data in the Keith Committee Report (1983), that is the *realpolitik*. Nevertheless, there are aspects of revenue policy and resources that are puzzling even within this purely financial logic: in July 1986, Customs and Excise officials argued for the recruitment of an extra 1700 staff. They claimed that there is £275 million owed in long-term outstanding debts from known traders who are not pursued because of limited staff resources and that if the extra staff were recruited, there would be savings to the Exchequer of £170 million *net* of staff costs. If the cost-benefit analysis is anywhere near correct, one must ask why the additional manpower is not approved by the Government? After all, in October 1986, the Government approved an increase of 500 social-security fraud investigators, justifying this with the assertion that in the previous two years, extra staff had saved £150 million in fraud.

The Office of Fair Trading

As with other regulatory bodies (including the police), much of the work of the Office of Fair Trading comprises advice of one kind or another, and may not be identified by any formal enforcement steps at all. It is thus improper to use these tabulations as the *sole* measures of performance. Bearing this in mind, there is no clear relationship between the number of complaints received against any particular business sector (such as food and drink) and the number of prosecutions instituted. In the UK, in 1983–84, there were 5292 convictions for offences of unfair trading, including the safety of goods. This dropped to 4835 in 1984–85. (In the following, the 1983–84 figures are in brackets.) The 1984–85 figures comprised 1301 (1491) convictions for false descriptions of goods, 86 (104) convictions for false price claimed, and 129 (129) convictions for false statements about services under the Trades Descriptions Acts. There were also 40 (49) convictions for offences involving Restrictions on Statements Orders and 96 (128) convictions for violations of Business Advertisements (Disclosure) Orders, contrary to the Fair Trading Act (1973). There were 73 (75) convictions for offences against the Consumer Credit Act (1974); 352 (347) for Weights and Measures Act violations; 1500 (1720) for Food and Drugs Acts violations; 2 (2) for offences against the Estate Agents Act (1979); 215 (205) for infringements of regulations under the Consumer Protection and Consumer Safety Acts; and 1020 (1402) convictions under other legislation enforced by Trading Standards and Environmental Health Departments.

In 1985, Trading Standards and Consumer Protection departments of local authorities in the UK administered 3201 oral and 1648 written warnings under the Consumer Credit Act (1974). (The latter figure doubled from the previous year.) Under that Act, 4 cases involving 8 defendants were prosecuted for giving false information to the Director-General of Fair Trading (s.7). Twenty-five cases involving 44 defendants were prosecuted under s.39(1) for unlicensed trading; 7 cases involving 8 people were prosecuted under s.39(2) for trading under a name not specified in the licence; and 2 cases involving 2 people were prosecuted under s.39(3) for failure to notify the Director-General of changes in particulars on the Public Register. There were 41 cases involving 69 defendants for breaches of credit advertisements and quotations; 2 cases involving 3 people for canvassing debtor-credit agreements off trade premises; 2 cases involving 3 defendants for soliciting entry into a debtor-creditor agreement; and one case of giving an unsolicited credit-token. (Figures for the previous year were substantially similar.) Not a particularly vast regulatory haul!

Department of Trade and Industry

The Department obtained 4267 convictions under the Companies Acts in 1985 (compared with 2733 in 1984). In 2616 more cases (over a third of the total) prosecutions – mainly for failure to forward an annual return or to deliver accounts – were withdrawn, normally because the company had complied with the rule after the issue of a summons. (This is the equivalent of not prosecuting motorists who rectify faults in their cars, or television licence dodgers who agree to take out licenses when caught: for reasons of economy, these measures too have become more widely adopted in Britain in the mid-1980s.) Almost all of these convictions were for regulatory rather than fraud offences. For example, there were only 10 convictions for fraudulent trading and 2 for frauds by officers of a company in liquidation. (There were also 3 acquittals for fraudulent trading.) By contrast, there were 2449 convictions for failure to deliver accounts; 17,327 for failure to forward an annual return; 57 for failure to keep accounting records; 10 for undischarged bankrupts acting as director or concerned in the management of a company; and 3 non-fraud offences by officers of companies in liquidation. (In Scotland, in 1984, 47 liquidators and 19 directors were fined, and 15 liquidators and 17 directors were admonished by the courts for company offences: 1985 figures are not available.)

The corporate form has become the dominant venue for malpractice by businesspeople, offering greater protection from creditors and from regulatory supervision than is the case with unlimited liability. However, in addition to companies offences, there are convictions under the

Bankruptcy Acts, of which there were 143 in 1984: 25 of them on indictment. (In addition, there were 10 bankrupts dealt with under the Theft Acts and Companies Acts.) It is not certain how many of these were offences committed in the course of trading (as opposed to bankrupts using credit cards for personal expenditure), but over a half of the convictions were for undischarged bankrupts obtaining credit, and over a quarter more for failure to keep proper books of account. No bankrupt who was prosecuted was acquitted: this is a measure of the clarity of the cases that reach the stage of prosecution rather than of prosecution-mindedness on the part of magistrates and judges.

Given the difficulty and expense of proving major intentional fraud and corporate crime offences, it may appear to be a rational strategy for agencies to go for 'trip-wire' regulatory offence prosecutions. However, the difficulty often is to get the courts to regard such offences seriously, partly because the background to the particular offence is not brought out in court. (See, further, Leigh, 1980; Levi, 1984a.) This is also discussed in the next chapter.

The Director of Public Prosecutions has statutory responsibility for the prosecution of certain categories of fraud and corruption. Until the Crown Prosecution Service came into being in 1986, the police (as well as the non-police agencies) were able to prosecute themselves frauds – the majority – that lie outside these categories, as an alternative to referring them to the Director. The extent to which they did so depended partly on the expertise of their solicitors: the Solicitors' Department in the Metropolitan Police was more capable of handling a fraud competently than those in smaller provincial forces. Before the 1980s, the police used to prepare their case fully and then, when they thought it was strong, pass it on to the Director of Public Prosecutions for a decision. However, some headline-grabbing prosecution failures led first to an 'early advice' *dirigiste* system and then to the formation of the Fraud Investigation Group in 1985, though this remained a half-way house between the old institutional separation of responsibilities for investigation and prosecution, on the one hand, and the co-ordinated Economic Crime Task Forces of the United States and West Germany, on the other. (Though in most US agencies, the prosecutions are decided on by a different division from the investigative arm.) Chapter 8 examines the current and proposed systems for prosecuting fraud, but since 1984, the absence of prosecutions against many scandalous commercial activities has been the subject of much criticism in the media and in élite commercial circles. In the light of these controversies, my 1985 survey asked executives for their views on fraud prosecutions (Levi, 1986a). Let us now review their opinions.

Executives' attitudes towards prosecution policies

It is always arguable that we cannot do everything, and this applies to prosecution decisions also. Members of the public may be able to avoid taking the hard political decisions that people in positions of responsibility cannot shirk. However, it is important to know how much support there is for current policy and since senior businesspeople may fairly claim a considerable interest in the consequences of fraud, not least because it affects their businesses, they are an important client group for fraud policing and prosecution services. Whereas there was little active lack of confidence in the police, there was strong dissatisfaction with the prosecution policies of the Director of Public Prosecutions, as they existed at that time.

For example, they were asked whether 'people from abroad who set up business here to defraud solely other foreigners should not be prosecuted'. Only 3.6 per cent agreed with this; 1.8 per cent were neutral; 33.9 per cent disagreed; and no fewer than 60.7 per cent strongly disagreed. This was the strongest response to any question in the whole survey. Another policy question asked was 'suspected fraudsters, no matter how major, should never be prosecuted unless there is a better than 50 per cent chance of the prosecution being successful'. Again, the question was set up in such a way as to avoid prejudicing respondents against currency policy in the Attorney-General's guidelines. Yet here, too, there was little support for the rigid application of the 50 per cent probability of conviction rule. The answers show that 28.6 per cent strongly disagreed and 44.6 per cent disagreed with the policy. Only 3.6 per cent strongly agreed and 7.1 per cent agreed, the remainder being neutral. Finally, the executives were asked to express a view on whether 'major frauds involving Britain's commercial reputation should be prosecuted whatever the cost'. This too provoked strong opinion in favour of a tough line on prosecution: 21.4 per cent strongly agreed; 58.9 per cent agreed; 7.1 per cent were neutral; 8.9 per cent disagreed; and 1.8 per cent strongly disagreed; the rest were 'don't knows'. So, and it should be borne in mind that the survey took place in September 1985 at a time when fraud had a much lower political profile than it did later, there was a strong mandate for taking action against domestic and overseas fraudsters, even in high-risk cases. (There are arguments against such a bold policy: for instance, a rash of failures might undermine the credibility of policing, though given the low credibility of deterrence at present, it is hard to imagine how such counter-productiveness could occur in practice.)

The trial of commercial frauds

Criticisms of the trial of fraud have been given an extensive airing during the mid-1980s. Some of these problems have become more acute as a result of the sheer growth in the number of frauds being processed through the system: in 1984, there were 8 times as many people found guilty of fraud at Crown Courts than in the Courts of Assize and Quarter Sessions 20 years earlier. From 1974 to 1984, fraud convictions rose 245 per cent at Crown Courts and 149 per cent at magistrates' courts. Only some of these complaints relate to the system of trial by jury: many relate to poor case preparation and the absence of a tough-minded system of pre-trial reviews of the allegations (which in the United States is often accomplished during the Grand Jury hearings). But the Fraud Trials Committee noted:

> 'An essential requirement of justice is that it be administered with reasonable dispatch. The evidence that we have received in fraud cases is that this is often not achieved . . . the average time in fraud cases at all stages is 30 to 40 per cent longer than that in all cases taken as a whole. . . . Cases are delayed or extended for long periods; they become stale through delay and are sometimes abandoned altogether for that reason. Essential witnesses die and, in any event, memories fade so that a fair hearing is impaired. Many of the procedures are time-wasting and they are sometimes used deliberately by one or other of the parties to cause delay.'
>
> (Fraud Trials Committee, 1986a:175)

Complaints by judges and by governments about the jury are centuries old (Harman and Griffiths, 1979; Thompson, 1980), but the development of criticisms of the jury system in relation to fraud dates from the 1960s (Finer, 1966; Levi, 1983; Morris Committee, 1965). These recent concerns arose within a context of police complaints that 'too many criminals' were being acquitted in other forms of major property crime (see Mack, 1976; Mark, 1973) and that juries were responsible.

During the 1970s and early 1980s, there were a number of major cases that ended in acquittal, and despite the relative lack of interest in fraud on the part of politicians and the media prior to 1985, there was episodic criticism of the fact that in spite of scandals in the financial services and property markets, very few – indeed, no – major City figures had been convicted of fraud. (The former Lord Mayor of the City of London, Sir Denys Colquhon Flowerdew Lowson, died upon receipt of a summons alleging fraud in his Unit Trust empire, thereby avoiding putting that immunity thesis to the test; and some other City figures have committed suicide when learning that their conduct was under investigation by the police or by the Department of Trade and Industry). Their future is reviewed in Chapter 8, but support for fraud juries is sustained by the pecuniary self-interest of the legal profession, with a minor supplementary role being played also by an unreflecting conservatism. There is a certain irony in the fact that in the debate on the Supreme Court Bill (1981), when proposing the abolition of the right to jury trial in *civil* cases, Lord Chancellor Hailsham criticized peers for being 'too conservative, with a small 'c'. (The proposal failed.)

The perspective within which the acquittal rate should be viewed is a matter of considerable dispute. Some appear to see any acquittal as a 'failure': sometimes a failure on the part of the jury (or, more globally, 'the legal system') to come to a 'proper' verdict (Mark, 1973). Others such as the former Master of the Rolls, Lord Denning, have a more schizophrenic approach to the jury. They approve of it as a bulwark of liberty when it appears to come to an 'equity verdict' with which they agree, i.e. an expression of dissent from an 'unjust prosecution', as is believed to have occurred when a senior civil servant, Clive Ponting, was acquitted after he leaked information to a Member of Parliament about British naval movements at the time of the sinking of the Argentine ship General Belgrano: but they disapprove of its 'bias' when they suspect – rightly or wrongly – that 'minority groups' are reluctant because of ethnic solidarity to convict their fellows of offences such as robbery (Denning, 1982). Analogously, many on the left who are keen to complain about the way in which the police label as 'criminals' those people whose names – convicted or not – appear on the Police National Computer display little compunction about referring to unconvicted criminals among the powerful. In short, consistency is not a highly-prized attribute in debates over criminal justice!

It should come as little surprise, then, that the rhetoric of blame occupies a significant role in the trial of commercial fraud. Business-people, professionals, and prosecutors commonly assert that cases are acquitted because juries do not understand them and/or that cases are not prosecuted because of the fear that juries might not understand them. There are problems in evaluating both these assertions: the first is hard to test conclusively because the Contempt of Court Act (1981) made it an offence for anyone (including academic researchers) to interview jurors about their decisions; the second is not readily susceptible to empirical refutation because unless one is a participant in the decision-making process – and even then, self-deception of motives can occur – it is self-justifying. With these limitations in mind, let us examine the evidence relating to the acquittal rate in fraud trials and the causes of those acquittals.

First, a brief comment on acquittals in the United States where, as in Canada and New South Wales, the defendant has the right to opt for trial without jury. (In Canada, if an offence carries a maximum of more than five years' imprisonment, the Attorney-General can override the defendant's choice of trial by judge alone and require him to have trial by judge and jury.) US statistics on this are not good, but many defendants do elect trial by judge alone, particularly if they have a technical defence or as an each-way bet to get a sentence discount without pleading guilty. The distribution of pleas and results in US District Courts in the year up to the end of June 1983 – the most recent year available – is set out in *Table 19*.

Table 19   *Convictions and acquittals in US District Courts, 1983*

	guilty plea	jury conviction	jury acquittal	court conviction	court acquittal
fraud	5019	622	183	145	43
embezzlement	1807	78	29	58	10
forgery and counterfeiting	2128	186	42	41	9
anti-trust	108	13	18	0	0
food and drug	71	6	0	1	1

Source: US Department of Justice (1985)

So of the comparatively small number of people who pleaded not guilty, the acquittal rate was 22.5 per cent overall: 23.1 per cent of those who pleaded not guilty before a judge alone, and 20.4 per cent of those who pleaded not guilty before a jury. Therefore, the acquittal rate was slightly higher in judge-only than in jury trials. In addition, 138 offenders pleaded *nolo contendere*: they agreed to be sanctioned without it being registered as a conviction. It is difficult to infer anything much about the social status of those on trial, and acquittal data are subject to the enthusiasms of prosecution agencies to take on high-risk cases as well as to different reasons for opting for jury and non-jury trial. However, to take what are the most likely high-status offender categories, we may note that in income-tax cases, 155 were convicted and 41 acquitted by juries, while 43 were convicted and 7 acquitted by the court; in securities and exchange prosecutions, only 1 out of 21 pleaded not guilty, and that led to a jury acquittal, there being no *nolo contenderes*; in anti-trust prosecutions, where there were 23 *nolo contenderes*, no-one opted for trial before the court, and 18 out of the 31 pleading not guilty were acquitted by juries: a very high proportion.

I will discuss in the final chapter the reform proposals made by the Fraud Trials Committee (1986a) – often referred to as the Roskill Committee – and by the Criminal Justice Bill (1986), but one of the traditional defences of democracy is that whatever the outcome of the decision-making process, popular involvement is an intrinsically good thing in itself. By that criterion, the only circumstances under which one could state definitively that an acquittal was unjustified would be if (1) the jury was unrepresentative, or (2) it was corrupt. But aside from the politics of reform, what does actually happen at fraud trials? The more one looks at the evidence, the more problematic some of the assertions about the role of the jury in accounting for the small number of convictions for major frauds become. Furthermore, there is often a concealed political assumption in statements which suggest that the acquittal rate is 'too high', that juries are 'too tolerant', or that trials are 'too expensive'. By what criteria is one judging the appropriateness of the baseline for excess? Bearing this in mind, let us review the assertions that *are* made about juries in fraud trials.

1 *Juries are prone to be corrupt.* Unlike in the United States, British jurors are not sequestered – kept out of circulation – during a trial. This does make them more vulnerable to 'nobbling' by either party. Since 1975, the police have detected at least five fraud cases in which jurors have been approached by a member of the public. However, there have been no convictions arising out of these approaches, partly because they usually have taken the form of 'chance discussions' – often at the end of a trial when prospects look bleak for the defendants – with a juror by some unknown third party, which the trial judge decides are too prejudicial to allow the trial to continue. (If corruption were frequent, one would expect to see a high acquittal rate: we will review that later.)

2 *Juries are too tolerant of fraud.* One reason why concern is often expressed about the jury is that jurors might be usurping the function of Parliament by applying their views about the morality of conduct rather than following legal rules about it. (It could be countered that the jury – if random – is more democratic than the law, particularly if the latter were passed by some previous Parliament.) There is a certain ambivalence about this issue, because many conservatives occasionally think it is a good thing for jurors to exercise their sense of equity against 'oppressive prosecutions', and the salience of popular views about morality is built into the notion of 'dishonesty' in English law of fraud and theft. However, whatever one's view about the *principle* of jury equity verdicts, the surveys of perceptions of crime seriousness discussed in Chapter 3 do not suggest much tolerance of fraud among the general public or among executives (except for tax offences committed in the course of otherwise legitimate business transactions). Indeed, most surveys show that there is *less* tolerance of property crime among people lower down the social-class scale than among the

better-off. Even convicted offenders rate fraud (and many other) offences only slightly less seriously than did the unconvicted public (Jones and Levi, 1983a).

Some sections of the public – probably including convicted offenders – may be less likely to believe police evidence, and this scepticism towards the police may be class, race, and/or age-related, but this is different from their being tolerant of offending itself. Besides, interviews with the accused play a relatively small role in fraud trials, and the tape-recording of interviews has long been routine in fraud investigations by the police and by the revenue departments. This means that there traditionally have been fewer disputes over 'verbals' – the alleged invention of admissions – in fraud than in other sorts of trials (though tape-recording has reduced such disputes – possibly by changing police behaviour as well as defence claims – in non-fraud trials). It also means that attitudes towards the police are largely insignificant in frauds, except in cases where corruption or oppression by the investigators is alleged. (It may be signficiant that in one large VAT evasion trial, the jury attached to their *conviction* verdicts a rider complaining that the crown had behaved oppressively.)

3 *Jurors cannot understand fraud cases.* There is much conceptual confusion over this issue. First, there is confusion between 'do not' and 'can not', so that where jurors do not follow a particular argument, it is inferred that they are incapable of so doing. (Some people may find sections of this book hard to understand, but this does not mean that they could not understand it if they re-read the bits they found difficult, or if I were able to express myself more simply or to make the issues more interesting to them. Naturally, like prosecutors and judges in fraud cases, I would *prefer* to believe that any faults lay in the reader/jury, but even if I have done my best to explain, this does not mean that others could not have done better, nor that I can absolve myself of any responsibility for incomplete comprehension.) Second, there is a lack of clarity in what we mean by 'understanding a fraud', and in specifying what levels of understanding are required.

There has been no adequate systematic research in Britain on juror comprehension of fraud trials. There are some anecdotes. Cornish (1968) mentions one accountant who had been a juror in a fraud trial. He stated that he had had to open up proceedings in the jury room by giving his own explanation of the mass of figures that had been produced in evidence, and that no fewer than nine of his fellow jurors had been unable to follow the evidence in any 'adequate' fashion. Four fraud jurors (including a distinguished professorial colleague and a bright student), who spoke to me of their experiences when they learned I was researching fraud, all expressed concern about their own lack of comprehension as well as about that of their fellows. However, they were all very critical of the way in which the prosecution and defence had presented their cases in court, so that leaves the question of inherent incapacity open. During the jury deliberations at the end of one trial that I observed, a juror who was not a professional person or a businessman asked the judge the meaning of 'estoppel', which appeared in the fine print among several hundred pages of documents and had not been referred to by any of the parties in the case. Research for and the views of the Fraud Trials Committee (1986a, 1986b) are examined in Chapter 8.

In the United States, where the right to jury trial is protected by the Sixth and Seventh Amendments, attempts have been made to carve out a 'complexity' exception in civil cases (criminal trials remaining sacrosanct) which argues that because juries cannot understand complex fraud trials, the use of them violates the constitutional right to due process and thus to a fair trial. This issue has still not been fully resolved (Judicature, 1982; Lempert, 1981), and it should be noted that some anti-trust (monopoly) cases may go on for well over a year and involve very difficult questions of economic theory and analysis which go far beyond any British criminal cases prosecuted hitherto. In a US criminal case in 1982, a reporter interviewed jurors after they had acquitted several lawyers and an insurance assessor of fraud after an eleven-week trial. All the jurors interviewed revealed faulty reasoning and misunderstanding of the judge's instructions on the relationship between fraud and the conspiracy charges and on their belief that to prove conspiracy, the fraud had to have been planned in advance (Hans and Vidmar 1986, p.114). After the acquittal of John de Lorean on racketeering and fraud charges in Detroit in 1986, the trial judge discovered from the jurors that the major reasons for the acquittal were that although some members of the jury thought he was guilty, they misinterpreted the judge's instructions to mean (1) that they had to bring in a unanimous verdict of either guilty or not guilty, and (2) that if they were not satisfied of his guilt on the racketeering charges, they had to acquit him on all other charges also (*Observer Business News*, 21 December 1986). However, it remains unknown whether (1) jurors *often* do not understand what people say to them and (2) any such lack of understanding is inevitable, rather than being the product of deliberately or incompetently obscure courtroom presentation by counsel and of ambiguous instructions by judges: see Chapter 8.

4 *Fraud trials are too long and expensive.* In an earlier study for the Royal Commission on Criminal Procedure (1981), I noted that of all cases

committed to the Old Bailey (London Central Criminal Court) in 1977 (and tried mainly in 1978 and 1979), the *average* length of contested conspiracy to defraud trials was 5½ working weeks, and that even the relatively simple fraud proseuctions taken out under the Theft Act (1968) lasted an average of 3 weeks. No fewer than one in five contested fraud trials lasted over 6 working weeks, and since less than half of those accused of fraud pleaded guilty – lower than the national, but similar to the London average for Crown Court trials – that imposed significant expenses as well as occupying the courts for considerable periods (Levi, 1981). Subsequent to that study, I examined 1978 committals, where there were four trials whose taxed costs exceeded £160,000 (two of which lasted almost 200 days). Indeed, the *average* taxed costs for cases committed for trial at the Old Bailey in the period 1977–80 exceeded £100,000, and only three fraud trials in that period cost less than £30,000. Fraud trials, therefore, are not cheap. In the period from 1979–84, the number of trials lasting over four weeks at the London Central Criminal Court (CCC) declined slightly but the number of long trials outside that court escalated dramatically. (See Fraud Trials Committee, 1986a, Appendix J).

Table 20   *Fraud trials lasting over four weeks*

	London CCC	other Crown Courts	total
1979	11	7	18
1980	10	8	18
1981	13	19	32
1982	7	16	23
1983	9	29	38

Source: Fraud Trials Committee (1986a)

No costs are given for fraud trials generally, but at the London Central Criminal Court, the average cost per case for each working *day*, including prosecution and defence costs, is £3000. Excluding the cost of Department of Trade and Industry inspections, the Roskill Report notes that 'the average cost of a commercial fraud case from the beginning of the police investigation to verdict, based on a sample of 10 cases lasting more than 20 days, on which verdicts were reached in 1981–1984' was £500,000 (Fraud Trials Committee, 1986a:174), though this figure may mislead, since it is an average only of the very long trials, *not* of trials as a whole. The average trial time in these cases was 46 days, which may be compared with my finding that cases committed for trial in 1980 averaged 24.5 days and their taxed costs (which excludes court time) averaged £103,000. So bearing in mind that the London Central

Criminal Court – being the Crown Court for the City of London – is more likely than courts elsewhere to hear detailed and arcane fraud cases, it does appear that trials there are both long and expensive. Whether they are 'too long' and 'too expensive' is a value judgment.

5 *Too many fraudsters are acquitted.* We have examined the mechanisms which sift out the weak cases from the strong, and the gatekeeping decisions by the police and Director of Public Prosecutions might be expected to weed out all but the very strongest cases, particularly given the application of the Attorney-General's guidelines that no case should be brought to trial unless there is a more than 50 per cent chance of conviction. (It is intriguing to speculate mathematically what the acquittal rate should be, given that criterion!) One would certainly expect a lower acquittal rate in fraud than in offences like burglary over which there has traditionally been great investigator pressure for prosecution and relatively low cost. Yet in spite of this, many fraud prosecutions fall by the wayside. For a number of reasons (including plea-bargains), a substantial number of fraud charges are left on the file or are dropped. Of those fraud prosecutions undertaken by the Director of Public Prosecutions in 1983, 180 out of 637 *charges* (not persons) proceeded with at Crown Courts ended in acquittal: a rate of 28 per cent. In 1984, the equivalent data were 61 acquittals and 159 convictions for obtaining property by deception; 9 acquittals and 37 convictions under the Bankruptcy Act (1914); 4 acquittals and 3 convictions under the Companies Acts; 26 acquittals and 71 convictions under the Forgery and Counterfeiting Acts; 27 acquittals and 17 convictions for false accounting; 43 acquittals and 131 convictions for corruption; and 9 acquittals and 2 convictions for conspiracy to defraud. The overall acquittal rate was thus 30 per cent in 1984. For cases prosecuted by the Director of Public Prosecutions, the acquittal rate in robberies was approximately the same; that for burglary much lower. But unlike fraud, many important robberies and burglaries were *not* prosecuted by the Director of Public Prosecutions but by individual forces.

More generally, in the period 1977–81, between 12 and 15 per cent of males tried for fraud and/or forgery at Crown Courts in England and Wales were acquitted: higher than burglary and robbery, but lower than theft, criminal damage, violent, and sexual offences (Butler, 1983). Of those people committed to the Old Bailey in 1977 for commercial fraud, 24 per cent were not in the end convicted: lower than the national or London average at that time. So although there may be grounds for concern about fraud trials, the acquittal data superficially give no greater reasons for concern than might arise generally for Crown Court cases.

Indeed, the Metropolitan Police Fraud squad were very happy about their conviction rate, which was 95 per cent in 1983. It may be that 'too many fraudsters' are being acquitted, but what criteria should we use to judge (1) how many are 'too many', and (2) whether those acquitted were 'fraudsters'?

A different method of approaching 'the acquittals problem' is to look at what sort of people *are* acquitted in fraud trials. Here, one encounters some difficulties in using the previous convictions of those acquitted as one's baseline, since many police critics – following Mark (1973) – state that it is the most devious 'offenders' who have the lightest conviction records: this very fact shows what sophisticated criminals they are! Thus, the signs of 'good character' become transmuted magically into those of 'bad character'. The only research into the backgrounds of those convicted and acquitted of *fraud* is my study of the 'downmarket' area of long-firm fraud (Levi, 1981), which found that out of 20 acquitted people alleged to have played a major role in fraud between 1962 and 1972, 14 had no previous convictions; of the remaining 6, only 2 had spent more than a year in prison prior to their current charges. Those acquitted tended to have lighter criminal records than those convicted, and those alleged to have been principals of fraudulent conspiracies were no more likely than non-principals to be acquitted. It is possible that these findings are out of date, and that in any event, they do not apply to fraud generally. However, there is no hard evidence that the 'whales' – whether previously convicted or not – are being acquitted in fraud trials while the 'minnows' are being convicted. The fact is that in the past, very few whales have been prosecuted, so juries have had no opportunity to acquit them.

A further method of approaching the acquittals issue is to analyse the reasons for the acquittals that have occurred in what – for reasons of length or notoriety – may be termed 'major frauds'. Of the cases from 1973–86 that led to widespread media coverage, the comments of lawyers, judges, and newspaper reporters suggest the following inferences about the causes of acquittals:

1 The trial judge ordered a re-trial in a multi-defendant case that had lasted over 100 days and allegedly had cost over £1 million in Legal Aid fees, following a report in the *Guardian* which implied that some of the accused had been convicted previously. (In the re-trial, they were all acquitted.)
2 A re-trial was ordered after a person – possibly connected with the defendants – approached jurors towards the end of a 137-day trial. (In the re-trial, the principals were convicted.)
3 The jury acquitted both defendants in an extremely involved

aviation insurance case. The trial judge earlier had ordered acquittals on some counts, after there was such a high level of disagreement between the expert witnesses that he thought it unsafe to leave the issues to the jury. Some who participated in this case stated that the charges had been wrongly drafted. (Despite the acquittal, one defendant was expelled from Lloyd's and the other censured following disciplinary hearings.)

4 The trial judge directed the acquittal of the accused in an alleged commodity broking fraud, when some expert witnesses declared that some of the accused's activities were established market practice, and some of the evidence could not be proved formally because the Bahamian authorities would not co-operate. The judge referred to the commodities market as an 'unregulated jungle' in which investors should venture only at their peril and added that in his view, *some* charges could have been sustained against the accused, but not those that were actually made. (There was some dispute over this: some parties to the case stated that the trial judge had got it wrong.)

5 The trial judge directed the acquittal of a Chartered Accountant on charges of conspiracy and false accounting after 11 days of legal submissions at the end of a 103-day trial. In a later trial, the accused was convicted of different charges of fraud.

6 A man with previous (and subsequent) convictions for fraud used to obtain jewellery partly through manipulating credit via Dutch banks. The trial judge dismissed charges of fraud against the bank and the jewellery firm, observing that although one of the defendants had admitted fraud, the Dutch case was outside the jurisdiction of the English courts, while the loss to the jewellery firm *might* have occurred as a result of the fact that the accused was under arrest and therefore could not pay them.

7 The trial judge ordered the acquittal of some of the directors of London and County Securities: a failed 'fringe bank'. He stated that the window-dressing of accounts – the object of which is to inflate the cash-in-hand figures at the year's end by borrowing money short-term (even overnight), thereby deceiving depositors and other creditors as to the health of the company – was such standard practice in the City of London during 1973–74 that it would not be right to leave the jury to assess the 'dishonesty' of the accused.

8 After ten days of a fraud trial, two women jurors got drunk at lunch time and in the afternoon session, one of them started to fondle a male juror's thigh! The judge thought it necessary to order a re-trial.

9 One major VAT fraud trial was abandoned after thirteen weeks

because of a technicality. After a similarly long re-trial, the jury convicted one person, acquitted six others, and failed to agree upon an eighth. The defence essentially was that the accused were legitimate dealers and had been innocent of any guilty knowledge about the criminal enterprise. (None of them gave evidence on oath. One, who had been imprisoned for his role in the 1963 Great Train Robbery, later agreed a very substantial settlement with HM Customs and Excise, in exchange for non-prosecution.)

10 The trial judge directed acquittal after he accepted defence legal submissions that two company directors could not be convicted of stealing from their wholly-owned company. These arguments were later rejected by the Court of Appeal (Criminal Division) on an Attorney-General's reference, but they cannot be re-tried (see Sullivan, 1984).

11 The directors of a company whose employees were caught in Germany sticking Johnny Walker labels on £76,000 worth of bottles of counterfeit whisky were acquitted on the direction of the trial judge, on the grounds that there was no jurisdiction to try the case.

12 The trial judge ordered the acquittal of four Iraqis accused of a £250,000 fraud after the Iraqi Government failed to produce diplomat witnesses who were essential to the prosecution.

13 The trial judge directed the acquittal of a deep sea diver and an official of the Salvage Association on charges of violating the Official Secrets act, and a jury acquitted them of dishonesty in relation to the awarding of the contract to recover (successfully) gold worth £45 million from HMS Edinburgh. (The defence was partly that the leaking of information was done to help break the monopoly of contracts enjoyed by an established firm, who allegedly had charged high prices for an unsatisfactory service.)

14 Two senior Home Office officials and a businessman were acquitted of corruption on the direction of the trial judge. It was alleged that they accepted holidays abroad in return for granting contracts for toys and games to be made by prisoners (at a lower price than labour in the 'open market'). The defence was that they had repaid the cost of the air fares and had not favoured him in any way with contracts.

15 A manager of a failed stockbroking firm and two brokers from another firm were acquitted of conducting illicit deals said to have caused the collapse of the manager's firm. The manager's defence was that what he had done was done with the knowledge of his firm's proprietors, while the others stated that they knew nothing of the way he handled the securities. (None of them gave evidence on oath.)

16 A former managing director was acquitted unanimously of insider

dealing (in thirty-five minutes after a week-long trial). It was alleged that he had purchased 100,000 shares in a public company after obtaining confidential information about its plan to take over his firm. His defence was that he regularly dealt in shares and had bought them without special knowledge. He denied being told in advance of the take-over and stated that if he had known, it would have been unethical as well as illegal to deal in the shares!

17 A director of a quasi-merchant banking firm which issued securities in fairly high-risk businesses, and a stockbroker with whom he had carried out transactions, were acquitted by the jury of theft and fraud charges in connection with a company that the former had floated. The trial lasted three weeks. In his summing-up, the judge stressed that the jury could not rely on the evidence of one key prosecution witness and that the evidence of another contained serious inaccuracies. The director still faced further charges of stealing £200,000 in shares, and the Director of Public Prosecutions later decided to proceed with them. However, a different trial judge pointed out during the pre-trial review that there would be a problem in proving dishonesty, since the defendant had written to the company whose shares he was alleged to have stolen, stating that the shares were a loan pending the reprinting of shares. Thus, the defendant might well succeed in a claim that he was negligent rather than dishonest. Following this, the charges were dropped, at an estimated total cost of £125,000 (*Observer Business Review*, 5 October, 1986).

What one may deduce from these cases is that even from a crime control perspective, it is mistaken to focus upon the jury as the source of the principal problems in *existing* fraud trials. Most of the acquittals are directed by the trial judge, not by the jury; a number followed the refusal of the accused to give evidence (though it is impossible to state what *causal* impact that had upon the verdict); in some international cases, there were disputes over the jurisdiction of the court that should have been anticipated by the prosecution and – on the assumption that the judge was correct in his ruling – in respect of which no prosecution should have been brought; and there is genuine room for dispute over whether the 'custom and practice' defences in two trials ought to have been accepted by the trial judge who ordered an acquittal.

The latter is an important moral issue: although the *civil* test of fraud may be whether or not the conduct involved real moral blame according to the contemporaneous notions of fair trading among businesspeople, the *criminal* standard for dishonesty is whether the defendants did realize or ought to have realized that what they were doing was dishonest according to the standards of ordinary people. (See *R* v. *Landy and others* [1981] 1 All E.R. 1181; *R* v. *Ghosh* [1982] 2 All E.R. 689; *R* v. *Cox and Hodges* [1983] *Crim. L.R.* 167–68: though Arlidge and Parry, 1985, appear to take the view that if something is not a civil fraud, it should not be a criminal fraud either.) There are times at which custom and practice in commerce may violate the moral standards of the public at large, though until someone is brought to trial, the public may not *know* what commercial customs are and may not have formulated an opinion about the morality or immorality of the behaviour in question. In such cases of normative conflict, it is not self-evident that it is the customs of businesspeople that should be given moral primacy: on what basis would we distinguish accepting the right to carry out window-dressing of accounts from the right of young unemployed blacks to extract 'street rent' from passers-by, or from the right of Rastafarians to smoke cannabis, or even from the 'customary right' of employees to take home 'spare' produce from the workplace? There is little doubt what line judges would take faced with such claims by lower-class defendants.

The Roskill report mentions a series of other problems with fraud trials. For example, it is asserted that 'Fraudsters and sometimes their advisers are skilful in exploiting delaying tactics and throughout that time fraudsters are free to continue their operations to the detriment of the public' (Fraud Trials Committee 1986a:52). (The Report does not address issues of bail, but this tactic actually is the result of the willingness of the courts to grant bail in serious fraud cases where the defendant has no previous convictions, despite the occasional tendency of the accused to abscond abroad, especially in VAT frauds.) It is unfortunate that a case cited in support of this contention was one in which the defendants were all acquitted at the Crown Court on the direction of the trial judge, who criticized the drafting of the indictment! (A fact that goes unmentioned in the Report.) Perhaps this supports their later argument that committal proceedings are used to help formulate a defence – is this so bad? – and to

> 'gain some advantage by reason of witnesses dying or going abroad or as a result of witnesses' memories fading by the time the case comes to trial. A more specific example is that the defence sometimes subject prosecution witnesses from abroad to such hostile cross-examination that they are reluctant to return for the trial.'
>
> (Fraud Trials Committee, 1986a:52)

In short, there are a host of difficulties that do arise, particularly in international cases, which conspire to make the prosecution of fraud more *technically* risky than other sorts of cases and which make fraud trials more prone than others to collapse after long periods, at great public expense. Some sorts of case (such as insider dealing) may be particularly risk-prone because they involve very detailed evidence and technical issues concerning activities to which jurors find difficulty relating. Whether jurors *inevitably* will find such issues incapable of resolution remains an open question. We shall discuss possible responses to these problems in Chapter 8.

7 The sentencing of commercial fraud

In this Chapter, I will address a number of important issues in relation to the sentencing of business criminals:

1 empirical questions about what punishments actually are imposed upon offenders, including sanctions imposed by some self-regulatory bodies such as Lloyd's and The Stock Exchange as well as court sanctions and administrative penalties imposed by the revenue departments;
2 empirical questions about what influences sentencing decisions in business crime cases;
3 analytic questions about whether there is discrimination in favour of (or against) white-collar crime.

Much of the controversy that surrounds the sentencing of white-collar criminals forms a continuum with the allegations of bias in the policing and prosecution processes. The latter receive more attention, particularly in Britain, not least because the low numbers prosecuted ensure that there are comparatively few sentences to examine! Arguments over bias are made more difficult to resolve by confusion over what constitutes the subject matter of the sentencing studies. Most of the empirical studies have focused upon fraud: Wheeler, Weisburd, and Bode state that 'White-collar crimes, for our purposes, are economic offenses committed through the use of some combination of fraud, deception, or collusion' (Wheeler, Weisburd, and Bode, 1982: 642). On the other hand, many ideological critics base their views more on the sanctions imposed (or not imposed) upon 'business regulatory offences' committed by corporations in pursuit of their organizational objectives, such as the production and marketing of dangerous products, pollution, and health and safety violations. (See, for example, Braithwaite, 1982b; Reiman, 1984.) Both are 'business crime', but their characteristics are somewhat different. Although this book has focused upon commercial fraud rather than on the regulation of corporate crime generally, I will include material on the latter in this review, as readers may think it interesting and important, particularly in relation to discrimination arguments. There has been some valuable work done on these topics in the United States, which I will discuss here, but as Walker (1985) has observed in his impressive summary and overview of sentencing theory and practice, British research on sentencing commercial crime has been scanty in the extreme. Let us begin by examining the evidence regarding what sentences fraudsters receive.

Sentencing levels in commercial fraud cases

The lack of illumination of commercial crime in the recorded crime and prosecution statistics is reflected also in the sentencing data: the categories used in compilation of the Annual Reports on Crime in England and Wales give no guide to the types of fraud committed and permit no direct and few indirect inferences to be made about the social status of those convicted and sentenced. Neither the police nor regulatory agencies keep and publish details on sentencing, and these can be examined properly only by laborious examination of court files. As I will argue later in this chapter, it would also be unsafe to infer much about general fraud sentencing levels from appellate guidelines. The data in this section have been obtained by supplementing the global crime statistics published by the Home Office with information from state regulatory and self-regulatory agencies, from press cuttings, and from appellate judgments.

Over the period 1979–85, the number of males over 21 given sentences of immediate and partly suspended prison sentences for fraud and forgery at Crown Courts rose from 1,300 to 2,400. There was a very slight upward trend in the *proportion* of males convicted at Crown Courts who were imprisoned – 48 per cent in 1979 and 51 per cent in 1985 – and it appears that this rise in imprisonment is attributable not to increased judicial punitiveness *per se* but rather to the increased numbers being convicted and to the introduction of partly suspended prison sentences in 1982. Separate figures for females were not kept until 1982, but the number of females over 21 imprisoned at Crown Courts rose from 175 in 1982 to 302 in 1985: a rise from 28 per cent to 33 per cent of those convicted (and note the low absolute numbers imprisoned). The principal sentences imposed at all courts in 1985 for commercial fraud offences are shown in *Table 21*.

This relative absence of imprisonment for fraud in courts overall would apply *a fortiori* to those convicted of indictable 'regulatory fraud' offences. For example, in 1984, thirty-two people were imprisoned in the UK in relation to offences of fair trading and consumer protection violations.

As regards the length of sentences, in 1985, the only persons in

Table 21   *Sentencing of fraud in 1985*

	frauds by company director	false accounting	other fraud	bankruptcy offences
fine	16	305	7585	66
suspended prison	19	132	2463	36
partly suspended imprisonment	12	32	440	6
unsuspended imprisonment	28	44	2488	21

Source: Home Office (1986d)

England and Wales to receive longer than 4 years' imprisonment – the cut-off point for the label of long-term prisoners – were 1 person convicted of fraud by company director and 16 in the broad category of 'other fraud'. As we move down the length of sentence scale, we find 33 imprisoned for more than 3 and up to 4 years, and 158 imprisoned for over 2 and up to 3 years for fraud. No-one was jailed for more than 2 years for false accounting. For fraud and forgery in 1985, the average number of days sentence for those sentenced to immediate imprisonment was 438 days at Crown Court and 93 days at Magistrates' Courts; for partially suspended sentences, it was 409 days at Crown Court and 146 days at Magistrates' Courts. Clearly, given both their numbers and the length of time they are serving, commercial fraudsters are not creating the crisis of overcrowding in the English penal system! In fact, the average length of sentence for fraud and forgery has dropped over the period 1979–85: from 17.1 months to 14.8 months at the Crown Court, and from 3.7 to 3.1 months at Magistrates' Courts. There are rare occasions when fraudsters receive extremely long sentences: in March 1986, one accountant who admitted specimen charges involving £115,000 (from a total fraud of £3 million) which he had taken from his employers was given a 14–year sentence. However, as we shall see later, such sentences are likely to be reduced on appeal.

Nor are the fines imposed draconian. Let us take £200 as a notional cut-off point of what one might consider to be a substantial fine. This is also a very crude measure of income and status, since the courts are supposed to take income into account when deciding upon the size of a fine: it represents one week's income for someone earning £10,400 annually, or considerably less to most executives. At Magistrates' Courts in 1985, fines over £200 were imposed upon 266 men, 24 women, and 1 company. Only 5 men and 1 woman received a fine over £1000. At Crown Courts, 168 men, 14 women, and 1 company were fined more than £200. Again, these were mainly for the offence of 'other fraud' which offers least guide to social status or type of act. Eight men and one woman were fined over £1000. *So in England and Wales in 1985, only 13 men and 2 women were fined in excess of £1000 for fraud and forgery.* To these may be added a small number jailed for revenue law offences, discussed separately.

Compensation and reparation are increasingly highlighted as key features of penal policy: see Chapter 8 and the Criminal Justice Bill (1986). In 1985, at Crown Courts, 104 offenders convicted of fraud and forgery were ordered to pay compensation of £501–1000, and another 135 over £1000. At Magistrates' Courts, 422 were ordered to pay £501–1000 compensation, and 144 over £1000 compensation. For fraud and forgery, the median compensation order was under £50 at Magistrates' Court and £200 at Crown Court. 1985 figures are not available, but in 1984, 74 Criminal Bankruptcy Orders (CBOs) – which can be imposed in cases where over £15,000 is proven to have been taken – were imposed by Crown Courts: of these, 60 were actually activated by the Director of Public Prosecutions, who has discretion to present them in his role as Official Petitioner. Unfortunately, the number of these that followed fraud trials is unknown, and some of the CBOs were imposed upon robbers and narcotics traffickers also.

Although the annual criminal statistics are far from helpful, it is possible to disaggregate some types of crime from other sources. As regards acts encompassed by the Office of Fair Trading (including those enforced by local trading standards officers), the following are the fines imposed on those convicted during 1985. (Corresponding fines for 1984 are given in brackets: the figures are deduced from information supplied by the Office of Fair Trading.) Fines for false descriptions of goods averaged £486 (536); false price claimed, £329 (299); false statements about services, £517 (326); Restrictions on Statements Orders, £206 (129); Business Advertisements (Disclosure) Orders, £292 (306); Consumer Credit Act, £487 (587); Weights and Measures Acts, £310 (245); Food and Drugs Acts, £246 (202); Estate Agents Act, £600 (1237); Hallmarking Act, £300 (–); Consumer Protection and Consumer Safety Acts, £310 (361); and other trading and environmental legislation, £333 (301). The average fine overall was £349: an increase of over one-sixth since 1984, which is considerably more than the rate of inflation. As regards full sentences of imprisonment, only three sentences in excess of 12 months were imposed (compared with one in 1984). There were 20 sentences of full immediate imprisonment; 5 partly suspended prison sentences; and 12 fully suspended sentences.

The Annual Report of the Department of Trade and Industry on Companies does not give any details at all of sentences, and the Annual

Report on Bankruptcy does not overwhelm the reader with information: that for 1984 tells us only that sentences on the 153 persons convicted ranged from 18 months' imprisonment to a conditional discharge.

Sentencing in tax cases

The great majority of suspected tax frauds are settled by negotiation with the Revenue departments, without recourse to prosecution (or public stigma). One must distinguish between 'ordinary' settlements and formal administrative penalties such as 'compounding'. The latter procedure requires evidence at a criminal standard of proof and at the end of the 1970s was used by Customs and Excise in 5 out of 6 alleged offences of fraud. Both informal settlements and compounding can often result in what are in effect very extensive fines, but names are not published, except in the case of 'Operation Nudger' in 1981, where a prosecution was withdrawn on the court-house steps, after the defendants paid £2.7 million in VAT arrears and penalties, but Customs and Excise made it a condition of the settlement that individual and corporate names *were* published. It may be that the desire of suspects to settle is motivated by their wish to avoid publicity and stigma and is unrelated to the sentences imposed by the courts. (We do know, however, that agency prosecution policies are affected by sentencing levels: Richardson, Ogus, and Burrows, 1983, suggest that low expected sentences deter pollution control agencies from taking cases to court, for their credibility would be undermined by light sentences.) Bearing in mind that court-imposed sanctions are only part of the picture, let us review the neglected area of sentences in criminal tax fraud cases.

Deane (1981) examined a sample of 98 cases between 1950 and 1974, and noted that (as one might infer from the prosecution criteria) they were generally serious cases that had gone on almost invariably for several years. On the other hand, 'there were only a handful of cases in which the fraud could be said to show any degree of sophistication' (Deane, 1981: 53). He excluded 40 'subordinate' offenders in multi-defendant cases – all of whom escaped with a light fine – and of the remaining 121 'major' tax fraudsters, two-thirds were imprisoned. One got a five-year sentence, 13 got 3 years, 7 got 2 years, 43 got 1–2 years, and 17 less than 12 months. Four received suspended sentences and 36 were fined. So the median sentence was 12 months' imprisonment (or a fine if one includes – as Deane did not – the subordinates).

The Keith Committee (1983: 356–57) adopted the same classification procedure as Deane in its review of sentencing in VAT fraud in 1981–82. There is a justification for examining companies separately –

on the grounds that they cannot be imprisoned – but in ordinary reviews of sentencing, one does not exclude 'minor' cases! Twelve companies and subordinates received fines, and two more conditional discharges. However, of the 113 major defendants, 54 per cent received fines: 2 per cent Community Service Orders; 29 per cent suspended sentences (half of whom were also fined); and 15 per cent were sent to prison, of whom only 3 people got more than one year's imprisonment. Indeed, the *total* immediate imprisonment 'awarded' in all VAT fraud convictions in 1981–82 in England and Wales was 14 years 1 month. (In 53 cases of arrears of £10,000 or less, only one person was jailed, and that was for *one* year.) So rates of imprisonment for tax fraud have dropped considerably from Deane's study period of 1950–74, when imprisonment was imposed in two-thirds of cases, to 1981–82, when it was 15 per cent. (This may be partly an artefact of Deane's non-random sample, however.) The Annual Reports of HM Customs and Excise are rather coy about sentencing levels, but in 1984–85, the courts imposed terms of imprisonment totalling 142 years upon 169 persons convicted of fraudulent evasion, ranging in length between 6 weeks and 4½ years. (One presumes that this prevalent practice of giving total prison sentences is aimed at maximizing general deterrence, but it offers little guidance to those interested in the distribution of sentences.)

However, it can be misleading to look crudely at penalty levels as a reflection of judicial sentiments, because these are constrained by legal maxima. Whereas in 'ordinary offences', such as theft and burglary, maxima are very high, in tax (and in corruption and many Companies Act offences) maxima have been historically quite low, reflecting legislative ideology and political concern to reduce parliamentary opposition to draconian penalties against business. In many cases, there is a maximum sentence of two years' imprisonment on indictment. There may be some kind of psychological scaling process by judges, whereby they look at the maximum sentence and try to work out how grave the fraud before them was compared with the gravest fraud they could imagine which *would* deserve the maximum. If this is the process they go through, it is hardly surprising that sentences are comparatively low: my calculations on the basis of figures provided in the Keith Committee Report (1983) are that in 1981–82, the average fine imposed in fraud cases prosecuted by HM Customs and Excise was £2120; that in 'regulatory' offences prosecuted by them (for example the failure to furnish VAT returns) was £308. Nor are the prospects for civil reparation high: over two-thirds of arrears in cases prosecuted are written off as irrecoverable, and this has increased (as have arrears generally) as the number of VAT officials has been cut back in the 1980s.

The use of figures for agency propaganda purposes tends to obscure their meaning, but the Customs and Excise data show that in 1984–85, the total sum of court fines, costs, and settlements under s.152 of the Customs and Excise Management Act (1979) amounted to £4,083,391, and the tax arrears in these cases amounted to £23,349,124. If we total up the 4526 prosecutions for failure to furnish VAT returns, 444 prosecutions for failure to pay tax, 169 convictions for fraudulent evasion, and 445 settlements under s.152 Customs and Excise Management Act (1979), we reach an average of £731 in fines, costs, and settlements, and £4181 in tax arrears for VAT violations in 1984–85. In the specific sub-category of VAT evasion on gold bullion – an activity often connected with 'organized crime' elements rather than professionals or businesspeople – the Report for 1985 states:

'39 persons were convicted in respect of evasion totalling £14,410,000. They were sentenced to terms of imprisonment ranging from 3 months to 6 years, were fined a total of £318,000 and were made the subject of Criminal Bankruptcy Orders totalling £14,178,000. However, there is considerable doubt whether much of this £14 m. or so will be realised [due to its possible removal to the] safe haven of inaccessible foreign bank accounts.' (p. 27)

There is a relationship between scale of offences and penal sanctions in fraud cases, which applies to imprisonment but not to fines: data from the Keith Committee reveal that fines totalling £100,000 were imposed upon 41 cases of over £10,000, with arrears totalling £2.3 million; fines totalling £100,000 were imposed in 53 cases of less than £10,000, whose arrears totalled £200,000. So the arrears/fine ratio is 23:1 in larger cases and 2:1 in smaller cases, possibly due to the greater use of imprisonment in large cases. The Keith Committee reviews sentencing practices somewhat drily:

'It appears that the congested state of the jails does not allow so many convicted tax fraudsters as formerly to be awarded an immediate custodial sentence. It has been suggested that fraudsters should be fined substantial sums in lieu of custodial sentences, but there is no indication from these statistics that the courts have adopted this approach. Indeed, compared with the scale of culpable arrears, the fines imposed in the larger cases are modest. . . . The recovery of arrears in prosecution cases . . . is slow and difficult . . . in VAT such arrears do not bear interest, and . . . a significant proportion of arrears, particularly in the larger cases, is never recovered. . . . Of the five largest frauds prosecuted in 1981/2, three cases, involving £750,000 of arrears, resulted in custodial sentences of 9 months, 21 months, and 2 years respectively, and in two cases involving £650,000 the defendants were awarded suspended sentences, together in the case of one defendant with a fine of £2,500. . . . Whatever the reasons, however, given the circumstances and scale of the larger tax frauds, it is questionable whether such sentences have significant deterrent value.'

(Keith Committee, 1983: 357)

In income-tax fraud cases, dealt with by the Inland Revenue, compounding does not exist, but settlements are negotiated by a more informal procedure. There, penalties are calculated according to a formula of 'culpable tax', meaning underpaid tax for which penalty proceedings would be competent and in time. From the total figure of culpable tax, up to 20 per cent is deducted for prompt and full disclosure, particularly prior to discovery; up to 40 per cent for co-operation during the enquiry; and up to 40 per cent for gravity of the offence. Thus, a minor offence readily admitted and speedily investigated would attract no penalty at all! This is despite the fact that in 'fraud' proceedings, the maximum penalty is a notional 200 per cent of tax due, as contrasted with 'neglect' proceedings, where the maximum is 100 per cent. No data are available for the results of sentencing in income-tax fraud cases.

Disqualification orders

An important and interesting type of punishment is the order which disqualifies a person from taking part in the management of a company or from a particular profession or occupation. In Britain and the United States prohibition from entry into business because one is not a 'fit and proper person' may occur in many areas: gaming, insurance, financial services, the law and accountancy professions, and the police. None of these are restricted to using convictions as a *necessary* condition of the prohibition, nor is conviction (particularly when the offence involves driving or alcohol) always a *sufficient* condition for being banned: the June 1986 draft rules for SIB, for example, require disclosure only of those criminal convictions 'connected with investment business or of a financial nature'. From the occupational group's standpoint, the prohibition on employment is properly viewed as an incapacitation sentence. However, there are circumstances under which the *courts* can impose disqualification, and this can arise from a mixture of motives: retribution, general deterrence, special deterrence, or incapacitation. For someone who makes a living from driving, a driving ban can be an occupational disqualification order, but although some such cases – where a bus or truck driver persistently speeds or violates the tachograph-checked rules on length of driving time in pursuit of profit, whether on direct company instructions or not – might be construed as a form of occupational or even 'white-collar' crime, I will concentrate here on commercial malpractice of a more conventional sort. (For US cases, see McDermott, 1982.)

The courts – as contrasted with commercial/professional bodies – are empowered to impose commercial disqualifications under two sorts of circumstances: as a sentence at the time of conviction; and in response to requests from liquidators or the Official Receiver, which may or may not follow a conviction. Under s.1(1) of the Company Directors Disqualification Act (1986) (hereafter CDDA, 1986), when a court makes a disqualification order, that person may not, without leave of the court, be a director, be a liquidator of a company, or be a receiver or manager of the company's property, or in any way, directly or indirectly, be concerned or take part in the promotion, formation, or management of a company. S.2 of the CDDA (1986) provides that where a person is convicted of an indictable offence in connection with the promotion, formation, management, or liquidation of a company, or with the receivership or management of the property of the company, the court *may* make a disqualification order against him or her. Magistrates' Courts can impose bans up to a maximum of 5 years; Crown Courts up to 15 years. Unfortunately, without a specific research study, it is impossible to ascertain the number of fraud cases in which disqualification orders *could* have been made, but in 1983, 86 orders; in 1984, 120 orders; and in 1985, 108 orders were made under what is now the CDDA (1986). So although increasing use has been made of it, it has never been a power that has been extensively employed. (My study of sentencing in all long-firm fraud cases at the Old Bailey revealed that between 1951–61, disqualification orders were made against 22.1 per cent of offenders; from 1962–72, this actually dropped to 18.1 per cent.)

S.11 of the CDDA (1986) prohibits bankrupts from engaging in corporate activities described above, without leave of the court by which they were adjudged bankrupt: in England and Wales, the Official Receiver must first be notified and be given the opportunity to oppose the lifting of the ban. The origins of the s.11 power are in bankruptcy legislation, where undischarged bankrupts have long been prohibited from obtaining credit and from engaging in trade without leave of the court. Gradually, the sanctions against bankrupts have come to be more refined, based upon a conception of misdeeds rather than incompetence, so that the onus is now upon the Official Receiver to show that there has been some element of *mala fides* if immediate discharge from bankruptcy is not to be granted. However, until they obtain their discharge, bankrupts cannot lawfully operate companies or obtain credit over £50 without disclosing the fact that they are bankrupt.

Because of the separate legal identity of the company, corporate malpractice or insolvency has always presented greater problems. No details are available of numbers of applications made, but the High Court has not been active in banning people whose conduct of liquidated companies makes them 'unfit' under s.9 of the Insolvency Act (1976) (later s.6 of the CDDA, 1986): the figures have soared from 3 in

1983 to 8 in 1984, to a record 12 in 1985! This section provides for a minimum ban of 2 years and a maximum ban of 15 years. Under s.3 of the CDDA (1986), the winding-up court *may* make a disqualification order where it appears that a director has been persistently in default in relation to the provisions of the Act requiring any return or other document to be filed with, delivered, or sent, or notice of any matter to be given, to the Registrar of Companies. If a director has been found guilty of three or more defaults within 5 years (whether or not on the same occasion), this conclusively proves 'persistence' under s.3(1). Similarly, disqualifications may be made under s.5 of the Act by a court before which defendants are convicted. The most likely director to be at risk of being sanctioned here is the Company Secretary, against whom proceedings are usually taken.

Moral fault does appear to be an important ingredient not only in taking action but also in determining the length of disqualification. There are two sets of issues here: first, what are the boundaries of the phrase 'in connection with the management of a company'? And second, what should the period of disqualification be? On the first issue, the Court of Appeal has taken a broad view and has ruled that management refers to the conduct of a company's affairs in relation to third parties as well as within the company: see *R* v. *Corbin* (1984) 6 Cr. App. R. (S) 17, and *R* v. *Austen* (1985) 1 BCC 99, 258. In *R* v. *Campbell* [1984] BCLC 83, CA, the court held that a disqualified person who took an active part in negotiations with banks and other institutions in relation to his role as a management consultant was acting in breach of his disqualification. As to the length of disqualification, a director of six British companies who had defaulted on the obligation to supply accounting material on 100 occasions in 1980 was convicted on 14 counts, for which he was fined £650. Nourse J. disqualified him for 4 years under what is now s.297 of the Companies Act (1985), observing that his defaults were aggravated by the fact that he made no attempt to remedy the situation between his conviction and the notification by the Department of Trade and Industry that disqualification proceedings would be initiated against him. Even at the time of the hearing, many unsatisfactory elements remained: see *Company Lawyer* 2 (174). By contrast, in *Re Civica Investments Ltd.* [1982] 126 *Sol Jo* 446, [1983] BCLC 456, Nourse J. imposed a disqualification order of only 1 year in the light of the substantial efforts of the director to remedy the 'failures' which led to his prosecution. In respect of 'planned' frauds, in the more recent case of *R* v. *Austin* (1985) 1 BCC 99, 258, the Court of Appeal took a very heavy line, confirming a 10-year disqualification upon a motor trader who had defrauded finance companies of some £300,000 by making false hire purchase applications and similar devices.

The CDDA (1986) consolidates the provisions of the Insolvency Act (1985) and the Companies Act (1985). This will make it easier to disqualify 'delinquent directors' from taking part in the management of a company, but it remains to be seen how the new criteria will actually be implemented. As discussed in Chapter 4, in the original Insolvency Bill (1985), there was to have been automatic disqualification of directors of companies subject to winding-up orders, unless the court chose to lift the disqualification. S. 7(3) as enacted, however, has a procedure whereby the Official Receiver, the liquidator, the administrator, or the administrative receiver 'shall forthwith report the matter' to the Secretary of State if it appears that the conduct of a director (including any past director, and including someone who is a 'shadow director', i.e. someone in accordance with whose instructions the directors are accustomed to act) of a company which has at any time become insolvent makes him unfit to be concerned in the management of a company. If the Secretary of State considers that it is in the public interest that a disqualification order should be made, he may apply to the court or direct the Official Receiver so to do. The disqualification period shall be not less than 2 years; the maximum period is 15 years. There is a statute of limitations: without leave of the court, no application can be made to the court after two years from the date when the company first became insolvent. In addition, s.8 enables the Secretary of State to apply to the court for a disqualification order following a report from inspectors appointed under the Companies Act (1985) that such an order would be in the public interest. These provisions place a considerable administrative burden upon the Department of Trade and Industry: by the end of 1986, some 10 per cent of liquidators' reports on directors – which may total 20,000 annually – have alleged unfitness. The Department of Trade and Industry is starting with the more clear-cut cases, but it remains to be seen how the courts will respond: in October 1986, on the Official Receiver's application, Mahmoud Sipra, the major debtor of Johnson Matthey Bankers, was disqualified for 12 years, but this was a far from routine, politically high-profile, spectacular commercial failure.

Sanctions imposed by SROs

In addition to any sanctions that are imposed by the courts, regulatory organizations have their own powers that are fixed either by statute or by contract. As in the case of court sanctions, these have legal maxima. For example, the maximum penalty the Swedish Stock Exchange can impose – short of expulsion – is a fine of ten times the annual registration fee of the company, which fee in turn reflects its size. In May 1986, Fermenta and Volvo were heavily fined for failing to disclose details of their activities to shareholders and to the Stock Exchange: Fermenta was fined over £100,000 – ten times its registration fee – but Volvo £200,000, only three times its registration fee. Culpability judgments are important there, but so too are reparative ones: the Swedish Stock Exchange stated that it would have expelled Fermenta if its chief executive had not promised to reduce substantially his stockholding in the company and if expulsion would not have affected innocent stockholders. (Revelations of vast accounting irregularities later led to his resignation, investigation by the Public Prosecutor, and in 1987 to Fermenta's becoming only the third company to be expelled from The Stock Exchange.)

In Britain, in the period 1983–87, Lloyd's has completed 16 disciplinary cases covering 34 individuals. Of these 10 have been expelled (in a total of 6 cases), 1 has been totally excluded and another given a lifetime exclusion from transacting business, and 15 have been suspended (including 2 for life). Additionally, there have been 7 censures, 10 reprimands, and 3 fines. The expulsion of one member – Ian Posgate – was reduced by the Law Lord on the Appeals Committee, Lord Wilberforce, to a suspension for six months, but Lloyd's subsequently refused to accept his re-registration as an underwriter on the grounds that he was not a 'fit and proper person'. Of those fined, one person – Peter Dixon – was fined £1 million (and ordered to pay £125,000 costs) as well as being expelled – though fining him is one thing, enforcing the fine on overseas assets is another; and the other person was fined £1000 as well as being censured. It should be noted that Lloyd's requires proof at the criminal standard of certainty rather than the civil one of balance of probabilities, but these do not count as criminal convictions, and none of the above cases have led to any criminal court proceedings.

The Stock Exchange has the power to expel members; suspend them from trading in any manner whatsoever; suspend their right to enter the trading floor of The Stock Exchange; censure them; and to reprimand them by the Council or by the Chairman. Moreover, under Rule 24.4, 'alternatively or additionally a fine of such amount as may be considered appropriate may be imposed'. Under Rule 22.1, for gross misconduct, any of the above penalties may be imposed; for misconduct, the penalty imposed shall not exceed a reprimand and/or 'a fine not exceeding £50,000 plus the amount of any improper profit which the Member may be found to have received'; and for minor misconduct, the maximum is a reprimand and/or a fine not exceeding £5000. The sentence is imposed by a Disciplinary Committee comprising at least three Members of the Council of The Stock Exchange. Sentences may be appealed to the Disciplinary Appeals Committee, comprising no more than nine persons, of whom a majority 'shall be non-Members with powers to co-opt additional members of the Council'. Between 1978 (when new disciplinary procedures were introduced) and November 1986, The Stock Exchange expelled 19 Members, suspended 22 others from trading in any manner whatsoever, suspended 3 persons from entering the Floor of the Exchange, and censured a further 24 publicly. (Information on reprimands is not available.) The ability to fine Members for disciplinary offences was introduced only in 1986 and, theoretically, the maximum penalty is infinite. However, ever since the introduction of the Talisman recording system, financal penalties have been imposed for late checking of financial returns, and from 1986, there will be formal fines for late delivery of financial returns: a 'technical' offence which can hide dishonest trading. Informally, it has sometimes been the case that members who have been found violating or even bending the rules have paid the profits improperly gained to charity: this occurred, for example, in the aftermath of the British Telecom flotation, when a leading investment trust manager paid back the profits he had made from using his privileged position to obtain shares for himself in the flotation. Only 2 out of 19 expulsions followed convictions for dishonesty in the Criminal Courts (which itself counts as a serious breach of the Rules), but they were all cases of high gravity and personal culpability.

Sentencing in the United States

In the United States, many studies make it hard to separate out the different types of business crimes: anti-trust cases are a kind of fraud, but in my view, judges may well perceive them as being different from securities violations in harmfulness and/or culpability. (Non-American readers should bear in mind that sentences in the US generally tend to be very much higher than in Europe or Australasia.) In 1983, in US District Courts – which cover federal offences – prison sentences were imposed upon 567 out of 1961 sentenced for embezzlement; 2487 out of 5867 sentenced for fraud; 1309 out of 2365 sentenced for forgery and counterfeiting; 68 out of 160 convicted for bribery; 31 out of 144 sentenced for anti-trust offences; and 5 out of 84 sentenced for Food and Drug Act violations. The average prison sentence for those sent to prison was 32.8 months for embezzlement; 36.3 months for fraud; 41.7 months for forgery and counterfeiting; 33.2 months for bribery; 3.3 months for anti-trust violations; and 31.5 months for Food and Drug Act offences (Administrative Office, 1984). I will discuss these futher when we review discrimination in sentencing.

Clinard and Yeager note that sentencing in anti-trust cases became more severe after 1976, with a marked increase in the rate of imprisonment from 7 per cent to 22 per cent of those sentenced for misdemeanours, and with 71 per cent imprisoned in the few felony prosecutions since some anti-trust cases were made felonies in 1974 (Clinard and Yeager, 1980:153). (Though even in the later period, sentences modestly averaged 192 days in felony and 71 days in misdemeanour cases.) There was also a six-fold increase in fines over this period. Their research in the period 1975–76 showed:

'In all 19 cases of violation, criminal fines were imposed on officers, while in only five were officers incarcerated. . . . In five cases individuals received suspended sentences, while in 11 probation was imposed. . . . In addition, for the 45 officers fined in the 19 cases of violation, the average penalty imposed was only $9,769; the nine corporate officials sentenced to confinement were given terms averaging six days. . . . The average length of probation time was just under 10 months (9.7) for those officials given probation.'

(Clinard and Yeager, 1980:152)

A study by the Bureau of National Affairs (1976) found that of the heavier sanctions imposed on 138 white-collar defendants, 26.8 per cent received fines, suspended sentences, or probation, though they had stolen or mismanaged an average of $21.6 million; 16.7 per cent received a sentence of 12 months or less, though the average loss in their cases was $23.6 million; and 37.7 per cent received prison sentences between 1 and 3 years, though the average loss from their actions was $16 million. A six-month survey by Orland and Tyler (1974) found that 36 per cent of white-collar defendants in the Southern District of New York were imprisoned. Clinard and Yeager state:

'In our study of 56 convicted executives of large corporations, 62.5 per cent received probation, 21.4 per cent had their sentences suspended, and 28.6 per cent were incarcerated. Almost all (96.4 per cent) also had a criminal fine imposed. Those convicted of price conspiracies and income tax violations frequently received the more severe sentences. . . . In view of the large salaries and benefits of most corporate executives, the fines imposed on officers . . . were not large. The maximum was $56,000, with an average fine of $18,250; the mean in financial cases was $22,700, and in manufacturing (one case) $2,000. The average fine for an officer in an antitrust conviction was $18,360.'

(Clinard and Yeager, 1980:278)

Wheeler, Weisburd and Bode (1982), in their study of eight federal crimes – anti-trust offences, securities and exchange fraud, postal and wire fraud, false claims and statements, credit and lending institution fraud, bank embezzlement, Internal Revenue Service fraud, and bribery – do not give the raw sentencing data, but they noted that other factors being held constant, around half of those defrauding $10–100,000 and 68 per cent of those defrauding over $2.5 million could expect to be imprisoned.

It is important to set sentences in the context of the influences that act upon them – to be discussed next – including national norms, but it can be illuminating to look crudely at the end result of prosecutions. To take the most sensational white-collar case of all, the median sentence imposed upon those convicted of making illegal campaign contributions to the Republican Party at the time of Watergate was a $1000 fine, and of the 21 convicted, only 3 received prison sentences. Indeterminate sentences in the United States provide a sentence range that makes median prison terms hard to work out, but a 10–30-month prison sentence was the median one imposed on the 20 convicted in relation to the Watergate break-in and cover-up: the median time actually *served* was 8 months. The longest sentences were served by former Secret Service agents Gordon Liddy (52 months) and Howard Hunt (33 months), followed by former Attorney-General John Mitchell (19 months) and senior Presidential advisers John Ehrlichman and Bob Haldeman (18 months each).

What factors influence the sentencing of business crime?

The relationship between causes of and reasons for behaviour is a fundamental difficulty in all attempts to account for human conduct. It is important, therefore, not to confuse the explanation of sentencing variations with the reasons given by judges for why sentences vary. The reason why this is a problem is that (1) we may be unaware of the reasons why we behave as we do, and (2) in the accounts we give to others, we may be seeking to justify our sentences even though we are aware that these are not the 'real reasons' for our conduct. In the light of this, there are two ways of going about explaining sentencing practice: one is to look at the reasons given by judges for their sentences; the second is to set aside what people *say* about their reasoning and to try to derive mathematically what those influences are by seeing what individual factors and combinations of factors can best predict sentence. When we carry out the latter exercise, we might well find that what judges say about their reasons for sentencing bear only a tangential relationship to what actually affects their sentence. For instance, judges might say that they are influenced by the social class of the defendant to give high-status people *tougher* sentences, but this may turn out not to be the case, even though they believe it to be true. I will review first the reasons given for sentence and then see how well these explanations fit the sentence-prediction models.

One sceptical approach is that principles of punishment are merely devices for justifying what we feel like imposing. This may be too cynical an interpretation: the elegant and acute review of sentencing psychology by Fitzmaurice and Pease (1986) suggests that our ability to discern why we behave as we do is very limited, so when we give reasons for sentences, we may be deceiving ourselves as much as deceiving others. Consequently, justificatory *rationes decidendi* for sentencing may tell us little about how sentences were 'really' arrived at, even when they are honestly put forward: they may be unconsciously rather than intentionally misleading. The authors do not address the question of whether judges tell the truth as they see it, though they might have argued that since the English judiciary so seldom give reasons for their sentences, and will not co-operate with any research into this subject, the need to deceive others does not arise! They do note, however, that 'it is virtually impossible to infer sentencing purpose from sentencing practice' (Fitzmaurice and Pease, 1986:51).

PLEA-BARGAINING AND FRAUD SENTENCES IN THE UNITED STATES

Looking at individual instances, one can find many examples of 'light' prison sentencing in 'serious' crimes. Plea-bargaining undoubtedly affects sentence, and in jurisdictions where the prosecution wishes to be proactive in taking cases to court, sentence bargains are frequently resorted to in exchange for the defendant's co-operation in providing evidence against others (Hagan, Nagel, and Albonetti, 1980; Katz, 1979). In June 1986, in what at that time was the largest insider-dealing case ever prosecuted, Dennis Levine pleaded guilty to earning $12.6 million from such dealing, and was promised a reduced sentence if he gave most of the money back and co-operated with the governmental investigation into other offenders. The maximum possible penalty on the four counts to which he pleaded was 20 years' imprisonment, so he had a considerable incentive for so doing: he implicated several former investment bankers who in turn repaid money. The most prominent of these was the leading Wall Street securities *arbitrageur*, Ivan Boesky, who in exchange for prosecution acceptance of a plea of guilty to one charge – with a maximum jail sentence of 5 years – and of the non-pursuit of triple damages against him, agreed (1) to record secretly conversations with other associates before news of his plea was released; (2) to be a co-operative witness in future insider-dealing probes; and (3) *personally* to disgorge $50 million in profits and to pay $50 million in penalties to SEC. He was also required to unwind all his shareholdings by April 1988 and was banned for life from securities trading.

Both defendants hoped to avoid imprisonment altogether, though sentence was postponed pending further SEC investigations. Levine was given a 2-year prison sentence and paid $11.5 million in fines, though he still faces other lawsuits from the Internal Revenue Service and Litton Industries (for $30 million). Much to the distress of the purchasers (who may be able to sue for damages), Boesky was allowed by SEC – 'to avoid causing panic in the markets' – to offload $440 million in securities just prior to the announcement of his settlement, which would have fetched much lower prices had the sales occurred afterwards. In late 1986, after paying all the back tax plus penalties, 81-year old fashion designer Aldo Gucci was jailed for a year and a day after pleading guilty to tax evasion charges totalling $6 million on his US operations; designer Albert Nipon was jailed for three years on tax evasion counts. White-collar defendants who wish to play Prisoner's Dilemma (or 'Supergrass') in this way can thus obtain bargain treatment for themselves, particularly if they can implicate other high-status defendants.

On other occasions, the corporation may engage in a plea bargain in exchange for the non-prosecution of individual executives or to minimize the publicity and vast legal costs that might ensue from fighting the case. In May 1985, one of the largest securities firms in the world – E.F. Hutton – was fined $2 million and ordered to pay the cost of the investigation (about $750,000) after it pleaded guilty to defrauding some of the 400 banks with whom it held accounts. It also promised to pay full restitution to any bank which had lost interest payments as a result of the frauds. It systematically paid cheques drawn on accounts in Bank A into Bank B, and wrote cheques on Bank B in favour of clients before the Bank A cheques had been cleared. This would not have been illegal had there been any money in the Bank A accounts, but there was not at the time when the cheque was drawn. This process, known as cheque kiting, was aimed at giving E.F. Hutton the interest-free use of millions of dollars between 1980 and 1982, for otherwise it would have had to pay overdraft interest on the full amount all the time. The company claimed that the practices represented violations of its policy and procedures, and that they had stopped in early 1982 after they came to the attention of senior management.

Another case, involving Marc Rich & Co., whose owners as well as whose corporate registration were domiciled in Switzerland, entailed breathtaking complexities of international jurisdiction. The Swiss would not grant judicial assistance to the US authorities, because the case involved fiscal evasion which was not covered by the US–Swiss Treaty of 1900 and because the US was trying to overturn its criminal code on economic espionage, which makes it an offence to reveal banking information except under highly-restricted circumstances. Marc Rich & Co. (and the individual defendants) refused to comply with US subpoenas, stating that they were not within the jurdisdiction of the US courts. The latter responded by freezing all of its US subsidiary's assets – over $90 million – putting it out of business. The US then got involved in wrangles with Cayman Islands and the Bahamas, where Rich had shifted $45 million to avoid the clutches of the US courts. In 1984, after almost two years of legal struggle, the company pleaded guilty to some less serious charges and in the plea bargain settlement, paid the Government $150 million, forfeited $21 million in court fines already levied plus future tax benefits, paid $780,000 in fines and $33,000 in costs: about $200 million altogether. This was the largest ever settlement for tax fraud charges. (Rich also paid nearly $10 million to his lawyers for their fees.) The United States also withheld nearly $37 million in cash of seized Marc Rich assets. Additionally, Marc Rich AG repaid debts of $130 million to fourteen creditor banks led by Chase Manhattan, and agreed to forfeit the right to use the payment of $150 million in fines as a tax liability in the United States: effectively costing the company a further $24–40 million in tax write-offs. One of Rich's co-directors pleaded guilty to one count of making false statements to the Government, and was given a suspended three-year sentence plus five years' probation on some form of community service work. In exchange, the Government lifted all restrictions on Marc Rich's US operations and allowed the Swiss parent company to pay the $130 million to the creditor banks. Rich and another director, Pinky Green, remain indicted on fraud and racketeering charges and would be arrested if they ever came within the jurisdiction of the United States, but they are safe from extradition in Switzerland. (For fuller accounts of the Rich saga, see Walter, 1985, and the fascinating insider account by Copetas, 1986.) These are examples of the more sensational plea bargains in the United States during the 1980s.

SENTENCING AND CONTESTED CASES

Though research on plea-bargaining has re-oriented thinking towards acknowledging the significance of prior negotiations between defence and prosecution lawyers which do not always include the judge, most perspectives on sentencing concentrate upon the *judge* as the only significant actor. A 'situational' approach to sentencing might suggest that we first examine the impact of immediate in-trial and post-trial influences. Nagel and Hagan (1982, pp.1432–35) have reviewed some of the American defence arguments and empirical sentencing surveys which are pleaded in mitigation on the grounds of fairness *between* white-collar defendants: thus, one might argue, *previous* light sentences justify *future* light sentences. Mann (1985) has shown how in the United States, wealthy defendants are able to pay for sophisticated defence memoranda on sentencing which raise what in effect are substantive issues of liability, the aim being to maximize the moral ambiguity in the judge's perception of 'what the offender did', thereby reducing the risk of a severe deterrent sentence. Criminologists may even be called in to present detailed analysis of the impact of punishment, at least where this might favour the defendant. In the cases he examined, defence counsel presented arguments on the following questions:

1 How much guilty knowledge did the defendant have of matters related to the offence?
2 Was there information that the defendant should have received if he had taken reasonable actions or paid reasonable attention, e.g. should we have read reports about a particular issue, even if in fact he had not done so?
3 What was the actual state of mind of the defendant in relation to the facts constituting the offence? For example, in one tax case, did he actually believe that non-reporting of income in the circumstances was permissible?

So in the United States, the sentencing stage becomes a highly adversarial process at which all the parties and the judge engage in detailed argument over the issues that usually have already been reviewed at numerous pre-charge and trial hearings. The judge is the central focus, but the parties – particularly the defence, but also the prosecution, who are normally keen to see a prison sentence, though they are less bothered about its length – are active in seeking to influence (1) the principles on which he sentences, and (2) the facts that he takes into account when arriving at his sentence. All of these matters are influenced also by the information-control strategies that are adopted at earlier stages in the litigation.

Except perhaps during the (non-judicial) negotiation of administrative penalties in tax cases, this sort of procedure does not occur in British fraud cases. Indeed, the idea of looking at sentencing issues in such a jurisprudential way would be viewed with horror by most English judges (see Ashworth, 1983; Fitzmaurice and Pease, 1986). Prosecution counsel play virtually no role in the sentencing process, except inasmuch as they may influence the type of picture the judge has of 'what happened' by the way they present the case during the trial or, when there is a guilty plea, in their brief summary of the case before defence counsel make their mitigation speeches. Indeed, the absence of such a presentation indicating culpability as well as harm may be one reason why sentencing tends to be so low in strict liability prosecutions: to the extent that he/she is unfamiliar with socio-legal research on regulatory agencies and is accustomed to routine prosecution procedures undertaken by the police, the magistrate may not realize that the prosecution has been undertaken only after numerous warnings, formal and/or informal, and thus confuses the *form* of strict liability with the *substance* of lack of culpability.

No systematic work has been done on mitigation in Crown Court *fraud* trials – Shapland's (1981) study does not touch specifically upon them – but my observations in court and discussion with lawyers can offer some perspective. The Social Enquiry Report prepared for the court will indicate (normally) prior convictions, family relationships, and economic circumstances: none of this is likely to enhance culpability. In cases of fraudulent trading, defendants with no prior convictions who had traded – apparently legitimately – for some time before becoming insolvent will argue that 'this is not a case where a company was set up with the deliberate intention of defrauding', thereby distancing them- selves from 'real' culpability and moving the judge away from a focus upon the harm done. Because of the low prosecution and conviction rate for insider dealing and 'Establishment' frauds, the highest-status defendants tend to be moderate-ranking solicitors who have 'invested' at the expense of their clients' accounts. In such cases (and most others involving professional people with no prior record), the lines of mitigation are clear-cut: disqualification and loss of community standing indicate severe moral and economic suffering; the money was spent to sustain a declining practice or gambling, or else resulted from marital stress rather than from greed; the defendant has paid back as much as he can/has sold his home, and this is not a case where he has salted away the proceeds in a foreign bank account! These are usually offered as reasons for sentencing below the tariff for whatever kind of offence has been committed.

Sometimes, however, ingenious lines of mitigation are found, which confirm Mann's (1985) observations that in pre-sentence hearings, the defence are able to raise again the question of blameworthiness which is central to the issue of guilt initially. For example, in September 1986, three directors of companies in the Portland Group were fined £750 each on each of six summonses of attempting to obtain British Telecom (BT) shares by deception. They had attempted to make a total profit of some million pounds and had actually made at least £95,000 by submitting at least 1500 applications for shares in BT, which were expected (correctly) to be massively oversubscribed, attracting a large premium on the offer price when dealings commenced on The Stock Exchange. The prosecutor acknowledged that this practice had been commonplace in the City and had gone on unchecked for many years. Their mutual defence counsel, George Carman QC, said in mitigation that the BT prospectus had not given any warning that the making of multiple applications – which he described as 'a hallowed practice in the City of London' – might be treated as a criminal offence. (Before imposing a severe sentence, do we have notices on doors in inner-city areas stating that burglary might be treated as a criminal offence? The magistrate was *not* told that despite the hallowed nature of 'stagging', prosecutions for it had occurred after some previous flotations.) Defence counsel further observed that all the main parties knew what was going on, and that the prospectus had stated that multiple applications might be either rejected (in the case of oversubscription) or aggregated (in the case of undersubscription): 'It is a very strange philosophy that says, after the event, it is a crime to put in multiple applications but on the other hand, if the issue is under-subscribed, we will add them all together and adopt them.' Indeed, there is some superficial plausibility in that argument, particularly when applied to a higher risk issue than BT. In fining the men £4,500 each (plus £500 each costs), the magistrate observed that this defence plea had been particularly persuasive. Given the profit involved, the size of the fine can only have indicated the magistrate's view that the offence was a very minor one.

However, one problem counsel have in presenting mitigation is they cannot always predict whether a line of argument will count as mitigation or as aggravation. For example, the longest English fraud sentence I have found is one of 14 years imposed upon Higgs, a 40 year-old management accountant (earning a mere £8,400 a year) who defrauded his American parent company of over £3 million over a five-year period, turning the subsidiary from a profit-making to a loss-making concern. The accountant also ran a book-making business, but spent virtually all the money gambling unsuccessfully himself: during 1984, he staked £889,000. The sum involved clearly was very large, though not by the standards of some operations in the City of London, but no-one (except the plant manager, an innocent whose signed cheques were altered by the accountant) lost his job. The only tangible benefits of his fraud were a detached house in a wealthy part of Cheltenham, a new car for his wife, and public school (i.e. in Britain, private) education for his three children (costing some £300 a term). He sold his house to repay the company. The size of the fraud plainly owed much to the lax financial control system of the American company as well as to his actions, and in some cases (of fraud against banks) this has counted as mitigation, as has the fact that the money was spent gambling rather than for profit (thus allowing an argument of 'diminished moral responsibility'). As Higgs put it, after he had been caught, to the parent company's accountants: 'It was not a devious conspiracy thing. I fell into a spiral trap. I used a flood of Prestolite funds to repair the damage.'

Some judges might have imposed a short prison sentence, or even a disqualification order plus a probation order combined with a requirement to attend Gamblers Anonymous. Yet here, the sentencing judge appeared to regard none of these features as mitigating his culpability, stating: 'We are not dealing with the Great Train Robbery but a simple theft from your employers, but the amounts involved are simply miles beyond any legal authority. You did this with your eyes open to feed your gambling habit' (*The Times*, 22 March, 1986).

Another feature that may be significant in accounting for sentencing in fraud cases is the lack of hostile media publicity about 'the low level of fraud sentences' in Britain (though not in the United States). In many years of research and general reading, I have yet to observe a single case of media hysteria about light sentencing of fraudsters, yet this is a fairly common feature of street and household crime reportage. Judges do like to feel that they are reflecting 'public opinion' – though some may have curious ideas about what that opinion is – and they do not like to see confidence in legal institutions undermined by media criticism, however unrepresentative they feel the latter to be. To the extent that they are constrained neither by a judicial audience – in the form of sentencing guidelines that are clear in their application and that can be appealed to by the prosecution as well as the defence – nor by a popular audience, refracted by the media, there will be no upwards pressure on fraud sentencing, and this can float, influenced by the idiosyncracies of individual judges and the particular mitigation arguments offered by counsel, at any level below the upper limits set out in the judgments of the Court of Appeal, which are discussed later.

In Britain, there is no research into the reasons for sentences in fraud cases which corresponds to that done in the United States. As Higgs above illustrates, it is hard to predict any particular sentence from any particular set of facts about a case: were the non-gambling solicitor and self-employed builder who received 2 years and 2½ years' imprisonment respectively (*The Times*, 18 June, 1986) for masterminding a plot to swindle banks of £1 million only one-seventh as culpable as Higgs, who got 14 years? As we shall see later this chapter, even in an appellate case, a fraudster with no previous convictions could be given 4 years' imprisonment on the basis of the gravity of his offence, or given a 6-month sentence on the grounds that he had already suffered professional disqualification and we should keep offenders out of custody wherever possible. (In a trial court, he might expect less than that.) Some interviews I conducted with judges suggested that the absence of violence, the relative lack of prior convictions, and the absence of public pressure for long sentences served to mitigate sentence. In multi-defendant cases, the demands of proportionality in relation to the role played in the fraud led to the scaling-down of sentences for minor actors: so if the principal was to be shown leniency for any reason – in one case, he had spent a lot of time in prison recently and 'deserved one last chance' – the others would have to get off lightly too. But whether these are typical – and how they translate into concrete sentences, for what are the anchor points for the scaling exercise? – is unknown.

Deane makes the optimistic assumption that trial judges follow the reasoning process suggested by the Court of Appeal and by Thomas (1979). However, in 2 out of the 4 suspended sentences imposed in tax frauds, the consideration

'appeared to have been the defendant's age and previously unblemished character (including a distinguished war record in one case). In the other two, the dominant factor seems to have been the subordinate role of the individual in the fraud: in one case the defendant was the nephew to the elderly gentleman with the distinguished war record, and his emotional dependence on a domineering father (who escaped prosecution by death) had been stressed; the second involved a lady whose accountant, charged with her, was found not guilty (since he had been under the continuing effect of brain surgery) – his unfortunate client had pleaded guilty, and in imposing a suspended sentence the judge said he was reluctant to send her to prison but equally reluctant to let her go without any reminder of what she had done.'
(Deane, 1981:55)

Although the rationales given by trial judges might not meet with approval by the Court of Appeal, particular problems arise where the individual being sentenced is considered by the judge – perhaps influenced by defence pleas – to be vital to continued employment of others or to the repayment of debts: the unreported case of *Young* is an example. In *Young* (20 October, 1981), a sentence of 2 years' imprisonment, suspended for 2 years, was imposed upon the defendant for a £3.5 million tax fraud committed by his chain of Chinese restaurants over a period of four years. The trial judge commented that only if Mr Young were free to run his restaurants personally could the money be repaid. Although his guilty plea and voluntary return from Taiwan doubtless assisted his mitigation – there may even have been a plea-bargain – it is clear that Mr Young bought his way to freedom. (Given this sentence upon the principal, his co-accused received suspended 12-month prison sentences, presumably on the grounds of fairness.) Clearly, cooking the books is more profitable than practising the culinary arts alone!

There appear to be similarities between what English and American judges regard as significant to sentencing white-collar cases, though many of the cases involving high-status persons that have been prosecuted in America would be unlikely to reach the English criminal courts. The basic problem, as US judges see it, is that they have a paradoxical problem of sentencing *offences* of high gravity but *offenders* of low 'essential' badness and light prior records. The difficulty is reinforced by the strongly positive relationship between the scale of the crime and the status of the offender: as Wheeler and Rothman (1982) show, offenders who use organizations as the medium for their offences commit crimes of greater duration, sophistication, and magnitude, but they also have fewer and less serious prior convictions than those who in non-organizational contexts commit frauds on businesspeople and the public. 'Organizational offenders' are also older and have more favourable Pre-Sentence Investigation Reports from probation officers than do other 'white-collar criminals'. Wheeler, Weisburd, and Bode observed that

> 'Repeatedly in the interviews, the judges came back to the nature of the criminal *act*. A more serious offense deserves a more serious sanction. . . . First, seriousness is measured by the dollar loss attributed to the offense. . . . A second consideration is the amount of complexity or sophistication shown in the commission of the offense. . . . Third, judges talk about the *spread* of illegality. . . . Fourth, judges report being attentive to the nature of the victim.'
> (Wheeler, Weisburd, and Bode, 1982:644)

They found that *actor*-related variables were important too, and these tended to produce what they called a 'paradox of leniency and severity' (1982:645). On the one hand, the high position of the offender makes his offence more grave; on the other, his impeccable prior 'community record' generates an overall picture of someone whose moral character is generally good.

From a statistical prediction viewpoint, the chances of being sent to prison rose dramatically and consistently with increased losses generated – from 27 per cent of those defrauding less than $500 to 68 per cent for those few who caused losses of over $2,500,000. It also rose with increased complexity/sophistication, with geographical spread, with role in the offence, and with number of prior convictions. Judges seemed reluctant to imprison the young or the old, particularly the latter. Other factors being held constant, women are 30 per cent less likely to be sent to prison than men, particularly in the less cosmopolitan areas, but still significantly in places such as New York, Los Angeles, and Chicago. (Once imprisoned, however, they receive only slightly shorter sentences.) There were variations by type of offence: tax offenders and securities and exchange violators stood a much stronger chance of being sent to jail (2/3 of those convicted) than bank embezzlers and those involved in bribery (1/3) and anti-trust violators (1/4). The authors discovered that judges were not always correct in what they said about their sentencing principles. They state:

> 'Judges frequently mentioned the direct loss to individuals as a sign of the seriousness of the offense, but net of the other variables in our analysis our classification of victim by type was not significant. Similarly, though judges mentioned the importance of the number of victims, we found a negligible relationship.'
> (Wheeler, Weisburd, and Bode, 1982:650)

Different criteria – particularly the importance of *actor*-related variables – come into play when deciding on the length of sentence, once the decision to incarcerate has been taken. The social background and prior convictions of the defendant, his plea, and the district in which sentencing occurs, seem most important. District variations could represent differences in local norms – suggested by Hagan, Nagel, and Albonetti (1980) – or the need of prosecutors to engage in plea-bargaining if they wish to have a high-prosecution profile: trade-offs become necessary (as they are in street and household crimes) to induce defendants to inform against their fellows, to keep the case-load moving along and allow time for the next set of prosecutions (Nagel and Hagan, 1982). This happened in 1986–87 insider dealing.

The inverse relationship between frequency of prosecution and levels of sentence has been noted in other studies also. It may be that in areas where white-collar cases are comparatively rare, and other sorts of crimes comparatively modest in seriousness, white-collar crimes may be viewed more negatively by judges: that is one possible explanation for my finding that sentences for long-firm frauds were higher at Manchester Crown Court than at the London Central Criminal Court (Levi, 1981). However, one possible interpretation for Braithwaite and Vale's (1985:155) unexplained finding that consumer violations were sentenced so differently in different Australian states is that active prosecution departments are likely to bring 'less serious' cases as well as 'serious' ones to court: under those conditions, even without any plea-bargaining or (slightly perverse) sentence *reductions* due to the fact that a particular offence had become so common as to count as routine, the 'gravity' criterion alone would reduce the average level of sentencing in high-prosecution compared with low-prosecution areas.

Wheeler, Weisburd, and Bode suggest three possible explanations for their findings, all of which may be true: heightened penalties to those few high-status offenders who trickle through to the sentencing stage, influenced perhaps by the post-Watergate atmosphere, but anchored also in historical patterns of *noblesse oblige* (Wheeler, Weisburd, and Bode, 1982:658).

In observations arising out of the same research project, Mann,

Wheeler, and Sarat elaborate the sentencing philosophies of the judges. They state: 'the sentencing purpose and rationale tends to be unidimensional: judges are concerned with general deterrence. . . . They tend not to be concerned at all with rehabilitation or incapacitation and . . . only minimally with punishment' (Mann, Wheeler, and Sarat, 1980:479). One judge justified his view that prison sentences deter:

> 'When I was still practising there were the electrical equipment antitrust cases. . . . They made screaming headlines. A few businessmen went to prison for terms like thirty, sixty, ninety days. I thought they were very sound sentences. And as a private practitioner I was made aware that all of a sudden businessmen were running into our firm wanting to know what the hell were the antitrust laws and how do you obey them. It really had an impact.'
>
> (Mann, Wheeler, and Sarat, 1980:483)

(A similar effect occurred in the aftermath of British scandals at Morgan Grenfell and Guiness in 1986–87.) The authors conclude that both retribution and special deterrence are satisfied by the stigma and economic losses consequent upon conviction; that by the time the offender has paid his legal bills, he has no money left because he has lost his job and has heavy routine financial commitments. Sometimes, a deterrent sentence will be passed for public consumption – an interesting elision of deterrence with denunciation – but in spite of their belief in the efficacy of deterrence, judges do not like to impose prison sentences unless they also feel that the offender deserves punishment. Moreover, judges perceive that white-collar criminals have a special sensitivity to imprisonment; that incarceration will harm innocent parties; that it may inhibit compensation; and that non-custodial 'reparations' are possible, such as community service. Perhaps, though there is no mention of it in their analysis or interviews, judges perceive that businesspeople, unlike the labouring and non-labouring poor, do not *need* the threat of severe sanctions to be generally law-abiding. This kind of perspective – added to paternalism/chauvinism – might also help to account for the lower risk of imprisonment for women, who are not seen as part of 'the dangerous classes' requiring harsh punishment to remain in line.

So what we end up with is a curious set of ambivalences in white-collar cases, which give judges dilemmas that are far more complex emotionally than in the more routine cases that normally preoccupy the courts. I will give three examples from different countries, which reveal the open-endedness in possible outcomes in high-status fraud cases. Any of these three cases could plausibly have ended in completely different outcomes.

1 In what appeared to be a specific plea-bargain between defendant and

prosecutor, Tan Koon Swan, the head of the Malaysian Chinese Association – the Chinese partner in the Malaysian Government coalition – pleaded guilty in Singapore in August 1986 to a charge of abetment in criminal breach of trust, which carries a maximum sentence of 3 years' imprisonment and an unlimited fine. He had manipulated the shares in the huge conglomerate Pan-Electric Industries, which was the first Singapore public company to go into liquidation. The Singapore authorities stated that they would not pursue other, more serious charges, for which the maximum was life imprisonment, subject to his paying £8.7 million restitution to Pan-Electric Industries and his easing the forward purchases of some $53 million made by that company. Prior to sentence, the judge was told that he had agreed to do this. It was anticipated by many (myself included) that he would get a substantial fine – like *Young*, the Taiwanese restaurateur mentioned earlier – but in fact, the trial judge stated that the public interest required a punishment that would not only fit the crime but would act as a deterrent. The crime 'struck at the very heart of the integrity, reputation and confidence of Singapore as a commercial and financial centre' (*Financial Times*, 27 August, 1986). So despite his plea of guilty, the fact that he and his family own and manage 40 per cent of companies capitalized at $234 million, and the fact that he was one of the most significant political and commercial figures in Malaysia, he was sentenced to 2 years' imprisonment and fined £155,400. Though not obliged to do so, because disqualification arises only for those convicted of offences in Malaysia (and not in Singapore), he subsequently resigned from the Malaysian Chinese Association. As I write, it seems unlikely that the promise of easing the forward contracts will be honoured because with him in prison, the share prices of his companies will not be high enough to make this viable. (To place this in perspective, one fellow Pan-Electric director who pleaded guilty much earlier received a 15-month sentence, while another, Peter Tham, was found guilty of forging share certificates and transfer forms and was sentenced to 8 years' imprisonment. So even though he was jailed, it appears that Swan did derive some *comparative* benefit from his plea and reparation.)

2 In May 1985, 65 year-old Paul Thayer, the former Reagan administration Deputy Defence Secretary, and a former stockbroker friend were each imprisoned for 4 years after pleading guilty to obstructing justice during an SEC investigation into an insider-dealing scheme. Thayer and a group of associates had made over $1.9 million illicitly in a year, and Thayer agreed to pay $550,000 in

settlement before sentence (presumably hoping to mitigate punishment). The trial judge rejected appeals for probation and community service, stating that a heavy sentence was needed to deter insider trading and that there was a 'necessity' for Mr Thayer to be sent to prison in order to protect 'the credibility of the criminal justice system' (*Financial Times*, 9 May, 1985). He might just as well have argued that although the crime was very serious, he was showing leniency because of the age of the defendant, his lack of prior convictions, and because he had suffered enough already. As Thayer himself pleaded in mitigation: 'I have paid a terrible price for an action that has, in effect, destroyed my life. I don't like myself as much as I used to.' The judge's reasons for imprisoning were clear – and note the implicit appeal to fairness in upholding the credibility of the criminal justice system – but as in Tan Koon Swan's case above, another set of reasons would have led to a completely different (and more lenient) sentence.

3 In Britain, by contrast, before 1987, no one went to prison for insider dealing, and those convicted in the period 1981–86 have received modest fines (though unlike the US cases referred to, they have all involved comparatively small sums and have not revealed any organized plots). For example, a former director of W.H. Smith (a leading firm of newsagent/retailers) was fined £800 plus £100 costs by the City of London magistrates. He had purchased 1500 shares in a company that W.H. Smith were researching for a possible take-over but subsequently, a rival bidder emerged and he sold the shares at a profit of £3000 (in 1984). Later that year, he resigned from the board on the grounds of ill-health. After the hearing, the W.H. Smith Chairman mitigated further the public image of the offence when he said later that there was no connection between the resignation and the share purchase, and that his former director:

> 'was at worst guilty of a technical offence. "It was a pure oversight, involving a tiny amount. Technically he was guilty." The company had "very strict in-house rules" stipulating that directors could not deal in the shares of any company it was researching.'   (*The Times*, 29 April, 1986)

English prosecutors are not yet allowed to play an explicit role in the sentencing process. But whether or not there is prosecutorial involvement, the public importance of the fraud *may* produce an environment in which a severe symbolic sentence appears required for at least one defendant. For instance, though other directors involved received lesser sentences, the owner of one Austrian wine company, Karl Peer, received an 8-year prison sentence in October 1986 for producing and selling 21 litres of wine contaminated by diethyl glycol.

Sanctions upon corporations themselves present different considerations from sanctions upon natural persons, for the fear of causing unemployment reduces sentences even where the offence is viewed gravely. This applies not only to pollution and to health and safety offences but to frauds. In December 1980, Mr Justice Jupp, sentencing a subsidiary of the textiles company Gannex Ltd in relation to an international fraud of over £500,000 upon HM Customs and Excise, almost £190,000 of which could not be traced, observed:

'Unfortunately, I have come to the conclusion that punishment will fall upon the innocent. There are people working in these companies whose jobs are in jeopardy. . . . It is going to be poor comfort to them if the Court imposes a fine which closes a factory and causes anyone to lose his job.'

He imposed a fine of £375,000 (plus £93,000 costs) upon the company, which was reduced on appeal, and whose payment still remains outstanding in 1986, the Inland Revenue finally agreeing to accept staged payments. Lord Kagan himself was sentenced to 10 months' imprisonment, fined £105,000, and disqualified for 3 years – including his spell in prison – from taking part in the management of a company: in mitigation was his plea of guilty and the fact that he had spent 3½ months in a French jail, albeit resisting extradition. As a 'surprise' bonus, charges against his wife and son were dropped since, as prosecution counsel observed, 'the prosecution of this matter would have been prolonged, difficult, and costly'. He is now supplying quality greatcoats to Soviet leaders!

Sometimes, though not consistently, the socio-economic implications of 'regulatory' but not fraudulent violation leads to the imposition of very substantial fines (in absolute terms, not necessarily as proportions of the company's assets or turnover), where offences have persisted for a long time. For example in 1985 and 1986, Pan-American and Eastern Airlines were given multi-million dollar fines for failing to make adequate airline safety checks. In a different set of cases, in August 1985, the Crocker National Bank was fined £1.6 million by the Treasury in settlement for 'failure' to report cash transactions exceeding $10,000 as required to do under US law; the Bank of Boston was fined $500,000 for helping customers to shift $1.2 billion to Swiss banks without reporting the transactions to the Treasury. This plainly was treated as a serious issue, partly because of the importance of money-laundering to the growth of organized crime. Thus, there is an intersection of 'white-collar' with 'organized' crime: a point which as we shall see later, complicates the examination of relationships between class, crime, and sentencing.

However, in other instances, sanctions are inhibited not only by fear of causing unemployment but also by the involvement of the company in activities considered vital to the state itself, particularly in the area of defence contracting. This raises problems both for judicial sentencing and for government policy. The generosity of the British Government in dealing with over-pricing by defence contractors has been examined elsewhere (Clarke, 1981), but in 1985, a number of scandals in the US defence industry led to General Dynamics being fined $676,283 for giving a top Pentagon official substantial gifts for his wife. In May 1985, the Navy Secretary banned General Dynamics from obtaining new contracts until it repaid $75 million in overcharges, but rejected a recommendation from the Pentagon's Inspector-General that three high-ranking senior executives be banned from taking part in military contracts. An even tougher deterrent line might have been taken, but sanctions may be influenced by the political and financial muscle of the 'military-industrial complex' (which directly or indirectly funds 1 in 10 employed Americans), and the monopoly or oligopoly in the building of missile systems like Trident weakens the bargaining power of government and makes it harder even for a government that *wants* to act to impose any major punishment short of nationalization.

PUNISHMENTS BY OFFICIAL SROs

As discussed earlier, the penalty options available to self-regulatory agencies are limited: the heaviest penalties are expulsion and fines. In the Stock Exchange cases, much argument appears to focus on culpability, for although it is a breach of the Rules to fail to regulate one's partners or employees, a limiting retributivist perspective appears to be adopted whereby severe sanctions such as expulsion are reserved for cases where *personal* malefaction rather than simple regulatory failure has been proven. However, culpability judgments are not self-evident: they are the result of constructions placed upon 'the evidence', and to the extent that people can insulate themselves from proof of having been involved in and having benefited from a particular course of conduct, they will have an advantage in rebutting culpability. This is a structural advantage for those committing offences – criminal or disciplinary – within an organizational context, for lines of responsibility become blurred there. (Braithwaite, 1984, in his analysis of corporate crime in the pharmaceutical industry, notes that lines of accountability which are very clear for internal managerial purposes suddenly become opaque when regulatory officials ask the company what they are: though cover-ups in the face of threats from outside or from organizational superiors are commonplace and are not restricted to criminal allegations.)

At Lloyd's, 10 out of 13 cases from 1984–86 had multiple defendants;

at The Stock Exchange, 14 out of 33 cases from the introduction of new disciplinary procedures in 1978 to November 1986 involved multiple defendants. Except in some rare cases, notions of scaling sentence according to culpability are generally employed, particularly where, as in these cases, defendants are all 'first offenders'. On the other hand, below expulsion, a utilitarian approach is adopted, inasmuch as despite their greater ability to distance themselves from direct involvement in breaches of the Rules, senior personnel tend to be given stiffer punishments to encourage them to display a high level of supervision. It should be noted that these sentences are imposed not for fraud but for breaches of rules which often impose a duty of care: for instance, a duty to enquire into the *bona fides* and the full name and identity of people for whom one acts. (I am grateful to The Stock Exchange and to Lloyd's for providing me with details of their disciplinary cases.)

Although those seeking precise sentencing guidelines will find nothing to assist them, the Disciplinary Committees set up by The Stock Exchange do give some account of reasons for mitigation and aggravation. These reveal the sort of admixture of sentencing 'principles' that one finds in appellate and trial court judgments. A good example is the case of a Member I shall term A, who in 1985 pleaded guilty to charges related to the placing of shares in an Unlisted Securities Market company that had been sponsored by a company controlled by someone not a Member of The Stock Exchange. We can see the way in which negligence considered to be short of 'wilful blindness' seems to act as a form of mitigation of culpability, when contrasted with active participation in the fraudulent scheme. It was not in fact the case that either he or his firm benefited – it was apparently done as a naive favour – and the absence of personal benefit did count as mitigation. Note also that the first charge was merely 'improper', while deceiving the Council investigator was 'disgraceful' (though the disgrace was mitigated by prompt recantation). Indeed, had he told the truth immediately, it is unlikely that he would have been charged at all. The charges and rationales were summarized out as follows:

'(1) At the request of the non-Member for names to be used as nominees A gave the names of his wife and infant daughter and the name of a discretionary client. This enabled the non-Member to use those names as initial placees for shares in the USM company. A made no enquiry about the use to be made of the names or about the purpose of such an arrangement.

Although the Disciplinary Committee are satisfied that A was unaware of the fact, the arrangement enabled shares in the USM company to be brought under the control of the non-Member who had been refused allocations by The Stock Exchange. By using the nominee names provided by A, the non-Member deceived the sponsoring brokers as to the identity of the beneficial owner of the shares.

The Disciplinary Committee found that A acted in a manner detrimental to the interests of The Stock Exchange and in an improper manner.

(2) When a series of questions in connection with the placing was subsequently put to A by an employee of the Council of The Stock Exchange, A intentionally misled the employee, falsely indicating that he had had no direct involvement in the matter. Following that interview A immediately requested a further interview at which he told the truth.

The Disciplinary Committee found that A acted in a manner detrimental to The Stock Exchange and in a disgraceful manner.

In considering its penalty, the Disciplinary Committee took account of the strain and stress which A was suffering at the time he agreed to supply the names to a non-Member and that he had not appreciated the full implications of what he was doing. The Disciplinary Committee also took account of the fact that he received no direct financial gain from his actions and that he immediately corrected his statements to the employee of the Council.'

In a 1986 case in which two partners and two employees of a small firm were expelled for defrauding a New York securities dealer of at least $264,000 in bogus Eurobond deals, the finance partner was suspended for trading for a year rather than expelled: it was held that he had been negligent, but not dishonest, to a very substantial degree and thus did not deserve expulsion. Although the formal sanctions may be thought to be fairly modest – 28 per cent of cases more severe than a reprimand led to expulsion, and the income of partners (though not of their salaried associates) may not suffer greatly due to their suspension, since they share in their firm's profits – comment is sometimes made about the higher responsibilities of senior personnel along with some general 'crime prevention' advice. A particular vice of securities dealers is booking purchases or sales of shares to a suspense account and then, depending on whether the share goes up, down, or stays roughly the same, booking it to their own account or a client's account: this has a very high gravity rating. Thus, in suspending a senior partner in one substantial broking firm for three months in September 1985, the Disciplinary and Appeals Committees

'took into account the fact that delay in issuing contract notes . . . and the misuse of a suspense account afford an easy avenue to fraud and other serious abuses. The proper administration of a broker's business requires that the rule be rigidly complied with and a Member should not accept instructions from a client that would result in a contravention of it. Many of the clients whose contract notes were delayed were personal clients of the Senior Partner. It is also an obligation of a firm (and in particular the Senior Partner) to ensure that the use of any suspense account is strictly and carefully monitored. . . . [The Senior Partner] failed to discharge that responsibility.'

On the other hand, where *active* complicity in a scheme with a high gravity rating is proven, expulsion is a likely outcome. In 1983, a broker and a jobber were both expelled following a case where mutual personal financial benefit occurred and the nature of the transactions was impossible to represent as a 'mere' regulatory breach committed without clear advantage to the Member:

> 'The Charges concerned dealings for his own account in the Short-dated Gilt-edged market by Mr. B, who became a partner in a Firm of Brokers in July 1974. Since 1973 Mr. B had been a close personal friend of Mr. C, who was an Associated Member with a firm of Jobbers and from 1979 a dealer for his Firm in short-dated Gilts.
> An arrangement developed between Mr. B and Mr. C. The two Members would discuss the state of the market: Mr. C would advise Mr. B on the Gilt-edged market and would assist him to deal at beneficial prices, and would conceal the fact from his own Firm by booking the bargains in other than chronological sequence.
> In recognition of the advice and assistance received, Mr. B made cash payments to Mr. C amounting to £20,000 during the period concerned.'

These examples do not tell the complete story. For offences completely beyond the pale and committed by people well outside the 'inner circles' – such as the Eurobond fraud – a public degradation ceremony is called for and this presents sentencers with no ambivalent emotions. But in a situation where there was no public, external pressure to impose heavy sanctions and where those accused were not generally seen to be 'rogues', professionals sitting in judgment on their fellows might be inclined to take the view that 'there but for the grace of God go I'. This would mitigate sanctions considerably, lest severity be applied to the sentencers themselves in the future. Some acts similar to those discussed above might have ended merely in reprimands: from these there would be no appeal or other public record. So this picture of quasi-judicial sentencing on The Stock Exchange is only a partial portrait.

There is no space for such detail on the reasoning employed by Lloyd's Disciplinary Committees when determining sentence. However, there too, notions of offence gravity and personal responsibility arise in what are usually multi-defendant cases. The more active the role, the greater the sentence; the greater the scandal and less genuine the transactions, the larger the sentences. The three solo defendants received punishments of a censure plus £1000 fine plus £400 costs; a 12-month suspension plus censure plus £5000 costs (settled by Lloyd's for £3000); and expulsion plus a £175,000 fine and £80,000 costs. Partly because of the scale and publicity attached to their offences, the principals of 'conspiracies' tended to be dealt with heavily. I will illustrate this with three examples.

1 In the syndicate run by Peter Cameron-Webb, who had the foresight of resign from Lloyd's before disciplinary action was taken, thereby evading the possibility of being dealt with by them (though in theory, he may still be prosecuted by the criminal courts), eight PCW directors paid away millions of pounds in PCW syndicates' premium income in the form of re-insurance to companies secretly owned by themselves. The seven who were available for discipline were sentenced as follows: Dixon – expelled, fined £1 million, with costs of £125,000; Wallrock – the former Chairman of Minet holdings, one of Britain's largest insurance brokers – expelled, no fine, but costs of £125,000 (reduced on appeal to £90,000); Sampson (the Members' agent) – expelled with £18,733 costs; Hardman – suspended 2 years with £56,200 costs; Oldworth – suspended 1 year with £37,466 costs; Davies – suspended 1 year with £40,172 costs; and Hill – reprimanded and censured, with £9,366 costs.

2 Four directors of the insurance brokers Alexander Howden purchased a Swiss bank with money obtained through re-insurance premiums paid to Panamanian companies controlled by Liechtenstein trusts associated with the directors. Three of the directors – known as the Gang of Four – were expelled with about £45,000 costs each, while the case against the fourth had been adjourned due to his heart attack. Posgate – who earlier had been reprimanded and censured in another case – was excluded, but this was reduced on appeal to a 6-month suspension plus his own costs. Benbassat, who had arranged the purchase of the Swiss Banque du Rhone, was expelled with costs of £25,000. In July 1986, another director of Alexander Howden was censured and ordered to pay £14,250 in costs after he was found guilty of 'dishonourable conduct' for failing to disclose the receipt of $50,000 in company funds which had been paid into a Liechtenstein *anstalt* (company) beneficially owned and ultimately controlled by him. (His appeal failed.)

3 Two underwriters set up their own re-insurance group (ironically named Fidentia) in Bermuda, assisted by two Bermudian lawyers. These companies re-insured genuine risks and paid the syndicates' claims, so were not a complete 'rip-off'. The principal underwriter, Brooks, was expelled with £39,688 costs; the 'stooge' underwriter, Dooley, was suspended for 21 months from doing business at and

from Membership of Lloyd's, with £12,153 costs; and the Bermudian lawyers were reprimanded with £1,000 and £500 costs respectively. (They continue in practice there.)

In his unsuccessful appeal against Ian Posgate's continued exclusion from Lloyd's as being not a 'fit and proper person', despite having had his sentence reduced from a life ban to a six-month suspension, his counsel requested the appeals tribunal to take account of his outstanding record of success as an underwriter (23 June, 1986):

> 'his errors which have been dealt with by disciplinary proceedings occurred at a time when Lloyd's standards were sadly lax in numerous ways and unclear in others . . . many aspects of Lloyd's conduct . . . created the climate of a market in which it was not easy to know where the boundaries of propriety were to be drawn.'

His acquittal on the more serious charges at his original hearing was used in an attempt to limit retribution. Moreover, his counsel stated that unlike others accused of irregularities who had protected themselves by seeking 'safe havens' abroad, Posgate had co-operated with all enquiries and had spent a lot of money to fight for the right to practise the only occupation he knew. To this was added the 'situational' point that if allowed to return to underwriting, he would be working under the supervision of an 'impeccable board of directors' and in a market where standards had been transformed. However, Lord Wilberforce – the President of the appeals tribunal – dismissed the appeal, observing that the authorities at Lloyd's were entitled to pay regard to the evidence that he showed a 'high degree of negligence and disregard' of the interests of members of the insurance syndicates which he had managed. This may be interpreted as a conflict between a 'social defence' (or 'dangerous offender') approach which seeks to maximize the discretion of regulatory bodies (in this case subject to the rules of natural justice), and a backward-looking retributivist approach which presumably would rule out the 'fit and proper person' test except where the past behaviour *itself* merited a ban.

The significance that is attached to different penalties is dealt with later in this chapter, but should give some cause for thought. Suspension from trading and membership can be highly expensive, if one is earning several hundred thousand pounds per annum. Therefore, to the extent that this does inhibit profit, the mere absence of a large fine or imprisonment should not be taken to reflect the absence of punishment. David d'Ambrumenil, a leading insurance broker, was suspended by Lloyd's for six months in July 1986 following criticism in a Department of Trade and Industry report of his alleged dishonesty in laundering funds from Minet's PCW syndicate on behalf of himself, Peter Cameron-Webb, and Peter Dixon: one presumes that his financial losses arising out of this suspension will be considerable. Ian Posgate was reputed to earn some £700,000 per annum from his underwriting, so a six-month suspension might have cost him £350,000! However, the impact of such prohibition orders is variable and some persons expelled from Lloyd's – for example Christopher Moran – have not suffered enormous financial hardship from that fact. The consequences of being disciplined is an important area for future research. I return to this theme later, but it is relevant when considering issues of sentencing discrimination to which I now turn.

Do commercial fraudsters receive discriminatory treatment?

The term 'discrimination' is not used in a morally neutral way: it implies that differences exist in the treatment of different people that are *unjustifiable*. (That may be why discrimination that one considers justifiable is labelled 'affirmative action'.) To show that people are treated differently is not in itself conclusive: few people think that different sentences for murder and shoplifting are examples of discrimination. The notion of disparity assumes that we are comparing like with like, and it is precisely this that is so difficult. What do we mean by 'like'? The trouble is that one seldom finds adult members of different social classes or status groups committing 'the same offence': even fraudulent trading, which might lay claim to being a rare example of an offence committed by both 'businesspeople' and 'villains', often is differentiated in terms of the degree of criminal intent in commencing trading initially (Levi, 1981). Likewise with many VAT frauds. It is one thing to argue over whether or not any given sentence or sentencing policy is 'too strict' or 'too lenient'. It is quite another to say that one set of sentences for one crime is unfair compared with a set of sentences for another type of crime as has been done, for example, by Snider (1982).

Moreover, the interpretation of differentials in one way rather than another is subjective. If we were to show that commercial fraudsters were sentenced more leniently than commercial burglars, but that first-offender commercial fraudsters were sentenced *less* leniently than first-time commercial burglars, what would this show? We might equally well counter that pound-for-pound stolen, first-time fraudsters got off more lightly. And what if 'fairness of punishment' incorporated a notion of the impact of punishment upon different offenders? How would we weigh the loss of employment prospects for the convicted fraudsters against the continued unemployment prospects of the convicted burglar?

(This issue will be addressed in Chapter 8 when we look at the impact and philosophy of punishment.)

The most sophisticated research on sentencing white-collar crime has been done in North America. Nagel and Hagan (1982) found that when they compared four groups – college-educated people convicted of (1) white-collar, and (2) common crimes, and less-educated people convicted of these crimes – only the category of college-educated people convicted of common crimes received preferential treatment: the college-educated convicted of the white-collar crimes did not. Wheeler, Weisburd, and Bode (1982) suggest that *once they reach the sentencing stage*, high-status *fraud* offenders are *more* likely to be imprisoned than lower-status fraudsters (though the former get slightly shorter sentences than the latter). But Hagan and Parker (1985) found that at least as regards securities offences, employers received more lenient treatment than managers, partly because employers tended to be prosecuted under the local Ontario Securities Act while managers (and lower-status employees) were more often prosecuted under the national Criminal Code. This in turn reflected the fact that employers were able to make their offences more complex and difficult to prosecute: judges would then regard these more as 'technical' than as 'real' criminal offences and would sentence employers accordingly. The authors hypothesized that in a form of capitalism where ownership and management are divorced, owners of capital may find it easier to distance themselves from responsibility: a point made also by many other authors in relation to the manufacture of dangerous products, anti-trust, pollution, and health and safety violations. (Perhaps this, combined with the fact that he was aged 68, explains why in June 1985, the head of a French waste-disposal firm was sentenced to only 18 months jail – 17 months of which were suspended – for receiving and concealing the highly toxic dioxin waste from the disaster at Seveso, Italy.) The arguments of Hagan and Parker (1985) might suggest that it is the notion of culpability itself, not any *deliberate* bias on the part of any individual judge or judges as a group, that generates leniency for white-collar criminals: the key role played by culpability attributions applies to the processes of prosecution and conviction also. Indeed, it is likely to operate in Britain by discouraging prosecution where there is no clear culpability nexus between the senior personnel and the 'criminals acts' that are carried out. The main exception to this is where the law imposes legal liability upon directors – for example for fraudulent trading – which it does not impose on employees.

The punishments imposed by The Stock Exchange and by Lloyd's discussed in the previous section cannot include imprisonment, but there was no clear evidence there that higher-status 'offenders' were sentenced more leniently. They enjoyed a structural favour, inasmuch as partners who are suspended from entering the floor of the exchange nevertheless continue to enjoy their share of the partnership income, so what looks like severe punishment may not affect their earnings (apart from the extra profits that their presence might have brought). By contrast, their lower-status associates lose their livelihood if they are suspended. But setting aside these critical economic consequences of censure, and quite apart from what sentencers *say* about the greater moral turpitude of malefactions by senior personnel, partners actually were normally given more severe *formal* penalties in multi-defendant cases. There were exceptions to this, however. In one case, a firm of stockbrokers gave 60 per cent kickbacks in commission in exchange for insurance brokers' falsely representing to insurance companies that the stockbrokers had introduced the business. B was suspended from trading for 1 year; C was suspended for 9 months; D and E were censured:

> 'In assessing the penalties appropriate in each case the Disciplinary Committee took into account that fact that it was B who was responsible for setting up the arrangement after C had been approached by the non-Member. Nevertheless, with the exception of the improper use of the [stockbroker] firm's stamp in the insurance broker's office, D and E were aware of the arrangement and as Senior Partner and Administrative and Finance Partner respectively, they should have either prevented its implementation or terminated it as soon as they became aware of its implications. In fact, the partners benefited from the arrangement for almost a year, and only terminated it when the introduction by the Council of a new financial return from firms made its discovery likely.'

So here, responsibility chains did benefit the senior partner. On the other hand, it does seem likely in this case that the senior figures actually were not responsible for devising and implementing the scheme, though they benefited equally from it. So in what sense is the sentencing differential 'unfair', given that all four were partners? It may be argued that compared with the sorts of sentences that someone involved in acts with similar costs outside the professional sphere might expect, the punishments are far from severe, but here we return again to the fact that these are not criminal cases and are judged in relation to the punishments available to The Stock Exchange, with expulsion being reserved for cases that are high both on the offence gravity and personal responsibility scales.

Part of the problem with these white-collar crime comparisons is that they tend to divorce the sentencing of different groups of offenders as if they were treated by different courts. In reality, except in those European jurisdictions such as West Germany that have special courts for economic offences, any given judge has a wide mix of cases. Given this, it follows that compared with the mass of offenders who come before him, the judge may feel greater moral ambivalence about white-collar than about other sorts of offenders. For one thing, the white-collar defendant typically will have a lighter criminal record than almost any adult being sentenced for burglary or robbery, and most people believe that people with prior convictions should be sentenced more harshly than those without.

The very great majority of those convicted of fraud and forgery are *not* the up-market offenders or even sophisticated professional criminals that would be the most interesting points of comparison. However, a statistical survey by the Home Office (1986c) of persons convicted in 1982 confirms not only that (unless recidivists on average commit far more serious crimes) the courts punish persistence, but that this is disproportionately likely to benefit those convicted of fraud and forgery, as against those convicted of burglary or robbery (see *Table 22*.)

Table 22 *Percentage of males 21 or over sentenced to immediate and to suspended custody in 1982, by offence and number of previous convictions*

	no previous convictions	1–5 previous convictions	6+ previous convictions
frauds and forgery	10 (18)	10 (13)	32 (20)
burglary and robbery	24 (22)	30 (14)	56 (20)

Note: Figures in brackets refer to percentage given suspended sentences.
Source: Home Office (1986c)

Those convicted of fraud and forgery were significantly more likely than burglars to be first offenders: 32 per cent of them were, compared with 19 per cent of those convicted of burglary within a dwelling, and 26 per cent of those convicted of burglary other than in a dwelling. At the other end of the spectrum, only 19 per cent of those convicted of fraud and forgery had 10 or more previous convictions, compared with 29 per cent of domestic, and 22 per cent of non-domestic burglars.

Moreover, the advantage has been increasing for fraudsters. Over the period 1977–82, the proportion of first offenders imprisoned for fraud remained constant at 10 per cent (though fines dropped, to be replaced by suspended sentences). For burglary and robbery, however, the rate of imprisonment for first offenders shot up from 13 per cent in 1977 to 24 per cent in 1982, while suspended sentences also increased from 11 per cent to 22 per cent (Home Office, 1986c). If one has a substantial number of prior convictions, one is much less likely to receive a fine: of males 21 or older convicted for fraud and forgery in 1982, 51 per cent with no previous convictions, 50 per cent with 1–5 previous convictions, and 29 per cent with 6 or more previous convictions received fines.

To the extent that each white-collar crime has on average a lower probability of being defined as such, reported, and prosecuted than any street or household crime (other than family violence), the importance of prior convictions is a form of structural advantage for white-collar criminals: some would call this indirect discrimination. For another, the notion of 'impeccability' referred to by Wheeler, Weisburd, and Bode (1982) is a form of social bias which results from the greater identification of the judge with the social world of the fraudster – particularly the fraudulent professional person – than that of the burglar.

However, let us reflect on what is meant by impeccable here. If the offender has been involved in various 'good works' in the community, that is one thing. But setting aside any possible Masonic influences (Knight, 1985), is the mere fact that the offender has been an employer, has not been a (known) cad to his family, is a loyal member of the golf club, and has pals with high-status jobs and without previous convictions who will speak for him in court an indicator of 'impeccability'? In practice, yes. But this is not a sign of superior moral worth but of superior *situation*. Indeed, there is even social-status discrimination *within* the category of white-collar crime: Wheeler and Rothman note that prior to sentence, those who committed their offences through their organizations were four times as likely as other 'white-collar criminals' to have a supporting letter in their file from someone in the community (Wheeler and Rothman, 1982:1422). It is hardly surprising that members of lower social classes (and even professional con-men) will find greater difficulty in producing persons of high standing to speak for their 'impeccability'. Sometimes, 'lower-class' individuals *are* the beneficiaries of a petition on their behalf from the local community, and judges give this as a reason for imposing a lower sentence. (As Hay, 1975, argues, the practice of the squirearchy pleading to the King for the commutation of death sentences was an important feature reinforcing local relations of allegiance in the seventeenth century.) But such petitions are hardly the preserve of the poor: they benefit high-status people also, as when local people plead for a local doctor to be treated leniently for fiddling his expenses 'because he is a good doctor'. Fitzmaurice and Pease (1986) note that judges tend to neglect situational influences upon crime in favour of views that see crime as the product of pathology: but white-collar criminals may be the exception to this generalization (as they are in criminological theory).

Mann makes the following comparison between white-collar and other crimes, noting that the white-collar defence attorney's objective in sentencing hearings 'is to characterize the defendant as having behaved in a normal manner, given the particular circumstances in which he acted. It follows that he says to the judge: the prosecution's understanding of the circumstances is incorrect. The argument does not fit the street-crime situation. There, the defense attorney must admit that his client's behavior was deviant. Any attempt to reduce the level of culpability attributed to the deviant must focus upon the defendant's personality. The attorney argues: the defendant is so abnormal that he – rather than a prosecutor – was incapable of appreciating the meaning of the circumstances in which he acted.' (Mann, 1985:218–19)

This is an oversimplification of street-crime defences, but Mann is right in arguing that the absence of substantive legal argument at the sentencing stage is a major difference between white-collar and other cases: this might be viewed as discrimination, though it is partly a function of differences arising out of the complexity of the acts themselves rather than from the social standing of the accused. Unfortunately, he does not compare white-collar with 'organized crime' cases, where sometimes there are similar problems in linking defendants to particular harmful acts. But quite apart from any bad publicity about 'gangsters' that might be generated by publicity-hungry prosecutors, in organized crime cases, the nature of the activity itself would tend to dominate as the *gestalt*. It is difficult to argue that one did not intend to cause harm by narcotics trafficking, vice racketeering, dumping toxic waste in the rivers, illegally transporting $1 million in cash out of the country, not to mention killing rival gang members! Besides, police and media campaigns make it a familiar concept that one can be 'a gangster' without having prior convictions – potential witnesses are 'too frightened to talk' or have been 'quietly eliminated without trace' – whereas cultural expectations mean that 'a businessman' or 'a professional' is seldom defined retrospectively as 'a fraudster all along' unless he or she has the convictions to support such an allegation.

Wealthy defendants can also afford more legal manoeuvres designed to keep them out of prison, though these do not necessarily succeed: in 1986, 32-stone international financier Alex Herbage was refused *habeas corpus* by the High Court despite his plea that he was being kept in 'outrageous' conditions of solitary confinement while remanded in Pentonville awaiting extradition charges to America involving an alleged £31 million fraud. (He was later granted judicial review of the 'cruel and inhuman' treatment he claimed to receive, but the courts did not uphold his claim for an interim relief against the Governor and the Home Secretary (*The Times Law Reports*, 21 May, 1986).) In Britain, unlike the United States, it is extremely rare for anyone to be granted bail while appealing against a prison sentence.

In the previous section of the chapter, we noted that American studies have examined in a statistical way and through interviews the relationship between sentencing and power. The evidence is not unambiguous – compare Wheeler, Weisburd, and Bode (1982) with Hagan and Parker (1985) – but it does suggest that high-status offenders convicted of fraud are not treated unduly leniently compared with others convicted of fraud, particularly if one holds culpability constant. Some further light may be shed upon this issue by raw comparisons of sentencing in US District Courts set out in *Table 23*.

Table 23   *Average sentences in US District Courts, 1983*

type of crime	% imprisoned	average sentence (months)
robbery	93	154.1
burglary	73	103.8
larceny and theft	46	42.7
auto theft	69	50.4
embezzlement	29	32.8
fraud	42	36.3
forgery and counterfeiting	55	41.7
bribery	43	33.2
anti-trust	22	3.3
Food and Drug Act	6	31.5

Source: US Department of Justice (1985)

These data do not take account of relevant variables such as prior convictions, which may be more common among typical burglars and car thieves than among fraudsters (particularly anti-trust offenders). However, leaving aside robbery – and its greater weighting for violence – the data are *prima˙facie* indicators of leniency for fraudsters: with the exception of forgery and counterfeiting – whose status as 'white-collar' is ambiguous – it is clear that the imprisonment rates and the average length of sentences for those imprisoned are substantially lower for fraud than for 'common crime' offences. As Hagan and Parker (1985) point out in a different context, the difficulty is that these aggregated data on fraud do not tell us much about the social class or status position of offenders, but looking at particular target groups for which comparisons may be made, we see that there are strong 'type of crime' differences in the rates and average lengths of imprisonment for offenders against banks, but a less clear relationship in the case of those who offend against the postal services (see *Table 24*).

However, there is an alternative way of viewing the sentencing data which might call into question the inferences of 'no favouritism for the powerful' that are being made here. This relates to the difficulties in defining who is and who is not an 'insider' (a category incidentally, that is flexible, since rumour about the character and conduct of a particular

Table 24 *Sentencing in US District Courts, 1983*

type of crime	% imprisoned	average sentence (months)
bank robbers	93	157.4
bank burglars	72	103.8
bank larceny/theft	68	65.8
bank fraud	30	34.5
postal robbers	94	148.2
postal burglars	52	57
postal larceny/theft	62	37.1
postal embezzlers	53	46.4
postal forgers	58	49.2

Source: US Department of Justice (1985)

individual may lead to his being reallocated, at least provisionally, to the status of being 'not quite one of us'). Let us assume that the members of élite groups who are selected for criminal prosecution (or, by self-regulatory bodies such as stock exchanges for non-criminal disciplinary prosecution over breaches of rules or regulations) are chosen because despite their high status *via-à-vis* most of society, they are not 'really' insiders: they are economic rivals, political opponents, personal enemies, or 'cads' who are too *successful* and who because of their selfishness in making profits are threatening the cosy cartel and thus the élite as a whole. Although such individuals would show up well on any of the scales used by the researchers – Duncan's SEI on impeccability, (see Wheeler, Weisburd, and Bode 1982) – would tough sentences on them really show that there was no class bias? Well, it might, but this would not show that there was no class bias in the system as a whole, and whether or not there was *sentencing* bias would depend on what factors influenced judicial decision-making and what sentences were imposed upon any 'real' former insiders who came up before the courts. So even if judges think that they are upholding the principle of social fairness in sentencing, they may still be the unwitting tools of the business élite.

The rise in the number of major figures who are taken to court for fraud makes it less plausible to 'explain' the apparent fairness of sentencing as an artefact of prosecutorial bias in selecting only fringe members of the élite. Chambliss (1978) and Katz (1980) have shown that prosecutors could make it appear as if the law applied equally to high-status people although in fact they were motivated by personal aggrandizement and political vendetta. Thus, it is not relevant to question whether judges – particularly at federal level – are affected by these political swings. Moreover, this approach is a little too easy on those who argue that 'the system' is fixed in favour of what Coleman (1985a) has termed 'the criminal élite'. For under it, the élite or ruling class or finance capital class is shrunk to a very much smaller body than it normally assumes in all but the most paranoid accounts of the power élite in the west: to focus upon a tiny body of persons as 'the élite' certainly contradicts the more subtle analysis of who governs which is to be found in most class hegemony theories (see Chapter 4). We must avoid special pleading when faced with awkward data!

In the United States, the evidence from the mid-1980s – later than the cases used in the sentencing studies quoted earlier – suggests that many companies and persons convicted in the courts and/or those sanctioned by the New York Stock Exchange *are* élite members: in the federal courts, in May 1985, major securities firm E.F. Hutton pleaded guilty to 2,000 counts of fraud upon banks; many top US banks have been sanctioned for violating the federal requirement to report cash deposits or movements in excess of $10,000; in 1986, fashion designers Aldo Gucci and Albert Nipon were jailed (in independent cases) for tax evasion; in October 1986, Antonio Gebauer, former Senior Vice-President of Morgan Guaranty Bank, pleaded guilty to charges of fraud on depositors; prominent securities dealers like Dennis Levine (who worked for the fast-growing merger specialists and investment bankers Drexel Burnham Lambert) have pleaded guilty to serious allegations of insider dealing. (Even though Levine's conspirators were not prosecuted in the criminal courts, but rather punished by having to pay back money following the much-criticized 'consent decrees', they are still barred permanently from working in the securities industry.) Despite membership of the Harvard Club, and major contributions to the Republican Party and numerous charities, *arbitrageur* Ivan Boesky, barred permanently by SEC in November 1986 from association with any broker, dealer, investment adviser, or investment company once he has put his own companies and shareholders in order (under SEC supervision) by April 1988, was never a member of the inner circles of East Coast Society. But anyone with a personal fortune of over $200 million – before paying $100 million to SEC – who was trusted by US and Asian banks to invest over $2 billion in funds on their behalf, cannot be regarded as too much of a down-market operator!

In the British context, where the *numbers* of élite members prosecuted are much smaller – approximately zero – the claim that only 'mavericks' among the élite are prosecuted has more plausibility. (Whether only the mavericks among the élite actually commit offences of fraud is a separate and highly important question, though with the exception of the media revelations in the wake of the DTI investigation of the 1986 take-over of Distillers by Guinness (discussed briefly in Chapter 8) hard evidence on this score is notable by its absence.) In the insurance sphere, such persons as Moran and Posgate were highly successful broker/ underwriters who were not 'really' insiders and who were punished heavily by Lloyd's in disciplinary hearings: but the former chairman of Minet, Sir John Wallrock, and the leading insurance broker, David d'Ambrumenil (the son of a former chairman of Lloyd's), who were expelled and suspended respectively, surely could not be described as 'outsiders'? In the period from the Second World War to the beginning of 1987, apart from Sir Denys Lowson, who had long been notorious for his dealings in the City and died before his trial, there were *no* élite insiders who have been convicted of fraud. John Stonehouse, a Labour Cabinet Minister, received a 5-year prison sentence for defrauding his insurance company after faking his death by drowning; Lord Kagan, a textiles manufacturer ennobled by Labour Prime Minister Harold Wilson, received a 10-month prison sentence for a £500,000 VAT fraud; Jim Slater, a prominent financier, received a £20 fine for violating the (now revised) section of the Companies Act that prohibited the purchase of company shares with its own money: but these were hardly Establishment men, and are a rather small sample from which to derive any review of sentencing discrimination. None of those prosecuted for 'stagging' (i.e. obtaining shares in an issue which they expected to be oversubscribed, either by giving false information or by misusing their preferential status) after the British Telecom flotation were high-status persons, even though there is strong evidence that such persons *were* involved in unlawful 'stagging': in some (though not all) cases where – rightly or wrongly – impropriety was alleged, a form of reparation took place, by donating the proceeds to charity.

We can interpret these kinds of data in two principal ways: (1) Establishment figures do not wish/need to break the law; or (2) law-breaking is fairly widespread, but it is only those outside the inner circle who are reported to the police or to the Council of the self-regulatory body for action. Note that to follow (2), one does not have to believe that those against whom action is taken are innocent, though as we saw in Chapter 2, *they* usually claim that they are victims of an Establishment frame-up (or, in those western and Third World countries where prosecutors are political appointments, victims of a political vendetta). All that is required is to see them as being not uniquely guilty. Given this background, it is not surprising – nor is it distressing to the élite – that sentences imposed by judges or by their peer group will punish them severely for abuse of trust (or, to the cynical, for being unwilling to play the game). Thus denunciation, retribution, and special deterrence are satisfied simultaneously by the same sentence, while the public – if it knows about the sentence at all –

is satisfied of the majestic equality of law. (Whether *general* deterrence is satisfied depends on whether other actual or potential offenders see the message as applying to them or see it as a sacrificial gesture to 'reassure the punters': clearly, in the Great Electrical Conspiracy anti-trust case referred to earlier (p. 236) they did see it as applying to them.) Judges then become the witting or unwitting victims of a prosecution charade, and the underlying reality of sentencing comparisons differs from their surface meaning.

With these observations in mind, let us examine the statistics on sentencing in England and Wales in relation to offence convicted. In each year of the 1980s, fraud and forgery has attracted the second lowest percentage of over-21s sentenced to imprisonment at the Crown Court for crime for gain, the least-imprisoned category being theft and handling stolen goods. Of males over 21 sentenced at Crown Courts in England and Wales in 1985, 66 per cent of burglars, 92 per cent of robbers, 43 per cent of thieves and 'fences', and 51 per cent of fraudsters and forgers were imprisoned. The total of male over-21s imprisoned for fraud and forgery at Crown Courts was 2400 (compared with 8300 adult burglars and 7200 adult thieves and handlers of stolen goods). As regards length of sentence, the rank order is the same. The average sentence for fraud and forgery was 14.8 months, compared with 15.9 months for burglary, 42.6 months for robbery, and 10.4 months for theft and handling. These figures are slightly misleading because they include the full terms of partially suspended sentences, and during 1985, 25 per cent of those (male and female) convicted at Crown Courts for fraud and forgery were given such sentences, compared with only 10 per cent of burglars, 14 per cent of robbers, and 16 per cent of thieves and handlers. So the average sentence imposed in fraud and forgery cases comes much closer to that in cases of theft and handling stolen goods, and drops lower still in relation to burglary.

In Magistrates' Courts in 1985, of males over 21 sentenced, 22 per cent of burglars and 8 per cent of thieves and handlers of stolen goods were imprisoned, compared with 9 per cent of those sentenced for fraud and forgery. There, the average sentence for fraud and forgery was 3.1 months, compared with 3.6 months for burglary, and 2.7 months for theft and handling stolen goods. In both courts, as in other areas of property crime sentencing, the average sentence for fraud and forgery has declined very slightly during the decade.

What these data imply in terms of *class discrimination* is rather more mysterious. Among adult offenders, we may take it for granted that nearly all burglars and thieves are working class and relatively poor. But it would be a mistake to assume that all fraudsters are middle class: most cheque and credit-card fraudsters, for example, are not, and though no separate statistics are kept for numbers convicted, inspection of court records suggest that they are the great majority of those taken to court for fraud. (This point about the social-class complexity of 'white-collar' *defendants* is confirmed in the work of Nagel and Hagan (1982) who found that in their US federal court sample, there were 8 less-educated for every 5 college-educated persons convicted of white-collar crimes: education level is a reasonable measure of social status in the United States.)

To the extent that sentences reflect 'the gravity of the offence', and that the cost is part of this, we should note that in 1985, the average value of property stolen in a *recorded* burglary – values in unrecorded ones being much lower – was £580; in robbery, £1283; and in theft (including car theft and unauthorized taking of motor vehicles), £393. As we have seen in Chapter 2, the sums involved in fraud tend to be much greater, which would inflate the average value considerably, though since the majority of frauds appear to be cheque frauds, the median value may be quite low. However, given that Court of Appeal judgments are unlikely to be followed in any consistent fashion by the lower courts, there is no immediate way of comparing high-value theft and commercial burglary sentences with those for fraud. Moreover, 'gravity' is more than just money: it also appears to involve diffuse conceptions such as 'being in a position of trust', the impact upon victims, offence prevalence, etc. Since all of these factors may run in diverse directions, and no-one (including the Court of Appeal) is willing to give guidance as to what weighting should be attached to each, it is hardly surprising that 'offence gravity' raises serious operational problems (see also Fitzmaurice and Pease, 1986, Ch. 5).

OPEN AND CLOSED PRISONS: THE TREATMENT OF FRAUD

A further element of possible discrimination is the within-prison experience of those incarcerated. White-collar criminals who are unconnected with organized crime groups have a good chance of going to an open prison. For offenders serving sentences of under two years – the majority of those fraudsters jailed – this is a very sharp contrast with the overcrowded local closed prisons, with their poor facilities, and itself constitutes a form of advantage. (A modest *dis*advantage lies in the fact that local prisons are often nearer to home, and therefore make visiting easier.) To be sent to an open prison is also an advantage compared with the tighter security arrangements (and tougher company) in closed training prisons.

A look at the data for 1985 illustrates the benefits to adult men of being convicted of fraud compared with other offences of a less 'genteel' nature, particularly burglary and taking and driving away a motor vehicle. For every category of offence, women are significantly more likely than men to be sent to an open prison. The sort of offence committed makes much less difference to women than to men in relation to the chance of being sent to an open prison, but in 1985 (though not in 1984), women were slightly *less* likely to be sent to an open prison for fraud than for any other offence. (To exclude young offenders, who are not involved in sophisticated fraud, I have eliminated data from youth custody and detention centres.) The figures in *Table 25* are the proportion of those in prisons – both training and local ones – who are in open prisons; in brackets are those in open prisons as a proportion of those sent to *training* prisons, normally reserved for longer-term prisoners.

Table 25   *Population under sentence in June 1985 in open prisons as a proportion of those in all adult prisons, by offence*

offence	males	females
fraud	36.6 (56.5)	47.7 (52.5)
forgery	28.2 (44.6)	63.0 (70.8)
burglary	14.2 (23.5)	48.9 (52.4)
other thefts	22.3 (39.8)	57.8 (67.4)
handling	25.6 (41.2)	53.8 (61.4)
taking and driving away	12.8 (24.9)	100 (100)

Source: Home Office (1986f)

On the other hand, it is arguable that this privilege of open prison only balances the greater sensitivity to prison conditions that white-collar defendants have, particularly since they are less likely than the typical prison inmate to have suffered any prior custodial experience. The measurement of the 'pains of imprisonment' is inevitably subjective, but the US 'country club' prisons such as Eglin, Florida, in which – despite overcrowding due to convictions of 'professionals' involved in fraud and drug money laundering in the 1980s – white-collar offenders play tennis and squash present a particularly sharp contrast with the state and federal penitentiaries like Sing Sing in which organized rape and violence abound. Again, this is not (or not *just*) deliberate favouritism: it is based partly on predictions of 'dangerousness' should the prisoner escape, and partly on predictions of the likelihood of escape. Not only are 'professional persons' less likely to commit offences 'on the run', but partly for that reason, their escape is less likely to create political heat for prison administrators. Furthermore, to the extent that their sentences are shorter and their confinement conditions more civilized, they are correspondingly less likely to try to escape, particularly if they believe that a closed prison full of 'criminals' and homosexual rapists beckons to them if recaptured. Thus, a self-fulfilling prophecy is created.

PAROLE

Although not strictly part of the sentence – a point reinforced by Court of Appeal judgments which forbid judges to take parole prospects into account when sentencing – parole is important when reviewing time actually served, and thus the fairness of punishments for different classes of offence and offender. I will not review the critiques that have been made about the inconsistencies of the principles applied to parole. Suffice it to note that parole applicants in Britain suffer from the 'double-sentencing' problem whereby the same criteria used by the trial (and appellate) judges in determining the initial sentence are taken into account a second time by the Parole Board and the Home Secretary when deciding whether they are 'fit to be released' before their one-third normal remission date. Retributivist and correctionalist criteria are mixed up in the manner with which we have become familiar in the review of sentencing 'principles'. Thus the Report of the Parole Board for 1984 states that granting parole 'must be a carefully calculated risk, particular care being taken with the cases of prisoners whose records show that, if they re-offend while on parole their offences may be grave crimes' (Home Office, 1985c:20). Some frauds would be examples of cases 'where the danger is grave': 'A person convicted of more than one sophisticated crime intended to produce a large reward, committed on different occasions, even if violence has not been used or contemplated.' At first sight, this may appear to be confusing offence gravity with risk prediction but in fact, the Parole Board is asserting that it is worse to let offenders out if they appear likely to commit a serious offence than a more minor one. Were it not for the double-sentencing problem, many would find this to be a morally acceptable position. However, since virtually no fraud offenders receive sentences in excess of five years – the cut-off point for grave crimes – they would generally be considered according to the criteria in lesser cases. The Report states:

> 'Most prisoners who have committed what is clearly the one offence they will ever commit may properly be granted early parole. . . . There are, however, a few exceptions for whom early parole will be less clearly justifiable. They include . . . notorious cases of fraud or breach of trust. It can only be said that each case must be considered in the light of the peculiar circumstances.'
>
> (Home Office, 1985c:21)

No particular research attention has been paid to parole in fraud, but we should note that as at the sentencing stage, 'major' fraudsters are advantaged by having typically fewer prior convictions than other substantial property criminals. Given the importance of prior convictions as a predictor of future criminality as well as of retributive deserts, this can be a significant advantage. Their within-prison behaviour also tends to be good, partly because they are more likely to be in open prisons, which have much better records of disciplinary offences, partly because they tend not to be violent people anyway (Levi, 1981), and partly because they are not seen as threatening to the *machismo* of either prison officers or other prisoners, and therefore are less likely to get involved in disputes.

Moreover, to the extent that post-release employment prospects improve chances of parole, fraudsters are unlikely to be worse off than other parole applicants: although Breed (1979) points to the difficulties white-collar criminals in prison have in finding jobs (at a time *before* the unemployment rate soared) and, in some cases, to the particular employment problems which resulted from professional disqualification, they may well be at an advantage compared with other sorts of prisoners. (In the absence of genuine jobs, the really devious can have their friends set up dummy companies to grant them employment!) They are also more likely to have a settled home and relatives waiting for them than many offenders, particularly petty persistent ones. The Report for 1985 states:

> 'The home circumstances and employment prospects can be critical for success on parole . . . a good home, a job to go to and the absence of the circumstances and temptations which led him into crime before are factors favourable to parole.' (Home Office, 1986b:17)

To the extent that criminal records are relevant to parole – and despite the statements quoted above, the Parole Board clearly thinks they are – comparing parole rates across categories of offence is slightly misleading, for one does not know whether any observable differences are due to the offences themselves or to variations in prior conviction records of people committing them. Nevertheless, in the absence of any other data, I will do so.

Those convicted of fraud have a better chance of being paroled at first review than any other category of property (or violence) offender: in 1985, no fewer than 77.6 per cent of those considered were recommended for parole, slightly higher than the rate for theft (72.9 per cent) and for handling, (77.2 per cent) and substantially higher than for burglary (66.3 per cent). In 1985, 100 per cent of those serving less than a year; 84.5 per cent of applicants serving from 1 to 1 year 11 months; 78.0 per cent of those serving 2 to 2 years 11 months; and 66.2 per cent of those serving 3 to 3 years 11 months received parole on the first review. At the upper end, only 2 out of the 22 offenders (3 out of the 11 in 1984) serving 5 years or more received parole at the first hearing, though even that was a higher proportion than for burglary.

The data from those considered for their *second* parole review included some who did not make a first application in that year – i.e. relate to a different prison population – but there were comparatively few fraudsters left in prison by then: 82 in 1985 (and only 48 in 1984). Inequalities had not only evened out by the time of the second review but actually worked against the fraudsters who remained: in 1985, 45.1 per cent of fraud applicants got parole, compared with 53.8 per cent of burglars, 54.3 per cent of thieves, and 65.4 per cent of handlers of stolen goods. Perhaps this indicates a bifurcation in fraud between the small 'hard core' who 'require' incapacitation – 40 parole applicants at second review were doing 5 years or more – and the majority who can be released without danger: 867 at first and 37 at second review in 1985. Altogether, 75.4 per cent of those fraudsters who applied for parole got it.

I do not have any data on the length of parole awarded for different offences, but there is no clear evidence of discrimination either for or against fraud on the basis of the above figures: burglars do worse, but thieves and handlers do about the same as fraudsters. On the other hand, to the extent that fraudsters' lack of prior convictions normally will have netted them a hefty discount in initial sentences, it could be argued that they have still done much better than other offenders in relation to the gravity of their crimes. It is impossible to separate out those receiving parole in relation to prior convictions but certainly, despite the comments of the Parole Board on the general unsuitability of fraudsters for early parole, there seem to be a remarkable number of exceptions to this general principle! It is plausible that despite perceptions of the gravity of fraud, they may look like better candidates for parole in correctionalist terms, partly because in most instances, any frauds (other than cheque frauds) committed would be unlikely to come to court – if at all – within the parole period. So again, the more sophisticated forms of fraud enjoy a comparative advantage arising out of their low reporting and prosecution rate.

Thus, we see British fraudsters generally benefiting from what one might term their low 'evilness rating' – a construct combined from moderate offence seriousness and comparatively light criminal records – and good behaviour inside prison (which in turn is assisted by their often being in open prisons and being not looked down upon as 'animals' or as character challenges by prison staff). In a very illuminating review of parole decision-making, Hawkins notes the importance of 'just deserts' considerations *as a starting-point* when considering the reasoning in one case of a sex offender who has served 10 years already:

'The wrong-doer, in other words, *has crossed the moral threshold*. He has atoned for his wrong-doing and in the absence of any powerful disqualifying condition (such as moral panic in the community demanding extra incapacitation for certain types of offender or institutional management concerns which compel the sanctioning of badly behaved prisoners) he is now ready.'

(Hawkins, 1983:110)

One 'structuralist' way of looking at the discrimination issue – though it may be an unacceptable one, since it is retributivist in its conception – it is to look at the relationship between public perceptions of offence seriousness and differential sentencing for offences. By this criterion, fraud should be treated *more* severely than theft and burglary – particularly commercial burglary. It does not appear to be so treated, judging from the data provided above.

In short, arguments of deliberate discrimination are hard to substantiate, particularly in a British context. Rather, there is a common mode of rationality from which white-collar defendants benefit, and benefit considerably. On the one hand, as the working paper *Criminal Justice* (Home Office, 1984b) confirms, retributivist considerations are supposed to be paramount in the sentencing of grave offences. This is expressed nicely in the sentencing *dicta* of (then) Mr Justice Edmund Davies when dealing with the Great Train Robbers in 1963:

'To some the degradation to which you have all now sunk will bring consequences vastly more cruel than to others. I have anxiously sought to bear in mind everything that has been urged on behalf of all the accused . . . but whatever the past of the particular accused and whatever his position, all else pales into insignificance in the light of his present offences.'

(Read 1979:214)

And yet many white-collar criminals who come before the courts – even those whose offences were clearly committed deliberately for gain – have 'characters' that present judges with far more ambiguity than other major property criminals, and psychologically incline them towards merciful sentiments even though they may see the offence as grave. Shakespeare was responding to similar notions in making such emotionally dramatic use of the fall from high esteem and power in his tragedies. Indeed, counsel for a financial director earning £18,000 a year – who was sentenced to 15 months' imprisonment (10 months of which was suspended) and ordered to pay £3,000 compensation after pleading guilty to stealing more than £13,000 from his employers – referred to his client as being 'like a flawed Shakespearean hero' (*The Times*, 16 July, 1985). Two examples from 1986 of fallen idols are the Chief Fire Officer of Derbyshire 'with a first-class degree' who had 'worked his way to the top' and, though earning £26,000 a year, was caught fiddling

£2,076 in expenses over a long period (partly suspended sentence of 8 months' prison plus 4 months suspended); the 'university graduate with a string of exam passes' who cheated an education authority 'to get students' grants illegally in his unceasing efforts to add to his brilliant academic record' (probation plus £1,250 compensation order). Note here the use of words such as 'fiddling' rather than 'stealing': there is no real analogue in fraud of the attempts of shopkeepers to get us to redefine shoplifting as theft by putting up in stores notices such as 'thieves will be prosecuted'. Note also that the social standing of the defendant is defined by his current class position, not particularly by his class origins, and that in rhetorical terms, having humble origins appears as mitigation. (One can visualize greater sympathy with such a defendant than with someone who has received 'every advantage of high birth and position'.) Almost by (social) definition, there are few working-class defendants who can produce mitigation of this sort: they have no 'long and distinguished career' to waste.

Fraud sentencing and the Court of Appeal (Criminal Division)

Finally, let us examine the views of the appellate courts as to what reasoning *ought* to be adopted by judges and review whether or not this results in some sort of bias in sentencing. If the sentence imposed appears to defence counsel to be too high, they may make a case to the Court of Appeal to have it reduced. That court has received somewhat muted praise from academic commentators for the internal intellectual consistency of its judgments, though it has tended to produce more general sentencing guidelines in recent years, even if it does not always adhere to them. The sentencing norms approved by it may shift slightly over time: during the 1980s, the Court of Appeal seems to have moved towards the position of acknowledging that long prison sentences can be shortened without doing much harm. However, since my previous research revealed that actual sentencing practice in long-firm fraud cases was generally much lower than these norms (Levi, 1981), the effect of these shifts on the general level of sentences is not self-evident. I will recount some decisions in fraud cases in the 1980s and the reasoning given for them by the appellate judges, where any reasons are given.

In *Murray* (1980) 2 Cr.App.R.(S) 379, the court considered the case of a small businessman of previous good character who started his business honestly but who falsely represented that he had an air transport operator's licence, resulting in a net loss to creditors of £2600. The court distinguished between this and the long-firm fraud type of case, which 'is all too common and when it occurs those who are guilty can expect to go to prison for a substantial time. . . . In this case the amount of money was not all that large, although each loser probably thought his loss was substantial.'

(p.379)

The precise weighting of the factors is unspecified, but the Court concluded:

'In all the circumstances, in our judgment, this was the kind of case where a less severe sentence than 18 months would have been appropriate. It was, however, a case for an immediate custodial sentence. In our judgment the appropriate sentence would have been one of nine months' imprisonment.'

In the important leading case of *Barrick* (1985) 7 Cr.App.R.(S) 142, the court issued some general guidelines about sentencing in cases of theft in breach of trust by employees and professional persons. It reviewed its recent prior decisions, so I will not reiterate them here. Instead, I will quote extensively from the judgement, so that readers may appreciate without any distortion from my editing the reasoning process adopted and recommended by the Court of Appeal. Barrick was 41 years old and was sentenced to 2 years' imprisonment for defrauding £9,000 from a small company to whom he had been an accountant over a period of time. He had pleaded *not* guilty. The court upheld the sentence:

'Mr Humphrey on his behalf has put forward all the points of mitigation which were available to him: the good character, the age at the time of the trial, the fact that he had no previous convictions, he served as a police officer and the fact that the mere term of imprisonment of any length is likely to be extremely unpleasant and deleterious for a person of this sort. . . . The type of case with which we are concerned is where a person in a position of trust, for example, an accountant, solicitor, bank employee, or postman, has used that privileged and trusted position to defraud his employers or the general public of sizeable sums of money. He will usually, as in this case, be a person of hitherto impeccable character. It is practically certain, again as in this case, that he will never offend again and, in the nature of things, he will never in his life be able to secure similar employment with all that that means in the shape of disgrace for himself and hardship for himself and also his family. It was not long ago that this type of offender might expect to receive a term of imprisonment of three or four years, and indeed a great deal more if the sums involved were substantial. More recently, however, the sentencing climate has changed . . . and certainly so far as solicitors are concerned, has changed radically.

In Jacob (1981) . . . a solicitor who had over a period of some three years stolen money from clients and his partners to the tune of between £40,000 and £57,000 had his sentence of four years' imprisonment reduced by the Court to eighteen months. In Milne (1982), this Court . . . substituted for the sentence of 3 years' imprisonment imposed upon a solicitor who had stolen some £40,000 from his client account, the term of eighteen months imprisonment, a quarter of which was suspended. . . . On the other hand, postmen do not seem to have fared quite so well. In Eagleton (1982) . . . a postman had been sentenced to five years' imprisonment for three offences of theft of packets in transit by mail, with 80 offences taken into consideration. A sentence of thirty months' imprisonment was substituted. Briggs (1982) . . . another postman . . . had stolen from the mail goods worth £1,300, most of which were recovered. On appeal a sentence of two years' imprisonment was substituted for three years which had been imposed by the trial judge.

We can see no proper basis of distinguishing between cases of this kind simply on the basis of the defendant's occupation. Professional men should expect to be punished as severely as the others; in some cases more severely . . . it seems to us that the sentence imposed . . . in Milne . . . was too lenient. *It is, we appreciate, dangerous to generalise where the circumstances of the offender and the offence may vary so widely from case to case.* In the hope that they . . . may lead to a little more uniformity, we make the following suggestions. [Italics not in original]

In general a term of immediate imprisonment is inevitable, save in very exceptional circumstances or where the amount of money involved is small. Despite the great punishment that offenders of this sort bring upon themselves, the Court should nevertheless pass a sufficiently substantial term of imprisonment to mark publicly the gravity of the offence. The sum involved is *obviously* not the only factor to be considered, but it *may* in many cases prove a useful guide. Where the amounts involved cannot be described as small but are less than £10,000 or thereabouts, terms of imprisonment ranging from the very short to about eighteen months are appropriate. . . . Cases involving sums between about £10,000 and £50,000 will merit a term of about two to three years' imprisonment. Where greater sums are involved, for example those over £100,000, then a term of three and a half years to four and a half years would be justified (see for example the case of *Strubell* (1982) 4 Cr.App.R.(S) 300). In that case the defendant was employed as an accountant. He pleaded guilty to offences involving it seems over £150,000. A sentence of three years' imprisonment was substituted for the five years imposed at trial.

The terms suggested are appropriate where the case is contested. In any case where a plea of guilty is entered however, the court should give the appropriate discount. It will not normally be appropriate in cases of serious breaches of trust to suspend any part of the sentence. As already indicated, the circumstances of the case will vary almost infinitely.

The following are some of the matters to which the court will no doubt wish to pay regard in determining what the proper level of sentence should be: (i) the quality and degree of trust reposed in the offender including his rank; (ii) the period over which the fraud or the thefts have been perpetrated; (iii) the use to which the money or property dishonestly taken was put; (iv) the effect upon the victims; (v) the impact of the offences on the public and public confidence; (vi) the effect on fellow-employees or partners; (vii) the effect on the offender himself; (viii) his own history; (ix) those matters of mitigation special to himself such as illness; being placed under great strain by excessive responsibility or the like; where, as often happens, there has been a long delay, say over two years, between his being confronted with his dishonesty by his professional body or the police and the start of his trial; finally any help given by him to the police.'　　　　　　　　　　(p.142ff)

The court went on to go through these 'criteria', making remarks such as in this case, the 'money was stolen from private individuals who could ill-afford the loss' (without showing how the sentence would have differed if they could have afforded it), concluding that the sentence of two years was 'in the circumstances not excessive'.

On the one hand, in the light of the general reluctance of the Court of Appeal to review the consistency of its decisions, this guideline practice is to be welcomed: it does at least set some kind of maximum and minimum for breach of trust in 'normal' cases, and reduces disparity between the sentencing of postmen and solicitors. On the other, though the narrowness of the range of possible sentences reduces the potential for disparity, one has to wonder what concrete guidance it truly gives. How does one weigh the ten factors that constitute *some* of the matters which the court will wish to take into account? In subsequent cases, we are given some rough idea of how to interpret the guidelines, but very little appreciation of how the sentencing intervals were arrived at, still less any justification for the original anchor points for sentence.

A number of cases were the subject of appeals in the wake of *Barrick*. In *Chatfield* and in *Colley* (1986) *Crim. L.R.* pp.71–2, a sentence of four months' immediate imprisonment was approved upon an honorary booking secretary with no prior convictions who stole £350 over two and a half years – about one-third of the cash received by the community centre; and a sentence of 6 months' imprisonment was approved on a clerk with no prior convictions who pleaded guilty to certifying false invoices submitted by a conspirator in another company for payment. (The latter did not appeal against his *suspended* prison sentence: presumably the sentencing logic was that breach of trust was more severe than fraud by an outsider.) In *Mossop* (1986) *Crim. L.R.* 72, a dentist unsuccessfully appealed against a sentence of 9 months for a fraud on the National Health Service involving £6,826 or more. The Court stated that 'it was a relatively short term of imprisonment, having regard to the gravity of the offences deliberately committed over a period of at least nine months'. In *Poulter* (1986) *Crim. L.R.* 73, a postman who had pleaded guilty to stealing £100 cash and goods from letters and parcels had his sentence reduced from 18 to 12 months' imprisonment. One might distinguish between this case and *Chatfield* above, on the grounds that the threat of damage to confidence in the Post Office does not apply to *Chatfield*, but in spite of the comments in *Barrick* about the importance of treating professional people no less severely than postmen, it is hard to reconcile the 12-month sentence for *Poulter* with the lack of criticism for the brevity of the 9-month sentence on *Mossop*.

In *Miller* (1986) *Crim. L.R.* 127, an accountant defrauded more than £500,000 over a period of nine years, but paid back some £200,000.

When the matter came to light, partly as a result of changes in accounting procedures, there was a deficiency of over £300,000. He was sentenced to 4 years' imprisonment. The special considerations of mitigation were his claim to have admitted the offences out of shame before he was detected; his co-operation with the police; and his plea of guilty. The money had been spent gambling. With some hesitation, the Court of Appeal reduced the sentence to 3 years, discounting about one-third from the upper limit of 4½ years because of the guilty plea. (Compare with the Crown Court sentence of 14 years upon *Higgs*, the gambling accountant who defrauded £3 million, discussed on pages 231–32.) In the case of *Offord* (1986) *Crim. L.R.* 102, a solicitor pleaded guilty to having defrauded clients and others of sums totalling £242,000 over a period of eighteen months. The Court reduced his 5 year sentence to 3 years:

> 'the courts had to deal sternly with those who abused trust at the expense of other: the greater the abuse of trust . . . the greater the need to punish severely and thereby deter others from being tempted in the same way. A solicitor who behaved dishonestly brought his profession into disrepute, and brought ruin at home. While those who were defrauded would be compensated by the Law Society, that was at the expense of solicitors generally, and the appellant could claim no credit for that . . . it was no longer thought necessary to impose very long sentences of imprisonment: more moderate sentences than used to be passed were thought to be sufficient to assuage the sense of public outrage.'
> (p.102)

So here we have a mixture of retribution – sentence mitigated implicitly by 'ruin at home' – general deterrence, and denunciation all being employed to 'explain' sentence. How the Court reached the view that 3 years – rather than 5 or 1 – would be sufficient to assuage the *public* sense of outrage remains mysterious. But it reveals once again that the maximum anyone of previous good character can expect if he pleads guilty is 3 years' imprisonment.

In *Grant* (1986) *Crim. L.R.* 127, however, the Court upheld a sentence of 4 years upon someone who had previously served a 4-year sentence for robbery and blackmail (committed over a period of time for money for gambling), who spent the life savings of one couple and the house purchase money of another for whom he had been acting as a cut-price conveyancer. In special mitigation was a psychiatric report which suggested that he was a psychopathic gambler. The Court of Appeal .

> 'did not consider that *Barrick*, which dealt with people who were of otherwise good character, who ruined themselves by making away with other people's money, to have any particular bearing on this case. The appellant was a thoroughly dishonest man who had resorted to robbery to feed his gambling

habit, and immediately after his release on licence had set up in a business that gave him access to other people's money in order to feed his gambling habit. Cases where persons of small means were deprived of their life savings caused a high degree of suffering, and if the appellant had contested the case the sentence would have been considerably greater. The sentence of four years included an appropriate discount.' (p.127)

So it appears that sometimes, if the defendant has been of previous good character, the fact that he has gambled away other people's money counts as *mitigation* – they have 'ruined themselves' without keeping the loot – whereas at other times, if a defendant has a 'gambling habit' and has shown himself to be 'thoroughly dishonest' already, it appears to count as *aggravation*. If we take the general view that a discount of one-third is given for a guilty plea, we are left with what would have been a 6-year sentence for someone with prior convictions who has defrauded people of small means, compared with a sentence of 2 years on a not guilty plea for *Barrick*, who defrauded people of slightly better but still not great means. Is this disparity? How do we justify this transformation from someone 'of good character' into someone who is 'thoroughly dishonest'? Many people do share this view of prior convictions as aggravation – including executives (Levi, 1986a), for example, – but why? It is noteworthy that the salience of prior convictions varies from offence to offence: in the 1985 rape guideline judgment of *Billam* (1985) 82 Cr.App.R. 347, the court stated that 'Previous good character is of only minor relevance' to mitigation of the 'normal penalty', though previous convictions for 'serious offences of a violent or sexual kind' should count as aggravating factors (351).

Where we move to other spheres that resemble 'traditional professional crime' more closely, we see that sentencing is quite tough. In *Silverman* (1983) 5 Cr.App.R. (S) 46, a 'front man' for a cheque-card fraud gang with no previous convictions had a sentence of 6 years reduced to 4. In *Lima* (1986) *Crim. L.R.* 129, an appellant with three prior convictions, who had been found with nine different passports and two identity cards, with stolen traveller's cheques to a value of £20,000, had his sentence reduced from 5 years to 3½ years: 'The Court thought ... insufficient allowance had been made for the appellant's plea of guilty, and the fact that the present sentence was to be served consecutively to the earlier sentence.' (p.129) (This reinforces the view that there is no simple addition of gravity scores for each offence, but rather a total 'deserved punishment' is built up more impressionistically.) But is *Lima* really a worse case than *Barrick* or *Miller*?

Some other cases are of interest to demonstrate appellate reactions to different sorts of fraud. In *Gupta* (1985) *Crim. L.R.* 681, the Court reduced the sentence on a car dealer with no prior convictions who pleaded guilty to several 'clocking' offences, from 12 months to a partially suspended sentence with 6 months to be served. It stated that this kind of fraud called for an immediate prison sentence combined with a substantial fine to take away the substantial profits made from this offence. The good character of the appellant was the rationale for reducing the sentence. It seems plain that anyone dealing in counterfeit currency will find the Court of Appeal upholding a custodial sentence: in *Horrigan* (1985) 7 Cr. App. R. (S) 112 – decided two weeks before *Barrick* – a sentence of 9 months' imprisonment was upheld on a woman – the only female considered here – who was convicted of passing four forged £50 notes and possessing seven others. In *Howard* (1986) 82 Cr. App. R. 262, a 2-year prison sentence was approved as being 'not a day too long' on a 21 year-old with no prior convictions who pleaded guilty to having bought counterfeit currency with a face value of £3000 and attempting to pass a forged £20 note:

> 'the most important consideration in cases of this type is the quantity of counterfeit notes found in the offender's possession, because that will demonstrate, with some degree of accuracy, the proximity of the source of the notes. . . . The issue of counterfeit notes undermines the whole economy of the country, and is likely to result in great loss to individuals who find themselves in possession of these notes. . . . It follows that this type of offence is one which in nearly every case will require a custodial sentence . . . first of all to punish the wrongdoer. The secondary reasons are to deter the wrongdoer himself from committing the same sort of offence in the future – that perhaps does not figure very largely in this case because it is unlikely that this man will offend again – but much more important, it is to indicate to others who are minded to make cheap and easy profit by the acceptance of counterfeit notes, that it is simply not worth the candle.' (p.262)

This reveals nicely the way in which notions of economic damage are employed to justify sentencing. There is a difference between the potential economic effects of counterfeiting and those of fraud by dentists upon the government, but from an alternative perspective, does this justify a sentencing differential of 15 months between this and *Mossop*? Or *Horrigan* and *Mossop* receiving the same sentence? Perhaps the underlying (and tacit) rationale is that a sentence of 9 months is enough to deter dentists from fraud but not to deter what are presumably the lower classes from dealing in what in absolute terms is not a very large amount of counterfeit currency? That may be justifiable on utilitarian grounds – wealthy people have enough going for them legitimately to make crime economically rational only for a much greater profit than would be needed to deter the poor – but on grounds of fairness, the difference is hard to justify.

In *Garner* (1986) Crim. L.R. 166, special problems arose because of the 2-year maximum sentence that then prevailed for conspiracy to contravene VAT. Garner was given two consecutive prison sentences of 2 years, fined a total of £150,000 (with 2 years' imprisonment in default), made criminally bankrupt for almost £2 million (the sum defrauded), and made to pay prosecution costs up to £90,000. The court reduced one prison term to 12 months, to reflect its smaller scale, and stated that in cases such as this where the Crown was the only creditor, if a fine was imposed, a Criminal Bankruptcy Order should be avoided. The court observed that if the offender had the means to pay and had made a profit from his crimes, 'it was wrong to look at terms of imprisonment to be served in default of payment of the fine as additional punishment: it was not being used as a punishment, but as a means to coerce the offender into surrendering his profit' (p.66).

In *Adams* (1986) *Crium. L.R.* 344, the court approved a 2-year youth custody sentence on a 20 year-old with prior convictions for dishonesty who pleaded guilty to obtaining £7,000 social security by fraud over a year. As in long-firm fraud cases, the Court distinguished between preconceived fraudulent schemes and those in which offenders did not disclose changes in their circumstances: 'This was a deliberate calculation and ingenious course of conduct, which put it into the category of the most serious offences of its kind.' So for a £7,000 social-security fraud, *Adams* might well serve only a year less than *Garner* or the gambling accountant *Miller*, and would serve the same sentence as counterfeit *Howard*, who had no prior convictions.

Another example of this (latent) difficulty in working out a justification for where the penalty scale starts is *Ford* (1986) *Crim. L.R.* 483, where the court upheld a sentence of 12 months upon the appellant who had pleaded guilty to a 'working and drawing' offence from which he had obtained over £7,000 over a period of six years. Rejecting precedents from earlier cases which suggested that sentences of 6 months might be appropriate, the court stated that:

> 'the facts of this offence were regrettably all too common and it might be that sentences which were appropriate in 1981 and 1982 were no longer useful as guidelines. Sentences of six months did not appear to be having an effect on those who are minded to tell lies to the DHSS in order to obtain money to which they are not entitled. It seemed to the Court that the time had come when it must be made even clearer than it had been in the past that those who defrauded the state must be dealt with by immediate custodial sentences longer than those which had been passed for several years.' (p.483)

So here, tougher sentences are justifiable because of failure of general deterrence and for denunciatory purposes. A similar line was taken in *Gilmore* (*The Times Law Reports*, 21 May, 1986), where a sentence of 7 years was upheld for possessing cannabis resin with intent to supply. The Court of Appeal stated that a very large quantity of drugs was involved and that the time had come when 'clearly' it was necessary to move up the level for serious drug offences: the number of such offences was on the increase, and had been since sentencing guidelines were given in *R* v. *Aramah* (1983) 76 Cr. App. R. 190. By this criterion, commercial fraud sentences (including those on solicitors who defrauded their clients' accounts) surely ought to be rising rather than falling, but in *Barrick*, the rising tide of fraud – albeit not against the state – did not appear to be considered at all or, if considered, was not thought relevant.

It may be tempting to some to 'explain' the sentencing practices of the English appellate courts simply as illustrations of the bias in the judicial system in favour of the rich and against the poor. However, as we have seen, many of the *victims* of fraud also are (or were) rich, and the process by which these sentencing differentials come about is a great deal more subtle than simple bias. It is far from certain that any judges sitting on the Court of Appeal have actually considered social-security fraud or burglary sentences in relation to commercial fraud ones, and it is most unlikely that they will have considered them in the way I have done here. So at a lower level of explanation, one might assert that judgments on tariffs and/or on the use of individualized justice criteria for different offences simply operate on different scales: judges somehow arrive at what they think is 'the right sentence' in 'this kind of case', without looking at crimes across the board. This is what lawyers often term 'taking each case on its merits' and whatever many academics might think about it, it is a highly valued *modus operandi* within the British legal culture. If I am right in thinking that judges do not systematically consider sentencing levels for different sorts of offences as a whole, then those searching for higher-order explanations of sentencing differentials might review the social learning (and/or, for Marxists, ideological) processes that lead to this moral pragmatism and to this compartmentalization of offences. (If judges consider that I am mistaken, then perhaps we could have more explicit justification for the differentials to which I have pointed.) But the explanatory task is far from easy, not least because it is hard for any of us to give reasons as to why we *do* start a tariff at one particular point rather than another.

What everyone might agree upon is that both the reasoning process and the sentencing guidelines recommended by the Court of Appeal allow a considerable latitude to judges faced with the task of sentencing the white-collar offender. After an internal political struggle between the Home Secretary – who wanted stronger measures such as the right of the prosecution to refer cases to the Court of Appeal – and the Lord Chancellor – who wanted to preserve the independence of the judiciary – clause 29 of the Criminal Justice Bill (1986) proposes modestly to give the Attorney General the right to refer sentences to the Court of Appeal – with the leave of that Court – 'to obtain their opinion on the principles which should be observed in sentencing in similar cases in the future'. This preserves the custom in England whereby, unlike the United States and continental jurisdictions, prosecutors have no real role in the sentencing process.

Actual sentences can only be changed if they are thought by the defence to have a chance of being reduced, so the impact of the Court of Appeal on sentences is limited to (1) those cases in which trial judges *try* honestly to follow its guidelines; (2) those in which trial judges seek to avoid potential criticism of their decisions by taking account only of the upper limit sentences that the Court would be expected to tolerate; and (3) those cases in which judges deliberately sentence 'over the top'. (After all, more publicity results from a trial than from appellate decisions, so judges might seek pragmatically to justify in terms of general deterrence the imposition of heavy sentences that they expect to be reduced.) It is also limited by the awareness that trial court judges have of the approved appellate sentencing norms. Since the Home Secretary failed in his attempt to enhance the role of the Judicial Studies Board to give greater publicity to appellate guidelines and to violations of them than has been the case in the past, it will remain the case that without further training, judicial awareness will be determined by defence use of guidelines in mitigation – i.e. when defence counsel have read them and when the guidelines suit them – and by judges' proactivity in reading the *Judicial Studies Board Bulletin*, the *Criminal Appeal (Sentencing) Reports*, academic works such as Thomas' *Principles of Sentencing* (1979) (which may be found in many Crown Court libraries but is now dated empirically), and the small number of sentencing cases that are discussed in the monthly *Criminal Law Review*.

8 Controlling the fraud business: current trends and future prospects

To Left, here's B., half-Communist,
　　Who talks a chastened treason,
And C., a something-else in 'ist',
　　Harangues, to right, on reason.

B., from his 'tribune', fulminates
　　At Throne and Constitution,
Nay – with the walnuts – advocates
　　Reform by revolution;

While C.'s peculiar coterie
　　Have now in full rehearsal
Some patent new philosophy
　　To make doubt universal.

And yet – why not? If zealots burn,
　　Their zeal has not affected
My taste for salmon and Sauterne,
　　Or I might have objected:–

Friend B., the argument you choose
　　Has been by France refuted;
And C., *mon cher*, your novel views
　　Are just Tom Paine, diluted;

There's but one creed, – that's *Laissez faire*,
　　Behold its mild apostle!
My dear declamatory pair,
　　Although you shout and jostle,

Not your ephemeral hands, nor mine,
　　Time's Gordian knots shall sunder, –
Will laid three casks of this old wine:
　　Who'll drink the last, I wonder?

'Laissez-faire' (1872),
from *The Collected Poems of Austin Dobson*

Introduction

Crime – all crime – is interwoven with the fabric of non-criminal social organization. Consequently, at least in developed states, it is hard to repress 'the criminal' without harming other liberties that are important to preserve. Containing street crime and industrial disorder may involve restraining freedom of movement, generally that of the poor but sometimes that of comparatively affluent strikers such as print workers and miners. It can be achieved – at a cost, and perhaps temporarily – by water cannon, rubber bullets, and other armorial bearings of the modern state which can physically seal off 'criminal areas' from the remainder of society, who can then go on about their business undisturbed, except by images of impending chaos in their minds. Commercial fraud cannot be handled in this kind of way. Bureaucratic redesign may reduce opportunities for fraud, but to place a ring of steel around any particular part of the commercial system would affect *directly* not only those who reside within but the entire populace. In this sense, it differs from public order control or even from changing the ecology of housing estates (Coleman, 1985; Newman, 1972).

Many different sorts of solutions (or, from the more modest, 'approaches') have been put forward about how to deal with 'crime'. Except for specialist books on fraud and white-collar crime, these seldom include any reference to business crime. But some of the same difficulties experienced in those general 'solutions' – few of which appear to have *reduced* crime, let alone eliminated it – apply also to remedies for fraud and corporate crime. For Conservatives, fraud is a growing economic and political problem for which simple repression is clearly inappropriate. As we saw in Chapter 2, there have been attempts by the Conservative Party Chairman in 1985 to link fraud and corruption with the decline of community and with 'permissiveness': but unless one accepts that the over-40s at Lloyd's somehow 'caught' this social disease late on in life – i.e. a secure and non-permissive family upbringing will not be sufficient protection against later temptation – this is hardly a plausible account. Current trends lead us to expect to see financial services fraud linked to drug-taking: I can envisage the banner headlines 'Morals of High-Flying Executive Crack Up Through Coke: "I started out on computer fraud but it led to harder stuff"' – or the pop-star type Sad Tale: '"I had it all too young" says former City whizz-kid at Old Bailey trial.' But the remedies are far from clear. We might – experience everywhere else in the world notwithstanding – succeed in cracking the cocaine problem, despite its efficaciousness in improving (in the short term, and until the nasal membranes disintegrate) one's concentration for those multi-million pound deals on the transatlantic telephone. But will this really increase the moral fibre of the young currency/commodities dealer earning his (or, more rarely, her) £300,000 a year until the burn-out comes in the thirties?

There are complaints by the Government and in the media that in the run up to the deregulatory Big Bang on The Stock Exchange in October 1986, salaries have shot up sky-high, and that this is bound to bring moral chaos to the recipients as well as extra costs for the consumer. But this is a free market area, and competition between the top (or would-be top) firms will ensure that these complaints are not heeded. In any event, they are partly 'special pleading' by those firms less well placed to offer the high salaries, who fear going to the wall in the future shake-out of the less successful securities dealers. It is all very well to lament the passing of the Golden Age of Community, but the world of aggressive international trading – whether in securities, commodities, tourism, or manufacturing – is unlikely to lend itself to any natural self-imposed moral order. As I have argued in Chapters 2 and 4, this is not just an example of the powerful being allowed to do as they please against the public interest: the 'invisible earnings' they bring to the balance of payments are all too visibly needed to counteract the trade deficit in the non-financial sector and, as North Sea oil runs out, this becomes more critical still in de-industrialized Britain.

For the left, the problem of Utopianism (or, in the words of Lea and Young, 1984, 'left idealism') remains for those seeking solutions to crime. The experience of all existing socialist societies gives no grounds for optimism regarding the prospects of eliminating fraud and corruption altogether: even if one rejects as overblown the claims of Simis (1982) about corruption in the Soviet Union, the socialization of the means of production tends to lead to the concentration of scarce resource allocation into the hands of powerful party figures and free-wheeling 'fixers'. If there are (justified) complaints about the secrecy of decision-making and about power élites in the west, then even less sunlight – that great disinfectant of fraud – shines upon those who exert power in the east. Most western Marxists now accept that the post-revolutionary withering away of the state and of law is a mirage rather than a serious proposition, and most eastern Marxists have accepted that to encourage production, there must be some sort of private sector to complement the public one. So if the chances are that where there is business, there will be fraud, Marxists and capitalists alike must consider what is to be done about business crime. As I have observed in Chapter 2, the Sino-Soviet preferred solution is execution, at least for those who have fallen out of favour. But this particular aspect of 'the China syndrome' has not yet produced any fall-out that has affected the west.

So, if the key radical platforms are unlikely to lead fraud to wither away, is it the case that in addition to being a criminal offence, fraud is also a major social problem? Well, in case potential readers turn to the final chapter before purchasing, I need hardly add that I have demonstrated its significance in many chapters of the book. As we saw in Chapter 2, frauds vary greatly in their economic and political impact, but in both capitalist and communist societies, they occasion very large losses to the state, to business people, and to private individuals. In Chapter 3, we noted that consistently over time and place, frauds of many types do appear to be rated very seriously by the general public. On the other hand, it seems unlikely that the general public go around in almost *constant* fear of becoming victims, as some do in relation to burglary and mugging (Hough and Mayhew, 1985; Jones, Maclean and Young, 1986). A recent survey on one British housing estate found that many people expressed anxiety at the risk of someone calling at the door and pressurizing them into buying something they did not want (Noaks, forthcoming). But this is not yet a crime, particularly not where the product is 'cold-called' insurance. The Financial Services Act (1986) makes it illegal for unauthorized persons to sell investments, but it is not a criminal offence for authorized insurance salespeople to pressurize sales, though there is a statutory 'cooling-off' period during which a contract may be cancelled. As regards securities, the sales technique of less reputable firms is often to lure 'punters' – whose names may have been obtained from a 'sucker list' or from their replies to offers regarding 'blue-chip' securities flotations such as British Telecom or the Trustee Savings Bank – into undertaking some sort of correspondence or securities transaction. Then, unless the members of the public have the presence of mind to state that they do *not* wish to be contacted in the future, the salespeople pester them on the telephone with a series of 'wonderful prospects', some of which 'unluckily' do not wholly fulfil expectations and go into liquidation soon afterwards. This is within the letter of SIB rules.

Some – though no-one has asked how many – of the six million adults in England and Wales who own securities may fear being defrauded, but though this is a potentially serious financial risk which objectively *could* materialize at any time, it is unlikely that it is something against which people feel they should take precautions every time they stay in or go out. The difficulty in preventing it by one's own actions may even make fraud *more* frightening, but although some research on the victims of fraud is under way (Levi and Pithouse, forthcoming), there are many issues relating to the fear of fraud which remain to be examined.

I do not propose here to outline a strategy for reducing crime or 'malpractice' by multinational corporations against nation states or the general working and consuming public, though I will occasionally present some analogies that are relevant to that task. There are many such texts available elsewhere – see, for example, the overview by Braithwaite (1984, Ch.9) – and the change of focus might blur the outlines of this work too much. What I will seek to do is to sketch the current trends and future possibilities in the ways in which the criminal justice system might tackle fraud, before making some final comments about the shape of public and privatized justice to come. The aim here is not to produce 'The Final Solution' to fraud but to clarify our thinking and to encourage more strategic analysis than one normally finds in polemical debates on law and order, whether related to upperworld crime or to other areas of criminality.

The theme of society under surveillance is one that has absorbed commentators from the classical political theorists such as Plato and Thomas More, through Bentham's Panopticon, The Ruler in Fritz Lang's brilliant film *Metropolis*, and Big Brother in Orwell's *1984*. Some claim that democracy legitimates that extension of surveillance, because the subversive minority might otherwise undermine the rights of the majority; others that individual minority rights are superordinate to majority opinion; and others still that the regulation of dissentient minorities is justified only under socialism, where substantive equality is guaranteed and therefore collective interests justly predominate. For some, the spread of regulation to cover the minutiae of social life – which Foucault (1977) argues is an integral part of the development of industrial capitalism – is Utopian; for others, it is profoundly dystopian. How do these issues relate to the control of commercial fraud? They are important because the organization of fraud and the laundering of the proceeds of commercial fraud, tax evasion, political corruption, terrorism, and narcotics are intimately linked via the need for secrecy and immunity from law enforcement that they all require. Increasingly, this has been achieved by the use of international tax havens as conduits for money and as legally registered bases for operations. It has also been achieved through using professionals – lawyers and accountants – as intermediaries in the perpetration of crime. Police powers and police organizations have always been based upon the principle of territoriality: outside national boundaries, mutual respect for sovereignty – the comity of nations – is supposed to apply. This has been equally true of the professions and of commercial SROs such as The Stock Exchange, whose disciplinary powers may extend across national boundaries to Members overseas, but which, prior to the passing of the Financial Services Act (1986), have been unable to do anything to non-Members. These territorially based control institutions with their attendant powers are becoming irrelevant to the serious commercial operator, fraudster and multinational alike. The name of the game is to maximize autonomy and to minimize tax and other sorts of costs (such as imprisonment or confiscation of assets). There will always be plenty of crime (including frauds costing hundreds of thousands of pounds) for the police to investigate without recourse to people or documents overseas, but the big-league players cannot be tackled on a purely domestic basis, nor without penetrating their professional advisers.

In some respects, we should feel sympathy for the fraudsters. As long as there was 'just fraud' involved, major state agencies would be unlikely to mobilize enough moral panic to overturn the barriers of international and domestic financial secrecy, even if they were interested in so doing. But the war on drugs has changed all that. American banks have been heavily criticized by the President's Commission on Organized Crime (1986a, 1986b), and all the major US law enforcement agencies – the FBI, the DEA, the IRS, and SEC – have become involved in the effort to break down territoriality and banking secrecy. This is the international parallel to the way in which the involvement of 'organized criminals' spoiled the cosy world of long-firm fraud ('bust-outs' in America) for the old-time business criminals (Levi, 1981). The comparative success of the Americans – backed by threats over foreign aid and the exclusion of foreigners from US markets – in negotiating mutual assistance treaties with some nations has not only encouraged the displacement abroad of North American fraudsters (in true criminal imperialist style), but has also provided an impetus for the development of measures by other major trading nations who do not themselves have banking secrecy legislation to press for anti-secrecy measures. The future control trends that I envisage consist mainly of extending social surveillance to increase the visibility of fraud to those who are not direct parties to it; enhancing inter-agency co-operation, domestically and internationally, to improve the capacity of policing agencies and the courts to cope with fraud investigations and trials; and deeper and less orthodox thinking about sanctions for fraud.

Business crime, being predominantly planned, looks as if it is susceptible to deterrence in principle, even though its visibility is low. Consequently, though *particular* control measures may generate disagreement, considerations not only of social equity but also of deterrence suggest that a higher crime control profile might be appropriate for commercial fraud (and, though this raises some different issues, for corporate crime generally). The increased use of the criminal justice system may not reduce the amount of fraud, just as it has not reduced other forms of crime. Indeed, there are some intriguing paradoxes in the politics of fraud regulation. Some prefer *laissez-faire* because they think that governmental intervention merely distorts the market and people will get round the rules anyway; others prefer it because they think deregulation will lead to more scandal and induce the collapse of capitalism. Conversely, some may prefer governmental regulation because it defuses scandal from the commercial world and transposes it to the regulatory world, while others see heavy governmental intervention as the only way of exposing enough of the unacceptable face of capitalism to undermine confidence in it.

In addition, there are the liberal reformists or political pragmatists who believe that limited intervention is the only way of ensuring that the system does not collapse under the weight of fraud: the upperworld equivalent of Kinsey, Lea, and Young's (1986) 'minimal policing'. Finally, there are the left idealists who are completely uninterested in any reforms at all, but interpret all possible moves as malevolent examples of the exercise of hegemony: if nothing is done, this proves the power of capital to insulate itself from the kind of state power that is used against the poor and the working class; if something is done, this is nothing more than a symbolic gesture to reassure the punters, sending a few marginal men to jail while the rich carry on exploiting. (For some penetrating discussion of interpretations of reform in penal settings, see Cohen, 1985.)

Total social structural overhaul – driving the money-changers from the Temple (and into Carey Street, the traditional home for bankrupts) – is the only way of eliminating fraud altogether, but whether or not we are attracted in principle to this solution, there remain the small problems of how revolution is going to be achieved and how we tell whether this road to socialism is going to be better than all previous roads. It may be that if fraud is seen to be widespread, this may de-legitimize the economic and legal system generally and speed the collapse of capitalism, but it has not happened hitherto. Meanwhile, there are some other, more modest reformist possibilities which emerge from looking at the regulation of fraud. If we overcome the Pavlovian conditioning that 'punishment' must always follow 'crime', we can start to think creatively about what is to be done about *all* sorts of crime. It is not evident to me that we ought to treat all crimes – from dropping litter to homicide – in the same way. But it seems *prima facie* unfair to treat petty persistent offenders or those who non-violently break into commercial premises at night *more* severely than people who steal much larger sums with a pen or computer, which is what seems to happen at present. This offends against the 'natural sense of rightness'.

The disadvantages of using penal law to regulate social conflicts have been stressed by some critical criminologists such as Christie (1977, 1986b). In the context of corporate worker and consumer safety violations, Braithwaite (1982b, 1984, 1985a) has argued that there are good reasons *not* to adopt a penal, retributivist approach: principally, that informal control works faster and more effectively than taking corporations through the criminal courts. It is possible that if changes were made to court procedures and sanctions for corporate law-breakers, his pragmatic cost-benefit analysis might give rise to a different solution. But Braithwaite's way of looking at corporate crime is an important corrective to the tendency merely to expose power-related inequalities such as the differential treatment of corporate and individual homicide (Box, 1983; Swigert and Farrell, 1981). (As a pragmatic method, I am in favour of provisions imposing strict and vicarious liability for corporate malpractice. However, as I have argued earlier, it is not simply ideological mystification to argue that the construction of causation and of culpability *are* different in a corporate from an individual context: it would be a strange conceptual world in which this was *not* so.) Braithwaite gives us a correctionalist promise that is implicitly or explicitly denied by most who write about reforming working-class criminals. If there are in fact *crime-reductive* reasons for dealing with fraud differently from the burglary of commercial premises, non-retributivists might find that defensible, but if there is no basis for the distinction in treatment other than 'that is the way it has always been', that is not – in my view – morally justifiable. There is an inevitable tension here between correctionalism and just deserts, just as there is between general deterrence and just deserts, or even between individual and collective just deserts: for example, was SEC morally right in 1986 to 'let off' Ivan Boesky with a mere $100 million fine, when this enabled them to expose other insider dealers who otherwise might have escaped any sanction? However, if we have neither deserts, nor corrections, nor deterrence for fraudsters, but we have heavy-handed justice for other sorts of offenders, that is a wholly unprincipled form of discrimination, even though it is one that has not been thought out deliberately as a sentencing policy.

The investigation and prosecution of fraud

Most British and American research – governmental and academic alike – suggests that whatever the announcement of more officers on the streets may do for the popularity of Chief Constables, this has negligible effects on the crime rate or on the clear-up rate. Nor has the contribution of detectives to the clear-up rate been as significant as they claim (Clarke and Hough, 1984). Combined with an attitude that 'lean is beautiful' – *nouvelle cuisine* served by supply-side monetarists – in government, this would seem to spell doom for extra recruitment to police forces. In Britain, for political reasons, this message has not been translated into serious restrictions on the pay or the resources of the police. But in an era of serious public-sector cutbacks, new expenditure has to be justified. This has had a significant effect on the struggle against commercial fraud, even if it does not appear to have inhibited to the same extent the drive against social-security fraud. As I have reiterated earlier in the book, this inequality of treatment should not be seen as a simple case of 'the powerful looking after their own': the principal victims whose cases are not dealt with satisfactorily are companies and wealthy individuals; and to the best of my knowledge, few of the principal suspects in uninvestigated but reported fraud cases are members of the inner circles of power. (Though this is only part of the story: people who *are* close to the centre of power – wherever that is – may fear that they might *become* fraud suspects, whereas they know that they are unlikely to fall foul of police officers dealing with burglary or picketing, or of social-security fraud investigators.)

Since arguments for extra resources are bound to be regarded with extreme scepticism, are there any grounds for thinking that fraud might be different from other offences? First, although many recorded frauds are committed by people using completely false identities, most of the larger and many of the smaller ones are not: they are committed by people who have positions in a chain of accountability. In other words unlike burglaries which, without a confession or an informant, tend to be virtually insoluble once the burglar has got away, the problem in reported fraud is not normally who the offender is but whether a criminal offence has been committed and can be proven to have been committed by a known suspect. This comprises at least two constituents: the transfer into the straightjacket of statute and case law of the feeling that one has been ripped off; and the linking of the *actus reus* with intentional or reckless behaviour on the part of the suspect. This takes time, and extra resources enable a more thorough judgment to be made about a report from a victim, and more interviews to be conducted, which may yield more awareness of the *organizational* ramifications of a fraud. Otherwise, as in most crime investigations, the tendency is to be content with 'knocking off' the front-line predators without worrying about what, if anything, lies behind them: after all, if we ignore issues of incapacitation and crime prevention, from the point of view of the statistical clear-up rate, it is not cost-effective to deal with crime as an organizational system. (This is a pragmatic objection to the view advocated by Walsh, 1977, that we should deal with theft and burglary more strategically as a stolen property system.)

In some instances, the resource issue is largely a question of money: is it worth a flight abroad and a week or more of an officer's time to see if a witness will come to Britain or if access can be obtained to an account?

(A different result might have been obtained in one securities fraud trial that resulted in acquittal had the police interviewed a potentially important witness who lived in France.) This is also a reflection of evidentiary rules: prosecutions have been abandoned because a judgment is made that it is not worth flying witnesses from Costa Rica or The Philippines to give evidence as simple as that company X was a duly registered company. The extra expenditure will not always yield a result, for evidentiary obstacles may exist which are insuperable: Panamanian banks, for example. Even with the most thorough investigation in the world, many fraud reports will end up being 'no crimed' because there is no evidence that what happened was a crime. (This, after all, is part of the difference between a subjectively defined social harm and a legally definable crime.)

The cuts in resources that the Metropolitan Police Company Fraud Department experienced in the 1980s forced them to prioritize cases more sharply on the basis of their *estimated* likelihood to yield a result. This may not have affected the numbers of recorded frauds or the clear-up rate but, *inter alia*, what the policy *has* done is to shift the economic burden of crime investigation onto victims, in particular corporate victims, and has thus transferred public law back into the sphere of private law. This public/private distinction has never been as clear-cut as many lawyers believe: the possibility of being prosecuted for fraud or theft has always been used as a lever to get fraudsters (and workplace thieves) to pay back the money and/or to resign. But there is something paradoxical about companies who complain that they have been defrauded of millions of pounds being told that because of the pressure of work on the Fraud Squad, the case cannot be investigated for 12 months, and that their best option would be to do their own investigation and come back later! What have they been paying their rates and taxes for?

However, *pace* the views of Kinsey, Lea, and Young (1986), as in other spheres of policing, the satisfaction of the public does not arise only from the fact of clear-up but from the way in which the public feel that the police dealt with the matter, including how seriously they feel the police took their grievance (Jones and Levi, 1983a, 1983b). So however accurate the police assessment of whether they would be able to take a case to court at the end of the day – and of course we can never know about the 'false negatives', i.e. the 'actual' fraud cases that they do not investigate fully because they mistakenly think that there is not enough in them – there has been a loss to the community if the reporter of the crime is dissatisfied. The feedback from my survey of executives (Levi, 1986a) demonstrates that many *are* dissatisfied, particularly but not exclusively with the Department of Trade and Industry. There is a certain amount of irrationality in this – as there is when people feel unhappy about police efficiency even if their burglary could not have been solved by anyone but Sherlock Holmes – but reducing people's sense of helplessness and isolation is a legitimate function of policing, even if it amounts merely to 'cooling the mark out' by going through the rituals of enquiry into the complaint.

Second, to the extent that there is a failure of credibility in the ability of the policing system to cope with frauds, many who would have legitimate complaints are not making them. This unaided group of non-reporters probably consists both of poor and wealthy individuals and although, as in any other public service, a decision might have to be made that their complaints should not be investigated because they are not serious enough or there is insufficient evidence, the rationing of demand for fraud policing may lead to inequitable results because it occurs largely by default. (An analogy might be with the under-policing of racial attacks.) If the police and government acted more positively over fraud, they might tap a latent demand for policing services to deal with offences that are perceived as serious by those who suffer from them.

Third, there are political reasons for redressing the balance between the policing of the suites and the streets. In a law and order society, where great significance is attached to crime, there is a great deal of political mileage in the unfairness of fraudsters – particularly those who are members of social élites – 'getting away with it' while poor ones go to jail. Simple comparisons such as the sums stolen to numbers prosecuted ratio in Chapter 2 are quite dramatic, even if they are a little misleading. And there is nothing quite like dramatic figures to mobilize media interest and public alarm. This may be one reason for the hint in October 1986 by the Home Secretary to the Commissioner of the Metropolitan Police that the latter might consider deploying some extra fraud squad officers when he received his increased force establishment. It certainly influenced the Government's more aggressive posture on the policing of the City of London in January 1987, responding to Opposition accusations that they were soft on their own political supporters.

Unless they lead to general deterrence, to asset disqualification under the Drug Trafficking Offences Act (1986) and the Criminal Justice Bill (1986), or to triple damages (as under the Insider Trading Sanctions Act, 1984, in the United States), higher levels of policing and prosecution for fraud are not – outside the Revenue sector – going to be fully cost-effective. But policing never is. There are all sorts of social disputes which could be privatized – industrial picketing, for example – but there are issues of principle in the privatization of law enforcement, such as the fact that private policing allows the state no independent voice and makes it harder still to minimize arbitrary and/or oppressive use of discretion. It can lead, also, to an increase in social costs: if more people turn to fraud as a result of the low level of reporting to the police and prosecutions, this imposes a cost upon other future victims, even if they in turn do not report their victimization and the social costs therefore remain hidden in the extra prices of goods and services passed onto the consumer.

This brings me to the value-laden question of what kind of policing is 'appropriate'. Although I have rejected a conspiracy theory approach to explaining the non-control of fraud, it must be acknowledged that if one were trying to set up a system that minimized the likely effectiveness of policing, it would come very close to the system as it existed prior to 1985, and even as it existed in the summer of 1986. Policing was divided among different agencies, whose co-ordination (except in Fraud Investigation Group cases) was minimal or even, as in the case of intelligence interchange from the Revenue departments to the police, officially prohibited. Fraud investigators in the Revenue departments and in the Department of Trade and Industry are appointed on a long-term basis but in the police, particularly the Metropolitan Police, they are not. There ensues a situation in which the most sophisticated offenders, possessing the greatest evidentiary protections of any criminal suspects even at a domestic – let alone international – level, are investigated by people of little training or relevant educational background, who then move on to a different job after periods normally ranging from 18 months to 5 years maximum. What is miraculous (or a tribute to police enterprise) is that any frauds at all – other than those investigated by private detective agencies or in-house security staff on behalf of the victim – get as far as a recommendation to prosecute.

There are no perfect cost-free solutions to this situation, even if it were agreed that it was a problem. Roskill proposed the urgent study of the possibility of setting up an integrated, interdepartmental investigation *and* prosecution unit to deal with 'serious' fraud (Fraud Trials Committee, 1986a:27). The Chief Secretary to the Treasury set up an interdepartmental working party (with police representation from the Commissioners of the City of London and the Metropolis) to enquire into this, and in October 1986, the Home Secretary announced as part of the £10 million package to implement the Roskill proposals the decision to establish a Serious Fraud Office: a statutory body responsible directly to the Attorney-General, headed by a Director who will be independent of the Director of Public Prosecutions. Its planned establishment of up to 80 accountants, lawyers, investigators, and clerical staff will be appointed on civil service pay scales, at an estimated total cost of £3–4 million annually.

It is important to review the background to the establishment of the Serious Fraud Office. During debates inside and outside Parliament on the Financial Services Act (1986) attempts were made by the Labour opposition to transform SIB into a fully-fledged investigative and prosecution agency along the lines of the American SEC. However, although City scandal was not sufficiently widespread to induce the Government to retreat substantially from its own more limited notion of the SIB's role, it was clear to everyone that the Fraud Investigation Group was an inadequate foundation for coping with a large amount of serious fraud and that a more specialized body was needed, particularly with the strong backing for change by the Roskill Report and by views expressed by senior executives such as those in my survey (Levi 1986a), discussed earlier in this book (pp.178–81).

Despite public expenditure cuts, and before the insider dealing and Guinness scandals at the end of 1986, the Government decided to set up the Serious Fraud Office to provide greater investigative and prosecutorial back-up for the control of fraud. It was hoped also that this would disarm the allegations by the opposition that the Government was holding back on 'cleaning up the City', but although the political environment was important, this should not be seen purely as a cynical political exercise: there had been a genuine shift of official opinion that the moral and economic, as well as the political, seriousness of commercial fraud had been insufficiently appreciated hitherto. In theory, one alternative possibility would have been to develop the SFO concept into a private-sector funded investigation and prosecution body: insurers Hogg Robinson devised one thoughtful scheme along these lines, though it foundered on the reluctance of the private sector to pay for it. However, for the Government to rely entirely upon private policing for major City crime would have been politically damaging, opening itself up to claims that it was prostituting the interests of the State to the moral criteria used by private institutions, so this possibility was not seriously considered. (As we saw in Chapter 5, to the extent that investigation and prosecution are reactive to complaints rather than proactive, they are in reality largely subservient at present to private-sector reports. Nevertheless, even though political pressures sometimes influence prosecutions, a constitutionally important distinction between private-sector prosecution and current practice is that once a crime is reported, the police and the Crown Prosecution Service do technically have control over subsequent decisions.)

The brief of the Serious Fraud Office, which supplements but does not replace the Fraud Investigation Group, and which is intended to collaborate and work closely with designated officers of the

Metropolitan and City Police Company Fraud Department, is to deal with 'serious' and/or 'complex' fraud, loosely defined as frauds involving at least £5 million 'at risk' where the details are 'complex'. I have pointed out later the problems in defining complexity and seriousness, and clause 1 (3) of the Criminal Justice Bill (1986) makes this remit quite open when its states that 'The Director may carry out in conjunction with the police investigations into any suspected offence which appears to him to involve serious or complex fraud.'

The Director of the Serious Fraud Office is given major powers as a result of the Bill, tougher in some respects than those available under the Police and Criminal Evidence Act (1984) and almost as great as those in the Financial Services Act (1986) (see Chapter 5). Under clause 2 (2), he may require the person under investigation 'or any person whom he has reason to believe has relevant information' to attend before him 'to answer questions or otherwise furnish information with respect to any matter relevant to the investigation'. Clause 2 (3) entitles him to require these persons to produce any specified documents or documents of a specified class which appear – without a requirement of reasonableness – 'to relate to any matter relevant to the investigation' or to state where the documents are. These provisions attracted hostile reactions from bankers and from lawyers' representatives, who argued that they were too draconian. Legal professional privilege is maintained, though a lawyer may be required to furnish the name and address of his client. Search and seizure warrants for documents may be obtained from a magistrate where (1) there are reasonable grounds for believing that a person has failed to comply with an obligation to produce documents; (2) it is not practicable to serve a notice in relation to them; or (3) the service of such a notice might seriously prejudice the investigation.

There are sanctions for non-cooperation, though they are much lower than the maxima for substantive fraud offences. As in s.105 of the Financial Services Act (1986), clause 2 (10) states that

'Any person who without reasonable excuse fails to comply with a requirement imposed on him under this section shall be guilty of an offence and liable on summary conviction to imprisonment for a term not exceeding six months or to a fine not exceeding level 5 on the standard scale or to both.'

Under clauses 2 (11) and (12), sentences of up to 7 years plus an unlimited fine on conviction on indictment, and 6 months and the statutory maximum fine on summary conviction, can be imposed where any person knows or suspects that an investigation by the police or the Serious Fraud Office into serious or complex fraud is being or is likely to be carried out and '(b) falsifies, conceals, destroys or otherwise disposes of, or causes or permits the falsification, concealment, destruction or disposal of documents which he knows or suspects are or would be relevant to such an investigation.'

Except for Revenue intelligence, which will be disclosed to others only for the purpose of a criminal prosecution by either the Serious Fraud Office or, in relation to an Inland Revenue offence, to the Crown Prosecution Service – see clause 3 of the Bill – information obtained may be passed on not only to the police but to Department of Trade and Industry Inspectors, the Official Receiver, and, under clause 3 (6), to

'(c) any body having supervisory, regulatory, or disciplinary functions in relation to any profession or area of commercial activity; and
(d) any person or body having, under the law of any country or territory outside Great Britain, functions corresponding to any of the functions of any person or body mentioned . . . above.'

So the possibility of developing international intelligence and supervisory interchange is very considerable: clause 3(4) also permits the Director to enter into agreements to supply for a (unspecified) specified purpose information that is in his possession.

Such a 'Fraudbuster' Squad is an important step, bringing Britain nearer to the Task Forces of North America, Australia, and some European countries. Quite apart from the powers of the unit, unless other agencies respond by *reducing* their fraud investigation staff, it will augment by a considerable proportion the (modest) total number of personnel available for dealing with commercial fraud, and aim to break down the artificial departmental barriers between fraud investigators and the police, the Department of Trade and Industry, and the Revenue. (Though [Inland] Revenue intelligence will still be passed on by them only in Serious Fraud Office cases.) It also represents a symbolic public change in the priority attached to City fraud by government and reduces the dependence of fraud investigation upon police valuation, which is influenced only indirectly by the Home Office. It creates the potential for more expert investigation and prosecution than hitherto.

However, without underestimating the potential significance of this development, no change is without its drawbacks. There are issues of principle in conceding that fraud should be different from all other areas of mainstream policing: for instance, the separation of investigation from prosecution was the central purpose of the establishment of the Crown Prosecution Service in 1986. Some, though not all, of these objections of principle are spurious. As Roskill observed, the non-police agencies already have integration of policing and prosecution, and no-one has sought to alter that position (Fraud Trials Committee, 1986a). But equally importantly, the purposes of separation included the tendency of the police to prosecute too readily, leading, in cases where the evidence was weak, to a large waste of public funds as well as to unfairness to the accused. This has hardly been the problem in fraud, where the principal complaint has been the inability to marshal an 'effective' (i.e. lawyer and/or jury-understandable) case to take before the court. If a combined unit will alter this, without prosecuting poor cases or behaving oppressively, then the substance, if not the form, of the equivalence with other crimes is maintained, and this will correspond more closely than the previous arrangement to the 'fairness principle' advocated by the Royal Commission on Criminal Procedure (1981b).

The establishment of such a squad is not a *sufficient* condition for fighting fraud more effectively. Salaries of the kind obtainable in the private sector will mean that unless there are some other forms of reward – for instance, pride in performing a public service recognized to be an important one, or the desire to learn some 'tricks of the trade' before going into more lucrative private work – the Office will not attract the highest calibre of staff. To achieve this, fraud work will have to change its status dramatically to become a prestige task, and this will require confidence that there is a serious intention on the part of the government to do something about fraud.

There will be other problems in the relationship between the Serious Fraud Office and the remainder of the policing system, which will require delicate handling. In what ways will the Office interface with other investigative agencies, particularly the traditionally secretive Inland Revenue? By analogy with the provisions of the Prosecution of Offences Act (1985), schedule 1 clause 7 of the Bill permits the Attorney-General to make regulations requiring chief officers of police to give information to the Director, but the loaning of officers for investigations will be voluntary, and this can create tensions if the police think that an investigation is taking longer than it deserves and is needlessly sacrificing other investigations. Designated police officers – hopefully an élite rather than those whom the Fraud Squad thinks it can spare – working in concert with the Serious Fraud Office will not be members of it but will be subject to police discipline. Organizational lines of accountability are hard to sustain where fraud investigators are drawn temporarily from different agencies: under clause 1(4) of the Criminal Justice Bill (1986), the Director of the Serious Fraud Office may take over the conduct of proceedings of any – undefined in the Bill – serious *or* complex fraud at any time, but who decides whether the fraud currently being investigated by officer X is more or less important than that under consideration by the Serious Fraud Office?

Moreover, the establishment of such an élite unit has its constitutional dangers: these arise from the contradictory problems of political independence and accountability. The risk of granting politicians and their friends effective immunity from the law is a principal plank of the police argument against increasing police accountability to local politicians. But insulation from political pressures is not just a problem in relation to *street* crime: as has been highlighted in the Third World and in countries such as Italy (Di Fonzo, 1983; Shipman, forthcoming), maximizing the independence of the investigators is particularly critical where the suspects are members of the élite themselves. In Britain, the risk of immunity for localized power cliques exists – albeit perhaps temporarily – under present constitutional arrangements (Doig, 1984; Fennell, 1983; Fennell and Thomas, 1983; Milne, 1976).

The ambivalent position of the Attorney-General – the senior Law Officer who at the same time is a political appointee and Member of the Cabinet – has been highlighted by the miners' strike and by other political controversies. Yet of the departmental ministers, it is arguable that he is in a position to be seen to exercise the greatest independence, so the decision to make the Serious Fraud Office accountable to him is defensible in those terms, even if it does not satisfy those who believe that there exists a deeper 'conspiracy of attitude' between law ministers and 'commercial interests'. What is the alternative? Although 'left realist' proposals by Lea and Young (1984) and Kinsey, Lea, and Young (1986) on enhanced local accountability may reduce the risk of the police being subservient to *central* political pressures, it is difficult to see how they will encourage the thorough investigation of commercial frauds or corruption. The City of London is unlikely to elect a radical left (or right) Common Council which will steamroller the police into prosecuting all and sundry fraudsters. If accountability ought truly to be local, this could not be called into question; and if people outside the City are defrau#ed, then in theory, *their* police can take care of the investigation. But the standard left critique of, and solution for, police accountability is rather vague on how the relationship between local and national interests is to be worked out, and this affects fraud as much as it does other offences. Established commercial and political groups do not need the help of local action committees to get their voices heard! The Director of the Serious Fraud Office will present an Annual Report to the Attorney-General and thence to Parliament, but useful though this will be, it is a modest degree of accountability and falls well short even of the Fraud Trials Committee's proposal that a Fraud Commission be set up to monitor the effectiveness of anti-fraud measures.

It is easier to advocate fraud investigative independence than to lay down a method for achieving it. From the 1970s onwards, a high prosecution profile has been adopted in the United States despite (or because of) the involvement of US Attorneys and SEC Directors who are political appointees, and this may be interpreted as 'proving' that there is little risk from *central* governmental influence. But I have argued already that there are important cultural differences between Britain and the United States, not only in how élites operate but also in the career prospects for lawyers who take on major fraud and corruption cases. Resources are finite and distrust of authority has its price, but if a check on political 'fixes' is wanted, it may be that the Police Complaints Authority offers a (limited) model: a small organization independent of the Attorney-General, perhaps reporting direct to the Select Committee on Home Affairs, might be given the power to re-investigate cases in which it is recommended that no action be taken. Claims of undue influence in protecting élites are likely to persist, whatever the system. Indeed, fraud prosecutors are in a situation from which it is hard to emerge unscathed: if they prosecute and the accused are acquitted, they are criticized for 'failing' and for wasting public funds, if not for political victimization; if they do not prosecute, they are criticized for incompetence or political favouritism or, since they give no reasons, for leaving a cloud over the investigated firm; and if they obtain a conviction, they are criticized for political victimization or for only catching the minnows while the whales remain beached in Miami!

Despite the establishment of a Serious Fraud Office, career structures and training will remain problems not only for it but for the police who will still prosecute the great majority of frauds. If the Office took over many of the cases currently dealt with (or at least reported to) the Fraud Investigation Group, there would still remain a large number of cases that present investigative difficulties to the police. There is a strong case for an extension of police training and for an increased component of problem-oriented learning in the training programme. As I argued in Chapter 5, the police generally remain unconvinced of the significance of fraud issues, particularly since the length of time they will spend on the Squad is currently small, but as financial transactions become more salient to organized crime as well as commercial crime investigation, this may enhance the perceived value of training in this area. Any such trend should not be overstated, however, for the police will overwhelmingly deal with small-scale localized crime which is unrelated to any significant organized crime connections. (This is generally true of the United States also, except for the FBI.) Finally, more thought should be given to how fraud investigation skills can be better transmitted 'on the job': by thorough post-investigation debriefing, for example, to communicate the positive and negative aspects of enquiries and the preparation of cases. Operational policing could become more efficient if there were more regular contact between Fraud Squad officers in different forces, for in policing

agencies throughout the world, there are traditionally both organizational and personal obstacles to inter-force and inter-agency
co-operation.

Career structures present different reform issues. If the more difficult
cases are hived off to the Serious Fraud Office, then the necessity for
improving the skills and continuity of *police* fraud investigators will
diminish (though skill development will be a problem for the SFO staff).
Higher pay means less turnover and less rapid promotion for the police,
so there will be less incentive to move from the Fraud Squad for
promotion purposes than there has been in the past. However, it is
undesirable to have officers dealing with fraud and corruption for only a
short period of two years, even if longer periods of service do increase
the risks of police corruption marginally: in the Metropolitan Police,
there could be a flexible system where there were some long-term, some
medium-term, and some short-term appointments. Moreover although,
as recent Metropolitan Police Commanders have shown, it is perfectly
possible to run the Fraud Squad highly competently without having had
any substantial prior experience working on it, it is easier to manage both
internal and external relations if one is familiar with fraud work. More
rapid handling of cases by prosecutors is needed to sustain the morale of
the police: otherwise, fraud investigation loses any sense of urgency and
victims may become yet more dissatisfied.

Finally, there are broader issues of policing strategies. As I have
observed in Chapter 5, the predominant British (and European) police
approach to fraud has been reactive. In the United States, by contrast,
'sting' operations have become commonplace, as the major enforcement
agencies have adapted to white-collar crime investigations the tactics
they tried out first on burglary and fencing. Apart from trading
standards officers, who apply a less sophisticated version of stings when
they pose as consumers to inspect the adulteration of food and to
examine weights and measures offences (such as the turning back of
mileage registers on cars), I see no signs of any strong move towards this
sort of policing methodology in mainland Britain: despite the absence of
clear constitutional rules against entrapment, the British police tend to
be more conservative than the Americans in their strategies. Nevertheless, whatever the implications for civil liberties, such methods may well
arrive in the future, if the authorities take seriously the notion that
enhancing the risk profile for financial intermediaries like banks and
securities traders is the only way of deterring them from co-operating
with fraudsters, and that setting themselves up as financial intermediaries is a good way of getting hard evidence against fraudsters (and
narcotics traffickers). Sting-type operations are more likely to occur in
the private commercial policing sphere, as anti-counterfeiting and

copyright protection groups develop further their use when they seek to break up organized rings of commercial pirates.

INTERNATIONAL DEVELOPMENTS IN POLICING

I have discussed in several places the internationalization of crime. This has not been matched by the internationalization of control agencies. Interpol is little more than a conduit for messages: it has no investigative arm and is unlikely to acquire one. SEC is flexing its international muscles, with the threat to ban overseas countries from its domestic securities markets unless they agree to the principle of 'waiver by conduct', i.e. that trading in the US implies the acceptance of US regulatory authority. But hitherto, that has not been accepted and in any event, SEC deals with only a sub-set of commercial fraud, albeit an important one. As regards Britain, the only significant international investigative body is the Commonwealth Commercial Crime Unit, whose mandate was extended significantly at the meeting of Commonwealth Law Ministers at Harare in July 1986 to include the collation of international intelligence on organized as well as on commercial crime. However, since there are only two operational staff, it will be appreciated that this mandate – though a valuable development in principle – is going to have a limited effect in practice.

Nevertheless, *conceptually*, these are important developments, particularly when taken alongside the view that here is an area where law actually can make a difference. For as I have argued in Chapter 5, in the policing of the powerful, procedural legal rules are necessary, though not sufficient, conditions for the enforcement of substantive prohibitions. Without the power to obtain *legally admissible* information from their own or other legal jurisdictions, the police are practically impotent. Although one may argue that existing rules are examples of what Reisman (1979) has termed *Lex Imperfecta* (i.e. laws which were *designed* to be inadequate, or 'imperfected'), during the 1980s, creative government lawyers have set about building international mutual assistance arrangements that will permit more international policing of commercial fraud. The occupational disease of many lawyers is to assume that a problem is solved once one has set up an appropriate legal framework: this is a delusion. But where powerful groups can be counted upon to avail themselves of every conceivable legal protection, sometimes with help from overseas governments, it is vital for law enforcement agencies to offer as few possibilities as possible for plausible excuses to be given to delay compliance or to prevent it altogether.

INCREASING THE FLOW OF INTELLIGENCE ON FRAUD

Changes in police powers present greater controversies than tinkering with the number and organization of police personnel, though ironically, the latter may be harder to change than the former. The development of criminal intelligence systems is one of the most serious issues in modern policing, and proactive information-gathering of sometimes dubious reliability has generated immense concern not only in Britain (Campbell and Connor, 1986) but also in the United States. In the US, I refer not only to the gathering of intelligence on political dissidents but also to the outcry when it was revealed in March 1985 that the Justice Department intended to develop a computerized system through which thousands of police agencies could exchange information about white-collar crime. The President's Commission on Organized Crime (1986a, 1986b) treats the improvement of criminal intelligence as a key part of the war on crime (and the Freedom of Information Act as a key obstacle, since it enables suspects to learn that they are under investigation). Hence, its stress upon the importance of the prompt and complete filing and collation of currency transfers under the Bank Secrecy Act. As the systems of production and distribution become more interdependent and vulnerable to sabotage, and as social divisions of different kinds intensify, total social surveillance becomes more attractive to administrators and more frightening to many citizens: perhaps, after all, we are not so very far from Bentham's vision of Panopticon. The only reassurance for libertarians, without in any way minimizing the risk arising out of state information-gathering and linked data-bases, is that in this era of the 'techno-police' (Manwaring-White, 1983), policing agencies tend to be obsessional about the collection of data but have very little idea of what to do with it when they have it.

International investigations which seek the production of bank records held overseas are dependent upon the mutual judicial assistance treaties which are a key part of future governmental strategies to combat organized and commercial crime, as they have been in the United States, not only in narcotics trafficking but also in commercial crime cases. As discussed in Chapter 5, the generation of intelligence comprises three elements: the provision of routine information largely unconnected with fraud (such as audited annual reports and currency transfer forms); the imposition of obligations on private-sector persons and bodies to report suspicions of fraud; and the provision of information about specific investigation targets.

POLICIES ON THE REPORTING OF COMMERCIAL FRAUD

There is great ferment within the professions – particularly the accountancy profession – about proposals to require them to report any frauds that they encounter (Allan and Fforde, 1986). To do so, it is argued, will damage the auditor/client relationship, breach the principle of confidentiality, and expose auditors to yet more lawsuits should they fail to disclose fraud. The traditional maxim that the auditor is a watchdog, not a bloodhound, is trotted out as a justification for this position: though with apologies to Mr Sherlock Holmes, one may ask why the watchdog did not bark in the night! Yet whatever the arguments, the tide of history is against them. S.82(8) of the Building Societies Act (1986) gives the auditors power 'if they are satisfied that it is expedient to do so in order to protect the investments of depositors or shareholders', or if requested by the Building Societies Commission to furnish information directly to the latter 'notwithstanding any obligation of confidence . . . and whether or not to do so would be contrary to the interests of the society'. In other words, even if it is not the case that the directors are personally 'on the fiddle', confidentiality may be breached with qualified protection against civil liability for auditors. Similar 'permissive' but not obligatory provisions are to be found in the Banking Bill (1986) and the Financial Services Act (1986).

There are some important issues here. The present duty of the auditor is to ensure that the accounts present a true and fair view of the company's trading position, and fraud is relevant only when it 'materially' – the crucial word – affects the extent to which the accounts can be relied upon. Auditors fear that if they report as 'fraud' an allegation which subsequently is not substantiated, they will be sued by their clients or at least will damage the financial standing of their clients if news of the investigation leaks out to the scandal-hungry media. They may also fear that a willingness to report fraud on their part may lead to other, less vigilant, auditors being appointed. In a free market situation, companies – who often regard auditors as a burden imposed upon them by the state – may prefer to 'chase the market down' to the least officious accountants. (This is known in the US as 'the race to the bottom'. There are analogies here with the choice of corporate domicile: in the United States, the State of Delaware is the most popular place to register partly because it is cheaper and imposes least regulatory supervision.) Moreover, though this does not necessarily lead to conflicts of interest in relation to fraud reporting, some accountancy firms are carrying out their audit functions barely at 'break-even' point, as a way of getting their foot in the business door to attract custom for their management consultancy and other services. In this respect, 'help' (albeit that few accountancy firms seek it) may be at hand, because under pressure from the European Community Eighth Company Law Directive, the Department of Trade and Industry (1986d) Consultative Document on *Regulation of Auditors* proposes that auditors' independence be enhanced by giving them fixed five-year terms with compulsory rotation and even canvasses the possibility of prohibiting auditors from providing services such as management consultancy to the companies they audit. This would reduce the temptation to turn a blind eye to fraud, whatever damage it might do to the profits of the large accountancy firms or chaos it might cause if, as seems certain, the auditors are still involved in negotiating tax liability with the Inland Revenue when the five-year spell comes to an end. It is not without a certain irony that these measures are being proposed at the same time that the Office of Fair Trading is suggesting the further dissolution of outmoded professional boundaries as part of its campaign against restrictive practices in the professions.

Rhetoric about the risk to professional/client relationships is as relevant as the complaints of social workers who, faced with child abuse, refer to the importance of maintaining social worker/client relationships. The crucial point is what are the advantages and disadvantages of imposing such an obligation? One starting argument is that there is no justification for state intrusion into what is essentially a private sphere of economic relations. The counter-argument is that there is a legitimate state interest because if, as happened at Johnson Matthey Bankers, a financial institution comes close to failure, this has considerable political and economic ramifications for others; and because the state effectively is paying a substantial proportion of fraudulent losses, which are offset against taxation. Another counter-argument is that it would actually make the position of both auditors and companies *easier* if there were a general rule about reporting fraud, because currently they fear the embarrassment of being seen to be particularly risk-prone rather than the embarrassment of reporting *per se*. (The latter view is one that may be deduced from my study of senior executives' attitudes to fraud: Levi, 1986a.) Opponents of compulsory reporting may argue that reporting may cause panic among depositors whose confidence in the firm may be unreasonably undermined: would you keep your money in a bank that was always being defrauded by its staff? Counter-arguments are that (1) this is unlikely unless one's institution actually is more risk-prone than others, and (2) compulsory reporting would provide an incentive to take more anti-fraud measures.

If one accepts that there *is* a case for compulsory reporting, the question then becomes what the threshold for doing so should be: it may be tolerable to leave 'serious' undefined in allowing police extra powers, but accountants certainly would not be happy with this if they can be sued or prosecuted for not reporting. Should it be fraud over a certain monetary sum? But corruption in the purchasing department or insider dealing by a director might be a serious matter whatever the figure. Or fraud of a certain type: fraud in an institution which handles people's money or investments may be more damaging than fraud in a manufacturing company. Then, there is the question of to whom one should report fraud. One reason why suspicions of fraud – and this will apply also to bankers' suspicions of narcotics trafficking – remain unreported is that they are most frequently experienced by comparatively junior audit clerks for whom there are few rewards for reporting, and potential disgrace if one's suspicions turn out to be unfounded. Where the 'high liver' is a member of senior management (as many Department of Trade and Industry inspectors' reports have noted), there are serious difficulties in knowing to whom one should report. Here, despite problems that they may have in getting information with which they may act to control executive directors, the role of non-executive directors is vital, though as the Guinness affair showed, major corporate activities can be concealed from them.

It is not surprising that professionals are reluctant to get involved in areas where there is a conflict of loyalties and a prospect of being sued if things go wrong. But how do other groups feel about the imposition of such an obligation to report? In my survey of attitudes (Levi, 1986a) on this issue, it might have been expected that executives would have tried to maximize their claims to autonomy, particularly since they were told that the survey would be used to inform policy-makers. However, this turned out not to be the case. Some of those interviewed admitted that they (and other companies) did not report some frauds because of embarrassment. However, the general view appeared to be that they would not mind reporting frauds if everyone else had to do it. They did not want the publicity consequences of being the only ones to report, and they certainly regarded improvements in the policing of fraud as a necessary trade-off for a requirement to report frauds.

Those who preferred directorial discretion did not necessarily take a soft line on fraud. Concern was expressed by a number of those interviewed about what constituted 'reasonable suspicion' of fraud. For example, what would happen if someone was strongly suspected of fraud but insufficient proof could be found to confirm that suspicion: might there be proceedings for defamation? A further argument against the obligation to report suspected fraud was that 'it would lead to a real decrease in white-collar crime but it would probably clog up the courts considerably'. One leading stockbroker – who was scathing about both police and Department of Trade and Industry competency in the policing of fraud generally – opposed obligatory reporting not because it would clog up the courts but because it would clog up the business, costing business money and lost time. Having discovered and dismissed a fraudster then you might not get a conviction but you would certainly be able to kill the firm. (This may or may not be a good thing.) He said that obligatory reporting would be absolutely chaotic, the police would go off with the books and the whole thing would be brought to a standstill. (This is a concern frequently expressed during parliamentary debates over tax official and police powers to inspect personal and corporate documents, from the Finance Act (1972) to the Police and Criminal Evidence Act (1984) and the Criminal Justice Bill (1986).)

So there is considerable variation in opinion among businesspeople themselves, and great scope for discretion in the identification of when 'fraud' has occurred which would make compulsory reporting within this 'grey area' hard to enforce. There is also the question of sanctions for failing to report fraud: what would be likely to happen to the companies (and to individual directors) if found out? Finally, there are important 'down-stream' implications of reporting requirements which have to be worked through. For example, there has long been a legal duty on company liquidators to report to the Official Receiver or the Director of Public Prosecutions cases in which they suspect a past or present director of having committed a criminal offence in connection with the insolvency: yet few prosecutions have resulted from the performance of this obligation. Unless these proposals are to be regarded merely as political ploys to divert criticism from the failure of state regulatory institutions to act against fraud, the enforcement agencies must be geared up to take action upon increased levels of complaint.

REPORTING CURRENCY TRANSFERS AND OVERCOMING BANKING SECRECY

There is no doubt that international and domestic banking secrecy will be a major battleground in the war on drugs. It is difficult to keep this in isolation from money flows generally, though the 1984 US–Cayman Islands treaty on mutual judicial assistance restricts the lifting of Cayman banking secrecy to narcotics cases as certified by the US Attorney-General. Banking secrecy and dummy 'front' corporations are useful to nations who wish to supply arms or oil to countries with whom they officially have trade bans – such as South Africa – and lifting the barriers of privacy is seen by many countries as merely a device to remove from other governments a source of income independent of US patronage.

Certainly, there seems little prospect – even with the most genuine of intentions – of eliminating all the commercial 'black holes' into which funds sink. In 1986, the Caymans having become more co-operative, the Turks and Caicos Islands having been returned to direct British rule, and inroads having been made into the Virgin Islands, Panama seemed to be the key target. From 1970, when banking secrecy laws were enacted in Panama, the number of banks rose from single figures to 121 in 1985. At the end of 1985, deposits in these banks totalled £33 billion, and foreign deposits were no less than £28 billion. In August 1986, the Panamanian Government promised to take (unspecified) steps to stiffen its criminal laws to halt money laundering, and stated that bankers who take part in laundering will be imprisoned. However, it has resisted to date all efforts by the United States to negotiate a bilateral treaty to open up Panamanian banking records, arguing that bringing down their banking secrecy will not solve the US drug problem. Even if Panama finally gives way, others will take its place. The Peruvian Government has eliminated the requirement to register one's name when purchasing certificates of deposit, thereby making them untraceable; many small countries like Vanuatu have fabulous protections for money-launderers, whereby even the government or the bank has no idea who either the beneficial or nominee owner of the securities is. But bilateral mutual judicial assistance treaties have been negotiated with Canada, Colombia, Italy, Morocco, The Netherlands, Thailand, Turkey, and the UK, as the US Government tries to weaken the links in the international money-movement chain.

In addition to its ventures against overseas banking secrecy, the principal US focus is at the point where the money moves either in or out of the United States. The Americans have adopted aggressive positions to get records: they have delivered subpoenas to foreign bankers on vacation in the US and to the Miami branch of an overseas bank for the records of its branches in the Bahamas, Caymans, and Antigua. They have moved into electronic surveillance: the Orozco case discussed in detail by the Presidential Commission on Organized Crime (1986b) was the first court-authorized telex intercept. From the viewpoint of the politics of crime control, it is difficult for the banks to oppose measures such as these which relate to the commonly perceived evil of drug-taking. Thus, even though banks themselves (as well as bank employees who may get individual rake-offs) benefit from money-laundering, they cannot openly argue that there is nothing wrong with it. They can simply not comply with the rules, but the US response to that has been to set up 'sting' operations in which FBI, IRS, or DEA agents ask banks to launder funds and, if they agree, charge them with criminal offences. In the future, it will be hard to argue successfully, as Maspeth Savings and Loan Association did in 1981, that non-reporting of currency transfers was unintentional and was the result of ignorance of the regulations (President's Commission on Organized Crime, 1986b:47). On the other hand, if bank employees are offered between 1 and 2 per cent of all laundered money – a price which should go up as investigation risks increase – this is a powerful incentive for voluntary co-operation, let alone that induced by 'an offer you cannot refuse'!

The President's Commission on Organized Crime (1986b) recommended rigorous compliance mechanisms with clear intra-bank responsibilities, and the amendment of the Right to Financial Privacy Act to permit financial institutions to disclose more information to the authorities without risking civil lawsuits; amendments to the Bank Secrecy Act to permit the Treasury department to pay rewards to informers for reporting violations and to permit interdepartmental information transfers; increased penalties for violations; and alterations to Title III of the Omnibus Crime Control and Safe Streets Act (1968), to permit currency transfer violations and other criminal provisions of the Bank Secrecy Act to trigger court authorization of the interception of telephone calls, telexes, and other forms of wire or oral communications (such as computer communications). Those who believe that capitalist institutions are immune from police surveillance should refine their analyses to take account of these efforts. These are tied up also with the attempts to confiscate the assets of drug traffickers, discussed later this chapter.

Finally, there are moves towards the international exchange of intelligence related to commercial crime. Some private-sector organizations such as the International Maritime Bureau already perform an international 'tracking' function. The Association of International Bond Dealers is beginning to co-ordinate supervision in the vast Euromarkets, and is likely to do so more in the future. In the public sector, Central Bank supervisors, through the Basle Concordat, liaise fairly closely about common problems. As for more formal policing agencies, Interpol maintains a small intelligence system, and the Commonwealth Commercial Crime Unit plays a role in collating intelligence. However, as the Boesky/Guinness affair shows, most significant of all are moves towards shared intelligence between SEC and securities regulators in Britain and Japan.

Indeed, there is something of a regulatory schizophrenia among the British groups. On the one hand, the Governor of the Bank of England called for closer regulation of international securities in the spring of 1985; on the other, by the summer of 1986, senior Bank officials were discounting the possibility of such harmonization and – much to the displeasure of the Americans – the Government was seeking to insert a clause in the Financial Services Bill which would have blocked the communication of information to foreign regulatory organizations. The harmonization initiatives, for instance the proposal that securities prospectuses issued in one country should be recognized as valid in another, emanate principally from the Americans – from John Shad, the SEC head, in particular. In the initial stages, the proposals on the co-ordination of intelligence encountered some resistance from the British Government, who were concerned about US legal imperialism in wanting the right to subpoena witnesses overseas to give evidence in insider-dealing cases. This is tied in with wider issues of attempts made by US courts to pressurize foreign nationals outside their jurisdiction into producing documentation to comply with American civil discovery procedures that are much more wide-ranging than those in other common-law jurisdictions. But initially, the insider-dealing issues have been resolved by compromise, partly on the basis that if non-US nationals *are* suspected of insider dealing, their authorization to trade in securities may be withdrawn by the UK SIB, whose general role is discussed later in this chapter.

So there are issues of legal principle here, related to concern about the vigorous and nationalistic way in which American courts might interpret 'comity', i.e. respect for foreign jurisdictions. The fear in Britain and other countries outside the United States is that the US is seeking to create what is tantamount to public international law, on the basis of US legal provisions which allow more readily than European courts for 'fishing expeditions' by the parties. (This is encouraged by the pursuit of cases by lawyers operating on contingency fees.) It is not pure nationalism, however. There may be some underlying economic fears, also, on the part of the British authorities lest some secretive financial operators in the Far and Middle East withdraw their funds from the UK because they are concerned that regulatory information may be passed on to the Americans. So here, too, conflicts of interest emerge, with the Department of Trade and Industry being more enthusiastic about trade (and employment) than about regulation, and with suspicions about the way in which particular regulatory developments may create benefits and losses to particular countries.

In spite of these problems, and after some very tough negotiations, the US and UK Governments signed in September 1986 a Memorandum of Understanding on the exchange of information between the Department of Trade and Industry and SEC (on securities) and between the Department of Trade and Industry and the US Commodity Futures Trading Commission (CFTC) on futures. Partly due to concern about the US Freedom of Information Act and partly to avoid endless litigation, para. 3 of the Memorandum expressly states that its provisions 'shall not give rise to the right on the part of any private party, directly or indirectly, to obtain, suppress or exclude any evidence or to challenge the execution of a request for assistance under this Memorandum', and para. 15 states that 'Each Authority will keep confidential to the extent permitted by law any request for information made under this Memorandum'. The range of uses of information is drafted widely. For example, although each authority must specify the grounds on which breach of the legal rule or requirement is suspected, para. 7(b)(iii) states that

> 'where the legal rule or requirement in question is that a person should be of good repute and competent ("fit and proper" or not "statutorily disqual-ified") if he is to set up or carry on an Investment, Securities Processing, or Futures Business, it is sufficient compliance with this subparagraph to specify that information is sought for that purpose.'

To avoid the risk of political or other interference with the exchange of intelligence, the authority to whom a certificated request for information is made may not challenge such a certification 'except on substantial grounds which shall be fully stated in writing' (para. 7). The information can be used in civil or administrative enforcement proceedings as well as in criminal cases, and the requesting Authority is enjoined to 'use its best efforts to ensure that it is not obtained by, any other person' (para. 9). Para. 12 of the Memorandum goes on to express, in diplomatic language, some of the tensions between the two governments by allowing investigators in one country to seek information by means other than under the Memorandum provided that they do so 'with moderation and restraint' and that except when a 'person within the territory of the investigating Authority . . . has possession, custody, or control of' the information sought, the host Authority shall be consulted first.

The Memorandum was given speedy effect by the exchange of information obtained from Ivan Boesky's statements to SEC about insider dealing on the part of prominent UK traders, which triggered off a wave of investigative activity within the UK in 1986–87. Much of this information might have been exchanged anyway at Stock Exchange level between London and New York, but the intergovernmental data interchange was certainly a comparatively new development. How the Memorandum will operate in practice remains to be seen, and it will be surprising if there are no moves towards tougher information exchange provisions at some time in the future.

REFORMING CRIMINAL PROCEDURE

There are two arenas in which procedural reforms are currently being played out: domestic and international. I will first discuss the domestic reforms that have been proposed to deal with fraud. The White Paper on *Criminal Justice* which prefigures the Criminal Justice Bill 1986 stridently proclaims: 'The Government is determined to bring about the changes in law, practice, and attitudes which are necessary to tackle serious fraud. This may, to be effective, involve making radical changes' (Home Office 1986e: para. 42). The aim is to bring commercial fraud – or at least 'serious' fraud – within the umbrella of the crime control model. The brunt of these changes will be borne by the system of criminal procedure, which has been attacked vigorously in a domestic context but has suffered grievous bodily harm from international fraud (and other aspects of organized crime). The essence of the complaint is that the criminal environment has changed, creating evidentiary problems of admissibility and proof that are frequently fatal to the trial of many sophisticated financial operations and/or that would be fatal if the cases were not marked No Further Action (NFA) by the Director of Public Prosecutions first.

I have reviewed some of the Roskill procedural recommendations in detail elsewhere (Levi, 1986b, 1986c), but I will comment briefly here upon the principal reforms in the Criminal Justice Bill (1986). Committal proceedings for some frauds are to be abolished: instead, where prosecuting authorities – the Director of Public Prosecutions, the Director of the Serious Fraud Office, the Revenue departments, and the Secretary of State – certify their opinion that there is sufficient evidence for a committal and that the evidence – clause 4 (1)(b)(ii) – 'reveals a fraud of such seriousness and complexity that it is appropriate that the management of the case should without delay be taken over by the Crown Court', a 'notice of transfer' may be issued. Following Roskill, clause 6 allows the accused to apply for a dismissal of the case, but oral evidence should be allowed only where it appears to the judge that 'the interests of justice require him to do so'. If the judge does dismiss the charges, no further proceedings on them may be brought except by a voluntary bill of indictment. These recommendations are a tough-minded approach to delay and to defence ploys aimed at maximizing their clients' chances of acquittal by making Crown witnesses uncomfortable. They reflect the irritation of the Fraud Trials Committee at the Alice-in-Wonderland (or Dickensian) quality that has surrounded the preliminary stages of some fraud cases, particularly since the introduction of Legal Aid.

Roskill noted the criticisms of the impact (or lack of impact) of pre-trial reviews in fraud cases: see also Leigh (1982); Levi (1981). Clause 7 of the Criminal Justice Bill permits trial judges to hold, in cases that are both serious *and* complex, preparatory hearings on his own motion or that of the prosecution or defence. He may order the prosecution to prepare and serve documents that appear to him to be relevant and, if they comply, he may order the defence to do likewise. At the preparatory hearing, both prosecution and defence may be ordered, *inter alia*, to outline their principal lines of argument and of law. Any order of the judge at a hearing is appealable to the Court of Appeal, but only with leave of the judge or that court. Clause 10 gives prosecution and defence the right to depart from the case disclosed by them at the preparatory hearing, but the judge or the other party may comment on this 'as appears . . . appropriate and the jury may draw such inference as they think fit'. Without the consent of the defence *or* the judge (who will consent only if he thinks that the defence have departed unjustifiably from their original case), *no* part of the defence case revealed at the preparatory hearing will be disclosed to the jury. These provisions certainly fall well short of the practice of the Star Chamber.

The Criminal Justice Bill (1986) took up many of the Roskill proposals to eliminate restrictions on the admissibility of documents: the general principle may be defined as being that documentary evidence other than witness statements should be admissible automatically unless (clause 15) the judge or magistrate considers that it would be in the interests of justice to exclude them. Thus schedules and charts, expert evidence, Department of Trade and Industry inspectors' reports, evidence given at insolvency proceedings, and perhaps even evidence taken in disciplinary tribunals may become admissible. This will apply also to documents held abroad, whose production is to be made simpler: on applications made *ex parte* or with defence representation, a magistrate or judge can send a letter of request to authorities overseas to take evidence on commission or to obtain documents, if proceedings have been instituted or are likely to be instituted if the evidence is obtained (clause 18).

Witness statements, however, present different problems, because the Government agrees that wherever possible, witnesses should be subjected to cross-examination if their evidence is in dispute: so it is not proposed, unless the judge considers that it is in the interests of justice to admit them without oral testimony, to alter the present rule whereby witness statements are not admissible evidence without defence agreement. This is particularly important in the context of documents which (clause 16) appear to have been prepared for the purposes of pending or contemplated criminal proceedings, or of a criminal investigation. It is stated that the court shall not give leave to admit the evidence unless it considers that to do so would be in the interests of justice, and one matter to which it should pay regard is 'any likelihood that the accused will be prejudiced by its admission if the person making it does not attend to give oral evidence in the proceedings'. Unless judges take a hard line, this may benefit defendants who make damaging admissions under questioning by the Serious Fraud Office or by Department of Trade and Industry Inspectors under the Financial Services Act (1986), and who subsequently choose not to give evidence on oath.

Clause 21 of the Bill adopts the imaginative Roskill proposal that overseas witnesses (other than the accused) could give evidence and be cross-examined via live video links. (It also extends this to under-14s in cases involving sexual offences and assaults or threatened assaults.) Videotaped evidence is used already in the United States, for example in the trial of John De Lorean for alleged fraud upon his creditors, which commenced in Detroit in October 1986. (It is interesting that in response to a request by a Californian court for depositions taken in England to be recorded on videotape, a High Court judge ruled that although video recordings of proceedings occurring *in* court would not be permitted, this method was appropriate elsewhere, and he could not uphold the defendants' claim that the presence of a camera would oppress them and cause additional stress: *J. Barber & Sons* v. *Lloyd's Underwriters* [1986] 2 All E.R. 845.

The general effects of these proposals in relation to the rules of evidence, which are *not* restricted to fraud cases, may be considerable in making some international cases prosecutable. By closing the gap between what investigative journalists can find (and can state without being sued successfully for defamation) and what the courts will allow as being formally proved evidence, this in turn may defuse some of the political heat over the absence of prosecutions against those whose conduct has been scandalous. (This is not to assert that all such scandals do involve fraud as defined by the criminal law: to the extent that there are improvements in the efficiency of the investigative and prosecution process, the way in which the substantive law draws the boundaries of fraud will become an even more critical factor in the future than it is at present. A case in point is the activities of those who assisted with the share support operation for Guinness when it took over Distillers in 1986.)

THE TRIAL OF COMMERCIAL FRAUD

Concern about the fate of the jury is evident in those countries which, unlike Canada and the United States, do not have the right to trial by jury enshrined in their written constitutions. Even in North America, there is considerable dispute about the role and ability of the jury (Hans and Vidmar, 1986), not least in mammoth civil anti-trust cases which can drag on for years. There are a number of different proposals to alter the jury system in relation to all trials: see also the Criminal Justice Bill

1986. The first – clause 86 of the Bill – is to abolish altogether the defence peremptory challenge. The Home Secretary has stated that it is intended to 'restrict in practice', but not formally abolish, the equivalent 'stand-by for the Crown'. Objections for cause will remain on exisiting principles, which make it very hard for anyone to challenge except where there is a specific relationship with the accused or prosecutors,or where the juror is disqualified under the Juries Act (1974) or the Juries Disqualification Act (1984). (Thus, quite lawfully, someone fined £1 million for serious fraud could sit on a fraud trial jury (1) after being charged but before conviction, and (2) the very day following his conviction.) Persons aged between 65 and 70 will be able to sit on juries (clause 87), but they will have the right to be exempted should they wish.

The abolition of the peremptory challenge might make a large difference to the composition of multi-defendant fraud juries in London, but since many objections at present are based upon the desire to show clients that one is active on their behalf and/or on unscientific assumptions about the relationship between juror characteristics and propensities to acquit, the effect on the fraud acquittal rate may be negligible. The Fraud Trials Committee (1986a, paras 7.34 and 7.38) recommended that jurors' occupations be disclosed on the jury panel, as was the case prior to 1973. This would make it easier to formulate objections for cause. For example counsel might argue that a juror had a *general* occupational interest – irrespective of direct personal knowledge of the accused or of any other direct party – either in conviction or in acquittal. However, it is not self-evident that similarity of occupation between juror and accused would count as a valid cause for objection: if it did, where would that leave the view that it is a good thing for jurors to have knowledge of the custom and practice of business under dispute?

Most controversially of all, the Committee – Walter Merricks dissenting – recommended that in 'complex fraud cases' – whose precise definition is regarded as impossible (Fraud Trials Committee, 1986a:133) – there should be no right to jury trial and that either prosecution or defence counsel should be entitled to apply to a High Court judge for the accused to be tried before a Fraud Trials Tribunal consisting of a specially chosen judge – not necessarily a High Court judge – and two 'lay members' who shall be 'selected from a panel of persons who have skill and expertise in business generally and experience of complex business transactions' (147). The Committee did *not* recommend that the court should have the right to dispense with jury trial of its own motion: if defence and prosecution agree on jury trial, that would be the mode of trial adopted (148). The verdicts of this Tribunal would be by majority vote – so the judge could be outvoted – but no dissenting opinions would be stated or acknowledged (151). (No reasons are given for this conclusion: perhaps, though majority verdicts are given in ordinary trials, it might be felt to undermine the confidence of the public and/or the accused in the decision of the court.) The potential advantage of this major reform is that unlike current verdicts of guilt or acquittal, where decisions may be reached on the basis of 'gut feelings' about the character of the person on trial, which may be the result of pure prejudice rather than reasoned assessment of the evidence, the Fraud Trials Tribunal will arrive at its decisions by processes that others can review and criticize. (Whether jurors do in fact reach their verdicts in this way in fraud cases – and if so, in how many cases – remains an open question.) The Committee assert that when the verdict is reached – whether guilty or not guilty – the judge should in every case deliver in open court either orally or in writing a statement of the law applied, together with the court's decisions on the facts.

If implemented – as is not government policy at present – this might have a dramatic effect upon the current temptations for trial judges to direct acquittals. This is not to deny that there are many legal issues which arise in fraud cases upon which expert judges may reasonably disagree, but given the caustic comments by the Court of Appeal on some judicial summings-up, inexperienced trial judges may find it less traumatic to take the view that there is 'no case to answer' than to proceed to sum up with a full jury decision. Though there is no hard evidence as to the *relative* importance of these factors, it has been suggested that this, combined with prosecutorial misjudgments and witness disillusion (or threats or bribery), may account for my research finding that most complex cases ending in acquittal were thrown out by the judge rather than by the jury: see Chapter 6. Unfortunately, it is not clear what would count as adequate reasoning on the part of the Fraud Trials Tribunal. We are not helped particularly by the statement of the Committee that 'We think that in principle the right of, and the grounds for, appeal against a decision by the FTT should be the same as those now prevailing in jury trials' (Fraud Trials Committee, 1986a:151). But there is a grey area between appeals on points of law and appeals on interpretation of 'the facts' that makes this a very restricted perspective: are the reasoning processes of judges and assessors so self-evidently superior to those of jurors?

The Committee proposed that this change should occur only for 'complex' cases. However, the guidelines on what constitutes complexity adopted by the Committee make it difficult to predict where its boundaries lie. It is stated that

> 'A complex case is not necessarily one in which enormous sums of money are involved, or one in which the documentation is copious, or the list of witnesses long, although it would be normal if some – if not all – of these

ingredients were present. It is a fraud in which the dishonesty is buried in a series of inter-related transactions, most frequently in a market offering highly-specialised services, or in areas of high finance involving (for example) manipulation of the ownership of companies.

The complexity lies in the fact that the markets, or areas of business, operate according to concepts which bear no obvious similarity to anything in the general experience of most members of the public, and are governed by rules, and conducted in a language, learned only after prolonged study by those involved.'

(Fraud Trials Committee, 1986a:153)

It appears, then, 'complex' frauds are those that involve the City of London, and that within this area of commercial transactions, the accused or the Crown would be left to select those that they want to be tried without a jury. This is a less draconian interpretation of 'complexity' than many appear to believe, but it leaves important difficulties of definition: if a pension fund administrator invests through a recognized market in overseas companies beneficially owned by himself, is this a 'complex fraud'? It is not within the general experience of most members of the public – little upmarket fraud is – and it is transacted through institutions with complex rules and special language. Yet can jurors not understand such a fraud? The Committee itself does not pretend that there is overwhelming evidence that juries either do or do not understand frauds as 'complex' as (or less complex than) these: indeed, the Contempt of Court Act (1981) makes it unlawful to interview actual jurors about their understanding. The research study commissioned by the Fraud Trials Committee concluded that jury understanding was very limited. However, since their method was to play an edited one and one half-hour transcript of a case to a mock jury panel, this is hardly decisive. (If anything, there is an argument for longer trials, on the grounds that jurors may absorb the reasoning behind a case after longer exposure to it.)

We are asked to make a leap of faith to agree that the specially selected judges and 'lay members' will unquestionably have the 'proper understanding' which jurors are alleged to lack. Moreover, unless we are to move towards the position where dishonesty becomes a matter of law – 'was a legal rule violated?' – rather than of fact – 'was what was done both a violation of a legal rule and morally wrong?' – there remains the difficulty of how we are to know what ordinary people regard as dishonest if we do not have ordinary people making the judgment but instead have a judge and members of professional élites making it? In other words, the Fraud Trials Tribunal may be better at applying legal rules to the facts of the case – and, in that sense, may be said to 'understand the issues better' – but *however independent-minded and impartial their members actually are*, their views about dishonesty may be open to criticism. This indeed is the moral and political danger of the proposal, just as it is in self-regulation by the City. If there is an acquittal, it may look as if this is an élite-group 'fix'. In other cases, particularly those overseas or where – as Ian Posgate unsuccessfully claimed in his regulatory dispute with Lloyd's – the accused claim that they are being victimized because they are not part of the City 'inner circle', 'fix' or 'scapegoat' may be alleged also if there is a conviction.

One alternative, proposed by solicitor Walter Merricks in his dissenting report (see Fraud Trials Committee (1986a)), is the establishment of a special court (along the lines of the old City of London one) with powers to impose very substantial fines, and disqualification orders. This would deal with regulatory 'trip-wire' offences which should be created and enforced rigorously. (He concedes the possibility of extending the maximum sentence that can be imposed by such a court from the normal 6 months to 18 months' imprisonment.) Merricks is notably silent on whether defendants would retain the right *not* to be tried before such a court. If – as in Scotland – the trial venue were at the discretion of the prosecution, some might regard this as a fair compromise, though given my observations on the sentencing of business regulatory offences (Levi, 1984a), there would have to be a substantial change in attitudes if the magistracy were to take such offences seriously. Possibly, the specialized nature of the court might assist in this respect. However although, as a matter of practice, those who commit 'complex' frauds may get below 18 months' imprisonment (see Chapter 7), to concede this officially might require us to make explicit some important questions about social equity and deterrence.

There remain ways of making fraud trials better *without* abolishing the jury. The least contentious changes in the trial of fraud are the proposed provision of glossaries and the increased use of audio-visual aids to assist juror understanding: the simulation research carried out for the Fraud Trials Committee (1986b) found that the provision of a glossary of technical terms prior to the summing up improved juror recall by 55 per cent; and the use of graphs and diagrams yielded a 20 per cent improvement in juror comprehension of specimen balance sheets. (Though given the brevity of the experimental trial, actual benefits in real trials may be expected to be substantially less dramatic.) Compared with overseas jurisdictions and with presentations in accountancy and commercial firms, there is a scandalous reliance upon 'talk-and-chalk'. This may change naturally, as later generations of lawyers appear who were brought up on (or even by) home computers. However hitherto, in practice, the courts have not greeted these new ideas of presentation with enthusiasm.

Another approach – not suggested by Roskill – is to allow jurors to play a more active role in court, instead of being discouraged from asking questions by lawyers who regard them as a nuisance or as children who should speak only when spoken to. Heuer and Penrod (1985) carried out systematic experimental research on real juries in Wisconsin and discovered that juror performance at post-trial multiple-choice questionnaries on issues that arose in the trial was significantly better among those jurors who were allowed to ask questions (via the judge) and who either were note-takers or were given legal instructions by the judge at the *beginning* of the trial. The paranoia in some legal circles about active juries is partly related to the risk of revealing hearsay evidence (or having to leave the jury speculating about why they cannot learn about a particular set of facts), but partly to the preference for status, distance, and *mystique vis-à-vis* lay persons. But there is much evidence from educational research that student involvement encourages understanding and attention.

In the United States and Canada, where there is a constitutional requirement to provide the right to jury trial, there has been a creative approach to helping jurors to assimilate material. The need for this is indicated by the findings of Elwork *et al.* (1977) that jurors given what were at that time standard Michigan instructions on how to define negligence were no better at evaluating the evidence and using it logically to reach a verdict than those given no judicial guidance at all! With assistance from psychologists, lawyers, and linguistic experts, instructions to the jury have been rewritten in language comprehensible to ordinary people that also meets legal standards: experimental studies by Elwork *et al.* (1977) and by Severance and Loftus (1982) found that jury deliberations were significantly improved when this was done. The appellate courts in Commonwealth jurisdictions currently spend a substantial amount of expensive legal time dealing with issues of alleged misdirections by trial judges on law, but they do so in the absence of evidence about what impact any of the changes would have had upon the jury. To disarm potential criticism from the Court of Appeal, trial judges sometimes simply read out the words used in earlier appellate cases to define the term (such as 'deception' or 'obtaining credit'). However, though judges' intuition about what meaning will be attached to the wording may turn out to be correct and some judges give what to *me* are superbly clear summings up, these appellate definitions have not been constructed systematically with lay people's perceptions in mind. Although much of the fault may lie with highly technical statutory drafting in English law, if the jury system is to work more effectively, systematic attention might be given to constructing what judges say in the light of how jurors interpret it.

Balancing the competing rights of the accused and 'society' is an emotive business. It also contains some paradoxes. Thus, the proposal of the Roskill Fraud Trials Committee (1986a) to abolish the right to trial by jury in 'complex' fraud cases was supported by the Lord Chancellor and several other senior judges, the City of London Fraud Squad, professional and business organizations, most of the senior executives in my survey (Levi, 1986a), the editors of *The Times, Daily Telegraph*, and *Financial Times*, and at least one civil-rights oriented academic (Leigh, 1982) and practitioner (Louis Blom-Cooper, QC), as well as some sociologists on the political left (Box, 1983). Opponents of the proposal were as mixed ideologically as its supporters: they included an impressively united front of lawyers of all political hues (from the National Council for Civil Liberties to the Society of Conservative Lawyers), Lord McCluskey – a High Court judge and former Solicitor-General of Scotland – in his 1986 Reith Lectures, plus the Metropolitian Police Company Fraud Department (and many Fraud Squad officers outside London to whom I have spoken), and prominent liberal academics such as Zander (1986).

Those who believe that fraud defendants should not be stripped of the right to demand trial by jury assert that there is no hard evidence that juries do *not* understand fraud cases and that it is impossible to draw a clear distinction between 'complex fraud' and all other sorts of cases. Since nobody has taken the trouble to explain what they mean by 'understanding' and how we could possible tell whether it was present or not, they have a strong prima facie case. But there is one key conceptual point of relevance to the trial of complex frauds as defined (loosely) by the Roskill Committee. The task that juries are generally expected to perform – whether they do so badly or well – is to make a judgment about whose explanation of 'what happened' is more plausible. In doing so, they call upon 'common sense', i.e. they make analogies between their prior experiences and what they see and hear in court.

Inter alia, what some hitherto rare insider dealing-type prosecutions ask jurors to do is not only to link the accused to share dealings that are seldom undertaken in their own names but also to make an inference about whether or not a particular transaction or set of transactions seems 'abnormal'. Let us take another rarely prosecuted situation. A company and/or its directors are accused of contravening s.151 of the Companies Act (1985) by using company money to purchase its own shares to inflate their price at the time of a contested take-over bid. In such a case, a jury might have to decide questions such as (a) whether moneys expended by the company or its bankers were intended directly or indirectly to buy shares or were for legitimate company purposes, however unwise these might be in the opinion of others, and; (b) whether particular directors were or were not 'in the know' regarding the nature of the expenditure. Granted that expert witnesses may be called to give evidence (and often to disagree), is not the critical examination of 'plausible accounts' likely to be more accurate if jurors have experience of how that particular person – or at least a person in his sort of position – might be likely to conduct himself and/or to record transactions?

This credibility evaluation factor is one reason why the Roskill Fraud Trials Committee (1986a) advocated the use of market professionals as assessors in tandem with the trial judge rather than trial by judge alone. One problem with this suggestion is that however fairly or unfairly, such market professionals may be not be viewed by defendants, the media, and/or the public as being wholly impartial: if senior personnel in a leading merchant bank were to be prosecuted, it might be hard to find a banker or even an accountant whose past, present, or potential future firm might not stand to gain from a particular trial outcome, or who had no prior dealings with the defendant firm that might have caused offence or gratitude. But although there may be excellent political or principled reasons for maintaining trial by 'common jury', it is mistaken to believe that one can maintain such a system without any cost at all to competent decision-making.

Whatever the motives of people on either side of the jury abolition debate, the absence of Cabinet consensus on the issue and the desire of the Government to avoid further contentious legislation in 1987 have led to the temporary abandonment of the Roskill proposals on removing the right to jury trial in fraud. However, the issue will doubtless return: (1) because the jury system serves as a useful scapegoat for the inadequacies of substantive legal drafting, police, prosecutors, and judges; and (2) because there are some genuine problems in presenting highly detailed information about matters beyond their everyday experience to people who are very intelligent, let alone to a randomly distributed sample of the population, minus those (primarily middle-class people) who are able to obtain exemption from long trials because they or their employer would lose money. Without suggesting that lawyers always make the most sensible judgments possible, those who think judging fraud is not hard in principle might fruitfully examine the notorious case of *Tarling (no.1)* v. *Government of Singapore* (1980), 70 Cr. App. R. 77, and see what a mess the Chief Metropolitan Magistrate and the appellate courts got into.

INTERNATIONAL DEVELOPMENTS IN CRIMINAL PROCEDURE

On the international front, 1986 witnessed a flurry of activities including not only the British Government White Paper on Extradition and the

Criminal Justice Bill (1986), but also the adoption of Commonwealth Schemes on Mutual Assistance in Criminal Matters (including the forfeiture of assets) and on the Transfer of Convicted Offenders. Much of the impetus for change came from Australia as well as from Britain, and was driven by concern about narcotics. However, the legislative proposals have ramifications for fraud also.

International agreements on legal matters always present difficulties due to personal and political rivalries, to divergences of legal systems – common law versus Napoleonic Code – and to distrust of the integrity of 'foreign' judicial processes. This has exerted a profound influence on extradition law, for example. These obstacles (known alternatively as 'rights') – which owe something also to cultural imperialism – are gradually being eroded. Clause 93 of the Criminal Justice Bill (1986) extends the case-law trend by allowing for extradition where – irrespective of any differences in legal labels – the offence could have attracted a sentence of 12 months or more had it occurred in the UK, *or* if it contravenes extra-territorial legislation punishable in both states, *or* if the foreign state bases its jurisdiction on nationality and the conduct constituting the offence took place outside the UK. This could assist fraud prosecutions overseas. But some alleged fraudsters claiming that they are victims of a political conspiracy may seek refuge in clause 95, which forbids extradition where the Secretary of State, the court of committal, or the High Court considers that the offence is of a political character, or if the purpose or possible result of return would be punishment on account of race, religion, nationality, or political opinions. (For a definitional overview of 'political offences', see Connelly, 1985.)

Committal courts reviewing extradition warrants must be satisfied that the offence is an extradition offence and – clause 98 – 'unless an Order in Council giving effect to general extradition arrangements otherwise provides, that the evidence would be sufficient to warrant the trial of the arrested person if the extradition crime had taken place within the jurisdiction of the court'. The passage of the Bill will enable the UK to sign the European Convention on extradition and, most controversially for the civil rights of suspects, enables the UK to make future treaties to abolish the overriding requirement that a foreign government requesting extradition should prove a prima-facie case against the defendant under UK law. Importantly, in the light of the extradition problems over *Tarling* (1980), there are provisions for appeal on the basis of a case stated by the committal court.

If it is finalized in the form agreed at the Commonwealth Law Ministers meetings in Harare on 1 August, 1986, the Scheme on Mutual Assistance (Commonwealth Secretariat, 1986) may be invoked not only when criminal proceedings have been instituted but also when there is reasonable cause to believe that an offence in respect of which proceedings *could* be instituted had been committed. These facts would be certified by the country requesting assistance, and the requested country would not normally look behind that certificate and would not examine the basis of jurisdiction asserted by the requesting country. Nevertheless, assistance may be refused in seven circumstances, of which the most relevant to fraud are (1) conduct which would not constitute an offence under the law of the requested country – para. 7(1)(a); (2) where 'it appears to the Central Authority ... that compliance would prejudice the security, international relations or other essential public interests of that country' – para. 7(2)(a); and (3) 'to the extent that the steps required to be taken in order to comply with the request cannot under the law of that country be taken in respect of criminal matters arising in that country' – para. 7(3). These could be significant limitations. For example, if Britain or Australia grant more draconian search powers in relation to fraud than the Caymans or Vanuatu – as has been the case following legislation in the 1980s – the request for judicial assistance can legitimately be frustrated. Furthermore, the scheme does not propose anything approaching an international subpoena for witnesses: paras 23, 24, and 25 relate only to those who are *willing* to give evidence.

In short, some important though limited steps are about to be taken within the Commonwealth to provide a procedural framework which could ease the prosecution and trial of international frauds. The extent to which the spirit of any such scheme will be complied with is a matter for speculation, however, and it seems unlikely that Panama will apply to join the Commonwealth!

Thinking about sentencing in commercial fraud cases

In some respects, a disproportionate amount of attention has been paid in this book to the sentencing process. As I argued in the previous chapters, commercial élites enjoy a structural advantage from the reporting, policing, and prosecution processes, so that the *practical* significance of the post-conviction sentencing process for members of the upperworld is comparatively minor, at least at present. Nevertheless, important issues of principle which currently may be taken for granted do arise in sentencing fraud, and I shall explore these in further depth here. My aim is not to set out 'the definitive sentencing principle', but rather to elucidate some issues that sentencers and authors of texts about sentencing ought to consider in the context of business crime.

However sceptical we are about the *causal* influence of the accounts we give for our actions, looking at reasons is important not only as a guide to what justifications are acceptable but also to see in what ways the requirement to give reasons might constrain our behaviour. There are many grounds upon which people seek to justify punishments. Apart from those who reject all punishment in capitalist society as illegitimate, most of us are inconsistent in our use of these justifications: in one case, we may favour a short sentence based on the prospects of rehabilitation; in another, despite our feeling that a prison sentence will not reform nor will it deter others, we might favour a retributive sentence; in another still, we might advocate a long sentence because although the offence was not grave, the offender is a persistent one who shows no sign of reforming whatever we do, so we have to teach him a lesson. These failings – if failings they be – are not the exclusive prerogative of 'ordinary people': judges who hear appeals against sentence in the Court of Appeal are prone to them, as a critical reading of Thomas (1979) would reveal. Indeed, Thomas – like the Court of Appeal itself – experiences some problems with the notion of 'sentencing disparity' when he notes, without enlightening us regarding how we might tell when the circumstances *are* 'appropriate' for sentencing one burglar to five years' imprisonment and his older co-defendant, with what appears to be a heavier criminal record, to probation, that 'in appropriate circumstances, the sentencer may deal with one offender by means of an individualized measure, while following tariff principles for sentencing his co-defendants. As different approaches have been adopted no question of disparity arises' (quoted in Wilkins, 1984:18). As Wilkins observes, in a brief but devastating critique of sentencing 'principles':

> 'The English courts seem to have provided themselves with a defence against any claims to show disparities in their dispositions. There are "different lines" and/or "different approaches" which are selected as appropriate, and in addition (or instead?) it is always possible to refer to the concept of "individualisation". While we are told that there is "no single theory", we are not told how many theories there are likely to be – clearly enough to ensure that there is no case to be made by those who would claim to see "disparity".'
> (1984:19)

Indeed, the individualization of sentence may justify almost anything, since almost no two offender/crime combinations are precisely the same. Wilkins is slightly unfair – unless he is implying caprice, how could the Court of Appeal ever overturn any sentence if there were no principles at all? – but he is right in pointing to the difficulty in constraining the Court of Appeal itself on the basis of *its* inconsistency of sentencing principles. (Walker, 1985, paras 8.40 ff. does seek to justify the position of the 'eclectic sentencer' who is not motivated solely by emotional reaction, but in my view, his efforts are not wholly successful. His argument does narrow the range of justifications – for instance, by excluding denunciation from the range of rational principles – but the choice *between* sentencing principles has an irreducible emotional and/or ideological base and it is unclear what criteria might guide 'objectively' the choice of any particular principle in any given case.)

The foregoing analysis, combined with the review of appellate judgments in the previous chapter, suggests that neither appeals to principle nor appeals to empirical research findings have any appreciable effects on British judges. There may be a certain amount of hubris in the complaints of some commentators that judges ignore their deeply-considered opinions (Ashworth, 1983; Fitzmaurice and Pease, 1986). Nevertheless, it appears to this author that whatever approach one adopts towards punishment – from abolitionism to 'an eye for an eye' – it is important to take into account the *effects* of different sanctions. In my view, this applies to retributivism as well as to other rationales, because it is impossible to make the punishment fit the crime without having some comparative scaling of the meaning of different punishments, whether we make this explicit or whether it remains merely implicit. There will continue to be differences of interpretation regarding what the effects of punishment signify: for example, some might think that the fact that the crime rate had risen despite fairly severe sentences *weakens* the case for longer sentences, yet in the drugs and social-security fraud (but not commercial fraud) cases mentioned in the last chapter, the Court of Appeal thought that the rise in the crime rate clearly meant that we required still longer sentences because punishment was not working. We thus reach an interesting paradox: unless we query the *possibility* of deterrence by increasing punishment alone, those offences that have been shown to be least deterrable in the past are those that require the longest deterrent sentences! Where would this end? We will review later the evidence on the impact of punishment, but let us first consider what retributivists have to offer in the way of thinking about the sentencing of fraud.

RETRIBUTION FOR FRAUDSTERS

Some argue that sentences should be proportionate in their severity to the gravity of the crimes committed. As Von Hirsch correctly observes, this is a view that is not restricted to retributivists, who believe that punishment should be proportionate to what an offence *deserves* (Von Hirsch, 1986:31). Utilitarians such as Beccaria and Bentham advocated on *deterrent* grounds a tariff of graded penalties in accordance with offence gravity, because otherwise offenders might be inclined to commit grave crimes more readily than trivial ones. The assumption that offenders can switch readily from one type of crime to another may not be warranted: though Walsh (1986) suggests that burglary and robbery are virtually interchangeable, and Levi (1981) has pointed towards the influence of sentence as one among several factors in the movement of professional thieves and robbers towards some types of fraud (such as long-firm and VAT fraud), it may be impossible for armed robbers or burglars (particularly juveniles) to get into insider-dealing circles. But to the extent that technical and social barriers to entry into particular forms of crime are modest and there is *actually* a realistic potential cross-elasticity of criminality, this utilitarian notion of steering offenders away from grave crimes by graduated punishments makes sense.

However, although such a principle may make sense, many believe that using crime prevention criteria in sentencing is unethical because it entails sentencing people not for the crime for which they have been convicted but for their 'essential characters', whether based upon their prior conviction record, family background, current employment or marital status, or perceived future criminal or other prospects. This is anathema to retributivists, who regard such sentencing criteria as fundamentally unfair, and therefore as impermissible even if they were good predictors of future crime scientifically (which they are not).

Readers will be pleased to learn that I will not review in detail the voluminous general literature on the philosophy of punishment. But it is worth noting the following attempt by Von Hirsch to set out the essence of a retributivist approach to sentence:

> 'As long as the state continues to respond to violence, theft, or fraud, or similarly noxious conduct through the institution of the criminal sanction, it is necessarily treating those whom it punishes as wrongdoers and condemning them for their conduct. If it thus condemns, then the severity of the state's response ought to reflect the degree of blameworthiness, that is the gravity, of actors' conduct. . . . The argument does not presuppose the idea of requiting evil for evil, or other arcane notions that have sometimes surfaced in the literature of retribution.' (Von Hirsch, 1986:36)

Setting aside the evasion of the difficulty faced by all retributivists – that although retribution does not *presuppose* any 'arcane notions' such as 'an eye for an eye', it does not rule them out either – immediately, we have a problem: are we blaming according to the effects of what the actor did – the gravity of *the* crime – or according to how much he is to blame for what occurred – the gravity of *his* crime? In many discussions of retribution, these distinct issues of harm and culpability become blurred. But they are important, not only in how we respond to 'ordinary crimes' – do people from wealthy and/or stable homes deserve more punishment than those from poor and/or unhappy ones, because the latter had 'more excuse' (i.e. less culpability)? – but also in how we respond to those frauds (and regulatory offences such as pollution) in which offenders may not foresee the *full* consequences of their conduct. Von Hirsch asserts that the consequences that should be considered in judging the harmfulness of an act 'should be those that can fairly be attributed to the actor's choice. This militates, for example, against including in harm the unforeseeable consequences of the act, or the consequences wrought by other actors who happen to choose similar actions' (Von Hirsch, 1986:65). Thus, according to this line of reasoning, the prevalence of an offence would not be part of the harm, because each individual burglar or fraudster has a negligible impact upon whether others engage in burglary or fraud. (Though presumably, if the fraudster actively recruited others into his activities, or even if the spread of public knowledge of the techniques he employed in, say, computer fraud or easy evasion of debts by the abuse of limited companies, made that crime more probable, that *would* increase the harmfulness of his conduct.) Crime seriousness surveys (see Chapter 3) are commonly used as the basis for assessing harm, but even though (*pace* Miethe, 1984) there is a considerable amount of consensus among different sections of the public about the seriousness of different crimes, the judgments of the public (and of police, judges, and even academics!) may be based on misinformation about the consequences of actions, e.g. overestimation of the damage caused by burglary (Maguire, 1982) or underestimation of the impact of fraud on those defrauded and/or on the economy as a whole (see the discussion in Chapter 2). Moreover if – as retributivists with a penchant for sentencing guidelines tend to do – we base sentencing norms on the previous practices of sentencers or, for that matter, on the expressed sentence preferences of the general public, we are incorporating sentences based not only on desert but on other rationales.

Again, there are some theoretical difficulties not addressed by Von Hirsch: to what extent does one incorporate the public's *fears* or their sense of social breakdown into one's analysis of harm? These do not always fall into the category of fallacious opinions discussed above: for even though the public may know that there were 'only' a small number of child kidnappings, rapes, or alterations of their bank accounts by computer hackers in any given year, they might still be alarmed very greatly by the fact that these phenomena existed at all. (Public perceptions of the prevalence of crime, which are important in police and judges' views about the seriousness of crime, *can* be smuggled in legitimately here. There may be some sort of take-off into sustained – or temporary – growth of public fears that results from the actions of a particular individual within the context of what other offenders are doing independently: the whole is greater than the sum of the parts. Von Hirsch presumably would reply that if these additional harms were allowable at all, they would not be culpable unless the offender had foreseen these possible risks from his actions.) One certainly can understand why 'soft-hearted' retributivists are so keen to exclude offence prevalence from the sentencing decision: as Fitzmaurice and Pease note, 'If "size of social problem" feeds directly into judgments of offence seriousness, deterrent sentencing and harsh retributive sentencing are almost inevitably indistinguishable, because offences judged to represent a social problem are *ipso facto* grave' (Fitzmaurice and Pease, 1986:76). We might add denunciatory sentences to this list, as they too are likely to be affected by perceptions of prevalence: indeed, many sentences conceived of as deterrent may 'in fact' be based on denunciatory emotions, particularly since there is so little evidence that longer sentences do deter many people from crime. Often, 'we' punish because 'something must be done', as a symbolic and cathartic gesture. Yet as Walker and Marsh (1984) have observed after some intriguing empirical work, there is no evidence for denunciatory effects, not least because few people have any idea about what sentencing levels are, even in highly-publicized cases.

Another problem, for all sentencers who are actually concerned about what they are trying to achieve, is judging the impact of their sentences. For retributivists and those aiming at special deterrence, this is a problem of gauging how much pain the convicted person will derive from a particular sentence: this variability is acknowledged whenever we think about the consequences of imprisonment for the offender's family or, more rarely, for an 'abnormally sensitive' individual's psyche. Those aiming at general deterrence are faced with the even greater complication of working out what the impact of their sentence will be on the statistical aggregate known as 'the public at large', and it is perfectly possible that the impacts will vary widely. There are ways of trying to standardize the effects of a given punishment: fines, for example, can be adjusted as a proportion of the income of the person fined. (Though even this may be unfair, inasmuch as the poor may suffer greatly from the loss of even a tiny sum, while different rich people may react very differently to the loss of the second BMW; and undeclared income presents further risks of inequalities, not only between white-collar and other offenders but also among working-class criminals.) But it is hard to argue that a year's imprisonment means the same to a stockbroker facing his first sentence or a woman who has murdered a drunken husband as it does to an old lag. Indeed, this has led one author (Newman, 1983) to argue for the graduated use of electric shocks as the standardized method in sentencing. It is the only punishment that affects everyone in a more or less uniform manner: except for capital punishment, of course, and even that may have differential consequences for surviving friends and relatives! So whatever our philosophy of punishment, we have rationally to take account of how much pain we are able to cause, and to whom.

People often talk about the need for punishment to fit the crime, and for sentence to be proportionate to the seriousness of the offence. Yet how do we operationalize this idea of 'proportionateness'? Von Hirsch – like many retributivists – does not consider relevant the problem of incommensurability of pain for different individuals, perhaps because the amount of pain we suffer is an unreliable self-reported phenomenon which those about to be sentenced are prone to exaggerate, and perhaps because it is a way of sneaking in unconscious social-class or gender bias into sentencing. But although it may be a problem to which those not attracted to the Newman short-sharp-shock method have no solution, it surely cannot be dismissed as a non-problem. Fitzmaurice and Pease (1986, Ch.6) have shown that the scaling of penal pain is a complex process, and that preferred sentence length does not rise in direct proportion to judgments about offence seriousness. (Indeed, in my view this is defensible, because a very long sentence – whatever that is – may produce disproportionate disruption to family life, to mental health, etc.: there is a larger gap between a non-custodial sentence and one year's imprisonment than there is between 1 and 2 years' imprisonment; and in terms of psychological deterioration, there may be a larger gap between 4 and 5 years' than between 1 and 2 years' imprisonment.)

In short, there is a long way to go before retributivism can be regarded as being wholly satisfactory – morally or intellectually – as a guiding principle of punishment for white-collar (or, for that matter, any other type of) criminals. It may be that for those who wish to play the punishment game at all, retributivism is 'satisficing', i.e. it is OK. But whether it is more satisfactory, or less unsatisfactory, than other principles is a matter for the reader.

THE IMPACT OF DIFFERENT PUNISHMENTS

The effects of punishments are themselves a matter of considerable dispute, but I will seek to review research – including my own – which is relevant to the principles of punishment that have been advocated in relation to business crime. We know comparatively little about how judges view the impact of different sentences on different people, but it is possible that ignorance of the impact of punishment upon 'ordinary' offenders may *increase* punishment levels in their case, while it acts in the converse way for white-collar criminals. There, judges may overestimate the impact of what they do to the offender and also the socio-economic consequences of conviction and of imprisonment. Perhaps, if we are to follow a retributivist policy, we should replace the Social Enquiry Report – based on an individualized notion of justice – with an Offence Impact Report, leaving it to the judge to decide whether the offender knew what he was doing? (This sort of offence impact notion is implicit in moves to 'bring the victim back in' to the sentencing process: see Shapland, Willmore, and Duff, 1985. Yet it does raise some important questions of consistency and foreseeability of concrete harms: fairness may be just as important in court disposals which incorporate victim views as in those which do not.)

THE SEVERITY OF DIFFERENT SANCTIONS

Although public views about the severity of different penalties has attracted considerable attention in recent research and theorizing (see Fitzmaurice and Pease, 1986; Hough and Mayhew, 1985), no systematic attention has been paid previously to this in relation to commercial fraud offences. In a questionnaire survey of 56 senior executives (Levi, 1986a), I asked businesspeople to judge the seriousness of a number of penalties – both those that could be imposed by a court and, since it is argued that the social and economic consequences of conviction *per se* are an important ingredient of punishment, those that might be imposed by the offender's reference group within the community – in relation to a case of fraudulent trading. To make this exercise more meaningful, I provided a mini-Social Enquiry Report about the offender's family and economic circumstances.

A deliberate attempt was made to focus executives' minds upon a particular sort of person (not too unlike themselves), in order to make the exercise more realistic. They were told that

> 'The offender is a 39 year-old businessman with no previous convictions. He has two teenage boys at public school, a non-working wife, and a mortgage of £30,000 on the jointly owned family home (which is worth around £120,000). Apart from their home, he has negligible disposable personal assets. He was earning £30,000 per annum when he was arrested for continuing to trade long after he knew that his company had become insolvent.'

On a 0–20 scale, the executives rated the sanctions as shown in *Table 26*.

The results are extremely interesting. First, they run counter to the official Tariff, whereby suspended prison sentences are regarded more severely than fines. *A two-year suspended sentence was viewed on average as being less severe than even a £5000 fine, and less severe than national publicity alone.* (This might make judges think again before imposing one in a

Table 26   *Executives' penalty severity scale*

	mean	median	rank
3 years' imprisonment	16.91	17.50	1
1 year imprisonment	13.25	14.50	2
6 months' imprisonment plus being banned for 5 years from taking part in the management of a business	12.52	12.00	3
6 months' imprisonment plus a further 18 months suspended prison sentence	11.04	10.00	4=
£50,000 fine	11.04	10.00	4=
being banned for 5 years from taking part in the management of a business	8.05	8.50	6
being struck off by the Institute of Chartered Accountants	7.18	6.00	7
publicity of one's offending in the national press and television	5.78	5.00	8
£5000 fine	5.55	5.00	9
2 years' suspended prison sentence	5.43	5.00	10
dismissal from one's current job	5.30	5.00	11
being shunned by former friends	4.75	3.00	12

Source: Levi 1986a

management fraud case.) Walker and Marsh (1984) also found that a suspended sentence was ranked lower in severity by many respondents than a fine of £40, community service, and probation. (By way of analogy, informal discussions with some Members of The Stock Exchange suggest that some view a notice of Censure – the lowest rung on the published penalty ladder – more seriously than a suspension from trading, because the words used in the notice imply a higher level of public disgrace.) Second, though it is dangerous to treat ordinal scales as if they were interval-level data (i.e. as if the gap between 1 and 2 was the same as that between 9 and 10), it does seem clear that *prison is seen to be very much more significant than other sanctions*, although a fine of £50,000 was as severe as a 6-month sentence without a management ban. (Methodologically, this lends support to the view that a 'combination sentence' is not as severe a punishment as the sum of its component parts taken separately.) Third, commercial incapacitation (via a ban on participation in company management or striking off by the Institute of Chartered Accountants) was considered to be a severe penalty for a businessman with a moderate mortgage (£30,000) and two boys at public school – for American readers, this means a private school! –

though the executives – who came from the ranks of high rather than ordinary commerce – may have overestimated the *general* impact of disqualification orders upon the business community at large. These can be evaded by operating from the background, using 'front men' (or women) to act for one (see Levi, 1981). Finally, publicity sanctions were considered important (though it is not clear how much this was because of the commercial consequences and how much because of the social consequences for one's family), but being shunned *oneself* by former friends was felt to be a quite minor punishment.

SENSITIVITY TO SANCTIONS

Radical critics are not keen to acknowledge the salience of the white-collar prisoner's *angst* at imprisonment, or if they do acknowledge it, they may welcome it on the grounds of retribution or deterrence. Many writers (and sentencers) take it for granted that the effects of conviction *per se* are severe for high-status persons and, inferentially, that they are higher for them than for other persons. For example, in the so-called 'paper label' case in the United States, Judge Renfrew (1977) sentenced a group of price-fixers to make speeches to the community, citing as his reasons their high social standing and implying their great suffering from social sanctions. It is almost as if a different penalty severity scale were in operation for white-collar compared with 'normal' offenders, resulting from their status rather than the nature of their offences. This might be defined as the 'fall from grace' effect.

However, what evidence is there about the impact of formal and informal sanctions and how they relate to different professional and commercial groups and to different sorts of offences? This is an important issue, for direct feedback to sentencers is negligible, so mistaken assumptions may never otherwise be corrected. In the case of Criminal Bankruptcy Orders, for instance, the trial judge is unlikely to learn whether the Director of Public Prosecutions – in his role as Official Petitioner – actually activated the order, still less what was successfully clawed back from the person sentenced. If this does not affect the *punishment* given (see the discussion of *Garner* (1986) in the previous chapter pp.269–70), the absence of feedback may not matter. But it is certain that perceptions – correct or incorrect – of the economic and social effects of 'fall from grace' do reduce sentences generally, so the assessment of the impact of conviction *per se* is crucial to the justification of reducing sentences here. (It may be that sentences ought to be low in white-collar cases, but we ought not to give spurious reasons for lowering them.)

In the case of *Patterson*, a blood specialist who was convicted of stealing large quantities of blood from the National Health Service for resale by conspirators abroad, netting £158,700 over a four-year period, the trial judge imposed a 3-year prison sentence, commenting that he was allowing for the fact that his career 'lies shattered for all time'. (The blood had been separated to make plasma by unqualified people in unhygienic conditions including a washroom and a garage!) Yet the General Medical Council subsequently ordered him to be suspended for only 12 months – a period that happily coincided with the remainder of his spell in prison – after which they would review the case (*Daily Telegraph*, 9 July, 1985). In July 1986, the GMC suspended him for a further 6 months, stating that his case would be reviewed again in February 1987. Why should the suspension have been for those particular periods? Would the judge have given him more than 3 years' imprisonment had he known that 'for all time' might mean 18 months?

Evaluating the social, psychological, and economic consequences of conviction and sentence is a far from simple task. There are a number of methodological errors to which commentators in this area are prone. A study in the United States by Benson (1984) compares pre-arrest and post-conviction socio-economic status of those convicted of a range of white-collar crimes. However, this may be misleading, because some businesspeople and professionals may have turned to fraud because their businesses or practices were in dire straits or because their expenditures greatly exceeded their incomes (even though the latter were high). Consequently, they would have gone 'bust' anyway and might well have found difficulty obtaining other high-status employment. In this sense, status loss may be a consequence of the business cycle, bad management, and/or vice rather than of conviction.

Studies based on the experiences of white-collar prisoners may not be generalizable to those who are not imprisoned, whose status and economic losses can be expected to be less. The length of the follow-up is also important: within-prison studies may focus on the anguish of imprisonment, and many white-collar ex-prisoners may have temporary difficulty in finding work, as the sympathetic study of 100 English prisoners by Breed (1979) indicates. Yet Watergate offenders are still making substantial sums of money from their memoirs and from lecturing, so eventual economic rehabilitation is possible, even if status is never fully restored. (Attorneys-General convicted of felonies in democratic – with a small 'd' – regimes are unlikely ever to return to their former positions!) White-collar convicts or persons expelled from self-regulatory bodies who possess any sophistication can set up companies registered in Liechtenstein, Netherland Antilles, or Panama without too much problem, and can get others to 'front' companies for them quite legitimately. They may be harmed in social status by conviction, or in some cases, undertaking these devious corporate manoeuvres may induce them to commit further offences by 'closing off' more straightforward options (Levi, 1981). However, one can push this labelling approach too far: if they were so lacking in deviousness and possessed such high moral standards, why did they ever get involved in fraud initially?

It is also important to be clear about who the reference group are for white-collar offenders. Benson states that the public may react more harshly to those convicted of manufacturing unsafe products or of health and safety violations (Benson, 1984:580). However, quite apart from the problem that public ratings of crime seriousness may not be reflected in their abstract sentencing preferences or their actual social behaviour, how relevant are general public sentiments to corporate executives? Surely what matters here is the group with which executives identify, and executives may have little difficulty in excusing crimes carried out for the benefit of the corporation rather than themselves. Even if their fellow executives rate those crimes seriously, they may not see the *personal* culpability of the convicted person as being very high: take, for example, the reactions to the former W.H. Smith director convicted of insider trading, discussed in Chapter 7. (This reference group difficulty is evaded also by Fisse and Braithwaite, 1983, in their study of the impact of publicity upon what they term 'corporate offenders', only some of whom had been convicted or even punished administratively.)

There is some American research that is relevant. Nathan (1980) examined the cases of 27 corporate executives who had been indicted or convicted for corporate crimes. Of the 27, 11 resigned as a result of indictment or conviction, 10 retained their original positions, and 6 assumed new positions within the same firm. A study of the 21 executives who admitted to the Watergate Special Prosecutor in 1973 and 1974 that they made felonious payments to candidates for federal elected office showed that despite convictions for felonies, many of them were still presiding over their companies (*New York Times*, 24 August, 1975). Bearing in mind that these are historic salaries that should be adjusted for inflation, etc., the Chairmen of the Boards of Braniff Airlines, Ashland Oil, and Carnation continued with their salaries in the £250,000 range; Goodyear's chief executive resigned, but was re-employed as a consultant with salary and pension exceeding $500,000 annually! Orland mentions the 1975 case in which Fruehauf Corporation was fined $10,000 and two of its executives were given suspended 6-month prison sentences and placed on unsupervised probation for 2 years, for evading corporate excise duties of $25 million over a decade (Orland, 1980:514–15). Based on the proposition that the offences had been committed for the corporation, the board of directors recommended the re-instatement of the convicted chief executive at a salary of $450,000 a year, and this was ratified by the shareholders. Cases collected by corporate counsel in support of this decision suggest that it was fairly typical. Plainly, neither the economic nor the social consequences of conviction were particularly debilitating. In this respect, one would expect to find distinctions based upon the perceived motivation for the corporate crime: was it done for or against the corporation?

Benson hypothesized (and found) that professionals and public-sector workers are susceptible to non-judicial sanctioning, whereas private businessmen or employees of private businesses are not (Benson, 1984:578). He found also that older offenders suffered less drop in socio-economic status, though those who did lose some status found it harder to recover than the young. However, 'the seriousness of the offense, at least as measured in terms of potential exposure to prison, had virtually no effect on loss of occupational status' (Benson, 1984:585). It appears that the criterion of exposure here is sentence *maxima* rather than sentence actually imposed. But this greatly weakens the force of the analysis, since maxima are frequently the residue of history rather than of coherent reflection and rationalization. In strict law, even if Parliament approves clause 31 of the Criminal Justice Bill (1986), which raises the maximum sentence for corruption to seven years' imprisonment on indictment, the maximum possible sentence for shoplifting will remain greater than that for VAT evasion or for corruption involving £100 million!

The impact of sanctions does not depend on whether those punished are in the public or in the private sector. First, the rise of consumerism and investor protection in the 1970s and 1980s has extended the 'fit and proper person' test to parts of the private sector, particularly in financial services, and consequently non-judicial sanctions have become broader in scope. Second, related to but not dependent upon formal 'fit and proper person' rules, there may be economic and/or social sanctions for *private*-sector personnel that arise from conviction, from adjudications by professional bodies, or even from bad publicity. I will illustrate this with examples which show the way in which *international* capitalism is affected.

In October 1986, Mr. Li Ka-Shing and four co-directors strove hard, but unsuccessfully, to overturn in the High Court a finding by the Hong Kong Insider Dealing Tribunal that they had engaged in insider dealing. Quite apart from any hurt pride or public shame, Mr. Li feared that it might affect his plans for corporate expansion outside Hong Kong. In November 1986, following the arrest of his *son* – the bank chairman – in connection with an alleged £416 million fraud upon the National Bank of Brunei, financier Tan Sri Khoo Teck Puat, though not himself under investigation for fraud, resigned his directorship of Standard Chartered Bank in the UK. This was partly because he was selling his Standard Chartered shares to get some money. However, given his family connection with the National Bank of Brunei scandal – he also owned 70 per cent of its stock – he might have been viewed as not a fit and proper person to be a bank director in the UK. In the United States in 1986, investment bankers Drexel Burnham Lambert took a lower profile in take-over bids after criticism of their entanglement with the insider dealing activities of Dennis Levine and Ivan Boesky.

The fall-out from Boesky's confessions and settlement with the SEC affected the British conglomerate Guinness, when it was revealed that soon after Boesky had supported its successful but bitterly contested take-over bid for Distillers in early 1986 – at a time when he was still admired as a brilliant *arbitrageur* – Guinness secretly took an unusual $100 million stake in high-risk investment syndicates organized by him. (The investments plummeted, partly as a result of Boesky's SEC settlement.) It was also revealed that a US liquor firm – Schenley – had supported Guinness by buying shares during the bid, allegedly in the expectation of having its distribution licences renewed if it did so: no doubt coincidentally, Guinness increased its business with Schenley on generous terms after the bid. The announcement of the Department of Trade and Industry investigation into Guinness greatly damaged the Guinness share price, and despite his protests and before any prosecutions were even contemplated, its chairman and chief executive, Ernest Saunders, lost his £375,000 per annum job, and although at the time of writing, it is not possible to predict what the long-term losses will be for him and for the other directors who resigned, their international market value as executives will have been considerably reduced.

The share price and reputation of Guinness market-leading merchant bankers, Morgan Grenfell, also suffered substantially when within a month of the Geoffrey Collier insider dealing scandal, it was alleged that its merger tactician star, Roger Seelig, had master-minded a scheme to buy up to £200 million of shares to help Guinness take control of Distillers: this 'price support' is crucial when the bidder's shares are offered in exchange for those in the target company. It was alleged by another merchant banker – Henry Ansbacher – that Morgan Grenfell had promised to indemnify its clients against any losses if Guinness share price dropped after the Distillers take-over. Morgan Grenfell angrily resigned as Guinness banker when the latter stated that the deal with Ansbachers had been made without its authorization and that a money transfer of £7,614,682.10 by Guinness to an Ansbacher nominee account was for an interest-free deposit rather than the purchase price for 2.1 million Guinness shares; for Guinness to have bought its own shares might have been a criminal offence under s.151 of the Companies Act (1985). Seelig resigned and, after great pressure from the Government and the Bank of England, he was followed by the Morgan Grenfell chief executive and by its corporate finance head – a former Director of the Take-over Panel – who, while not admitting personal wrongdoing, accepted responsibility for their inadequate supervision. Their salaries were over £200,000 per annum each, so the financial impact on them was considerable; and their future prospects are also uncertain.

Some institutional investors are wary of people involved in public scandals, not just for moral reasons but because scandal is likely to damage the prospects for the growth in share prices. Yet where the entrepreneur continues to make high profits, many investors will remain 'loyal'. The hostile reactions of Prime Minister Edward Heath and the Department of Trade Inspectors' Report which criticized 'Tiny' Rowland's options dealings (*Lonrho Limited*, 1976, pp.622, 632, 636, 643) did not prevent him from expanding his highly successful business empire, although they may have influenced the Thatcher Government's rejection of his attempt to take control of Harrods. Similarly, the castigation of Robert Maxwell as a man unfit to manage a public company (*Pergamon Press Limited*, 1971, p.207) did not halt his entrepreneurial rise: in his successful libel suit against satirical magazine *Private Eye*, Maxwell claimed that long after his troubles at Pergamon, he had been offered (and had declined) a seat in the House of Lords by senior figures in the Labour Party (Jackson *et al.*, 1986). It is plausible that indictment or expected indictment on serious criminal charges makes credit hard to find, unless acquittal is perceived as a public vindication of entrepreneurial activities: the business prospects of John De Lorean – acquitted of drug-trafficking and fraud at separate US trials – remain uncertain in 1987, but even before his trials, his reputation for commercial success had been destroyed.

As for the consequences of *imprisonment*, at least some of those jailed for investor fraud make a success of new careers, though the proportion who do so is unknown. Former Swiss banker Paul Erdman became a best-selling author of excellent financial novels. Trevor Pepperell – who served two years and four months in open prison for his role in the fraudulent secondary bank, London and County Securities – used his time (and that of fellow prisoners) to invent some successful financial board games, and now his company is quoted on The Stock Exchange's Unlisted Securities Market. As he observed, in a way that unconsciously stresses the conflict between retribution and rehabilitation:

'Freed from the worries of earning a living to pay for food, clothing, and accommodation, I was able to concentrate on writing a book and inventing the games. Fate had dealt me a bad hand, but I decided to use my prison sentence as a sabbatical rather than a punishment.'

(Financial Times, 20 December, 1986)

In the United States, apart from the best-selling books by Watergate conspirators, R. Foster Winans (1987), quondam author of the 'Heard on the Street' column on the Wall Street Journal, profitably spent his time awaiting an unsuccessful appeal against his 18 month jail sentence by writing a popular account of his insider dealing career. So for some, free enterprise triumphs in the end! But many, such as former Labour Cabinet Minister John Stonehouse, never recover commercially or psychologically following their imprisonment. The variation revealed by these examples suggests the value of caution in drawing conclusions about the typical consequences of bad publicity and penal sanctions, whose effects may be quite subtle and hard to measure by income and job position. For example, whether or not former British Champion Jockey Lester Piggott is convicted in relation to income tax fraud charges involving millions of pounds for which he was arrested (in a blaze of publicity) on 19 December, 1986, it seems unlikely that unless his competence declines, racehorse owners will cease to employ him as a trainer. However, both they and he may be very careful in future about how and where the fees are paid, and prosecution for fraud – in addition to conviction earlier in 1986 for unlawful firearms possession charges – would certainly rule out his being mentioned in the Queen's Honours List. Even if people do not lose their formal positions, stigma of some kind may affect their lives, though they may seek to neutralize shame (to themselves and to others) by claiming that they are victims of some establishment conspiracy.

The reasons for the imposition of stigma in business remain complex and ambiguous. Benson (1984:579) may have overstated the self-interested nature of reactions to fraud, by supposing that the business community will react more harshly to crimes that victimize business than to those that victimize government or private individuals: the crime seriousness ratings discussed in Chapter 3 show that fraud by professionals and mail-order fraud are rated more severely by British executives than crimes against business (though these in turn are viewed as being more serious than tax fraud). To pursue the theme of the social and economic consequences of exposure for fraud, the executives in my survey (Levi, 1986a) were asked how they would react (1) socially, and (2) in business dealings, to someone in their business or social circle in three different circumstances:

1 if he was *convicted* of fraud against other businesspeople or investors;

2 if he was *suspected*, on the basis of statements from a trusted friend or a reliable newspaper, of having committed fraud against other businesspeople or investors;
3 if he was *convicted* of income tax evasion.

In the case of the person convicted of fraud against other businesspeople or investors, 79.2 per cent replied that they would avoid him socially; 4.2 per cent that they would overtly snub him socially; and 12.5 per cent that it would make no difference socially. (The remainder did not specify what they would do.) The reaction in business dealings was even stronger: 92.5 per cent stated that they would avoid completely business dealings with him and 7.5 per cent that it would make them more careful in business dealing with him.

The reaction to suspicion of fraud was more modest, thus supporting the validity of this exercise. (One respondent commented caustically that a reliable newspaper report was a contradiction in terms! 'There is no such thing as a paper is as good as its reporters who, in the mass, are not reliable.') In answers 52.5 per cent stated that they would avoid him socially; 5 per cent would overtly snub him; and 35 per cent stated that it would make no difference socially. The remainder did not express a view. Again, there was tougher reaction in the business sphere: 53.8 per cent stated that they would wholly avoid business dealings, and 46.2 per cent that they would take care in business dealings.

The reaction to conviction for income-tax fraud was mildest of all. Forty per cent stated that they would avoid him socially; 4 per cent that they would overtly snub him socially; and 48.9 per cent that it would make no difference to social relations. The remainder did not express a view. With reference to business dealings 29.4 per cent stated that they would avoid them completely; 60.8 per cent that they would take greater care in business dealings; and 9.8 per cent that it would make no difference at all to their commercial dealings.

It does seem plain that a distinction is made between types of fraud in terms of implications both for social acceptability and for commercial trustworthiness. The income-tax fraudster is not generally perceived as a serious risk for other businesspeople, but he is not wholly in the clear, since only 9.8 per cent stated that the fact that someone had been convicted of tax evasion would make no difference to them in commerce. The whiff of exposure for suspected commercial fraud would be enough to make a bare majority of the executives stay out of the way socially and cut off commercial dealings altogether. Whether the difference in the reactions to convictions and suspicions of fraud against businesspeople or investors is due to the extra stigma of conviction or the burden of proof is unknown, but it is interesting nonetheless. In no case would many people overtly snub a fraudster socially. (Reactions to other types of offender would make an interesting comparison.) Finally, for all categories, conviction or suspicion of fraud made a much greater difference to business than to social intercourse. There may be a gap between expressed attitudes and actual behaviour, but the variation in responses encourages one to regard them as honest replies.

PUBLIC OPINION AND SENTENCING THE FRAUDSTER

As discussed in Chapter 3, the populist appeals to seriousness ratings in political measures to 'get tough with crime' have been used by white-collar crime writers to suggest that the balance of policing should change towards the heavier policing of corporate crime. These studies equally may be used when seeking support for tougher sentencing of business criminals, both absolutely and in relation to 'common criminals'. (See Braithwaite, 1982b, Cullen *et al.* 1983, Gibbons, 1969, Newman, 1957, 1976, Reed and Reed, 1975, Walker and Marsh, 1984.) Business executives also took a very hard line on what commercial fraudsters should get compared with burglars: their tough views applied both to professional men who defraud their clients and to businesspeople who defraud their creditors.

To sum up, there are good grounds for believing that on retributivist criteria – whether determined by the opinion of the general public or of senior businesspeople – fraudsters of various types ought to be punished severely, in absolute terms and relative to other sorts of offenders. This is equally the case if one adopts a more abstract, philosopher-king approach to setting retributive penalties. However, to state that fraud rates high in the retribution stakes offers little guide to where the penalty scaling process should start and end, and there are many problems such as the commensurability of pain between different individuals which must be addressed rigorously by those who favour this approach to punishment. Let us now consider information relevant to other candidates for principles of punishment: deterrence and incapacitation.

EXECUTIVES' EXPECTATIONS OF SANCTIONS FOR FRAUD

Such sentencing principles as general deterrence and denunciation rest upon assumptions not only about the rationality of offending but also about knowledge of penalties. Such knowledge is difficult to come by, not least because under the English system, there is so much discretion that it is difficult to predict with certainty what precise sentence might be imposed in any given set of circumstances. This makes the choice of 'typical sentences' problematic, to put it mildly.

Previous research on fraud sentencing (Levi, 1981) suggested that Crown Court judges did not appear to follow appellate guidelines. Consequently, rather than select Court of Appeal judgments on fraud, which seldom attract public attention, I decided that the best method of proceeding would be to take recent cases reported in the 'quality press' that executives might read – *The Times* and *Daily Telegraph* – and to pick some that might be relevant to the executives themselves. In this way, we would have a clearer idea of whether expected sentences might be likely to deter *them* should they contemplate frauds of this type, and also examine feelings about the appropriateness of these expected penalties. After all, if people expect penalties to be lighter than they actually are, there is no deterrent or denunciatory point in increasing sentence without ensuring that there is accompanying publicity. On the other hand, if executives think that sentences are heavier than they actually are, increasing publicity for sentences without increasing the sentences themselves might actually decrease the deterrent effect. To enable the respondents to picture the circumstances of the offence, a little more detail was given in the vignettes than is normally the case, though the gravity of the tax fraud was understated by the absence of information about its duration and the involvement of other parties.

The vignettes were as follows:

1 A 39 year-old travel agent pleaded guilty to trading long after his limited company had become insolvent. Two thousand families lost £620,000 for tickets that had not been received. He had paid back £10,000 to the liquidators.

2 A 43 year-old businessman was convicted after pleading not guilty to trying to defraud an insurance company of £214,000 by setting fire to the premises of his ailing business. His secretary reported the plot before he was able to put it into effect, and the police recorded a conversation between them discussing the plot.

3 A 50 year-old managing director pleaded guilty to milking £40,000 from the firm he was brought in to save.

4 A 45 year-old banker pleaded guilty to obtaining £67,000 from insider tradng on shares tipped by his wife, who worked for the tipped company's bankers.

5 A 42 year-old managing director of a private limited company hotel group pleaded guilty to defrauding the Inland Revenue of £363,000 by filling in false tax returns, failing to deduct tax for employees, and using company funds for personal expenses. All the money was repaid.

6 A 38 year-old accountant pleaded guilty to defrauding employers of £500,000. Except for his home and £21,000 that was repaid, all the

money had been spent gambling. As a consequence, the firm went into liquidation.

Because of the difficulty of weighting combined penalties, it is difficult to arrive at a clear analysis of the accuracy of expectations of punishment. Overall, except for insider trading, the executives *under*-estimated the chances of receiving a custodial sentence, and greatly *over*estimated the chances of being disqualified from company management. Where prison sentences were anticipated., they were often expected to be longer than was actually the case. This complex picture is interesting because in so far as one can write about 'typical' penalties for the relatively rarely sentenced offences of fraud, the actual sentences in the vignettes here are fairly high compared with other sentences in my media, Crown Court, and appellate samples, particularly in respect of the under-utilization of suspended and partially suspended sentences. We should recall also that suspended sentences were rated by the executives as minor penalties.

Insider dealing was the only offence for which less than half expected some kind of immediate prison sentence (including partially suspended ones): even this was over-pessimistic, since no one has yet been jailed for this offence in Britain. Respondents – many of whom had had some contact with the police over fraud – were realistic in not expecting very much use of compensation, though they predicted more compensation than actually occurred. Those who thought that sentences were too lenient did not greatly underestimate what they were likely to be. However, because of the small number of people who wrote in what they would like sentences to be, it is impossible to know whether there would be general support for a tougher line on sentencing or for more use of compensation, possibly via the asset confiscation principles that are proposed in the Criminal Justice Bill (1986). The executives plainly expected much greater use of disqualification orders than was the case in practice: the legislative framework has changed subsequently (see Chapter 7), but radical increases in the use of disqualification may take longer.

In short, the survey findings suggest that if sentences themselves are to remain unchanged, there is some scope for increasing possible deterrence by heightening businesspeople's perceptions of the chances of being imprisoned should they be convicted. However, it would be as well to keep silent about the length of the jail terms they might expect to receive. The results also suggest possibilities of enhancing fear by requiring publicity of the offence, perhaps paid for by the offender himself. Given the nature of social networks, it seem likely that convictions for fraud will be known to their current peer groups –

though they can always move – so publicity might not make much difference to deterrence. However, it is a point being considered also in the context of 'compounding' fines by Customs and Excise, which are carried out at the criminal burden of proof. This practice of anonymous settlement does raise issues of fairness *vis-à-vis* other sorts of offenders, as well as questions of general deterrence. The non-publication of compoundings (and of settlements with the Inland Revenue) increases the temptations to settle without a fuss, and thus saves criminal justice costs: but if this is *ipso facto* a good thing, why is it not extended to other spheres of the criminal justice system?

One final point on deterrence should not be ignored. It is theoretically mistaken to assume that everyone who 'objectively' is in a position to defraud is faced at every moment with active temptations to commit fraud, and that if we are to deter such people, what is needed is a set of penal sanctions that will be feared by all of them 24 hours per day. Many businesspeople and professionals – from ethical socialization or from lack of imagination – never think to commit fraud even though they could commit it if they had it in mind to do so. 'Active' deterrence comes into play only when crime is contemplated. Even then, the set of beliefs and commitments independent of the criminal process (though dependent upon perceptions of the risk of discovery) may have more influence than the fear of prison or even of being 'cut' at the Club.

Deterrence is situational, and varies according to the nature of the occupation and personal circumstances of prospective offenders, as well as their perceptions of how the offence in question is likely to be viewed by those whose opinions they value. If bank employees are caught 'at it', they may escape prosecution but they will almost certainly lose their jobs and their preferential rate house mortgages at 2–3 per cent per annum. The former head of the equities dealing section at bankers Morgan Grenfell, who in November 1986 resigned after he admitted breaching the company's share dealing rules, lost his £300,000 per annum job and was prosecuted. Irrespective of any conviction that might ensue, it seems unlikely that he will get another similarly paid job. If insider dealing of the kind alleged in his case were as widespread as has been claimed, there is plainly ample scope for deterrence, though future dealers may be more inclined to consult their lawyers before making admissions to their employers.

Whether insider dealers actually *will* be deterred is an open question: extraordinarily, only days after the Morgan Grenfell case attracted headline news in all the 'quality press', television, and radio, a fairly junior but long-serving clerk in British Commonwealth and Shipping was dismissed after he bought shares in a company about to be taken over by his firm, making £850 profit. These purchases were channelled through the same broker, Scrimgeour Vickers, as the Morgan Grenfell dealer used! Both of the above cases were crudely carried out, and sophisticates contemplating insider dealng may consider that they are less vulnerable. (Despite the resources of SEC and the hi-tech of the New York Stock Exchange, it is far from certain that Dennis Levine and Ivan Boesky would have been exposed had it not been for an anonymous tip-off from Venezuela!) On the other hand, provided that they think that they have some chance of avoiding detection, unless they expect to be prosecuted and penalized heavily, securities dealers facing 'burn-out' in their mid-thirties may feel that they have less stake in avoiding exposure and dismissal than do ordinary bank employees or senior managers. *A fortiori*, in areas of business criminality that are expected to attract less public opprobrium than insider dealing or embezzlement, there are few deterrents, except where the corporate bosses are hoping for a title or for some other form of public honour, or where they fear that they may be banned from trading altogether: illegal Sunday traders, facing fines that are much lower than their marginal daily profits, may carry on their business unabashed. Some traders adopt the moral and financial compromise of opening on Sunday only in the busy pre-Christmas period. O stigma, where is thy sting?

CONFISCATION OF ASSETS

Asset-confiscation is a form of punishment that can mean all things to all people. It may be viewed as a general or individual deterrent, as retribution, and – inasmuch as money may be needed as capital to commit other major crimes (including the establishment of businesses as fronts for crime) – as incapacitation. Attacking crime through the forfeiture of assets is a major police and customs as well as criminal justice goal, which is attaining high priority throughout the developed world. Given space constraints and the changes that have been made by the Drug Trafficking Offences Act (1986), which are extended in a more modest form in the Criminal Justice Bill (1986) to cover fraud and other crimes where over £10,000 has been obtained, it is pointless to review existing legislation in detail. However, it is important to note that prior to the above legislation, both Criminal Bankruptcy Orders and other forfeiture provisions which aroused concern in relation to drug offenders were very modest yielders of funds (Advisory Council on the Penal System, 1978; Hodgson Committee, 1984; Levi, 1981, Ch. XII). The reason for this is simple. For assets to be confiscated, they have to be (1) unspent, (2) traced, *and* (3) retrieved. If any one of these conditions is not met, any order imposed by the courts will be inoperative. Although the willingness of tax havens to assist the police and other regulatory agencies varies – even in relation to narcotics trafficking, where there is the most pressure exerted for co-operation – there will always be some who are unwilling to co-operate at all. This is a matter of global political economy, resulting from the desire of rich and poor states to avail themselves of income from the lawfully and unlawfully wealthy who wish to hide their assets and/or to utilize favourable tax residence legislation.

The Drug Trafficking Offences Act (1986) and clause 39 of the Criminal Justice Bill (1986) impose substantial sentences – on a sliding scale related to the sum involved in the order, from 12 months for £10–20,000, to 10 years for over £1 million – in default of payment under a confiscation order. Prior to these provisions, prisoners subject to a Criminal Bankruptcy Order had little incentive to co-operate with investigators. (Though in principle, if there was evidence of the existence of undisclosed assets held by them, they could have been prosecuted under the Bankruptcy Act for failing to disclose their existence, thereby 'earning' an extra sentence that might be consecutive to their present one.)

The Drug Trafficking Offences Act (1986) places the onus on the convicted person to demonstrate that *any* assets under his control are *not* the result of drug sales if they are not to be confiscated. This is an important enhancement of official powers, and attracted considerable reservations in Parliament and in the conservative press such as the *Daily Telegraph*. On the grounds that drug trafficking is uniquely evil (and for more pragmatic reasons of getting the legislation passed), the Criminal Justice Bill (1986) does *not* extend this draconian method to those convicted of fraud or other serious offences. Instead, clause 46 enables the court to make a confiscation order for 'such sum as the court thinks fit', provided that the sum is at least £10,000 and that this does not exceed

'(i) the value of his proceeds of the offence or, as the case may be, the aggregate value of his proceeds of the offences in respect of which the order is made; and
(ii) the amount appearing to the court to be the amount that might be realised at the time the order is made.'

If the court imposes both a confiscation order and a compensation order and the offender cannot pay both in full, the compensation order takes priority: the victim gets priority over the state. So for fraud and other offences, the sum confiscated is to be tied much more closely to the charges made out and proven in the indictment. To a greater extent than has been the case in the past with Criminal Bankruptcy Orders – which are abolished in the Bill – this will open up interesting avenues for plea-bargaining and charge-bargaining in fraud trials, particularly if judges and magistrates make extensive use of them.

But even the reversal of the normal burden of proof is no magic retrieval formula. In the more substantial frauds (or drugs cases), unless success is achieved in the freezing of assets – see Chapter 4 and clauses 51–64 of the Criminal Justice Bill (1986) – the proceeds may well be overseas. Even if the actual proceeds are overseas, any of the offender's assets held within the jurisdiction of the English courts may be confiscated in their stead. If they are under the control of persons other than the convicted offender, then those other persons must be able to show that they acquired the assets for full market value: otherwise the assets become liable to confiscation.

For those with a reasonable 'front', this liability is not difficult to evade: as when goods are sold by long-firm frauds, the goods or assets are sold for a substantial market value sum, but the purchaser is given a secret kickback in cash (or, perhaps, narcotics) of whatever amount is agreed between them. Moreover, there are three major *legal* difficulties facing asset-confiscation in international cases, which added to the lack of technical and personnel resources, helps to explain the low returns from 'financial' penalties in fraud (and narcotics) cases:

1 the lack of a domestic power to order the preservation of property pending the outcome of a *foreign* judicial proceeding;
2 the lack of jurisdiction to transfer the right of ownership regarding movable property or money that is situated abroad (i.e. getting the money back);
3 the inability of the courts of one country to enforce the criminal judgments (including forfeiture orders) of another country.

Section 19 of the Drug Trafficking Offences Act (1986) and clause 67 of the Criminal Justice Bill (1986) enable provision to be made for foreign confiscation orders to be registered in England and Wales, and clause 66 of the Bill makes provision for British orders to be enforced abroad in 'designated countries'. Proposals to extend this to cover the location of the proceeds of crime, taking forfeiture proceedings, and enforcing confiscation orders made within the Commonwealth were adopted by the Commonwealth law ministers at their meeting in Harare in 1986. These will apply to all crime (including fraud), and were a direct response to alarm about international organized crime.

In the United States, the Organized Crime Control Act (1970) included a section (title IX) which gave extensive powers – including criminal forfeiture – to the courts against Racketeer Influenced and Corrupt Organizations (RICO). There is a large legal literature on the scope of RICO which I will not review here (see Blakey, 1986; Ita, 1984 for some overviews). Suffice it to state that these provisions, aimed at inhibiting the spread into commerce of organized-crime groups – whatever they are! – apply to many fraudulent conspiracies. A leading case is *Russello* v. *United States*, 104 S Ct 296 (1983) which related to a large arson insurance fraud scheme in Florida. The Supreme Court held that moneys obtained by Russello from the insurance scheme could be forfeited, so not only enterprises but also financial 'interests' were within the scope of RICO. Nevertheless, even armed with wide powers, forfeiture proceedings under the RICO statutes yielded only $35 million between 1970 and 1980 in narcotics cases. The Drug Enforcement Agency enthusiastically appropriated planes, boats, and cars of narcotics traffickers for recycling in the war against drugs. However, the US authorities began to take *financial* asset-tracing seriously only in the mid-1980s, and such 'intangibles' are particularly relevant to frauds, where the *physical* 'instruments of crime' – such as a pen, a rented telex machine, and a 'shell company' registered in a tax haven – tend to be relatively valueless.

The US authorities have become much more sophisticated in their approaches to money-laundering. These developments have been accompanied by greater yields from confiscation under RICO and Customs statutes, which netted $250 million in 1984, compared with $62 million in 1981 and $35 million in 1980, though the sums are still modest compared with the gains from trafficking. In treaties with Switzerland and the Cayman Islands, some strides have been made towards increasing the visibility of narcotics trafficking transactions, but the effectiveness of these provisions is seen more in political rhetoric than in real economic gains. There is a novel form of incentive for overseas co-operation, insofar as the Swiss are able to keep drug-dealers' assets that they freeze, rather than having to return them to the US: this approach is more justifiable morally in relation to crimes which have no identifiable victims than in relation to fraud, however. Indeed, strategic foreign policy interests are significant inhibitors of international agreements, as may be witnessed in the difficulties that the United States is facing in obtaining co-operation from Panama, whose role in the international money-laundering trade is counterbalanced by its opposition to the spread of communism in a crucial part of Latin America. Furthermore, the CIA also utilizes banking secrecy havens to launder funds for foreign ventures, so improved access for US officials might turn out to be a double-edged sword for US administrations concerned to conceal some of their activities from Congress and the public. This theme is taken up again later in this chapter. But if the hope is that confiscation of assets can somehow replace traditional penal sanctions, it is unlikely to be a hope that will be borne out by the reality, unless measures are developed to enhance the visibility of commercial transactions and to improve international civil litigation. As that great criminologist Dashiell Hammett might have said, if you scratch the falcon, there will be jewels. But before we can scratch it, we first have to find the Panamanian falcon!

INCAPACITATION STRATEGIES AND THE CONTROL OF BUSINESS CRIME

As the fiscal crises of modern states deepen, and as prisons become increasingly overcrowded, the thoughts of penal administrators turn towards incapacitation of 'dangerous offenders', so that we can prioritize those whom we do and do not imprison in terms of the harm that they would be likely to cause if released. Motives for incapacitation normally comprise two elements: the seriousness of the harm to be done in the future, and the likelihood that the individual or group will offend. Although discussions of 'the dangerous offender' do not normally refer to business crime, there is no reason why this should be so. One of the principal points made by many authors on corporate crime is that 'crimes of the powerful' threaten the moral fabric of society as well as causing serious physical injuries (as in health and safety offences and the dumping of toxic waste). From my review of the social and political effects of fraud and corruption in Chapter 2, it is hard to argue that such actions are not seriously damaging, and Chapter 3 shows that they are perceived as such. (Though one of the key difficulties with notions like 'fabric of society' is working out what one would *exclude* from them.) Nevertheless, it is one thing to argue that commercial fraudsters and corporate criminals – categories which overlap only in some respects – are 'dangerous offenders', but quite another to work out an incapacitation strategy which is appropriate for them, assuming that one regards incapacitation as an ethical position anyway.

In the area of corporate crime, one of the real problems facing sentencers – including those official and self-regulatory agencies and courts with power to revoke trading licenses – is the damage that may be done to employees and investors by punishing the corporation. For example, when licensed securities dealers Prior Harwin, who had aroused controversy by their dealings in the 'grey market' in new share issues prior to investors' receiving confirmation that they had been allocated shares, were raided and closed down by Department of Trade and Industry officials immediately before Christmas 1986, their directors claimed that although they had made a loss in previous years, they were now solvent and that investors had been placed at risk by precipitate DTI action. (On the other hand, as in previous scandals like the £4 million failure of licensed dealers McDonald Wheeler in 1986, if the DTI waits for the full picture to emerge, they are criticized for their inaction!) One of the justifications claimed by the US SEC for allowing Ivan Boesky to unload $440 million in securities, just prior to the announcement of his $100 million insider dealing settlement with them, was that to have forbidden these transactions would have destabilized the market and damaged other investors besides Boesky himself. To the extent that the individual executive has unique skills, punishing him/her and punishing the company are inseparable, and this affects incapacitation as much as retribution.

In some cases, 'naughty' corporations might be reformed and incapacitated by having their previous directors replaced by 'public interest directors' who would apply principles of 'social audit' to the running of the business (McDermott, 1982); compulsory divestment is a long-established way of dealing with anti-trust or with conflicts of interests (as with brokers and underwriters at Lloyd's). But the primary commercial incapacitation techniques are (1) imprisonment and (2) banning particular individuals (or 'sorts of individuals') with 'bad reputations' from taking part in management of either business in general or specific sorts of business which are deemed to be particularly vulnerable (a) because they are easy to use as vehicles for fraud and/or (b) because of the social harm done if violations occur. A prime example of (b) is the securities industry.

In critiques of incapacitation such as that offered by Von Hirsch (1986), much is made of the immorality of punishing the innocent. This is a rather spurious objection in practice: most offenders who are incapacitated have actually done something unpleasant, so the 'unjust sentence' is the gap between what they deserved and what they got. It is not that they are innocent: it is that 'they are not as bad as all that'. Except for those who are prepared to applaud fraudsters for their entrepreneurial initiative, the analysis in the previous chapter and in my discussion of 'just deserts' here suggests that many fraudsters (and, with reservations on my part about the difficulty of attributing *personal* responsibility to organizational actors, corporate criminals) do *not* get what they deserve: they get *less*. This is the converse problem to the one for which incapacitators are normally attacked, which is that the latter leads to punishment for persistence rather than for crime gravity. Moreover, as I argued in a previous book (Levi, 1981, Ch. XII), very few offenders who commit 'substantial' frauds (over, say, £100,000) have a long string of prior convictions. Consequently, if the discriminant point was about five convictions, after which further reconviction becomes very likely – a pragmatic position acceptable to those who are not opposed in principle to incapacitation (Walker, 1980, 1985) – very few fraudsters would be incapacitated. (The use of a standardized trigger-point itself would count as a further discrimination in favour of fraudsters.) On the other hand, if the incapacitation threshold were to go down to as low as one or two convictions, which it would need to do to have much effect, such a practice – though it may be *deserved* – might well be seen as unjust: certainly, the proportion of 'false negatives' (i.e. those predicted to be dangerous who would not in fact have committed offences if released) would rise.

It may be helpful at this point to remind the reader of some data derived from a Home Office statistical bulletin on the backgrounds of those convicted in 1982 (Home Office, 1986c). Those convicted of fraud and forgery contained a higher proportion of first offenders than those convicted of burglary: 32 per cent, compared with 19 per cent for burglary within a dwelling and 26 per cent for burglary other than in a dwelling. (The category of theft by employee was highest of all offenders: 63 per cent were first offenders.) At the other end of the spectrum, 19 per cent of those convicted of fraud and forgery had 10 or more previous convictions, compared with 29 per cent of domestic and 22 per cent of non-domestic burglars. (Only 3 per cent of those convicted of theft by employee had 10 or more previous convictions.)

Some reservations are appropriate here. Data on the reconviction rates of fraudsters are extremely crude, since they are based on the Home Office offence categories which merge the major and the comparatively trivial fraud offences. Thus, it is not particularly illuminating to discover that many of those convicted for fraud in 1982 were recidivists, for this tells us little about recidivism among those who commit 'major frauds'. To some extent, discussion of elite recidivists is misleading: if elite members committed acts that were severely disapproved of by their group, they would cease to be elite members, so by definition, retrospective surveys would not find elite members with heavy recidivism rates for 'serious frauds'. However, one does not need to be a member of the elite to commit a major fraud involving millions of pounds. Furthermore, one reason for the comparative absence of large numbers of convictions among fraudsters may be the low visibility and low prosecution rate of commercial frauds and, *a fortiori*, of 'regulatory' offences by companies. Thus, the presence of non-criminal formal and informal sanctions is more significant in the context of business activity than in other sorts of offending behaviour. To sum up, one can incapacitate commercial fraudsters on the basis of their previous convictions, thus keeping out of circulation many persistent fraudsters. However, even more than is the case with petty persistent offenders of other kinds, this would be unlikely to prevent many major frauds from occurring. No systematic analysis has been done on the criminal records of professional fraudsters, but the work of Mack (1975) and my earlier narrower study of long-firm fraud (Levi, 1981) suggested that they were modest. Even though they may never have reached the Criminal Courts, the major scandals involving Lloyd's, licensed deposit-takers, and small firms of solicitors that have arisen in Britain in the 1980s have been perpetrated by people with impeccable backgrounds who have breached the trust of their investors, depositors, or clients to massive effect. The major damage, then, has been done by criminal professionals rather than by professional criminals. It is this which makes conviction-based incapacitation strategies largely irrelevant to the control of the more up-market forms of commercial fraud.

INCAPACITATION WITHOUT CUSTODY: THE KEY TO THE FUTURE?

Both present practices and future prospects for controlling fraud induce a profound scepticism about the value of reliance on post-conviction remedies and suggest a focus instead on the wider networks of commercial regulation. If we had tough sanctions for fraudsters, this might reduce fraud by lowering its attractiveness compared with other forms of lawful and unlawful activity. For more modest infringements, the disgorgement of profits would at least provide some compensation for victims, though we should bear in mind that fraud is often reported only when the prospects of reparation are or seem to be low. If the scepticism that I displayed earlier in this chapter about the prospects for the natural achievement of a Golden Age of Community in the commercial world is justified, there remains some chance of subjecting commerce to the 'omnipresent discipline' that Silver (1967) views as being the essence of policing.

As I noted earlier, incapacitation can occur outside prison as well as inside it. A key role here is played by (1) entry controls into commerce and the professions, and (2) procedures for monitoring complaints against members of the professions. All the professions – particularly accountants, doctors, lawyers, and surveyors – are coming under increasing attack from many sources: from the public, concerned about the quality and integrity of the advice that they receive, and about the proper investigation of complaints; from the media, in search of scandal; from professional indemnity insurance rates, sky-rocketing from increased litigation expenses over actions for negligence, particularly in the United States; and from the pressures of the marketplace, as price competition increases and as financial services conglomerates exert their muscle in active trading markets. Professional anxiety about public confidence is not misplaced: there is widespread criticism about the apparent lack of concern among regulatory bodies for the standards of work of their members, and about their reluctance to suspend or strike off members for poor quality work or even for negligence. This legitimation crisis has spread far beyond the anti-professional radical fringe of writers like Ivan Illich. People are afraid that they are being ripped off by professionals as a class, not just by deviant individuals: that immorality is *structural*. The opportunities for insider dealing by professionals have always been considerable, but with enhanced market activity at times of merger and take-over booms, they mushroom. Consider the following situation.

Many companies are content to leave their property assets under-valued, since this makes their return on assets look more impressive. Sharp corporate raiders with an eye for opportunities to buy companies cheap and sell off the undervalued assets move in and bid for the shares, and become labelled as 'asset-strippers'. Target companies who either anticipate a bid or have actually received one call in a surveyor to revalue their assets. The surveyor is in a perfect situation to know whether the company's shares are overvalued or undervalued, and the temptations to make a fortune by insider dealing are considerable. In a commercial climate of 'merger mania' and deregulation such as the one Britain and the United States have been witnessing in financial services in the mid-1980s, the moral justifications are easy. A real estate surveyor, accountant, or solicitor who is called in to advise on a take-over or is asked to revalue the company's assets (including property assets) can do well by insider dealing, whether or not the purchasing or target company directors and their secretaries/wives/lovers are doing so as well. This is not all. As building societies and other financial institutions become desperate to deploy the money they have borrowed, there is pressure on 'independent' surveyors – normally recommended or even specified by the lending institution to the prospective buyer – to inflate their assessments of the value of houses so that they can lend the money. (If the professional succumbs, he may end up being sued for negligence; if he does not, he may be struck off the list of recommended surveyors.)

As we move towards conglomerates where banks own estate agencies, insurance companies, in-house accountants and solicitors, corporate finance, and merger and take-over sections, the risks increase of gaps appearing in the invisible Chinese Walls which separate these functions, policed as they are by corporate Compliance Officers who are frequently seen as unproductive functionaries who are not making money but are there only to make life difficult. (In this sense, they resemble credit managers in commerce and Custody Officers in the police.) Further-more, disparities in regulatory standards between different professions become absurd: whereas chartered surveyors are not allowed to pay or receive 'backhanders' for obtaining clients from or recommending clients to solicitors, solicitors apparently can give part of their conveyancing fees to any real estate agents who recommend them to their clients. This scarcely reinforces moral standards. An atmosphere is created in which professionals feel that they too must show that they are dynamic and move with the times, partly because they do not want to *feel* old-fashioned and partly because they want to retain their membership. Consequently, spurred on by the Office of Fair Trading's hostility to restrictive trade practices such as barriers to cross-profession links, they advertise their services aggressively. This in turn leads to new problems of civil liability. If one advertises that chartered surveyors or accountants are *real* professionals without whose assistance one is bound to encounter problems, then when something goes wrong, it is hard for the professional to claim that he has not been negligent, for negligence is judged against the level of professionalism one portrays oneself as possessing. There is so much literature emanating from the professional bodies in Britain and the United States – accountants are an excellent example here – that almost anyone might be adjudged negligent by the highest standards of his profession.

I have introduced some of these themes, which suggest ample ground for concern about conflicts of interest in the professions and commerce, and that many actual conflicts are likely to go unobserved by outsiders. There is no room here for a full-blown discussion of professional self-regulation. Let us focus instead upon one area in which much concern has been expressed, which reveals an important regulatory trend which will intensify in years to come. The Financial Services Act (1986) makes it a criminal offence, punishable by up to two years' imprisonment and/or a fine, for any unauthorized person to engage in investment business: the latter is defined in the Act to include dealing in, managing, and giving advice about investments including securities, rights to securities, certain money market investments, options, futures, contracts for differences, unit trusts and other 'collective investment schemes', and long-term life assurance contracts. (In other words, it excludes 'real' commodities dealings, where actual delivery of goods takes place, and other matters like genuine trade debts.) Authorization can occur either directly by SIB or indirectly through membership of Recognized Professional Bodies (such as the Institute of Chartered Accountants) or of approved SROs – AFBD, FIMBRA, IMRO, LAUTRO, and The Securities Association (The International Stock Exchange) – which apply tests of propriety acceptable to SIB.

These tests are expected – perhaps a more accurate term would be 'intended' – to be standardized in terms of level of morality and competence right across the financial-services sector. Whether the *formal* standardization of rules will apply in *substance* is a matter for speculation at the present time. There are grounds for scepticism, though, on the basis that (1) prior to the establishment of SIB and the passage of the Financial Services Bill, self-regulatory bodies in the securities industry operated with very different standards of supervision and of enthusiasm for timely preventative action; and (2) they have highly variable resources for vetting applicants for licenses and for inspecting firms in operation.

The notorious English laws of defamation provide excellent reasons for lack of specificity here. However, on the political heat-defusing use of self-regulation, it is worth noting the remarks of the Chief Executive of Deak-Perrera, the largest (and oldest established) foreign exchange dealers in the United States, who were alleged to have been substantial money-launderers during the 1970s and early 1980s for both organized and corporate criminals (see Chapters 5 and 8). In an interview with the *New York Times* on the subject of how to regulate improper dealing in gold bullion, Nicholas Deak stated: 'We in the business can usually spot a phony operator faster than anyone else. What our industry ought to do is to form a self-regulating group' (President's Commission on Organized Crime, 1986a:138). This should be read within the context of the discussion in Chapter 4, which suggested that business interests – like most other interest-groups – will generally seek to neutralize the harm done to their trade by any legislation that is passed to regulate them.

The criteria that SIB considers to be relevant to the decision as to whether someone is a 'fit and proper person' to be authorized to engage in investment business are set out in para. 1.19 of the Draft Rules, June 1986, and represent one response to my earlier analyses of the problems of incapacitating on the basis of convictions alone. The relevant section, to be filled in by all applicants, states:

> 'The applicant should answer all the questions in this section, and where applicable, supply full details.
>
> (i) Has a petition been served for the bankruptcy or winding up of the applicant at any time over the previous ten years? Has the applicant been connected (not as a creditor) or involved with the management of a company which has been wound up over the previous ten years? Is the applicant aware that any such petition is pending or contemplated?
>
> (ii) Has, over the previous ten years, the applicant had a receiver or administrator appointed, failed to satisfy a debt adjudged due, or come to an arrangement with its creditors or been the subject of a reconstruction?
>
> (iii) Has the applicant ever had a licence or authorisation relating to any activity refused or withdrawn either in the UK or elsewhere?
>
> (iv) Has the applicant ever been refused membership of an SRO, exchange or other professional body in the UK or overseas, had its membership

revoked or resigned from any such body; or decided, after making an application, not to proceed with it?

(v) (a) Has the applicant ever been criticised, censured, or disciplined by any body of which it is a member or by any other regulatory body in the UK such as the CSI or Take-over Panel, or by any overseas regulatory body; or had its affairs investigated by any such body except in the course of an investigation conducted as part of normal monitoring and surveillance procedures, with no adverse findings? (b) Has the applicant ever received any communication from the Registrar of Companies concerning compliance with the requirements of the Companies Act or had its affairs investigated under other civil or statutory enactment?

(vi) Has the applicant ever been refused an investment business agency or had such an agency withdrawn?

(vii) Has a person carrying on a relevant activity ever refused to have further dealings with an applicant?

(viii) Has any of the applicant's principal bankers, legal advisers, or auditors changed over the previous three years? If so, the applicant should provide details and the reasons for the change.

(ix) (a) Has the applicant been involved over the past year in civil litigation (excluding litigation concerning bad debts) with any of its customers or investors? (b) Is the applicant at present involved in such litigation, or is such litigation pending?

Several things are noteworthy about these rules. First, they appear to be very comprehensive in their disclosure requirements, including overseas 'records' as well as domestic ones. However, this inevitably opens up questions of consistency in international enforcement practice: the chance of an investment dealer being sanctioned in the US is very high compared with the chances in Panama or the Bahamas! But apart from the fairness aspect, it *may* keep out some American professional fraudsters, who have been involved in some major securities scandals in Britain in the mid-1980s. There appears to be no requirement to notify prior Department of Trade and Industry or other investigations into *previous* companies which have *not* led – as most do not lead – to licence revocation or any measures such as winding up mentioned in the above sections, though this might be important and surely is relevant information. Second, there is the problem of what SIB is going to do with these data, even if the applicants are honest in completing the forms. Given that up to 40 per cent of companies in England and Wales have failed to comply with the requirements to supply annual reports on time, what will be made of admissions of non-compliance under s.(v) (b)? And what if an investigation has not led to any action? Issues of fairness in the implementation of discretionary rules are important even if SIB has legal immunity against being sued in performance of its regulatory functions. Furthermore, we return again to the question of enforcement: for perfectly good reasons of constitutional principle, SIB and other SROs, not being statutory bodies but being merely bodies authorized under the delegating powers of the Secretary of State, do not have access to the Criminal Records Office in their vetting procedures, and even with excellent media sources and commercial contacts, may find it hard to confirm the veracity of the declarations that are made.

In the view of this writer, not too much reliance should be placed upon the effectiveness of disqualification orders except in high visibility situations such as the professions, banking, and the City, for it is comparatively easy for disqualified persons to operate *sub rosa* as 'shadow directors' via 'front men', although those banned might be held criminally and/or civilly liable to repay losses under s. 13–15 of the Company Directors Disqualification Act (1986) should they be discovered. Restrictions on who is authorized to act as a liquidator via the licensing procedures of the Insolvency Act (1986) may inhibit some abuses. In the 1970s and 1980s, one practice of certain 'accountants' who were not members of professional bodies was to advertise themselves as company doctors to ailing but respectable firms, and then to use them as vehicles to defraud creditors: a severe case of iatrogenic illness!

However, the very notion of 'good character' which is a key component of the entry prohibition approach to fraud prevention runs counter to the situational crime prevention approach, since it stresses some essentialist notion of honesty and neglects the influence of more immediate variables, whether they be of the fast women and slow horses variety or merely a sense that one is not prospering as much as one deserves and/or that 'everyone is at it, so I might as well join them'. The fact that the perpetrators of many of the worst scandals that have rocked the British financial establishment – particularly at Lloyd's – were leading figures of impeccable background should cast some doubt upon the predictive value of 'good reputation' in the control of 'serious' fraud. In December 1986, scandal was extended to a particularly sensitive part of the public sector when the Department of Trade and Industry announced that it had appointed outside Inspectors to investigate allegations that officials in it or in the Office of Fair Trading had engaged in insider dealing on the basis of advance information they had about crucial governmental decisions such as whether or not a particular take-over bid would be permitted to go ahead. (The Guinness affair of 1986–87, which revealed that creating a false market in shares during take-over bids was endemic even among some of the most notable firms, raises rather different issues, since it is arguable that this was done largely to benefit the firm rather than just for directors themselves, though with performance bonuses, the distinction is a little academic.)

What in the context of the security services one might term the Philby/Blunt syndrome – that if someone is a 'good chap', he is not a 'criminal type' – is actually conducive to the perpetration of fraud: in this sense, ideological myths (though comforting socially) get in the way of social defence. The sceptical American-based companies traditionally have an advantage here over their British counterparts. In any case, the social homogeneity of the City is breaking down under the pressures of meritocracy, the invasion of hugely capitalized US and Japanese corporate finance and securities traders, and internationalization generally. So to the extent that entry control by 'bad reputation' and conviction is acknowledged to be theoretically inadequate for fraud prevention, the focus of surveillance rationally ought to shift to monitoring the conduct of people while they are transacting business and in their domestic lifestyles. If fraud prevention is really a high priority, companies and/or SROs may begin to examine employees' and directors' personal credit card bills and the value of their homes, to ensure that they are not spending more than they earn; reporting requirements should be imposed upon betting shops and casinos, to inform about who is spending the money. The President's Commission on Organized Crime (1986b) does indeed propose the inclusion of casinos within the currency reporting requirements.

As for monitoring, many of the larger market-makers in securities have installed telephone systems which automatically record all conversations made with persons in the dealing room and, perhaps, the settlement room of the brokerage house. The principal purpose of this is to have an objective means of settling disputes with buyers and sellers of securities over what was actually requested. But a side effect is that it becomes possible for corporate compliance officers to check for insider dealing carried out from the office, even if they have not yet gone so far as to track the dealers physically to make sure that they do not go around the corner to make their improper call from a public booth, or to check the people with whom they have lunch or furtive meetings in the park! Despite the 'know your customer' rule, which obliges authorized investment dealers to make proper enquiries about the *bona fides* of persons with whom they transact business and which, if broken, may lead to the firm's de-authorization, it should not be hard to set up a company – offshore tax haven or domestic – to use for one's illicit transactions: the problem for the insider dealer arises not from the technical difficulties in carrying out transactions but from the risk of exposure following detailed investigation of major dealings, particularly in take-over bid situations. Without intensive monitoring of employee expenditure patterns, the chances are that any misconduct will be discovered not by internal corporate compliance officers but by other securities institutions – who may have an interest in getting insider dealers sacked and generating bad publicity for their rivals – or by Stock Exchange surveillance officials. However, the computerized transaction recording systems in London, New York, and all major stock exchanges make for easier proof of evidence and for less scope for documentary tampering.

Technology has also come to the aid of merchant banks in charge of securities flotations, who can try to spot 'stagging' – covert multiple applications for shares by the same parties – by means of handwriting examination, computer databases that contain and cross-check lists of the names and addresses of 'known staggers' and that perform random checks on the *bona fides* of applicants, and even fingerprinting (to prove links once or if they have suspected them).

In addition to the SIB and other self-regulatory organizations, the Office of Fair Trading plays a (modest) incapacitatory role in relation to commercial fraud (Borrie, 1984). Under Part III of the Fair Trading Act (1973), traders can be required to give written assurances that they will desist from further violations, but these have not been particularly effective. Apart from the considerable difficulties of enforcing bans, given the problem of tracking 'offenders', the obstacle here – and this was seen during the debates on the Insolvency Bill – is the attitude that trading at the risk of others is a right to be curtailed only under the most rigorous conditions. It may be that this is morally appropriate, and should be applauded as a libertarian position. However, if this attitude remains, then entry control into commerce as a whole is doomed as a way of reducing the risk of fraud. By contrast, the New York Stock Exchange has a draconian general catch-all provision which enables it to prohibit conduct which is 'contrary to just and equitable principles of trade'.

Clearly, there is a problem of balance, but from the viewpoint of consumer and commercial creditors, the incompetent may be a greater risk than the evil company director, not least because there are more of the former than of the latter. Major changes have been proposed to this system by the Office of Fair Trading in its 1986 discussion paper *A General Duty to Trade Fairly*, which contemplates decriminalizing some areas of malpractice and replacing them with informal mechanisms of enforcement by trading standards officers in relation to transactions between traders and consumers. As in the Financial Services Act, a distinction is drawn between groups who are professionals and others. The ideological foundation for this is expressed in the following statement:

> 'Those in business are normally better equipped than consumers to look after their own interests. There may also be a basic difficulty in determining

what, as between traders, constitutes fair or unfair trading. If unfair trading is taken in the sense of advantage being taken of a relatively weaker position, much in trader-trader relationships can be held to be of its nature "unfair".'

(Office of Fair Trading, 1986:35)

So the conditions under which the state is prepared to referee commercial conflicts become clearer. It is those who are in a *relatively* weak position to protect themselves who are to be helped; elsewhere, *caveat emptor* rules. The distinction here is a morally uneasy one, as the quotation above implies, for there are immense inequalities of power between different traders so that the difference is one of degree rather than kind. However, in the securities and investments field, the Government already took for granted that to impose the same levels of rules upon all traders would generate compliance costs that were 'too high' and would thereby deter trade. To have acted on any other basis would have required a fundamental change in the way we conceive of commercial competition: hence the distinction between the individual investor, on the one hand, and the 'business' and 'professional' investor, on the other.

But even if one accepts that differentiation, other regulatory policy problems exist which do not square completely with the new focus upon free and open competition. If syndicate members know that someone has been disciplined for malpractice by Lloyd's but still want him to act for them, as was the case with Ian 'Goldfinger' Posgate in 1986, is denying this possibility not an unfair restrictive trade practice in a system that operates on a disclosure principle? Should there be provisions akin to the Rehabilitation of Offenders Act (1974) that apply to this area of commercial life, so that there should be a requirement of disclosure of prior activities but not necessarily an automatic ban? Along with the prior commercial and criminal activities of those who are banned or censured, this aspect of regulation by the 'paternalist state' deserves closer attention than it has received hitherto.

So although some of the outrage of some of the victims may be defused by the requirement to compensate victims of investment fraud and insolvency, it appears that whatever way the regulation of fraud moves, there are political risks: if we have state licensing of securities and other firms, then when things go wrong, the regulators get blamed for inducing false confidence into investors by granting the official imprimatur such as 'licensed dealer'; if we do not have state regulation, then blame arises because the state has left the market to its own devices and Aunt Agatha has lost her money.

The state can intervene in other ways to alter commercial policies. In a remarkable Downing Street seminar on crime prevention for leading businesspeople in December 1985, the British Prime Minister criticized insurance companies for failing to give discounts for people who took burglary prevention measures and for not doing enough to improve locks on motor vehicles: insurance discounts were introduced by many companies soon afterwards. She might have gone further, had she or the Home Secretary had time to discuss fraud prevention. As regards cheque and credit-card frauds, much has been done without direct government intervention, though with Home Office encouragement: there are now difficult-to-counterfeit holograms on all credit cards; since 1986, the start date on new Barclaycards is the day after the expiry of the old one, rather than one that overlaps; addresses are written by hand on envelopes of varied sizes and mailed from small towns in different parts of the country rather than just from the tell-tale Northampton headquarters; card authorization limits are varied in different stores or in the same store over time; shop assistants who retain cards that have been stolen are given cash rewards (from £50–500); and in many cases, cardholders living in theft-prone areas now have to collect their new cards in person. Nevertheless, though many credit-card frauds result from customer carelessness – leaving Person Identification Numbers with their cards – and/or from theft, it is arguable that even if there is a fall-off in custom, companies have a responsibility to require customers to display their photographs on cards. In principle, companies could also institute greater checks on those who apply for cards, since there appears to be fairly widespread potential for the use of fake personal data – including the use of nominee 'off-the-shelf' companies or simple accommodation addresses – to establish creditworthiness. This does cost money, but it is difficult to justify expensive police time and court/penal costs if victims are so lax about fraud prevention. (The only thing that can be said in favour of current anti-fraud policies here is that it may be less injurious socially to enable credit cards to be obtained fraudulently than as a result of mugging or burglary: however, the hitherto low, though rising, security which enables the cards to be re-used readily means that there is every incentive to mug and burgle anyway.)

So quite apart from the financial-services sector, there are many spheres in which a benevolent state could act to encourage self-regulation in the interests of crime prevention. One can see the political attractions of such a trend. Not only does it not cost the hard-pressed Treasury any money, but it also devolves *blame* for crime onto the private sector, while claiming the credit for initiative oneself. Whether, and in what contexts, these anti-crime exhortations will take place is a matter for speculation: designing out commercial crime may turn out to be a more difficult task than even the most sagacious politician can manage.

Concluding thoughts

In the preface, I observed that criminology was a somewhat artificial boundary for the analysis of social control. This has been recognized by all classical social theorists, who treated penality, i.e. the liability to punishment by the courts, as being only a subsidiary part of the means by which social regulation – if not social harmony – was or could be accomplished. Yet regulation is no longer what it was. Lawyers and politicians may still treat the criminal law as if it denoted some separate sphere of control: it is true that the sanction of imprisonment is one that only Criminal Courts can impose, and the absolutist nature of the classification of people – guilty/not guilty, rather than 'a little bit guilty' – is a particular feature of Criminal Courts. But one cannot treat crime in isolation from the remainder of the social and economic system, and in particular not from informal and civil dispute settlement.

Nor can one justifiably ignore the obligation to think more rigorously about the use of discretion. There is a certain schizophrenia about the role of discretion in the criminal justice process, particularly in policing. On the one hand, everyone agrees that discretion is inevitable and is part of 'good policing'; on the other, we keep repeating incantations such as 'a crime is a crime is a crime' and 'the law has to be obeyed ', particularly when adults – who have no excuse because they have grown up already – commit offences. Yet every day, regulatory agencies allow serious crimes in the business world – pollution and health and safety at work offences – to go unpunished. Every Sunday, I see shops trading illegally, despite the fact that Parliament – by rejecting the Shops (HL) Bill (1985) – has clearly expressed its view that this should not be allowed. If it is not the case that we should always prosecute because 'a crime is a crime is a crime', then let us think harder about why we prosecute those we do *and* why we do not prosecute those we do not. We may come to the conclusion that we are doing the right thing at present. But we should think through the justification for doing so.

Those who have written imaginatively about the way in which some aspects of specifically *penal* control have been replaced (and have been made more pervasive) by measures of social regulation 'in the community' have written about these phenomena in the context of regulating the poor (Cohen, 1985; Garland, 1985). We can close down the asylums and give the insane 'community care'. We no longer need to worry about insufficient room in our Youth Custody Centres: we can give our delinquents electronic 'bleeper' bracelets that allow them to be tracked in the community twenty-four hours a day. We no longer need the death penalty or transportation: we have the welfare state, which is a far more effective means of regulating what seventeenth-century politicians in England termed 'the ungovernable people'. We do not need to prosecute every person we believe to be abusing the social security system: we can cut off their benefits instead, and save ourselves the expense of prosecution and incarceration. (Unless they go off and commit other offences to replace the funding they have lost, in which case they become, say, 'burglars', rather than 'social security fraudsters', and this confirms our initial judgment that they were dishonestly claiming social security, as well as defuses the image of social security enforcers as persecutors of the poor.)

Yet there is no reason why we should confine to the poor this analysis of the dispersion of penality. The upperworld, too, has its methods of civil and informal regulation. In parallel with the self-regulatory disciplinary procedures that have resulted in fairly severe penalties for some senior figures at Lloyd's, there are criminal investigations by the Fraud Investigation Group and civil lawsuits – both in operation and pending – by the insurance syndicate members against their agents and against Lloyd's itself, alleging regulatory negligence in failing to ensure compliance with the rules. If not settled out of court, the legal costs alone of these civil proceedings could amount to £20 million in the UK alone, and more as they spread during 1987 to the United States. Thus, we see an intriguing overlap between systems of criminal, self-regulatory administrative (at a criminal burden of proof), and civil law.

Similar overlap applies in the United States, where one of the attractions of the *nolo contendere* plea for defendants is that an ordinary conviction opens up the route to easier proof for claims of damages in the civil courts. As we saw earlier, in 1986 Dennis Levine agreed to pay $11.5 million to the state in relation to charges of insider dealing. But in addition, he faces *civil* claims by the Internal Revenue Service and is a co-defendant in a lawsuit for $30 million by Litton Industries who claim that as a result of his insider dealing activities, they paid much more for a company called Itek Corporation than they needed to. These lawsuits, however, pale into insignificance compared with those launched against Ivan Boesky in the wake of his settlement with SEC. It is this liability to civil suits which makes it difficult to dismiss as merely token punishment the fact that Boesky was not sent to jail but 'only' had to pay $100 million and agree to a permanent ban from dealing on or through the US Stock Exchange. Part of the concern about the supposed leniency of Boesky's sentence may have emanated from suspicions that the willingness to accept a plea bargain that did not entail imprisonment was related to his being a former contributor to Republican Party funds. But it was fuelled by the coincidental upholding by the US Court of Appeals in December 1986 of an eighteen-month prison sentence on a former Wall Street Journal columnist (Winans, 1987) who dealt in shares before discussing them in his column: if you are going to be found out, it is better to be part of a large conspiracy that you can expose!

Apart from strengthening possibilities for civil redress – more affordable in Britain, with its absence of class actions and contingency fees, for the very rich and for the very poor (who may sometimes get Legal Aid) than for those of moderate incomes, and more useful against fraudsters whose identities we know and who remain within the jurisdiction than for those who have vanished elsewhere – one of the lessons of these cases is that we *can* do something more about fraud if we take measures to create more effective and durable audit trails. Here technology, often regarded with alarm and suspicion as an instrument of oppression, can be used to identify suspicious currency or securities movements and, through automation, to provide more accurate and difficult-to-alter records of the times and circumstances of commercial transactions. If self-regulatory and/or state agencies are allowed free or freer access to such records, then the risks of being found out are enhanced; if compliance officers are required to report suspected frauds and/or 'irregularities' to external sources such as SROs, who can check on whether action has been taken, then this will reduce the ability of small firms and of very senior personnel in large firms to conduct themselves corruptly in the knowledge that they can 'keep the lid on'. With more expert, independent and committed regulators, and the sorts of evidentiary reforms discussed earlier in this chapter, some inroads could be made into upperworld malefaction. Whether we *want* this sort of control is a separate moral and economic question, but without it, levels of fraud will certainly not abate.

Another interesting development in regulation imposes some degree of liability for fraud on regulators themselves. A man who had lost £10,000 which he had invested with a licensed securities dealer run by two former directors of another company that had gone 'bust', complained to the Ombudsman (Parliamentary Commissioner for Administration, 1986). Castigating their regulatory inactivity, the Ombudsman concluded that the Department of Trade and Industry's administrative deficiencies in failing to suspend the dealer's licence when they clearly should have done were sufficient to justify redress. The repayment (plus interest) was made *ex gratia*, but the potential consequences of this idea of governmental responsibility for regulatory negligence are enormous. It would certainly lead to a substantial improvement in the resources allocated for fraud control, and would provide an economic incentive for effective regulatory performance. Christie (1977, 1986a) wants us to think about resolving conflicts more creatively: well, here we have some examples. Except, of course, that the regulators – or rather, those who pay for the regulators, i.e. the members of Lloyd's (plus the taxpayer, when these costs are offset against tax) in the first case, the taxpayer alone in the second – usually end up paying, and the fraudster gets away with it. But the principle is there. We have regulation without criminal law, though in both cases there is a criminal law there that potentially might be made use of.

If all the changes discussed in this final chapter were implemented, would this cease to be the case? Probably not. For the primary interest of most victims is the return of their money. And the criminal law is important here not just for symbolic reasons but as a stick with which to threaten the fraudster. Fraudsters, however, are not easily frightened: they can figure out what the chances of being prosecuted and convicted are. And the stick at present is rather small. So the consequence of giving victims access to a bigger stick might be not an increase in prosecutions but rather an increase in informal or civil settlements of debts owed. This might even induce more – we must talk always of more or less, never of absolute – deterrence, since fun and greed, not need, drive this kind of fraud. But this is only a limited development and one which, in a sense, *increases* penal inequality. It still leaves the poor in the formal system, because generally speaking, they have spent the money; they have nothing left to trade. Creating non-penal remedies for them (or, to be more honest about it, *against* them) is rather more difficult. So the consequences of these criminal justice reforms would be that we end up with a slightly different system from what exists at present: the fraudster no longer gets quite so much richer, but the poor still get prison.

Endnote: the shape of things to come in the punitive City

Post-industrial society is characterized by a desperate search on the part of government to find responsible non-governmental bodies to carry out key regulatory functions. The inspection of factories in the nineteenth century was a comparatively easy task: hours of work, and health and safety provisions were *visible*, even if they were not vigorously enforced. But technological changes and increasing consumerism mean that it becomes harder and harder to tell whether or not a rule is being violated. How do we know if food sold to the public contains contaminated and/or banned substances? This, at least, is a problem that can be resolved by forensic analysis, *if anyone reports it or if government or commercial compliance officers inspect it*. But how can we tell if insurance or securities are being sold by an unauthorized person? Or if a director or professional is engaged in insider dealing? For tasks like this, social control must be dispersed and, at least in part, privatized. To borrow from Foucault (1977), a new 'carceral archipelago' – i.e. a new area of imprisonment – must be created within the metaphorical 'punitive city'. Thus, 'responsible corporations' – those with a comparatively good track record of violations – are permitted to police their own health and safety violations, leaving (reduced) resources to be focused upon the higher risk firms; SROs, set up alongside the established professional bodies, police their members who in turn have their own corporate compliance officers: upperworld community policing, with as few state police officers as possible to upset the delicate mechanisms of control.

For the remainder of society, however, this sort of strategy is labelled in advance as being doomed to failure. It is a common misunderstanding in some circles that large numbers of police and extensive police powers are positively *desired* to police the working-class city. This is foolish: self-policing is always preferable. But the family defects and the other pathologies of the poor give them (and us) inadequate protection against the forces of greed. Their crimes are highly visible; their police are already in place; there are all too few responsible bodies – schools, churches, youth clubs, football supporters' clubs (for the 'true' soccer-lovers) – to do the control work that is necessary. Fortunately, there are other regulatory factors – work prospects for some; social-security benefits for others; leisure activities (or, in the case of television and video, *in*activities); narcotics; and even, perhaps, the 'black economy' – which serve to counteract the risk of revolt that is 'caused' by the ineffectiveness of family, school, and religion. We see now why we need the police: even in Japan, with its increasing geographical mobility and recently privatized families, social disorganization is rife. So Foucault's punitive city was designed to regulate the workers and the unemployed, because they were *the* dangerous classes from whom 'social problems' (i.e. problems for both capitalist and communist governments) originated. Or so it was said.

But now we have a different set of disciplinary problems, created by people who live, not in the slums or even the suburbs of the punitive city, but in leafy Oxfordshire villages (or, in the US, Yuppieville), from which their Porsches zoom forth at 5 am *en route* for the City. (Though with 24-hour trading in commodities and securities, and the abolition of the requirement to trade on the floor of The Stock Exchange, they need never leave home at all: they can operate, Hefner-style, from their electronic bedrooms.) They work hard, sustained by adrenalin (with the occasional nutrition offered by 'coke') as they play on the great financial casinos of the world with other people's money. What if *they* break the law? Well, with a bit of luck, nobody will notice, and 'everybody knows' that there are strong economic reasons why insider dealing is actually beneficial to the markets, though governments are forced to act tough because the public are ignorant and might misunderstand what was going on. But as for corporate embezzlement, computer fraud, commercial credit fraud, etc., there is general agreement that something must be done. When professionals actually run off with all our money (rather than merely secretly diverting a part of it), causing the hard-working 'little men' to lose their cash from Savings and Loan Banks in Ohio or from Pension Funds in the South of England, this is both morally and politically intolerable. So the professions and the SROs, under the overall supervision of Big Brother in the Department of Trade and Industry (or, in the US, the Department of Justice and the Treasury) must prevent this as best they can. They must set up insurance compensation funds and they must watch vigilantly over their members and discipline them when they break the rules. Thus we see the intensification of surveillance within the commercial City.

But the professions, too, are no strangers to social disorganization. They are disintegrating under the combined pressures of the envy and greed produced by the huge salaries in some sectors; of conglomerates which make it hard to maintain independence of judgment; of conspicuous consumption in the fast lane; and of the need to move all that money which has been borrowed from depositors and has to make a profit. If scandals break, then the regulators are thrown to the wolves and Something Must be Done: otherwise trade will be damaged when people go elsewhere with their money. Then, almost certainly in the opinion of most professionals in 1986, comes increasing state regulation – for Britain, a Securities and Exchange Commission under a more English name – but supplemented by a self-regulatory army. To train and pay for all these troops, however, is no simple matter, and there is the problem of where to station them to police the invisible crimes that may occur anywhere, at any time, and be committed by anybody.

This shape of regulatory things to come is naturally overdrawn: for to stop the embezzlers and the money-launderers *completely* would make life too uncomfortable for the money-makers, and in a fast-changing global market in which, once behind, we may never catch up, we all depend upon the money-makers. So the terrain upon which this new carceral archipelago has to be built is difficult: even more difficult than the slums of the inner city with their unwelcoming inhabitants and their continual crises in police/public relationships. In the building process, we might fracture the mains carrying the water supply to the rest of the city. Moreover, people on the whole work better when they are happier and freer, and their contentment is important if we want to stop them moving (with their assets, freely transferrable *sans* exchange control restrictions) to more pleasant foreign climes. So although we may try to develop our upperworld equivalent of the punitive city, we cannot try too hard: for whether they are market-makers, first-class chefs, or Presidential advisers, those who are socially useful and create our wealth have to be allowed the occasional peccadillo. The ironic circle is complete: to fund the punitive city for those who are too young or too old or too ill-equipped to join the ever-shrinking ranks of the merchants, or the labouring poor, or 'the middling people', we must give the City the latitude to police itself, even if this means that the striving for prosperity triumphs over law. Persistent offenders who steal £1 go to prison; persistent insider dealers who steal £10 million pay back the money – perhaps in addition to a substantial fine – on the rare occasions that they are caught. *De maximis non curat lex*: for the greatest things, the law provides no remedy.

Bibliography

Adams, J. (1986) *The Financing of Terror*. London: New English Library.
Adams, S. (1984) *Roche versus Adams*. London: Andre Deutsch.
Administrative Office (1984) *Annual Report of the Director, 1983*. Washington, DC: US Government Printing House.
Advisory Council on the Penal System (1978) *Sentences of Imprisonment*. London: HMSO.
Allan, R. and Fforde, W. (1986) *The Auditor and Fraud*. London: Consultative Council for the Accountancy Bodies.
Aris, S. (1985) *Going Bust*. London: Andre Deutsch.
Arlacchi, P. (1986) *Mafia Business: the Mafia Ethic and the Spirit of Capitalism*. London: Verso.
Arlidge, A. and Parry, J. (1985) *Arlidge and Parry on Fraud*. London: Waterlow.
Ashworth, A. (1983) *Sentencing and Penal Policy*. London: Weidenfeld and Nicholson.
Aubert, W. (1952) White-collar Crime and Social Structure. *American Journal of Sociology* 58:263–71.
Audit Commission (1985) *Computer Fraud Survey*. London: HMSO.
Auditing Practices Committee (1985) *Draft Auditing Guideline on Fraud and other Irregularities*. London: Consultative Council for the Accountancy Bodies.
Baldwin, J. and McConville, M. (1981) *Courts, Prosecution, and Conviction*. Oxford: Oxford University Press.
Baldwin, R. and Kinsey, R. (1982) *Police Powers and Politics*. London: Quartet Books.
Bax, M. (1986) The Will Found to Control Boiler Room Companies. *Company Lawyer* 7:172–73.
Beattie, J. (1986) *Crime and the Courts in England 1660–1800*. Oxford: Oxford University Press.
Becker H. (1973) *Outsiders*. New York: Free Press.
Benson, M. (1984) The Fall from Grace. *Criminology* 22(4):573–93.
Bequai, A. (1978) *White-Collar Crime: A Twentieth Century Crisis*. Lexington, Mass.: Lexington Books.
Blakey, G. (1986) Asset Forfeiture under Federal Criminal Law. In H.

Alexander and G. Caiden (eds) *The Politics and Economics of Organized Crime.* Lexington, Mass.: Lexington Books.

Block, A. (1980) *East Side-West Side.* Cardiff: University of Cardiff Press.

Block, A. and Chambliss, W. (1981) *Organizing Crime.* New York: Elsevier.

Block, A. and Scarpitti, F. (1983) Defining Illegal Hazardous Waste Disposal: White-Collar or Organized Crime. In G. Waldo (ed.) *Career Criminals.* Beverly Hills, Calif.: Sage.

—— (1985) *Poisoning for Profit.* New York: William Morrow.

Bok, S. (1982) *Secrets.* Oxford: Oxford University Press.

Bologna, J. (1984) *Corporate Fraud: The Basics of Prevention and Detection.* Boston: Butterworths.

Borrie, G. (1984) *The Development of Consumer Law and Policy – Bold Spirits and Timorous Souls.* London: Stevens.

Box, S. (1983) *Power, Crime, and Mystification.* London: Tavistock.

Bradley, D., Walker, N., and Wilkie, R. (1986) *Managing the Police.* Brighton: Wheatsheaf.

Brady, J. (1983) Arson, Urban Economy, and Organized Crime: The Case of Boston. *Social Problems* **31**(1):1–27.

Braithwaite, J. (1982a) Enforced Self-Regulation: A New Strategy for Corporate Crime Control. *Michigan Law Review* **80**:1466–1507.

—— (1982b) Challenging Just Deserts. *Journal of Criminal Law and Criminology* **73**(2):723–63.

—— (1984) *Corporate Crime in the Pharmaceutical Industry*, London: Routledge & Kegan Paul.

—— (1985a) Corporate Crime Research: Why Two Interviewers are Needed. *Sociology* **19**(1):136–38.

—— (1985b) *To Punish or Persuade.* Albany, NY: State University of New York Press.

Braithwaite, J. and Vale, S. (1985) Law Enforcement by Australian Consumer Affairs Agencies. *Australian and New Zealand Journal of Criminology* **18**(3):147–64.

Breed, B. (1979) *White-Collar Bird.* London: John Clare.

Bringhurst, B. (1979) *Antitrust and the Oil Monopoly: the Standard Oil Cases, 1890–1911.* Westport, Conn.: Greenwood Press.

Bryant, J., Chambers, M., and Falcon, D. (1968) *Patrol Effectiveness and Patrol Deployment.* Unpublished Ph.D thesis: Department of Operational Research, Lancaster University.

Bureau of National Affairs (1976) *White-Collar Justice: A BNA Special Report on White-Collar Crime.* Washington, DC: Bureau of National Affairs.

Butler, S. (1983) *Acquittal Rates.* London: Home Office Research and

Planning Unit Paper.

Cain, M. (1975) Rich Man's or Poor Man's Law. *British Journal of Law and Society* 2:61–6.

Calavita, K. (1983) The Demise of the Occupational Safety and Health Administration: A Case Study in Symbolic Action. *Social Problems* 30(4):437–48.

Caminer, B. (1985) Credit Card Fraud: The Neglected Crime. *Journal of Criminal Law and Criminology* 76(3):746–63.

Campbell, D. and Connor, S. (1986) *On The Record: Surveillance, Computers, and Privacy*. London: Michael Joseph.

Carlen, P. (ed) (1985) *Women Criminals*. Oxford: Polity Press.

Carroll, R., Pine, S., Cline, C., and Kleinhaus, B. (1974) Judged Seriousness of Watergate-Related Crimes. *Journal of Psychology* 86:235–39.

Carson, W. (1970) White-Collar Crime and the Enforcement of Factory Legislation. *British Journal of Criminology* 10:383–98.

—— (1981) *The Other Price of Britain's Oil*. Oxford: Martin Robertson.

Chambliss, W. (1978) *On the Take*. Bloomington, Ind.: Indiana University Press.

Chambliss, W. and Seidman, R. (1982) *Law, Order, and Power*, second edition, Reading, Mass.: Addison-Wesley.

Chibnall, S. and Saunders, P. (1977) Worlds Apart: Notes on the Social Reality of Corruption. *British Journal of Sociology* 28(2):138–54.

Christie, N. (1977) Conflicts as Property. *British Journal of Criminology* 17:1–17.

—— (1986a) Crime Control as Drama. *Journal of Law and Society* 13(1):1–8.

—— (1986b) Images of Man in Modern Penal Law. *Contemporary Crises* 10:99–106.

City of London Police (1983) *Annual Report of Commissioner for the City of London, 1982*. London: City of London.

—— (1985) *Annual Report of Commissioner for the City of London, 1984*. London: City of London.

—— (1986) *Annual Report of Commissioner for the City of London, 1985*. London: City of London.

Clarke, M. (1981) *Fallen Idols*. London: Junction Books.

—— (ed.) (1983) *Corruption*. London: Frances Pinter.

—— (1986) *Regulating the City*. Milton Keynes: Open University Press.

Clarke, R. and Hough, M. (1984) *Crime and Police Effectiveness*. Home Office Research Study No. 79. London: HMSO.

Clinard, M. (1952) *The Black Market*. New York: Holt, Rinehart.

—— (1978) *Cities with Little Crime*. Cambridge: Cambridge University Press.

—— (1983) *Corporate Ethics and Crime.* Beverly Hills, Calif.: Sage.

Clinard, M. and Yeager, P. (1980) *Corporate Crime.* New York: Free Press.

Clinard, M., Yeager, P., Brissette, J., Petrashek, D., and Harries, E. (1979) *Illegal Corporate Behaviour.* Washington, DC: Department of Justice.

Coffee, J. (1986) Understanding the Plaintiff's Attorney: The Implications of Economic Theory for Private Enforcement of Law through Class and Derivative Actions. *Columbia Law Review* 86(4):669–727.

Cohen, S. (1985) *Visions of Social Control.* Oxford: Polity Press.

Cole, D. (1983) *The Attitudes of Manufacturing Executives to Offences against the Environment.* Adelaide: Social and Ecological Assessment.

Coleman, A. (1985) *Utopia on Trial.* London: Shipman.

Coleman, J. (1985a) *The Criminal Elite: Sociology of White-Collar Crime.* New York: St Martin's Press.

—— (1985b) Law and Power: The Sherman Anti-trust Act and its Enforcement in the Petroleum Industry. *Social Problems* 32(3):265–74.

Commonwealth Secretariat (1986) *Mutual Assistance in the Administration of Justice: Report of a Meeting of Senior Officials to Consider Three Draft Schemes.* London: Commonwealth Secretariat.

Conklin, J. (1977) *Illegal but not Criminal.* Englewood Cliffs, NJ: Prentice-Hall.

Connelly, A. (1985) Ireland and the Political Offence: Exception to Extradition. *Journal of Law and Society* 12(2):153–82.

Consensus Research (1985) *Attitudes of Companies in Britain to Fraud.* London: Ernst and Whinney.

Copetas, A. (1986) *Metal Men: Marc Rich and the Ten-billion-dollar Scam.* London: Harrap.

Cork Committee (1982) *Insolvency Law and Practice: Report of the Review Committee.* London: HMSO.

Cornish, W. (1968) *The Jury.* London: Allen Lane.

Cotterrell, R. (1984) *The Sociology of Law: An Introduction.* London: Butterworths.

Cox, B., Shirley, J., and Short, M. (1977) *The Fall of Scotland Yard.* Harmondsworth: Penguin.

Cranston, R. (1979) *Regulating Business.* London: Macmillan.

Cullen, F., Link, B., and Polanzi, C. (1982) The Seriousness of Crime Revisited. *Criminology* 20:82–102.

Cullen, F., Link, B., Travis, L., and Wozniak, J. (1985) Consensus in Crime Seriousness: Empirical Reality or Methodological Artifact? *Criminology* 23(1):99–119.

Cullen, F., Maakestad, W., and Cavender, G. (1984) The Ford Pinto

Case and Beyond: Corporate Crime, Moral Boundaries, and the Criminal Sanction. In E. Hochstedler (ed.) *Corporations as Criminals.* Beverly Hills, Calif.: Sage.

Cullen, F., Mathers, R., Clark, G., and Cullen, J. (1983) Public Support for Punishing White-Collar Crime: Blaming the Victim Revisited. *Journal of Criminal Justice* 11:481–93.

Deane, K. (1981) Tax Evasion, Criminality, and Sentencing the Tax Offender. *British Journal of Criminology* 21(1):47–57.

Deloitte, Haskins, and Sells (1986) *Regulation and the Financial Services Bill.* London: Deloitte, Haskins, and Sells.

Denning, Lord (1980) *Due Process of Law.* London: Butterworths.

—— (1982) *What Next in the Law.* London: Butterworths.

Department of Trade and Industry (1984) *A Revised Framework for Insolvency Law.* London: HMSO.

—— (1985a) *Financial Services in the United Kingdom: A New Framework for Investor Protection.* London: HMSO.

—— (1985b) *Companies in 1984.* London: HMSO.

—— (1985c) *Bankruptcies in 1984.* London: HMSO.

—— (1986a) *Handbook of the Companies Investigation System.* 2nd edn. London: HMSO.

—— (1986b) *Annual Report of the Office of Fair Trading for 1985.* London: HMSO.

—— (1986c) *Companies in 1985.* London: HMSO.

—— (1986d) *Regulation of Auditors.* London: DTI.

Di Fonzo, L. (1983) *St. Peter's Banker.* Edinburgh: Mainstream Publishing.

Ditton, J. (1977a) *Part-Time Crime.* London: Macmillan.

—— (1977b) Perks, Pilferage, and the Fiddle: The Historical Structure of Invisible Wages. *Theory and Society* 4:39–71.

Doig, A. (1983) "You Publish at Your Peril" – The Restraints on Investigatory Journalism. In M. Clarke (ed.) *Corruption.* London: Frances Pinter.

—— (1984) *Corruption and Misconduct.* Harmondsworth: Penguin.

Downes, D. (1979) Praxis Makes Perfect. In D. Downes and P. Rock (eds) *Deviant Interpretations.* Oxford: Martin Robertson.

—— (1983) *Law and Order: Theft of an Issue.* London: Fabian Society.

Durant, M., Thomas, M., and Wilcock, H. (1972) *Crime, Criminals, and the Law.* London: HMSO.

Elwork, A., Sales, B., and Alfini, J. (1977) 'Juridic Decisions: in ignorance of the law or in light of it', *Law and Human Behaviour* 1:163–90.

Ericson, R. (1981) *Making Crime.* Toronto: Butterworths.

—— (1982) *Reproducing Order.* Toronto: University of Toronto Press.

Ermann, D. and Lundman, R. (1982) *Corporate and Governmental Deviance*. Oxford: Oxford University Press.

European Community Information Technology Task Force (1984) *The Vulnerability of the Information Conscious Society: European Situation*. Unpublished research monograph.

Farrar, J. (1985) *Company Law*. London: Butterworths.

Fennell, P. (1983) Local Government Corruption in England and Wales. In M. Clarke (ed.) *Corruption*. London: Frances Pinter.

Fennell, P. and Thomas, P. (1983) Corruption in Britain: An Historical Analysis. *International Journal of Sociology of Law* 11:167–89.

Finer, M. (1966) Company Fraud. *The Accountant*:583–88.

Fisher Report (1980) *Report*. London: Lloyd's.

Fisse, B. and Braithwaite, J. (1983) *The Impact of Publicity on Corporate Offenders*. Albany, NY: State University of New York Press.

Fitzmaurice, C. and Pease, K. (1986) *The Psychology of Judicial Sentencing*. Manchester: Manchester University Press.

Fletcher, G. (1978) *Rethinking the Criminal Law*. Boston: Little, Brown.

Foucault, M. (1977) *Discipline and Punish: The Birth of the Prison*. London: Allen Lane.

Frank, N. (1983) From Criminal to Civil Penalties in the History of Health and Safety Laws. *Social Problems* 30:532–44.

Fraud Trials Committee (1986a) *Report*. London: HMSO.

—— (1986b) *Improving the Presentation of Information to Juries in Fraud Trials: A Report of Four Research Studies*. London: HMSO.

Galanter, M. (1985) Judicial Mediation in the United States. *Journal of Law and Society* 12(1):1–18.

Gamble, A. (1985) *Britain in Decline*. 2nd edn. London: Macmillan.

Gandhi, J. (1982) *Lawyers and Touts: A Study in the Sociology of the Legal Profession*. Delhi: Hindustan Publishing Corporation.

Gardiner, J. and Lyman, T. (1985) *The Fraud Control Game: State Responses to Fraud and Abuse in AFDC and Medicaid Programs*. Bloomington, Ind.: Indiana University Press.

Garland, D. (1985) *Punishment and Welfare*. Aldershot: Gower.

Gartner, W. and Wenig, A. (eds) (1985) *The Economics of the Shadow Economy*. Berlin: Springer Verlag.

Gatrell, V. (1980) The Decline of Theft and Violence in Victorian and Edwardian England. In V. Gatrell, B. Lenman, and G. Parker (eds) *Crime and the Law: The Social History of Crime in Western Europe Since 1500*. London: Europa.

—— (1987) Crime, Authority, and the Policeman-State, 1750–1950. In F. Thompson (ed.) *The Cambridge Social History of Britain, 1750–1950*. Cambridge: Cambridge University Press.

Geis, G. (1984) White-Collar and Corporate Crime. In R. Meier (ed.)

Major Forms of Crime. Beverly Hills, Calif.: Sage.

Gibbons, D. (1969) Crime and Punishment: A Study of Social Attitudes. *Social Forces* **47**:391–97.

Gottfredson, S., Young, K., and Laufer, W. (1980) Additivity and Interactions in Offence Seriousness Scales. *Journal of Research in Crime and Delinquency* **17**:26–41.

Green, M., Moore, B., and Wasserstein, B. (1972) *The Closed Enterprise System*. New York: Grossman.

Greenberg, D. (ed.) (1981) *Crime and Capitalism*. New Brunswick, NJ: Rutgers University Press.

Griffith, J. (1985) *The Politics of the Judiciary*. 3rd edn. London: Fontana.

Gunningham, N. (1974) *Pollution, Social Interest, and the Law*. Oxford: Martin Robertson.

—— (1985) *Safeguarding the Worker*. Sydney: Law Book Co.

Gusfield, J. (1962) *Symbolic Crusade*. Bloomington, Ind.: Indiana University Press.

Hadden, T. (1983) Fraud in the City: The Role of the Criminal Law. *Criminal Law Review*:500–11.

Hagan J., Nagel, I., and Albonetti, C. (1980) The Differential Sentencing of White-Collar Defendants in Ten Federal District Courts. *American Sociological Review* **45**:802–20.

Hagan, J. and Parker, P. (1985) White-Collar Crime and Punishment: The Class Structure and Legal Sanctioning of Securities Violations. *American Journal of Sociology* **50**:302–16.

Hall, J. (1952) *Theft, Law, and Society*. New York: Bobbs-Merrill.

Hall, S., Critcher, C., Jefferson, T., Clarke, J., and Roberts, B. (1978) *Policing the Crisis*. London: Macmillan.

Hall, S. and Scraton, P. (1981) Law, Class and Control. In M. Fitzgerald, G. McLennan, and J. Pawson (eds) *Crime and Society: Readings in History and Theory*. London: Routledge and Kegan Paul.

Hans, V. and Vidmar, N. (1986) *Judging the Jury*. New York: Plenum.

Harman, H. and Griffith, J. (1979) *Justice Deserted*. London: National Council for Civil Liberties.

Harris, P. (1986) Socialist Graft: The Soviet Union and the People's Republic of China – A Preliminary Survey. *Corruption and Reform* **1**(1):13–32.

Hawkins, G. (1969) 'God and the Mafia.' *Public Interest* **14**:24–51.

Hawkins, K. (1983) Assessing Evil. *British Journal of Criminology* **23**(2):101–27.

—— (1984) *Environment and Enforcement*. Oxford: Oxford University Press.

Hay, D. (1975) Property, Authority, and the Criminal Law. In D. Hay, P. Linebaugh, and E. Thompson (eds) *Albion's Fatal Tree*. London:

Allen Lane.

Health and Safety Executive (1985) *Health and Safety Executive Report, 1984–85*. London: HMSO.

—— (1986) Report by *HM Inspector of Factories 1985*. London: HMSO.

Henry, S. (1978) *The Hidden Economy*. Oxford: Martin Robertson.

—— (ed.) (1981) *Can I have it in Cash?*. London: Astragal.

—— (1983) *Private Justice*. London: Routledge and Kegan Paul.

Hermann, A. (1983) *Judges, Law, and Businessmen*. Amsterdam: Kluwer.

Heuer, L. and Penrod, S. (1985) *Draft Report: A Field Experiment on Improving Jury Communication*. Madison: Wisconsin Judicial Council on Improving Jury Instructions.

Hodgson, G. (1984) *Lloyd's of London: a Reputation at Risk*. London: Allen Lane.

—— (1986) *Lloyd's of London: a Reputation at Risk*. 2nd edn. Harmondsworth: Penguin.

Hodgson Committee (1984) *The Profits of Crime and their Recovery*. Aldershot: Gower.

Hogg Robinson (1986) *Computer Security in Practice*. London: Hogg Robinson.

Holdaway, S. (1983) *Inside the British Police*. Oxford: Basil Blackwell.

Home Office (1971) *Report of the Commissioner for the Metropolis for the Year 1970*. London: HMSO.

—— (1973) *Report of the Commissioner for the Metropolis for the Year 1972*. London: HMSO.

—— (1974) *Report of the Commissioner for the Metropolis for the Year 1973*. London: HMSO.

—— (1976) *Report of the Commissioner for the Metropolis for the Year 1975*. London: HMSO.

—— (1977) *Report of the Commissioner for the Metropolis for the Year 1976*. London: HMSO.

—— (1978) *Report of the Commissioner for the Metropolis for the Year 1977*. London: HMSO.

—— (1983) *Report of the Commissioner for the Metropolis for the Year 1982*. London: HMSO.

—— (1984a) *Report of the Commissioner for the Metropolis for the Year 1983*. London: HMSO.

—— (1984b) *Criminal Justice: A Working Paper*. London: HMSO.

—— (1985a) *Criminal Statistics in England and Wales 1984*. London: HMSO.

—— (1985b) *Report of the Commissioner for the Metropolis for the Year 1984*. London: HMSO.

—— (1985c) *Report of the Parole Board 1984*. London: HMSO.

—— (1986a) *A Police for the People: Report of the Commissioner of Police for the Metropolis for the Year 1985.* London: HMSO.

—— (1986b) *Report of the Parole Board, 1985.* London: HMSO.

—— (1986c) *Previous Convictions of Persons Convicted in 1982.* London: Home Office.

—— (1986d) *Criminal Statistics in England and Wales 1985.* London: HMSO.

—— (1986e) *Criminal Justice: A Working Paper,* revised edition, London: HMSO.

—— (1986f) *Prison Statistics for England and Wales 1985,* London: HMSO.

Hough, M. and Mayhew, P. (1983) *The British Crime Survey: First Report.* Home Office Research Study No. 76. London: HMSO.

Hough, M. and Mayhew, P. (1985) *Taking Account of Crime: Key Findings from the 1984 British Crime Survey.* Home Office Research Study No. 85. London: HMSO.

Hough, M. and Moxon, D. (1985) Dealing with Offenders: Popular Opinion and the Views of Victims. *Howard Journal of Criminal Justice* 24(3):160–75.

Hopkins, A. (1978) *Crime, Law, and Business.* Canberra: Australian Institute of Criminology.

Hoyle, B. (1985) *The Mareva Injunction.* London: Lloyd's of London Press.

Hunt, A. (1981) Dichotomy and Contradiction in the Sociology of Law. *British Journal of Law and Society* 8:47–77.

Hutter, B. (1986) An Inspector Calls. *British Journal of Criminology.* 26(2):114–28.

Institute of Chartered Accountants (1987) *Countering Computer Fraud.* A report of the Information Technology Working Party. London: Institute of Chartered Accountants in England and Wales.

Ita, T. (1984) RICO-Criminal Forfeiture of Proceeds of Racketeering Activity under RICO. *Journal of Criminal Law and Criminology* 75(3):893–939.

Jackson, J., Donnelly, P., Haines, J., and Maxwell, R. (1986) *Malice in Wonderland. Robert Maxwell v Private Eye.* London: Macdonald.

Jackson, R. (1967) *Occupied with Crime.* London: Harrap.

Jefferson, T. and Grimshaw, R. (1984) *Controlling the Constable: Police Accountability in England and Wales.* London: Frederick Muller/Cobden Trust.

Johnston, M. and Wood, D. (1985) Right and Wrong in Public and Private Life. In R. Jowell and S. Witherspoon (eds) *British Social Attitudes: the 1985 Report.* Aldershot: Gower.

Jones, K. and Cassidy, B. (1986) Review of B. Fisse and J. Braithwaite, *The Impact of Publicity on Corporate Offenders.* In *International Journal of the Sociology of Law* **14**(1):77–87.

Jones, S. and Levi, M. (1983a) *Police-Public Relationships.* Unpublished research monograph. Department of Social Administration, University College, Cardiff.

—— (1983b) The Police and the Majority: The Neglect of the Obvious. *The Police Journal* **LVI**(4):351–64.

—— (1987) Some Police and Public Perspectives on Law and Order and the Causes of Crime. *Howard Journal of Criminal Justice* **26**(1):1–5.

Jones, T., Maclean, B., and Young, J. (1986) *The Islington Crime Survey.* Aldershot: Gower.

Judicature (1982) *Helping Juries Understand Complex Cases. Judicature* Special Issue, March/April.

Karmel, R. (1982) *Regulation by Prosecution: The Securities and Exchange Commission versus Corporate America.* New York: Simon and Schuster.

Katz, J. (1979) Legality and Equality: Plea Bargaining in the Prosecution of White-Collar and Common Crimes. *Law and Society Review* **13**:431–59.

—— (1980) The Social Movement Against White-Collar Crime. In E. Bittner and S. Messenger (eds) *Criminology Review Yearbook*, Vol. 2. Beverly Hills, Calif.: Sage.

Keith Committee (1983) *Report*, Vols 1 and 2. Committee on Enforcement Powers of the Revenue Departments. London: HMSO.

Kinsey, R. (1985) *The Merseyside Crime Survey.* Edinburgh: report prepared under the auspices of Edinburgh University.

Kinsey, R., Lea, J., and Young, J. (1986) *Losing the Fight Against Crime.* Oxford: Blackwell.

Klockars, C. (1980) Jonathan Wild and the Modern Sting. In J. Inciardi (ed.) *History and Crime.* Beverly Hills, Calif.: Sage.

—— (1985) *The Idea of the Police.* Beverly Hills, Calif.: Sage.

Knight, S. (1985) *The Brotherhood.* London: Granada.

Kramer, R. (1984) Corporate Criminality: The Development of an Idea. In E. Hochstedler (ed.) *Corporations as Criminals.* Beverly Hills, Calif.: Sage.

Lampert, N. (1985) *Whistleblowing in the Soviet Union.* London: Macmillan.

Lea, J. and Young, J. (1984) *What is to be Done about Law and Order?.* Harmondsworth: Penguin.

Leigh, L. (1982) *The Control of Commercial Fraud.* Aldershot: Gower.

—— (1985) *Police Powers in England and Wales.* 2nd edn. London: Butterworths.

—— (ed.) (1980) *Economic Crime in Europe.* London: Macmillan.

Lempert, R. (1981) Civil Juries and Complex Cases: Let's Not Rush to

Judgment. *Michigan Law Review* **80**:68–132.

Levi, M. (1979) Long-Firm Fraud, Sentencing, and the Advisory Council. *Howard Journal of Criminology and Penal Reform* **18**:92–9.

—— (1981) *The Phantom Capitalists: The Organisation and Control of Long-Firm Fraud.* Aldershot: Gower.

—— (1982) The Powers of the Revenue Departments: An Overview. *British Tax Review* **1**:36–51.

—— (1983) 'Blaming the jury: frauds on trial', *Journal of Law and Society*, **10**(2):257–70.

—— (1984a) 'Business Regulatory Offences' and the Criminal Law. *The Company Lawyer* **5**(6):251–58.

—— (1984b) Fraud Trials in Perspective. *Criminal Law Review* (July):384–97.

—— (1985) Police Powers and Police-Public Relationships. In E. Alves and J. Shapland (eds) *Legislation for Policing Today: The Police and Criminal Evidence Act.* London: British Psychological Society.

—— (1986a) *The Incidence, Reporting, and Prevention of Commercial Fraud.* Unpublished monograph prepared for the Home Office Crime Prevention Unit.

—— (1986b) Fraud in the Courts: Roskill in Context. *British Journal of Criminology* **26**(4):394–401.

—— (1986c) The Future of Fraud Prosecutions and Trials: Reviewing Roskill. *Company Lawyer* **7**:139–45.

Levi, M. and Jones, S. (1985) Public and Police Perceptions of Crime Seriousness in England and Wales. *British Journal of Criminology* **25**(3):234–50.

Levi, M. and Pithouse, A. (forthcoming) *The Victims of Fraud.* Report of Economic and Social Research Council Project.

Lidstone, K., Hogg, R., and Sutcliffe, F. (1981) *Prosecutions by Private Individuals and Non-Police Agencies.* Royal Commission Research Study No. 10. London: HMSO.

Lonrho Limited (1976) *Department of Trade Inspector's Report on Lonrho Limited.* London: HMSO.

McBarnet, D. (1981) *Conviction.* London: Macmillan.

McCormick, A. (1979) Dominant Class Interests and the Emergence of Antitrust Legislation. *Contemporary Crises* **3**:399–417.

McDermott, M. (1982) Occupational Disqualification of Corporate Executives: An Innovative Condition of Probation. *Journal of Criminal Law and Criminology* **73**(2):604–41.

McIntosh, M. (1975) *The Organisation of Crime.* London: Macmillan.

McNee, D. (1983) *McNee's Law.* London: Collins.

Mack, J. (1975) *The Crime Industry.* London: Saxon House.

—— (1976) Full-Time Major Criminals and Courts. *Modern Law*

Review 39:241–67.

Magnusson, D. (ed.) (1985) *Economic Crime – Programs for Future Research*. Stockholm: National Council for Crime Prevention.

Maguire, M. (1982) *Burglary in a Dwelling*. Aldershot: Gower.

Mann, K. (1985) *Defending White-Collar Crime*. New Haven, Conn.: Yale University Press.

Mann, K., Wheeler, S., and Sarat, A. (1980) Sentencing the White-Collar Offender. *American Criminal Law Review* **17**:479–520.

Manwaring-White, S. (1983) *The Policing Revolution*. Brighton: Harvester.

Mark, R. (1973) *Minority Verdict*. London: BBC Publications.

—— (1981) *In the Office of Constable*. London: Collins.

Mars, G. (1982) *Cheats at Work*. London: Allen and Unwin.

Mattera, P. (1985) *Off the Books*. London: Pluto Press.

Maxfield, M. (1984) *Fear of Crime in England and Wales*. Home Office Research Study no. 78. London: HMSO.

Mersey Committee (1913) *Jury Law and Practice*. London: HMSO.

Miethe, T. (1984) Types of Consensus in Public Evaluations of Crime: An Illustration of Strategies for Measuring Consensus. *Journal of Criminal Law and Criminology* **75**:459–73.

Millen, E. (1972) *Specialist in Crime*. London: Harrap.

Milne, E. (1976) *No Shining Armour*. London: Platform Books.

Moody, S. and Tombs, J. (1982) *Prosecution in the Public Interest*. Edinburgh: Scottish Academic Press.

Moran, M. (1986) *The Politics of Banking*. 2nd edn. London: Macmillan.

Morris Committee (1965) *Jury Service*. London: HMSO.

Murphy, D. (1983) The Journalistic Investigation of Corruption. In M. Clarke (ed.) *Corruption*. London: Frances Pinter.

Murphy, J. and Carratu, V. (1986) *Brands and their Protection*. New York: Elsevier.

Nader, L. (1986) Review of S. Shapiro *The Wayward Capitalists*. *Harvard Law Review* **99**:1362–373.

Nagel, I. and Hagan, J. (1982) The Sentencing of White-Collar Criminals in Federal Courts: A Socio-Legal Exploration of Disparity, *Michigan Law Review* **80**:1427–465.

Nathan, R. (1980) Coddled Criminals. *Harper's Magazine* (January):30–5.

Neill, P. (1987) *Regulatory Arrangements at Lloyd's: Report of a Committee of Enquiry*. London: HMSO.

Nelken, D. (1983) *The Limits of the Law*. London: Academic Press.

Newman, D. (1957) Public Attitudes to a Form of White-Collar Crime. *Social Problems* **4**:228–32.

Newman, G. (1976) *Comparative Deviance*. New York: Elsevier.

—— (1983) *Just and Painful: A Case for the Corporal Punishment of Criminals*. London: Collier Macmillan.

Newman, O. (1972) *Defensible Space*. London: Architectural Press.

Niang, L. (1986) Corruption and Economic Crime. *Company Lawyer* 7(2):81–2.

Noaks, L. (forthcoming) *Attitudes to Crime and Community on Bettws Estate*. MSc dissertation, University College, Cardiff.

Noonan, J. (1985) *Bribes*. Cambridge, Mass.: Harvard University Press.

Norton, P. (ed.) (1984) *Law and Order and British Politics*. Aldershot: Gower.

Office of Fair Trading (1986) *A General Duty to Trade Fairly: A Discussion Paper*. London: Office of Fair Trading.

Orland, L. (1980) Reflections on Corporate Crime: Law in Search of Theory and Scholarship. *American Criminal Law Review* 17:501–20.

Orland, L. and Tyler, H. (eds) (1974) *Justice in Sentencing*. Mineola, NY: Foundation Press.

Parkin, F. (1979) *Marxism and Class Theory: A Bourgeois Critique*. London: Tavistock.

Parliamentary Commissioner for Administration (1986) *Fourth Report, 1985–6*. London: HMSO.

Pearce, F. (1976) *Crimes of the Powerful*. London: Pluto Press.

Pearson, G. (1983) *Hooligan*. London: Macmillan.

Pease, K. (forthcoming) The Seriousness of Crime: Findings from the 1984 British Crime Survey. Home Office Research and Planning Unit Paper. London: Home Office.

Pepinsky, H. (1974) From White-Collar Crime to Exploitation: Redefinition of a Field. *Journal of Criminal Law and Criminology* 65:225–33.

Pergamon Press Limited (1971) *Department of Trade Inspectors' Interim Report on Pergamon Press Limited*. London: HMSO.

Poggi, G. (1979) *The Development of the Modern State*. London: Hutchinson.

Policy Studies Institute (1983) *The Police and the People in London*. London: PSI.

Ponting, C. (1984) *The Right to Know*. London: Sphere Books.

Posner, R. and Scott, K. (1980) *The Economics of Corporation Law and Securities Regulation*. Boston: Little, Brown.

President's Commission on Law Enforcement and the Administration of Justice (1967) *The Challenge of Crime in a Free Society*. Washington, DC: US Government Printing Office.

President's Commission on Organized Crime (1986a) *Organized Crime and Money Laundering*. (Record of Hearing II, 14 March 1984). Washington, DC: US Government Printing Office.

President's Commission on Organized Crime (1986b) *Organized Crime and Money Laundering: Interim Report*. Washington, DC: US Government Printing Office.

Punch, M. (1985) *Conduct Unbecoming*. London: Tavistock.

Read, P. (1979) *The Train Robbers*. New York: Avon.

Reed, J. and Reed, R. (1975) 'Doctor, Lawyer, Indian Chief': Old Rhymes and New on White-Collar Crime. *International Journal of Criminology and Penology* 3:279–94.

Reiman, R. (1984) *The Rich Get Richer and the Poor Get Prison*. 2nd edn. London: Wiley.

Reiner, R. (1985) *The Politics of the Police*. Brighton: Wheatsheaf.

Reisman, M. (1979) *Folded Lies*. New York: Free Press.

Reiss, A. (1983) The Policing of Organisational Life. In M. Punch (ed.) *Control in the Police Organization*. Cambridge, Mass.: MIT Press.

Reiss, A. and Biderman, A. (1980) *Data Sources on White-Collar Lawbreaking*. Washington, DC: National Institute of Justice.

Reiss, A. and Bordua, D. (1967) Environment and Organisation: A Perspective on the Police. In D. Bordua (ed.) *The Police*. New York: Wiley.

Renfrew, C. (1977) The Paper Label Sentences: An Evaluation. *Yale Law Journal* 86:590–618.

Reuter, P. (1983) *Disorganized Crime*. Cambridge, Mass.: MIT Press.

Richardson, G., Ogus, A., and Burrows, P. (1983) *Policing Pollution*. Oxford: Oxford University Press.

Rider, B. and Leigh Ffrench, H. (1979) *The Regulation of Insider Trading*. London: Macmillan.

Riley, D. and Shaw, M. (1985) *Parental Supervision and Juvenile Delinquency*. Home Office Research Study No. 83. London: HMSO.

Rossi, P., Simpson, J., and Miller, J. (1985) Beyond Crime Seriousness: Fitting Punishment to the Crime. *Journal of Quantitative Criminology* 1(1):59–90.

Rossi, P., Waite, E., Rose, C., and Berk, R. (1974) The Seriousness of Crimes: Normative Structure and Individual Differences. *American Sociological Review* 39:224–37.

Roth, J. (1978) Prosecutor Perceptions of Crime Seriousness. *Journal of Criminal Law and Criminology* 69:232–42.

Royal Commission on Criminal Procedure (1981a) *Law and Procedure*. London: HMSO.

Royal Commission on Criminal Procedure (1981b) *Report*. London: HMSO.

Rutter, M. and Giller, H. (1983) *Juvenile Delinquency: Trends and Perspectives*. Harmondsworth: Penguin.

Samuels, A. (1986) Non-Crown Prosecutions: Prosecutions by Non-

Police Agencies and Private Individuals. *Criminal Law Review* January:33–44.

Sanders, A. (1985) Class Bias in Prosecutions. *Howard Journal of Criminal Justice* 24(3):176–99.

Schrager, L. and Short, J. (1980) How Serious a Crime? Perceptions of Common and Organisational Crimes. In G. Geis and E. Stotland (eds) *White-Collar Crime: Theory and Research.* Beverly Hills, Calif.: Sage.

Scott, J. and Al-Thakeb, F. (1980) Crime Statistics and the Perception of Crime. In G. Newman (ed.) *Crime and Deviance: a Comparative Perspective.* Beverly Hills, Calif.: Sage.

Scraton, P. (1985a) The State v. The People: An Introduction. *Journal of Law and Society* 12(3):251–67.

—— (1985b) *The State of the Police.* London: Pluto Press.

Scraton, P. and South, N. (1984) The Ideological Construction of the Hidden Economy: Private Police and Work-Related Crime. *Contemporary Crises* 8:1–18.

Scull, A. (1982) *Decarceration.* 2nd edn. Oxford: Polity Press.

Sealy, L. (1984) *Company Law and Commercial Reality.* London: Sweet & Maxwell.

Sedgemore, B. (1986) Bent: Britain's Banking Frauds. *New Socialist,* February:34–35.

Sellin, T. and Wolfgang, M. (1964) *The Measurement of Delinquency.* New York: Wiley.

Senate Permanent Subcommittee on Investigations (1980) *Illegal Narcotics Profits,* Hearings held 7, 11, 12, 13, and 14 December 1979. Washington DC: Government Printing Office.

Severance, L. and Loftus, E. (1982) Improving the Ability of Jurors to Comprehend and Apply Jury Instructions, *Law and Society Review* 17:153–98.

Shapiro, S. (1983) *Wayward Capitalists.* New Haven: Yale University Press.

Shapland, J. (1981) *Between Conviction and Sentence: The Process of Mitigation.* London: Routledge and Kegan Paul.

Shapland, J., Willmore, J., and Duff, P. (1985) *Victims in the Criminal Justice System.* Aldershot: Gower.

Shearing, C. and Stenning, P. (1981) Modern Private Security: Its Growth and Implications. In M. Tonry and N. Morris (eds) *Crime and Justice,* Vol 3. Chicago: Chicago University Press.

—— (1983) Private Security: Implications for Social Control. *Social Problems* 30(5):493–507.

Sherman, L. (1978) *Scandal and Reform: Controlling Police Corruption.* Los Angeles: University of California Press.

Shipman, T. (forthcoming) *One Step Ahead of the Law: The International Heroin Business.* London: Fontana.

Silver, A. (1967) The Demand for Order in Civil Society. In D. Bordua (ed.) *The Police.* New York: Wiley.

Simis, K. (1982) *USSR: The Corrupt Society.* New York: Simon and Schuster.

Skolnick, J. (1966) *Justice without Trial.* New York: Wiley.

Smith, A. (1982) The Idea of Criminal Deception. *Criminal Law Review*:721–31.

Smith, D. (1982) White-Collar Crime, Organized Crime, and Business Establishment: Resolving a Crisis in Criminological Theory. In P. Wickham and T. Dailey (eds) *White-Collar and Economic Crime.* Lexington, Mass.: Lexington Books.

Smith, L. and Burrows, J. (1986) Nobbling the Fraudsters: Crime Prevention through Administrative Change. *Howard Journal of Criminal Justice* **25**(1):13–24.

Smith, R. (1985) Who's Fiddling? Fraud and Abuse. In S. Ward (ed.) *DHSS in Crisis.* London: Child Povery Action Group.

Smith, S. (1986) *Britain's Shadow Economy.* Oxford: Clarendon Press.

Smithies, E. (1985) *Black Economy in England since 1914.* London: Gill and Macmillan.

Snider, L. (1982) Traditional and Corporate Theft: A Comparison of Sanctions. In P. Wickham and T. Dailey (eds) *White-Collar and Economic Crime.* Lexington, Mass.: Lexington Books.

—— (1987) Towards a Political Economy of Reform, Regulation, and Corporate Crime. *Law and Policy* **9** (1):37–68.

Social and Cultural Planning Office (1986) *Social and Cultural Report, 1984.* Rijswijk, The Netherlands: Social and Cultural Planning Office.

Spangler, E. (1986) *Lawyers for Hire.* New Haven, Conn.: Yale University Press.

Sparks, R. (1980) 'Marxism and Criminology' in Tonry, M. and Morris, N. (eds) *Crime and Justice*, Vol. I. Chicago: University of Chicago Press.

—— (1982) *Research on Victims of Crime.* Rockville, MD.: US Department of Health and Human Services.

—— (1983) Britain. In E. Johnson (ed.) *International Handbook of Contemporary Developments in Criminology*, Vol. 2. Westport, Conn.: Greenwood Press.

Sparks, R., Genn, H., and Dodd, D. (1977) *Surveying Victims.* Chichester: Wiley.

Strom, S. (1985) Economic Crime. In D. Magnussen (ed.) *Economic Crime – Programs for Future Research.* Stockholm: National Council for

Crime Prevention.

Styles, J. (1983) Embezzlement, Industry, and the Law in England, 1500–1800. In M. Berg, P. Hudson, and M. Sonenscher (eds) *Manufacture in Town and Country before the Factory*. Cambridge: Cambridge University Press.

Sugarman, D. (1983) Law, Economy and the State in England, 1750–1914: Some Major Issues. In D. Sugarman (ed.) *Legality, Ideology, and the State*. London: Academic Press.

Sullivan, G. (1984) 'Company Controllers, Company Cheques, and Theft – a Reply', *Criminal Law Review*, 381–444.

Sutherland, E. (1983) *White-Collar Crime: The Uncut Version*. London: Yale University Press.

Svensson, B. (1985) *Economic Crime in Sweden*. Paper presented as background material for a conference on economic crime at Saltsjobaden, Sweden, later published as Magnussen, D. (ed.) (1985) *Economic Crime – Programs for Future Research*. Stockholm: National Council for Crime Prevention.

Swigert, V. and Farrell, R. (1981) Corporation Homicide: Definitional Processes in the Construction of Deviance. *Law and Society Review* 15:161–82.

Sykes, G. (1978) *Criminology*. New York: Harcourt Brace Jovanovitch.

Szasz, A. (1986) The Process and Significance of Political Scandals: A Comparison of Watergate and the 'Sewergate' Episode at the Environmental Protection Agency. *Social Problems* 33(3):202–17.

Szasz, T. (1973) *The Second Sin*. London: Routledge and Kegan Paul.

Tanzi, V. (1982) *The Underground Economy in the United States and Abroad*. Lexington, Mass.: D.C. Heath.

Thomas, D. (1979) *Principles of Sentencing*. second edition, London: Heinemann.

Thompson, E. (1975) *Whigs and Hunters*. London: Macmillan.

—— (1980) *Writing by Candlelight*. London: Merlin.

Thorp, A. (1954) *Calling Scotland Yard*. London: Allen Wingate.

Tiedemann, K. (1985) International Research Tasks in the Field of Economic Crime. In D. Magnussen (ed.) *Economic Crime – Programs for Future Research*. Stockholm: National Council for Crime Prevention.

Tremblay, P. (1986) Designing Crime: The Short Life Expectancy and the Workings of a Recent Wave of Credit Card Bank Frauds. *British Journal of Criminology* 26:234–53.

Tunc, A. (1986) 'The Judge and the Businessman', *The Law Quarterly Review*, **102**:549–68.

Turk, A. (1980) Analyzing Official Deviance: for Nonpartisan Conflict Analyses in Criminology. In J. Inciardi (ed.) *Radical Criminology: The*

Coming Crises. Beverly Hills, Calif.: Sage.

Tutt, N. (1985) *The Tax Raiders*. London: Financial Training Services.

Uglow, S. (1984) Defrauding the Public Purse. *Criminal Law Review* February:128–41.

UK Anti-Piracy Group (1986) *International Piracy*. London:UK Anti-Piracy Group.

US Department of Justice (1985) *Sourcebook of Criminal Justice Statistics – 1984*. Washington, DC:Bureau of Justice Statistics.

Von Hirsh, A. (1986) *Past or Future Crimes*. Manchester: Manchester University Press.

Walker, M. (1978) Measuring the Seriousness of Crimes. *British Journal of Criminology* 18:348–64.

Walker, N. (1980) *Punishment, Danger, and Stigma*. Oxford: Blackwell.

—— (1985) *Sentencing: Theory and Practice*. London: Butterworths.

Walker, N. and Marsh, C. (1984) Do Sentences Affect Public Disapproval? *British Journal of Criminology* 24(1): 27–48.

Walsh, D. (1986) *Heavy Business*. London: Routledge and Kegan Paul.

Walsh, M. (1977) *The Fence*. Westport, Conn.: Greenwood Press.

Walter, I. (1985) *Secret Money: The World of International Financial Secrecy*. London: George Allen and Unwin.

Weatheritt, M. (1986) *Innovations in Policing*. London: Croom Helm.

Wheeler, S. and Rothman, M. (1982) The Organisation as Weapon in White-Collar Crime. *Michigan Law Review* 80:1403–26.

Wheeler, S., Weisburd, D., and Bode, N. (1982) Sentencing the White-Collar Offender: Rhetoric and Reality. *American Sociological Review* 47:641–59.

Wilkins, L. (1984) *Consumerist Criminology*. Aldershot: Gower.

Williams, G. (1985) Letting off the Guilty and Prosecuting the Innocent. *Criminal Law Review* (March):115–23.

Wilson, J. (1975) *Thinking about Crime*. New York: Basic Books.

Winans, R. (1987) *Trading Secrets*. London: Macmillan.

Wolfgang, M., Figlio, R., Tracy, P., and Singer, S. (1985) *The National Survey of Crime Severity*.Washington, DC: Department of Justice.

Wong, K. and Farquhar, B. (1987) *Computer Related Fraud Casebook*. London: BIS Applied Systems.

Woolf, E. (1985) *Legal Liabilities of Practising Accountants*. London: Butterworths.

Zander, M. (1985) *The Police and Criminal Evidence Act 1984*. London: Sweet and Maxwell.

—— (1986) The Report of the Roskill Committee on Fraud Trials. *Criminal Law Review* (July):423–32.

Zietz, D. (1981) *Women Who Embezzle or Defraud: A Study of Convicted Felons*. New York: Praeger.

Name index

Subject index